The Sung Theology of the English Particular Baptist Revival

Monographs in Baptist History

VOLUME 15

Ours is a day in which not only the gaze of western culture but also increasingly that of Evangelicals is riveted to the present. The past seems to be nowhere in view and hence it is disparagingly dismissed as being of little value for our rapidly changing world. Such historical amnesia is fatal for any culture, but particularly so for Christian communities whose identity is profoundly bound up with their history. The goal of this new series of monographs, *Monographs in Baptist History*, seeks to provide one of these Christian communities, that of evangelical Baptists, with reasons and resources for remembering the past. The editors are deeply convinced that Baptist history contains rich resources of theological reflection, praxis and spirituality that can help Baptists, as well as other Christians, live more Christianly in the present. The monographs in this series will therefore aim at illuminating various aspects of the Baptist tradition and in the process provide Baptists with a usable past.

The Sung Theology of the English Particular Baptist Revival

A Theological Analysis of Anne Steele's Hymns
in Rippon's Hymnal

Joseph V. Carmichael

FOREWORD BY
Michael A. G. Haykin

✎PICKWICK *Publications* · Eugene, Oregon

THE SUNG THEOLOGY OF THE ENGLISH PARTICULAR
BAPTIST REVIVAL
A Theological Analysis of Anne Steele's Hymns in Rippon's Hymnal

Monographs in Baptist History 15

Pickwick Publications
An Imprint of Wipf and Stock Publishers
199 W. 8th Ave., Suite 3
Eugene, OR 97401

www.wipfandstock.com

PAPERBACK ISBN: 978-1-7252-7084-8
HARDCOVER ISBN: 978-1-7252-7083-1
EBOOK ISBN: 978-1-7252-7085-5

Cataloguing-in-Publication data:

Names: Carmichael, Joseph V., author. | Haykin, Michael A. G., foreword.

Title: The sung theology of the English particular baptist revival : a theological analysis of Anne Steele's hymns in Rippon's hymnal / by Joseph V. Carmichael ; forword by Michael A. G. Haykin.

Description: Eugene, OR: Pickwick Publications, 2021 | Series: Monographs in Baptist History 15 | Includes bibliographical references and index.

Identifiers: ISBN 978-1-7252-7084-8 (paperback) | ISBN 978-1-7252-7083-1 (hardcover) | ISBN 978-1-7252-7085-5 (ebook)

Subjects: LCSH: Particular Baptists—Hymns | Baptists—England—History—18th century.

Classification: BX6276 C37 2021 (print) | BX6276 (ebook)

To
Craig and Emily Kaplowitz,
Lincoln and Melinda Speece,
and
Michael and Tracy Utley,
friends in life,
friends in the faith.

Contents

Foreword by Michael A. G. Haykin | ix

Preface | xi

Acknowledgments | xiii

1. Introduction | 1
2. Biography of Anne Steele | 42
3. The Setting of Anne Steele's Hymns and John Rippon's *A Selection of Hymns* | 62
4. Anne Steele as a Hymn-writer | 102
5. Anne Steele's Hymns and Psalms in Rippon's *Selection of Hymns* | 117
6. Conclusion | 201

Bibliography | 219

Index | 229

Foreword

THE INTRODUCTION OF HYMNS into the worship services of English Dissent at the close of the seventeenth century was a major turning point in the history of Protestantism and its spirituality. Up until that point, English Protestants, be they members of the state church or Dissenting communities outside of the establishment, sang only the Psalter. The introduction of hymnody was not without opposition, but eventually the arguments made for the use of hymnody by men such as Benjamin Keach or the more well-known Isaac Watts, the so-called father of the English hymn, won the day. The century that followed these pioneers was in many ways a golden age for the English hymn with hymnwriters like Charles Wesley, Philip Doddridge, William Cowper, John Newton, and Benjamin Beddome. And with these great hymnwriters must be ranked Anne Steele, the subject of this monograph. Though deeply shaped by the hymnic skill of Isaac Watts, Steele crafted a corpus of such powerful hymns that she was easily the leading Baptist hymnwriter down to the dawn of the twentieth century.

As with any hymnwriter from the long eighteenth century, not all of Anne Steele's hymns were used in the decades after her death. Her influence on Baptist life and thought must therefore be examined through those hymns that appeared in Baptist hymnals, of which the most important one was that produced in multiple editions by the London Baptist John Rippon. In this vital monograph Joseph Carmichael examines those hymns of Steele that were printed in these editions of Rippon's hymnal and thus is able to detail the potential impact that this portion of Steele's hymnody had upon the Particular Baptist community who sang her hymns.

In Baptist worship there are two key texts: the Scriptures and the hymnal, whether or not the latter is found in a print copy or in a digital format.

As such, hymnody has shaped Baptist thought and life far more than most Baptist leaders realize. This important study shows the how and why of the influence of the hymns of one Particular Baptist—Anne Steele.

Michael A. G. Haykin

Dundas, Ontario
July 30, 2020.

Preface

ANNE STEELE'S HYMNS OUGHT to be sung by the Christian church. They deserve every bit of the scholarly study they have received in recent years. Profoundly theological and deeply experiential, they are appropriate for both congregational worship and the devotional practice of personal piety. Their literary quality and poetic value continue to stimulate my study of them.

The origin of the present book was my doctoral work at The Southern Baptist Theological Seminary. I wanted to research the English hymn, considering its corporate and personal use, its doctrinal and practical value, its literary and poetic depth, and its spiritual and personal import on both Christian congregations and the individual believers making up those congregations. After much consideration of the place of psalms and hymns in the worship of the Christian church since the Protestant Reformation, I finally focused on the specific hymns of Anne Steele as published in John Rippon's widely successful *Selection of Hymns*. The reasons for this decision are explained in the chapters that follow.

Chapter 1 introduces the English Hymn and considers recent scholarship on Anne Steele and John Rippon's *Selection of Hymns*. Chapter 2 offers a biographical sketch of Steele. Chapter 3 examines the cultural and religious setting of both Anne Steele's hymns and Rippon's popular and successful hymnal. Chapter 4 considers Anne Steele's approach to her craft as a hymn-writer. Chapter 5 examines the fifty-two hymns of Steele found in Rippon's hymnal, especially as they demonstrate the theology of the *Second London Confession* and illustrate the characteristics of evangelicalism. Chapter 6 summarizes the picture of Steele that emerges from a consideration of her hymns in Rippon's hymnal and considers her influence on the revival of the English Particular Baptist community.

Acknowledgments

THE REVEREND KEVIN TWIT first suggested I study the hymns of Anne Steele. I took his advice. I am glad I did.

Redeemer Church (PCA) offered me a place to serve as part-time Assistant Pastor for the five years I lived in Louisville, Kentucky, working on the dissertation that eventually became this book. It was an honor, privilege, and great joy to serve there. Words cannot express what Redeemer's founding pastor, Dr. David Dively, means to me. He took me in as his assistant when he barely knew me. He gave me the freedom to grow and develop as a minister of the gospel. He was never critical of me, but always instructive. His and his wife Kathy's generosity to my family and me was overwhelming. Dave has been to me "the friend that sticketh closer than a brother."

The First Presbyterian Church of Greensboro, Alabama, also deserves recognition. They took the risk of calling a pastor with a half-written dissertation. They gave me the time and a warm and inviting place at which to finish my dissertation. While serving as the stated supply minister of the faithful New Covenant Presbyterian Church in Selma, Alabama, I was able to edit this book for publication.

Dr. Michael Haykin is not only the supervisor of my doctoral research, but also my friend. When I had doubts about why God's providence led me, a Presbyterian, to Southern, a Baptist seminary, he often was the answer. Dr. Haykin's patient counsel, wise advice, and shrewd editing, helped me to persevere and this book to be published.

Thanks to Roy M. Paul of the Andrew Fuller Center for Baptist Studies for his meticulous proofreading. I am grateful for his efficient work.

I am thankful for the wonderful work of each Anne Steele scholar quoted within this book, especially J. R. Broome, Cynthia Aalders, Sharon

xiii

James, Nancy Cho, and J. R. Watson. Without their research before me, this book would not have been possible.

My mother and late grandparents have shown financial generosity all through my life, but especially during the two sets of seminary years. I am thankful for my sons, Fulton, Morris, Milledge, Henry, Thomas, and Joseph. I am proud to have these young men as my sons. They handled the "PhD years" with grace and dignity. They have given me undying support—years worth of it! And I am blessed beyond measure with Betsy, my beloved wife. She is a wonderful pastor's wife. She accompanied me to two seminaries and has supported me through what is now our eighth place of pastoral service. She would not let me quit researching and writing, and she picked me up in times of deep discouragement. She gave birth to two living children in Louisville. In between she mourned the death of three other babies in the womb. She trusted God. He was indeed the "dear refuge of her weary soul," as Anne Steele wrote.

Finally, three couples deserve special recognition. Craig and Emily Kaplowitz, Lincoln and Melinda Speece, and Michael and Tracy Utley have been faithful friends to us for many years, dare I say decades! Without their prayers and encouragement I do not think this book would exist. It is to them that it is affectionately dedicated.

Joseph V. (Josh) Carmichael

Quiet Harbor, Montgomery, Alabama
August 2018.

1

Introduction

Anne Steele, the English Hymn, and Rippon's *Selection of Hymns*

ANNE STEELE (1717–1778) WAS an early pioneer of the English hymn. Celebrated as "the female 'Poet of the Sanctuary,'"[1] Steele was among many other early English Particular Baptists as well as other Dissenters and Nonconformists in her hymn-writing efforts.[2] From the end of the seventeenth century through the first three quarters of the eighteenth century, a group of English Particular Baptists joined Anne Steele in a broader movement that later came to be known as the "Golden Age of Hymnody."[3] This period, which coincided with the rise of evangelicalism, is certainly known more for its two leading hymn-writers, Isaac Watts (1674–1748) and Charles Wesley (1707–1788), both still well-represented in modern hymnals. However, there is a group of English Baptists, whose evangelical and theologically compelling hymns—once received warmly—have been practically forgotten.[4] At the head of this group, otherwise made up entirely of pastors,

1. Hatfield, *Poets of the Church*, 570.

2. See Stevenson, "Baptist Hymnody, English," 1:110–12.

3. See *Christian History* 10, no. 3 (1991), which is dedicated to the topic of the hymns of the eighteenth century. The title of the issue is "The Golden Age of Hymns." It is proper, for the purposes of this book, to date this "Golden Age" as beginning in 1707, the year of the publication of Isaac Watts's landmark *Hymns and Spiritual Songs* and the year of the births of both Charles Wesley, writer of thousands of hymns, and Selina Hastings, Countess of Huntingdon, who founded a branch of Calvinistic Methodists and published more than ten hymn collections.

4. Dudley-Smith, "Why Wesley Still Dominates," 9–13, and Wright, "Hymn Writers' Hall of Fame," 20–23. Baptist authors collectively wrote 263 of the 588 hymns in

is Steele, a pastor's daughter, who has been called the "all-time champion Baptist hymn-writer of either sex."[5] J. R. Broome points out that, writing among a generation of hymn-writing giants such as Watts, Wesley, William Cowper (1731–1800), and John Newton (1725–1807), Steele is "in fact the only woman of that period whose hymns have stood the test of time."[6] Other notable Particular Baptist hymn-writers[7] of the era include Joseph Stennett I (1663–1713), Benjamin Wallin (1711–1782), Benjamin Beddome (1717–1795), Samuel Stennett (1727–1795), Benjamin Francis (1734–1799), John Fawcett (1739–1817), and John Ryland Jr. (1753–1825).[8]

Writing her hymns originally not only for personal devotional purposes but also to supplement the collection of Watts's hymns sung in her father's congregation, Steele finally allowed them to be published in 1760, though under a pseudonym, Theodosia. W. R. Stevenson calls the thirty years that followed the first publication of Steele's hymns in 1760 "the palmy days of Baptist Hymnody."[9] Hymnologist Louis F. Benson adds that the publication of Steele's volumes launched Baptist hymnody into its own golden age.[10] Paving the way for Steele and the other English Particular Baptist hymn-writers had been Benjamin Keach (1640–1704), who argued for the propriety of singing hymns in worship and who introduced the practice to his Baptist church in 1673. Keach in fact published two hymn books of his own compositions.[11]

Rippon's *Selection of Hymns,* and have a substantial number of hymns in *The Baptist Hymnal* of 1883, but have many fewer hymns in *Baptist Hymnal* published in 1991. Anne Steele has none. See also Doane and Johnson, *Baptist Hymnal.* See Forbis, *Baptist Hymnal* (1991). Finally, see Young, "History of Baptist Hymnody in England from 1612–1800," 122–24, for an analysis of several early Baptist hymnals, including Rippon's *Selection of Hymns.*

5. Fairchild, *Religious Trends in English Poetry,* 2:111, in Arnold, *English Hymns of the Eighteenth Century,* 318.

6. Broome, *Bruised Reed,* 151. Stevenson regards Steele as "by far the most gifted Baptist hymn-writer of this period." Stevenson, "Baptist Hymnody, English," 1:111–12.

7. The following writers are mentioned, along with Steele, because Stevenson lists them as the prominent early Particular Baptist hymn-writers. Further, they have substantial representation in all the editions of the major Baptist hymnal of the period: Rippon's *Selection of Hymns.*

8. Stevenson, "Baptist Hymnody, English," 1:111–12.

9. Stevenson, "Baptist Hymnody, English," 1:112.

10. Benson, *English Hymn,* 213.

11. McBeth, *Baptist Heritage,* 94–95. Tom Nettles notes that Benjamin Keach "was in the forefront of arguing for the use of hymns in worship as a part of the ordained worship of God." On that issue he wrote and published a number of early Baptist hymns and hymnals. See Nettles, "Benjamin Keach," 99n8. On Keach and hymns see also Martin, *Benjamin Keach (1640–1704),* and Walker, *Excellent Benjamin Keach.* As early as

Benson suggests that "the year 1750 begins a new period in Baptist hymn writing" in "the school of Watts."[12] That is the year Benjamin Wallin's *Evangelical Hymns and Songs* was published, which Richard Arnold believes to be the first congregational hymnal to use the word "evangelical" in its title. The Particular Baptists thus wedded themselves to this word, which meant at the time, "'Agreeable to the gospel; consonant to the Christian law revealed in the holy gospel,' and 'contained in the gospel.'"[13] Wallin's publication therefore placed the Particular Baptists self-consciously in the evangelical stream.

Now, in a recent morphology that has received wide acceptance, David Bebbington has grouped the attitudes and convictions of early British evangelicals under four qualities or characteristics.[14] First, there is what he calls *conversionism*, the belief that lives need to be changed. Second, there is *biblicism*, a commitment to and belief that all spiritual truth is to be found in the Bible. The third characteristic is *activism*, the commitment of all believers to lives of service for God, especially through evangelism (spreading the good news) and mission (taking the gospel to other societies). Finally, there is *crucicentrism*, the conviction that Christ's death on the cross was the sacrifice providing atonement for sin (i.e., providing reconciliation between a holy God and sinful humans).[15] As the high point of the English hymn coincided with the rise of evangelicalism, it will be seen that Steele's hymns also reveal Bebbington's quadrilateral.

In his study, *The Anatomy of Hymnody*, Austin C. Lovelace defines a hymn as "a poetic statement of a personal religious encounter or insight, universal in its truth, and suitable for corporate expression when sung in stanzas to a hymn tune."[16] The singing of hymns served a number of functions in the evangelical circles within which Steele and the other Particular Baptist hymn-writers of her day composed their hymns. Louis F. Benson, leading early twentieth-century hymnologist, for example, lays out a typology of such functions based on the content of the hymns: the hymn of praise, the hymn of prayer, the doctrinal hymn, the didactic

---

1663, Hanserd Knollys (1598–1691) is also reported to have commended "the singing of hymns and spiritual songs along with the psalter as an ordinance of God's worship." See Howson, "Hanserd Knollys," 50–51.

12. Benson, *English Hymn*, 213.

13. Johnson's *Dictionary* in Arnold, *English Hymns of the Eighteenth Century*, 244.

14. For the reception history of Bebbington's work, see Larsen, "reception given *Evangelicalism in Modern Britain* since its publication in 1989," 21–36.

15. Bebbington, *Evangelicalism in Modern Britain*, 2–3. He explains these characteristics on 3–17.

16. Lovelace, *Anatomy of Hymnody*, 5.

hymn, the sermonic hymn, liturgical hymn, and the hymn of personal experience, among others.[17]

For example, regarding the sermonic hymn, J. R. Watson notes that the pioneering Particular Baptist hymn-writer Benjamin Keach "used hymn-singing as an aid to worship and for the exposition of scripture."[18] Benjamin Beddome followed suit, supplementing his own church's hymn-book by often "composing a hymn to be sung after his sermon on the Lord's Day morning."[19] The didactic function of hymns involves the doctrine being declared by the congregation through song and received into the minds and hearts of those who sing. As Keach argued, "Singing is not only sweet and raising to the Spirit, but also full of Instruction."[20] "Accordingly," note Madeleine Marshall and Janet Todd, "many hymns are the artful expressions of religious truth, designed to be learned in song as musical recitation."[21] Concerning Particular Baptist churches, the "doctrinally acceptable" hymns of Isaac Watts filled the gap between the time of Joseph Stennett I's early hymns and those of Anne Steele and her contemporaries.[22]

With respect to the hymn of personal experience, Jan Anderson notes, "Hymns were designed not to glorify the poet but to aid worshipers in expressing their feelings to God."[23] Lovelace suggests as a chief reason for the abiding popularity of Watts and Wesley "their ability to express lyrically as well as simply the Christian's experience."[24] In point of fact, when it comes to the hymn of personal experience, Broome states, "No one has excelled Anne Steele in her tender, memorable, sensitive expression of the heart feelings of a tempted, exercised, tried Christian."[25] In short, Richard Arnold says that eighteenth-century "hymns were expected to educate, arouse, or spiritually benefit or satisfy a congregation, to propagate and support certain religious and theological principles and specific orientations toward Christian experience, and to provide hope or assurance for one's beliefs and aspirations."[26] Hymns were thus sung to give worshipers an opportunity to offer corporate

---

17. Benson, *Hymnody of the Christian Church*, 141–85.

18. Watson, *English Hymn*, 111.

19. Cramp, *Baptist History*, 519.

20. Keach, *Breach Repair'd in God's Worship*, in Arnold, *English Hymns of the Eighteenth Century*, 244.

21. Marshall and Todd, *English Congregational Hymns in the Eighteenth Century*, 2.

22. Benson, *English Hymn*, 143.

23. Anderson, "Were Hymns Good Poetry?" 29.

24. Lovelace, *Anatomy of Hymnody*, 5.

25. Broome, *Bruised Reed*, 175.

26. Arnold, "Veil of Interposing Night," 374.

praise to the triune God, to teach the Scriptures and theology, and to express devotion to God and the cause of the gospel.

Benjamin Keach has been credited with permanently laying the foundation for hymn-singing among the Particular Baptist churches.[27] Benson notes that he printed some of Keach's hymns as early as 1676 in his *Wars with the powers of darkness* (4th ed.) and three hundred of them as *Spiritual Melody* in 1691.[28] Samuel J. Rogal credits the ingenuity of Keach: "He managed to form a primitive model for what would come early in the eighteenth century—the hymn and the hymnbook as instruments to complement publicly moral and religious expression."[29] Though Keach's hymns were doctrinally sound, it is often observed that they simply lacked the poetic quality necessary to press his hymn-singing movement forward.[30]

Joseph Stennett I followed Keach by just a few years, publishing a collection of evangelical hymns celebrating the Lord's Supper in 1697 and another for use with the service of Baptism in 1712.[31] Stennett, in contrast, was not only said to be a "good poet" by poet laureate Nahum Tate (1652–1715), but was praised by Isaac Watts for his "beautiful language" as Watts "was not ashamed to confess that he borrowed some of his lines from Stennett's hymns."[32] Stennett's success is attested by the fact that each of his collections had subsequent editions published a decade after their first printings. B. A. Ramsbottom points out the importance of Stennett in the fledgling Particular Baptist hymn movement: "Humanly speaking, Joseph Stennett's hymns are the reason why hymn-singing did not sink into oblivion" among the Baptists.[33]

It was following the beginnings by these two men and prior to the explosion of hymn-writing during the generation of Steele, Wallin, Beddome, and others, that the Independent Isaac Watts burst upon the scene with the publication of his *Hymns and Spiritual Songs* in 1707 and *Psalms of David* in 1719.[34] Eventually published together, these texts, as they gradually made their way into Particular Baptist congregations, filled the gap in the worship of Particular Baptists until 1769 when John Ash (1724–1779) and Caleb Evans (1737–1791) published that group's first hymnal, *A Collection of Hymns*

27. See Benson, *English Hymn*, 99–100.

28. Benson, *English Hymn*, 100.

29. Rogal, *General Introduction to Hymnody and Congregational Song*, 81.

30. For example, see Benson, *English Hymn*, 110–14.

31. Benson, *English Hymn*, 100.

32. Ramsbottom, "Stennetts," 1:137.

33. Ramsbottom, "Stennetts," 137.

34. Watts, *Hymns and Spiritual Songs*; and *Psalms of David Imitated*.

Adapted to Public Worship.[35] This hymnal, which later came to be known as the *Bristol Collection*, due to its editors' association with the Bristol Baptist Academy, contained 412 hymns, including some of Watts's most popular ones. This hymn-book is not only widely known as the first Baptist hymnal, but was also one of the early successful attempts at collecting hymns from a variety of authors from a variety of denominational backgrounds in the same volume. According to Benson, however, it was the desire of the editors that it supersede Watts as the Particular Baptist hymnal of choice which eventually led to their hymnal being superseded. Its successor was John Rippon's (1751–1836) *A Selection of Hymns, from the Best Authors, including a Great Number of Originals; Intended to be an Appendix to Dr. Watts's Psalms and Hymns*, first published in London in 1787. Ken R. Manley explains the Particular Baptist community's affinity for Watts: "Baptists found the hymns of Watts eminently suitable: they were doctrinally orthodox, objective in tone, rich in emotion but free from frivolities. The grace of God, the person of Christ and his redemptive action were central themes of his hymns."[36] Rippon wisely chose to supplement Watts rather than trying replace him, as it was Watts's own "homiletical hymnody" that endeared him to the Baptists, inspired some of their own hymn-writing endeavors, and spurred Rippon on in his idea of publishing a new hymnal.[37] The first edition of Rippon's *Selection of Hymns* contained 588 hymns, 45 of which were by Anne Steele. His expanded editions added more of Steele's hymns, bringing the total to 52.[38] The success of Rippon's *Selection of Hymns* was phenomenal, with approximately 200,000 copies being sold in Britain and over 100,000 in America.[39] Manley posits that Rippon's *Selection of Hymns* was one among the many ways he encouraged the revival among Particular Baptists during the last quarter of the eighteenth century and the first quarter of the next, in that it "introduced to the Baptist community many of the songs of the Revival, endorsing their Evangelical piety."[40]

---

35. Ash and Evans, *Collection of Hymns* (1769).

36. Manley, '*Redeeming Love Proclaim*', 86.

37. See Manley, '*Redeeming Love Proclaim*', 86–87.

38. See Manley, '*Redeeming Love Proclaim*', 287–89. Manley's table lists fifty-three hymns for Steele in Rippon's hymnal, but for this research only fifty-two were identified. See Manley, '*Redeeming Love Proclaim*', 289, for his numbers.

39. Rippon, "Preface," in *Selection of Hymns*, iii–iv.

40. Manley, '*Redeeming Love Proclaim*', 6.

Thesis and Methodology

Through his *Selection of Hymns* John Rippon disseminated the sung theology and piety of the golden age of Baptist and evangelical hymnody.[41] Writing of this hymnal, Manley notes that "Rippon understood that hymns are a force for unity as well as for shaping and strengthening faith."[42] Through a theological examination of the fifty-two hymns and Psalm paraphrases of Anne Steele included in the various editions of Rippon's phenomenally successful *Selection of Hymns*, this book will argue that Steele played a significant theological and spiritual role in Baptist faith and life in Great Britain from the 1780s to the 1830s. The thesis is that Anne Steele's hymnody as mediated through Rippon's *Selection of Hymns* nurtures through song the revival in the English Particular Baptist community that occurred in the closing decades of the eighteenth century and continued through the first decades of the nineteenth century. Rippon's *Selection of Hymns*, a central vehicle of sung piety in the British Baptist context, especially within the revival and expansion of Particular Baptist faith and piety from the 1780s to the 1830s, met specific theological, pastoral, and devotional needs among the Baptist community. Steele's inclusion in the *Selection of Hymns* was a key part of this influence and its impact on the person in the pew.

Manley's extensive study of Rippon's life and Rippon's *Selection of Hymns* demonstrates the usefulness of this hymnal as the primary source of data for this research. One aspect of its usefulness is that it is a collection of hymns from a variety of authors carefully arranged and organized according to theological, ecclesiological, and devotional concerns. Rippon's collection of hymns, according to Manley, is also illustrative of "the devotional content of Baptist worship during his lifetime and [is] a valuable pointer to Baptist spirituality for the period."[43] Similarly, Donald Davie argues that the "great congregational hymns of the eighteenth century are certainly devotional writings; they appeal to experience, . . . yet their

---

41. Steele's hymns will be evaluated as printed in Rippon, *Selection of Hymns*. Rippon's *Selection of Hymns* became a standard of Baptist hymnody, increasing its reach and influence. Louis Benson notes the enormous impact of Rippon's *Selection of Hymns*: Not only was it a "standard of Baptist hymnody, . . . it also served as a source book for makers of many hymn books in the church outside, . . . carried forward Particular Baptist Hymnody to our own time [1915], being used in Spurgeon's Tabernacle till 1866 in connection with Watts. It also was a link of connection between Baptist hymnody in England and America, and was reprinted in New York as early as 1792." Therefore, "Rippon's *Selection* put American Baptists in early possession of much of the Evangelical Hymnody." See Benson, *English Hymn*, 145 and 362.

42. Manley, '*Redeeming Love Proclaim*', 82.

43. Manley, '*Redeeming Love Proclaim*', 84.

peculiar glory is that at their best, they are doctrinally exact, scrupulous and specific. Theological niceties are *not* sterile – not so long as they can be translated into worshipping experience."[44] Thus a study of one of the leading authors represented in Rippon's *Selection of Hymns* offers a window into the sensibilities of Baptist thought, theology, and piety, as well as worship practices valued by the English Baptist community and other evangelical congregations during the period under consideration.

Manley makes the claim that the widespread use of Rippon's *Selection of Hymns* "among Baptists was a theologically unifying force of almost incalculable significance."[45] Watson explains that the congregations that sing hymns "interpret the hymns . . . in the way they have come to understand them, almost unconsciously, in the light of doctrine, belief, and history. Hymns are sung by those people who share certain things: Bible-reading, doctrine, common prayer, and moral precept. . . . Congregations sing because of what they believe, and believe because of what they sing."[46] An analysis of Rippon's *Selection of Hymns* in general and Steele's hymns in particular promises to reveal much of the theology and piety of the Baptists in the period under examination.

The focus of this book on Steele's hymns in Rippon's hymnal stands in contrast to the work of a number of other scholars, who have examined Steele's entire literary corpus of 144 hymns, 47 Psalm paraphrases, miscellaneous poems, and prose pieces as published in the two volumes of *Poems on Subjects Chiefly Devotional* as well as several other unpublished hymns, poems, and letters. The question may be asked: Why examine only fifty-two of these hymns and Psalm paraphrases? As the chief disseminator of the evangelical and Baptist hymnody available in his day, Rippon's hymnal was the key introduction of Anne Steele's hymns to the larger Particular Baptist worshipping community.[47] Rippon's hymnal provided the vehicle by which the English Particular Baptist community received their sung theology and piety. It can even be said that among Baptists and other Dissenters, this hymnal functioned practically as a "prayer book."[48] Rippon's *Selection of Hymns*, which gave Steele's hymns life for the persons in the pew, was the channel by which the congregations communally came to know Anne Steele and through which her theological perspective was communicated to them.

44. Davie, *Eighteenth-Century Hymn in England*, 14.

45. Manley, 'Redeeming Love Proclaim', 85.

46. Watson, *English Hymn*, 18–19.

47. Though it has been noted that Ash and Evans introduced Steele's hymns through their *Bristol Collection*, it was Rippon who first actually listed her as the author of her hymns. Further, he offered a balanced selection of Steele's hymns in his hymnal.

48. See Manley, 'Redeeming Love Proclaim', 84.

Rippon organized his *Selection of Hymns* into seventeen distinct subjects with various subheadings.[49] These subjects and Steele's inclusion within them reveal what Rippon wanted to communicate through the hymns he chose. His headings show an understanding of the theological emphases of the Particular Baptists, doctrines that needed to be emphasized in the face of errors, and of the overall outline of the major theological convictions of the Particular Baptists. Rippon begins his topical index with the foundational doctrinal themes of God, Creation and Providence, the Fall of Man, Scripture, Christ, and the Spirit. Having laid a theological base, he moves to the realm of Christian experience, both individually and corporately, with the Christian Life, Worship, the World (its vanity), the Church, Baptism, and the Lord's Supper. The final group provides hymns for Times and Seasons, Time and Eternity, Death and Resurrection, Judgment, and Heaven and Hell. Steele's fifty-two hymns are proportionally distributed throughout the major sections.[50] An examination of Steele's contribution to these themes will reveal her value to the British Baptist community between the 1780s and 1830s.

Manley concludes, "Like any good hymnbook Rippon's helped to define and interpret the Christian faith for its own generation."[51] It met specific theological, pastoral, and devotional needs among the Baptist community. And from its beginning, Rippon's hymnal made its way across denominational lines, making it a part of larger evangelical sensibilities as well. A study of Anne Steele's fifty-two hymns in the *Selection of Hymns* will thus offer a glimpse into the theological, spiritual, experiential, and evangelical tenor of Baptist life during the period under consideration. It was the worshippers in the pew who sang the hymns of Rippon's *Selection of Hymns*. As they sang they were influenced by such hymnwriters as Anne Steele in the shaping and strengthening of their faith.

---

49. J. R. Watson laments the lack of organization among other Dissenters' hymn books. See Watson, *English Hymn*, 91. Rippon was innovative in his careful arrangement, marking, and indexing of hymns in the *Selection of Hymns*.

50. It should be noted that she does not have hymns in the following small sections: the Fall of Man, the World, and Judgment, which contain only five, five, and ten hymns, respectively. She also does not have a hymn on baptism. She has notable and balanced representation, however, in the other thirteen sections. See Manley, *Redeeming Love Proclaim*, 286.

51. Manley, '*Redeeming Love Proclaim*', 135.

The English Eighteenth-Century Hymn:
Recent Studies

"For nearly three hundred years the commonest and most sustained poetic experience of English people, and their only regular, shared, and public enjoyment of poetry, has been provided by hymns,"[52] writes N. H. Keeble. Yet, the most recent study of the English hymn has focused on its literary form as worthy of detailed academic study. Why is there a need for such study? Professor of English and literary critic J. R. Watson answers, "The hymn has been badly treated."[53] It has been dismissed by literary critics as "restricted and churchy," and of little literary value.[54] For example, in his introduction to *The Oxford Book of Christian Verse*, David Cecil says, "A large proportion of religious verse is poor stuff. . . . Hymns are usually a second-rate type of poetry."[55] The label that the hymn is restricted and second-rate art is based in part on at least five items: its form, typical use, nature, content, and purpose.[56] Its existence within a religious community adds another layer upon this perceived restriction within each of these characteristics.

The Metrical Form of the English Hymn

Concerning the hymn's form, Erik Routley, a longtime professor of church music, hymn-writer, and the leading hymnologist of the last century, who promoted "the godly and sensible pleasure of *reading* hymns . . . in solitude, reading them as lyric poetry," wrote in describing the hymn as literature, "There is a level beyond which literature cannot rise if it is to be good hymnody. The most obvious restraint on poetic inspiration and technique is the need, in a hymn, to use regular stresses, which gives its text, in the reading, a sing-song monotony which no master of poetry would tolerate in his verse for a moment."[57] Routley continues his critique, "the more natural flow of the words . . . in a true poet's hands, [are] never constricted by that framework" of regular meter.[58] So while Routley enjoys reading hymns as poetry, his obvious presupposition is that due to the hymn's "restraining

---

52. Keeble, review of *The English Hymn*, 804.

53. Watson, *English Hymn*, 16.

54. Watson, *English Hymn*, 16.

55. Cecil, *Oxford Book of Christian Verse*, xi, xxiii.

56. These categories overlap, but are still helpful in examining hymns and the criticisms thereof.

57. Routley, *Panorama of Christian Hymnody*, v.

58. Routley, *Panorama of Christian Hymnody*, v.

itself" to a simple form within a strict observation of meter, it is therefore less than truly poetry.[59] When the early hymn-writers such as Watts began moving beyond the Psalter texts to hymn-writing, however, they did not try to change the form dramatically, but to improve on the quality of existing hymnody. Benson describes their aim with the metrical form they used: They desired to cast God's word "into measured and rhyming lines which plain people could sing to simple melodies, as they sang their ballads."[60] For this they have been criticized.

The Congregational Use and Common Nature of the English Hymn

Since Routely specifically mentions his particular preference for the private reading of hymns, it is worth noting that his complaint against the restrictions of meter also touches on the criticism the hymn receives due to its use. One of the reasons for the hymn's simple form is to facilitate congregational singing within the church. Due to the fact that hymns have such a narrow use, and a religious one at that, it has been said that hymns "receive no grace from novelty of sentiment, and very little from novelty of expression."[61] Cecil adds, "Composed as they are for the practical purpose of congregational singing, [hymns] do not provide a free vehicle for the expression of the poet's imagination, his intimate soul."[62] Another critic in this same vein observes, "In a good hymn you have to be commonplace and poetical. The moment you cease to be commonplace and put in any expression at all out of the common, it ceases to be a hymn."[63] But Donald Davie suggests this common nature of hymns also caused them to become such a part of the English national consciousness "as to furnish allusions and commonplaces even for those not religiously disposed."[64] There was a time when the average Englishman was familiar with a wide range of hymnody.[65] Richard Arnold says of the eighteenth-century hymn in its

59. See Watson, *English Hymn*, 24–25.

60. Benson, *English Hymn*, 46. See also 207–8 for a discussion of Watts's use of the hymn form as compared to that of psalm tunes.

61. Johnson, *Works*, 2:267, in Watson, *English Hymn*, 1.

62. Cecil, *Oxford Book of Christian Verse*, xxiii.

63. Tennyson, *Tennyson*, 754, in Watson, *English Hymn*, 1.

64. Davie, *Eighteenth-Century Hymn in England*, 2.

65. Davie demonstrates this through a discussion of a scene involving hymn-singing from some surprising characters in Rudyard Kipling's story, "At the end of the Passage." See Davie, *Eighteenth-Century Hymn in England*, 1–5.

own time, "When one considers the sheer numbers of people who would have experienced them, it seems not unlikely that hymns were probably the most widely known and memorized of any verbal phenomenon."[66] For some, this fact also works against the hymn. Davie continues, "Because certain hymns have become so thoroughly incorporated into a notion of English nationhood, English people will be affronted by any attempt to consider them judiciously, as poems."[67] Similarly, Arnold says, "Hymns are primarily a *popular* rather than *literary* genre."[68] So the charge goes against the hymn that the common form written for the most common of people to sing as they have gathered for worship results in a common, i.e., unimaginative and simplistic, literary composition. But these are not the only restrictions for which hymns have been criticized.

The Theological Content and Religious Purpose of the English Hymn

Though hymns can be read and used privately by individuals, they are written primarily for congregational singing *in the Church*. Watson says of hymns, "They were given to the Church by those who wrote them, for the use of the faithful in worship."[69] As congregational songs, hymns offer the opportunity for corporate praise to God, encouragement of God's people, and the call to repentance and faith. The perceived narrowness of this religious purpose, which obviously results in the religious content of the English hymn, has not gained a favorable reception from critics of hymns. When combined with the theological and experiential content of hymns, the criticism increases. Regarding these issues, and relating them to the literary value of hymnody, it has been said, "The essence of poetry is invention; such invention as, by producing something unexpected, surprises and delights. The topics of devotion are few, and being few are universally known; but, few as they are, they can be made no more."[70] The charge in this case is that the theological and devotional nature of hymns limits their subject matter to such a small selection of well-known material that they have no power to surprise or delight. Cecil does not mince words in his criticism in this area: "The average hymn is a by-word for forced feeble sentiment, flat conventional expression."[71] Routley

---

66. Arnold, *English Hymns of the Eighteenth Century*, xi.

67. Davie, *Eighteenth-Century Hymn in England*, 2.

68. Arnold, *English Hymns of the Eighteenth Century*, xiii.

69. Watson, *Annotated Anthology of Hymns*, 4.

70. Johnson, *Lives of the Poets*, 2:267 in Watson, *English Hymn*, 1.

71. Cecil, *Oxford Book of Christian Verse*, xi.

complains of what he calls "the 'in-group' language, mythology and thought-forms of evangelical hymnody," yet he does admit that the significance of the biblical vocabulary of hymns, at least in earlier periods, was how it connected the author to the reader.[72]

Regarding the specifically theological content of hymns and their biblical imagery, Routley suggests that modern readers of hymns may not appreciate such "rough places" in hymns as "the pervasive blood" and "the whole complex of Atonement theology," yet he still argues that the "pressure of devotion" in evangelical hymn-writing required "the discipline of doctrine."[73] Nicholas Temperley has harsher words on this point. Regarding what he sees as the personal, emotional, and immediate imagery of hymns he declares,

> One of the most extreme Evangelical [Anglican] hymns was Toplady's "Rock of Ages, cleft for me" (1776), with its explicitly Calvinist theology, helpless dependence on God's grace, morbid sense of guilt, and disturbing images of the human body which suggest Freudian meanings to the twentieth-century observer. These elements explain both the wide appeal of Methodist and Evangelical hymns, especially among the uneducated, and also the distaste for them felt by many sincere Christians of a more conservative mind and fastidious taste.[74]

In all of these criticisms of the hymn as a poetic form, it is really by way of its very definition that it has been criticized. And even the singers of the English hymn are indirectly included in these criticisms. Further, the worldview of the critic, often very different from that of the hymn-writer and of those for whom the hymn was written to sing, affects the analysis. There also seem to be presuppositions underlying these criticisms, namely, that the process of writing verse for "narrow religious purposes" will result in a product of poor literary quality, limited subjected matter, and shallow imaginative and emotional value. Lovelace succinctly sums up the problem here regarding hymns: "Perhaps few forms of poetry are so widely known and used, and so generally misunderstood and unappreciated."[75]

---

72. Routley, *Panorama of Christian Hymnody*, v.

73. Routley, *Panorama of Christian Hymnody*, v, 25. For a contemporary criticism of the historic Christian understanding of Jesus's shed blood and its use in hymns, see Bell, *Love Wins*. For a contemporary response to Bell's criticism, see "The Blood-Drained Gospel of Rob Bell," at Moore to the Point Blog, posted March 15, 2011: http://www.russellmoore.com/2011/03/15/ the-blood-drained-gospel-of-rob-bell/.

74. Temperley, *Music of the English Parish Church*, 1:209.

75. Lovelace, *Anatomy of Hymnody*, 5.

The Literary Value of the English Hymn

So, there has been a recent movement to rehabilitate both the English hymn as an art form and the hymn-writer as a poet. Watson, for example, in his book *The English Hymn: A Critical and Historical Study*, exams the English hymn as literature generally and as poetry specifically. He describes his work,

> One of the purposes of this book is to try to rescue the hymn from its 'common' image; another is to see how the hymn works—what kind of text it is, how we read or sing it, what kind of pleasure we get from it, how we interpret it; in the process it may be possible to see whether there are, in hymns, traces of the great contradictions and confusions of our fallen and redeemed nature; and to question the idea that hymns—because of their lack of irony, their apparent simplicity, and their doctrinally confined expression—are unable to represent these things with any subtlety or imaginative power.[76]

Watson's work is critical for the present examination of recent studies of the English hymn as well as the examination of Steele's hymns to follow. N. H. Keeble reviewed Watson's book and said, "Through a whole series of careful and percipient readings of particular hymns Watson alerts us to their structural shapeliness, their textual ingenuity, and their metaphorical complexity. . . . There is no study comparably rich and generous, nothing to match either the wealth of material covered or the catholicity of its insights."[77]

Watson pointedly answers each of the criticisms mentioned above in his recent work on the English hymn.[78] Watson's approach to the question of whether hymns deserve to be considered poetry is simple: "This is, in my view, an old-fashioned and unnecessary question, based on some idea of 'poetry' which is almost certainly subjective and indefensible, if only because poetry can be so many things."[79] In a seminal essay that Watson calls "the best essay on hymns ever written,"[80] James Montgomery says, "We are not without abundant proof, that hymns may be as splendid in poetry as they are fervent in devotion."[81] Thus, Watson seeks to "demonstrate

---

76. Watson, *English Hymn*, 4.

77. Keeble, review of *The English Hymn*, 805.

78. See Watson, *Annotated Anthology of Hymns*, 1–9, and *English Hymn*, vii–x and 1–41.

79. Watson, *English Hymn*, viii.

80. Watson, *Annotated Anthology of Hymns*, 5.

81. Montgomery, "Introductory Essay," x. He does address, however, the problem of having so many hymns of poor poetic value: "Hymns, looking at the multitude and mass of them, appear to have been written by all kinds of persons, except poets; and

what kind of poetry hymnody is, its characteristics as a genre with its own rhetoric and language."[82]

Regarding the metrical restrictions of the hymn, Watson notes that T. S. Eliot finds the most interesting verses in English written within a metrical pattern such as iambic pentameter: "It is this contrast between fixity and flux, this unperceived evasion of monotony, which is the very life of verse."[83] So rather than resulting in monotony, the form of the hymn is seen here as avoiding it. Watson observes that certain meters were particularly frequent in the eighteenth-century English hymn—86.86., or Common Meter (C.M.), 66.86., or Short Meter (S.M.), and 88.88, or Long Meter (L.M.)—and demonstrates how "each of the forms has its own character, which shapes the material and becomes part of the meaning."[84] Watson goes a step further, explaining that within a metrical shape biblical content becomes something different than a patchwork of biblical themes and images, "it becomes a new experience in and through the metre. . . . In many of the finest hymns, the metre implies the passion" which the hymn both expresses and generates.[85] Finally, he summarizes, "It is through these limitations [of meter] that the hymn works in the way that it does: it is because it is so circumscribed that it becomes such an interesting poetic form, containing the human and religious sensibility within its regularity, and finding within the enclosed forms a freedom of its own."[86] So rather than being an obstacle to clarity, depth, and creativity in hymn-writing, the metrical form when used skillfully helps to create the literary art of the hymn.

Throughout his discussion of the English hymn Watson answers the other criticisms, those of the hymn's typical use, nature, content, and purpose, though not necessarily in these strict categories. A few examples will illustrate. Watson says, "Hymns speak to those who are united in a common belief."[87] This belief is often neither shared nor understood by the critic of

---

why the latter have not delighted in this department of their own art, is obvious. Just in proportion as the religion of Christ is understood and taught in primitive purity, those who either believe not in its spirituality, or have not proved its converting influence [e.g., many of our eminent poets], are careful to avoid meddling with it." Montgomery, "Introductory Essay," viii–ix.

82. Watson, *English Hymn*, viii.

83. Eliot, "Reflections on Vers libre," in *Selected Prose*, ed. Hayward, 88–89, cited in Watson, *English Hymn*, 25.

84. He also explains the primary uses of each of these meters. Watson, *English Hymn*, 32–33. It will be demonstrated that Anne Steele skillfully used these three primary meters to her advantage.

85. Watson, *English Hymn*, 40–41.

86. Watson, *English Hymn*, 15.

87. Watson, *Annotated Anthology of Hymns*, 3.

the hymn. So the hymn's use for a worshipping community and its common nature as a simple and popular literary device are often dismissed out-of-hand. Watson further notes that the believers within the worshipping community for whom the hymns are written interpret the hymns "in the way they have come to understand them, almost unconsciously, in the light of doctrine, belief, and history. Hymns are sung by those people who share certain things: Bible-reading, doctrine, common prayer, and moral precept."[88] An unwillingness to meet this interpretive community and the hymn-writers who compose for its benefit on their own terms results in a misunderstanding of the value of the hymn's use and nature.

It is complained that hymns are restricted by a narrow subject matter and religious purpose. Watson notes, however, that "hymns could, be quarried from any part of the Bible, and that they could encompass all the religious moods of the human soul."[89] Perhaps some critics have simply not taken the time to gain an understanding of the breadth and depth of the subject matter in the Scriptures nor of the variety of emotions found in hymn lyrics. Further, Watson lists just a few hymn topics: "Hymns can contain systematic theology, Christian doctrine, praise, prayer, jubilation; they can express patience and trust, and also faith, and hope, and love. . . . They are full of information about Father, Son, and Holy Spirit."[90] But hymns are also about the practical religious experience of the doctrines about which they teach. Concerning the Trinity, they are concerned with an "awareness of sinning against the Father, of mercy through the Son, of power through the Holy Spirit."[91] And Watson observes that hymns are universal because they "are rooted and grounded in the simplest of human emotions" such as "the knowledge of wrongdoing, and the hope of forgiveness," which are "essential parts of the day-to-day life of most people."[92] Hymns satisfy deeply felt human needs. Watson, thus, finds the hymn to be an art form that is valuable "both as an aid to devotion and as an expression of the human soul."[93] As the only poetry known to most people, Watson concludes, "The special characteristics of [the hymn's] genre are a stability," not always found in some literary genres, "which comes from its use of consistent codes, especially the great code of the Bible; and a firmness of reader-response which comes

---

88. Watson, *English Hymn*, 18.

89. Watson, *Annotated Anthology of Hymns*, 2.

90. Watson, *Annotated Anthology of Hymns*, 2.

91. Watson, *Annotated Anthology of Hymns*, 2.

92. Watson, *Annotated Anthology of Hymns*, 3.

93. Watson, *Annotated Anthology of Hymns*, 7.

from the interpretive community of the Church."[94] These answers would also collectively explain why common worshippers, often to the surprise of the more sophisticated literary critics, are not offended by being referred to as "worms" who need their sins to be "washed away by Jesus' blood." So to gain a full understanding of the hymn, the critic or student of hymnody must gain "a complex awareness of the way in which hymns function in worship today, and have their origins in the worship of yesterday."[95]

Other critics, some who even have various qualms with the English hymn as an art form, still offer insight into the literary value of the English eighteenth-century hymn. For example, Watson's dismissal of the argument that hymns are by definition *not* poetry does not diminish the fact that certain hymns can be *bad* poetry. Lovelace acknowledges the legitimate concerns of the hymn's critics: "The hymn is one of the most difficult of all poetic forms to master, for its small palette and vast subject matter make demands on technique which give pause to the great poets yet seem to encourage the versifiers—those carefree souls who 'have a feel for meter' and 'can rhyme,' even though the results are doggerel."[96] The existence of poor poets within a specific literary genre, however, does not negate the value of that genre itself. When applying skill and creativity, along with theological understanding and conviction, to the hymn-writing task, valuable work of poetic art can result. Davie in fact writes of "castigating an English audience . . . for perpetuating the outrageous fiction that eighteenth-century poetry was barren of devotional lyrics."[97]

Lovelace also begins to answer some of the other criticisms of the hymn. His observation suggests that the hymn should not be discounted from a literary perspective simply due to its commitment to meter or for its theological content. Lovelace, as opposed to some of the fiercest critics of the hymn, also sees the "vast subject matter," not the lack thereof, as actually adding *difficulty* to the task of hymn-writing. This further means that the hymn's role as poetic literature and in doctrinal instruction should not be unnecessarily separated. Cynthia Aalders states the case for examining the hymn on both counts: "Just as a hymn should be understood as a work of literature, its effectiveness contingent on how it functions within the bounds of a specific genre, it likewise represents a particular theology,"

---

94. Watson, *English Hymn*, 21.
95. Watson, *English Hymn*, 19.
96. Lovelace, *Anatomy of Hymnody*, 5.
97. Davie and Stevenson, *English Hymnology in the Eighteenth Century*, 9.

its effectiveness thus being contingent on how it functions within a specific ecclesiastical tradition.[98]

Finally, the literary value of the hymn should not be divorced from its use as a vehicle of service to both the personal and corporate devotional lives of believers. Highlighting Charles Wesley's contribution as a writer, especially within the Church of England, Nicholas Temperley says, "In his hymns, it is not too much to say, Christianity was first brought home to the minds and hearts of millions of uneducated people, who had previously known it only as a mysterious rite to which they were expected to conform."[99] In a similar vein, Davies suggests that among Dissenters, the introduction of the hymn allowed for a new stress on "the importance of the congregation," at times allowing for even "a subjectivity in the worship."[100] Yet he quickly adds that though the subjectivity may be open to some criticism, the "subjective emphasis in Watts and Doddridge was always clearly related to a historic stress on dogma."[101] Temperley adds, "The cardinal point about singing for Methodists and Evangelicals was that it should be a heartfelt and spontaneous act of worship by the people."[102] In examining Anne Steele's hymns as literature, Cynthia Aalders echoes all the aforementioned sentiments succinctly: "Ideally, the singing of hymns will give voice to a worshipper's heartfelt devotion to God, and for this reason alone they have great value."[103]

Isaac Watts as the "Father of the English Hymn"

As noted above, Keach and Stennett are credited as being among the early English hymn-writers. Davies points out that the "Particular Baptists had an important contribution to make to English Worship as the forerunners of Isaac Watts in effecting the major transition from metrical paraphrases to hymns proper."[104] But he adds that their penchant for viewing the hymn as a pedagogical device to aid in remembering the subject of the sermon

---

98. Aalders, *To Express the Ineffable*, 33.

99. Temperley, *Music of the English Parish Church*, 1:208.

100. Davies, *From Watts and Wesley to Maurice*, 99–100.

101. Davies, *From Watts and Wesley to Maurice*, 100. He further notes that "for real subjectivity and wallowing in sentimental feelings we must turn to Victorian hymnody."

102. Temperley, *Music of the English Parish Church*, 1:209.

103. Aalders, *To Express the Ineffable*, 36. Steele's hymns serve as an example of both the criticisms and successes of the English hymn as literature.

104. Davies, *From Watts and Wesley to Maurice*, 135.

perhaps contributed to a lack of artistic quality.[105] Isaac Watts, who "viewed himself as a poet," followed them in time.[106] J. R. Watson says,

> Watts, who was born in 1674, came on to the scene at exactly the right moment. He took the struggling and experimental hymn form, and transformed it by a combination of poetic energy and high devotional seriousness. His poetry in *Horae Lyricae* (1706, 1709) shows his love of inspirational verse, written with passion and excitement; and his hymn-writing shows his ability to discipline himself to write in a few well-known metres, and with a purposeful clarity.[107]

He further argues that Watts—pastor, theologian, and poet—both "set the standard for a century and more" and also inspired those who came after, and thus "has been rightly seen as the first really great hymn-writer in English."[108] Marshall and Todd explain two sides of Watts's craft, he "shared the moral concern of the more rigorous believers at the same time that he delighted in the literary imagination and its pious possibilities."[109] Rogal describes Watts's achievement,

> The key to Watts's legacy was the relationship between hymnody and literature. He was one of the few poets of the Augustan Age who managed to preserve the spiritual enthusiasm of Protestant Dissent and to demonstrate that it could achieve poetic expression. As both preacher and poet, he formed an obvious link between the Calvinist zeal of the late seventeenth century and the evangelical revival within the eighteenth-century Established Church represented by the Wesleys and George Whitefield.[110]

---

105. Davies, *From Watts and Wesley to Maurice*, 136.

106. Rogal, *General Introduction to Hymnody and Congregational Song*, 85.

107. Watson, *Annotated Anthology of Hymns*, 121.

108. Watson, *Annotated Anthology of Hymns*, 121. Montgomery says, "Dr. Watts may be almost called the inventor of hymns in our language; for he so departed from all precedent, that few of his compositions resemble those of his fore-runners,—while he so far established a precedent to all his successors, that none have departed from it, otherwise than according to the peculiar turn of mind of the writer, and the style of expressing Christian truths employed by the denomination to which he belonged." Montgomery, "Introductory Essay," xx–xi.

109. Marshall and Todd, *English Congregational Hymns in the Eighteenth Century*, 32.

110. Rogal, *General Introduction to Hymnody and Congregational Song*, 86.

Lovelace describes Watts's place in hymnody (and Wesley with him) as "towering over the landscape" of the small number of "masters of the art of hymn writing."[111]

Most studies of the eighteenth-century English hymn, Watson's included, begin their study of the golden age of hymnody with a review of Watts and his work and style. Watts wrote as a well-studied theologian who desired to teach the sturdy doctrines of the Christian faith in a poetically pleasing style and a language that the common worshipper in the pew could understand. He desired to help the believer engage his or her emotions while praising, learning about, and growing in piety toward the Triune God. Marshall and Todd comment on Watts's desire and quest to encourage the singers of his hymns toward spiritual devotion, "A piety that stressed the lively feelings of the believer turned naturally to poetry. The power to move the singers' emotions in response to recognition of absolute truth belongs to pure poetry uncompromised by any ulterior motives."[112] Watts used his poetic talents not to make a name for himself—something he could have certainly done—but to bring home the ideas of the majesty of God and the believer's complete dependence upon God to the people in the pew in their day-to-day existence in a fallen yet redeemed world. Arthur Pollard catches the sense of Watts's success in this endeavor: "There is something rugged, something of the character of the pioneer, in Watts's Christianity. It is marked by the feeling of danger and adventure, struggle and hardship, and yet confidence in ultimate victory."[113] Rogal describes Watts's approach to his craft and his legacy,

> Watts conveyed in his hymnody the soul of the poet and the conviction of the conservative preacher, but as minister, he cast aside the theological mantle and bowed in the direction of the humblest Christians. He beckoned to them to walk with God on the high ground of Christian piety, thus providing the model—for the last half of the eighteenth century—for a group of hymnodists who continued his vitality and his frankness.[114]

A brief look at a few of those who were influenced by Watts follows.

---

111. Lovelace, *Anatomy of Hymnody*, 5.

112. Marshall and Todd, *English Congregational Hymns in the Eighteenth Century*, 57.

113. Pollard, *English Hymns*, 14.

114. Rogal, *General Introduction to Hymnody and Congregational Song*, 86.

The English Hymn after Watts

In *The Music of the English Parish Church*, Nicholas Temperley offers his analysis of the English hymn from the standpoint of the Anglican Church. This is valuable because a few Evangelical Anglicans, who came after Watts, are known as some of the best of the hymn-writers of the eighteenth century. Temperley, pairing Charles Wesley with the Independent Watts as the greatest hymn-writers of the eighteenth century, says that Wesley "must be regarded as an Evangelical [Anglican] quite as much as a Methodist."[115] Wesley is regularly known as the hymn-writer who contributed more emotive and exuberant hymns of heightened spiritual experience to the genre. Watson notes that he was an extreme example of hymn-writers who used "Biblical language . . . to find a 'voice', to express emotion or to crystallize a thought."[116] So, it is not only the emotion in his hymns, but the biblical language as well, for which Wesley is known. Bernard L. Manning finds that his "constant reference to the classical language of the faith—the written Word of God—gives Wesley's hymns themselves a classical poise and accent which marks them off . . . from all other modern hymns."[117] And this lends itself to a confidence found in Wesley's lyrics "rooted in the orthodox, catholic, evangelical faith."[118] Much more could be said about Wesley, but suffice it to say, as Manning observes, "The heart of Wesley's religion is sound doctrine."[119]

Beyond Wesley, Temperley says, "Many hymns of lasting value were contributed by other Evanglicals, especially John Newton, William Cowper, and Augustus Toplady [1740–1778]."[120] Horton Davies lists Newton and Cowper as having written the highest quality of the Evangelical Anglican hymns. He describes these hymns, "Essentially, they were songs of individual experience, marking the successive stages of penitence, conversion, justification, pardon, and sanctification in the life of the Christian pilgrim through

---

115. Temperley, *Music of the English Parish Church*, 1:208. In contrast to Temperley, this study is focusing more narrowly on the English eighteenth-century hymn in the Nonconformist tradition. The Methodist movement was within the Anglican church, at least until the very end of the eighteenth century. Montgomery says of Wesley, "Next to Dr. Watts as a hymn-writer, undoubtedly stands the Rev. Charles Wesley. . . . He has celebrated [his own hymn themes] with an affluence of diction, and a splendour of colouring, rarely surpassed." Montgomery, "Introductory Essay," xxiii.

116. Watson, *English Hymn*, 231.

117. Manning, *Hymns of Wesley and Watts*, 37.

118. Manning, *Hymns of Wesley and Watts*, 74.

119. Manning, *Hymns of Wesley and Watts*, 75.

120. Temperley, *Music of the English Parish Church*, 1:208.

this vale of sorrow to eternity."[121] As has already been noted, Nonconformists sang the hymns of these Anglican hymn-writers as well.[122] Summarizing their study of several major hymn-writers in a way that would be agreeable to most of the scholars of hymns examined here, Marshall and Todd list as accomplishments of the English eighteenth-century hymn:

> Watts' desire to rouse his singers from indifference, to raise devotional consciousness, Wesley's call to conversion and spiritual fervor, Newton's vision of Christian life in its large providential frame—these inspired courage in the hearts of the poets and led them to experiment with different means of affecting their singers.[123]

Davie finds in Newton a pastor who spoke the language of his people and who, even if he was not a great poet, yet offered the moral poetic virtue of honest lyrics that ministered to the everyday lives of those for whom he wrote.[124] Davie praises Cowper for his plain style and notes that Cowper's ability, more than that of his contemporaries, to write "for dispersed and anxious individuals (of whatever denomination or persuasion) is what gives his hymns a distinctive urgency and pathos."[125] Davie also finds "not doctrine, but experience" lying at the center of Cowper's hymns.[126] Three of the other hymn-writers who Watts, already famous by the time of his death in 1748, influenced tremendously were the Nonconformists, Steele, Benjamin Beddome, and Philip Doddridge (1702–1751).[127] Davies compares Particular Baptist pastor Beddome to the Independent Doddridge in his desire to teach the sermon through the vehicle of the hymn, calling Beddome "the indefatigable sermon summarizer in verse."[128] Watson halts the anticipated criticism for this in Beddome, noting that though he was self-consciously teaching Baptist doctrine through his hymns, Beddome's "clarity and balance, however reveal a strong imagination which is closer

121. Davies, *From Watts and Wesley to Maurice*, 234–35. Montgomery says that Cowper "stands alone among 'the mighty masters' of the lyre." Montgomery, "Introductory Essay," viii.

122. These latter three hymn-writers of the Church of England had a total of forty-one hymns in Rippon's expanded edition of his *Selection of Hymns*. See Manley, *'Redeeming Love Proclaim'*, 286.

123. Marshall and Todd, *English Congregational Hymns in the Eighteenth Century*, 151.

124. See Davie and Stevenson, *English Hymnology in the Eighteenth Century*, 14–19.

125. Davie, *Eighteenth-Century Hymn in England*, 153.

126. Davie and Stevenson, *English Hymnology in the Eighteenth Century*, 14

127. Watson, *Annotated Anthology of Hymns*, 147.

128. Davies, *From Watts and Wesley to Maurice*, 136.

to the Evangelical Revival of Newton and Cowper than the sweet tones of Doddridge."[129] Watson credits Doddridge, a disciple of Watts, with his own "awareness of the emotional power of hymns, and the ability to move a congregation."[130] Anne Steele, the subject of this book, was also a skilled and popular contemporary of these hymn-writers who has only recently begun to receive the study she is due.[131]

Conclusion

The value of the English eighteenth-century hymn as a literarily pleasing, theologically instructive, and devotionally compelling art form both in its own time and up to the present should not be underestimated. Watson notes that for some, "hymns have been the only poetry that they have ever known."[132] He continues, "The lines and verses they have sung at school or on Sundays have satisfied their sense of rhythm and form, and the emotions and ideas of those familiar hymns have given expression to some of their most deeply felt longings and aspirations."[133] As confirmation of Watson's point, the controversial novelist, D. H Lawrence, though admitting his personal distaste for the poetic value of hymns as well as their theological imagery, yet famously wrote, "They mean to me almost more than the finest poetry, and they have for me a more permanent value, somehow or other. . . . They are the same to my man's experience as they were to me nearly forty years ago."[134] Hymns have indeed the capacity to make a deep and lasting impression. Marshall and Todd conclude that the hymn "incorporates the common poetic values of its day, most particularly the sought-after balance between specific expression and general experience and the careful alliance of poetic delight and instruction."[135] Concerning the hymn's contribution to a stress on the congregation's participation in the worship service, Davies suggests, "The great significance of this eighteenth century Dissenting hymnody was that if 'enthusiasm' was banned from the sermon

129. Watson, *English Hymn*, 201. Montgomery offers a similar assessment of Beddome and says, "His compositions are calculated to be far more useful than attractive, though, on closer acquaintance, they become very agreeable, as well as impressive, being for the most part brief and pithy." Montgomery, "Introductory Essay," xxvii.

130. Watson, *English Hymn*, 179.

131. An evaluation on the recent literature on Anne Steele follows below.

132. Watson, *Annotated Anthology of Hymns*, 1.

133. Watson, *Annotated Anthology of Hymns*, 1.

134. Lawrence, "Hymns in a Man's Life," 380–81.

135. Marshall and Todd, *English Congregational Hymns in the Eighteenth Century*, 149.

it was reintroduced in the praise, and thus emotions were not starved, as was so often the case in Established worship during this period."[136] Hymns allowed for Christians to express their emotions through biblically appropriate language as they gathered for worship. In concluding her overview of the English eighteenth-century hymn, Aalders discusses the capacity of the hymn to serve the expression of both Christian doctrine and devotional experience while also being artistically pleasing to its participants.[137] She sums up this discussion, "Thus, eighteenth-century hymnic efforts took place during a time when the prevailing aesthetic sensibility held that art could both edify and delight, a fact that requires the hymn to be considered as a work of both theology and literature."[138]

Anne Steele: The Current State of the Scholarship

After many years of neglect, there have been four recent significant studies on the life of Anne Steele and her hymnody. The authors of each of these studies, J. R. Broome, Sharon James, Nancy Cho, and Cynthia Aalders, have immersed themselves in the Steele Collection housed at the Angus Library, Regent's Park College, Oxford, and were given access to Karen Smith's unpublished DPhil thesis on the Calvinistic Baptists of Hampshire and Wiltshire.[139] Additionally, Ken Manley has written an invaluable monograph on John Rippon and his *Selection of Hymns*. These four studies on Steele and the one on Rippon provide essential background information to research on Steele's hymns as found in Rippon's *Selection of Hymns*. There have been other recent studies on particular aspects of Steele's hymns and hymn-writing that are also relevant to our topic and need to be noted.

In *A Bruised Reed: The Life and Times of Anne Steele*, J. R. Broome does just what the subtitle expresses. His thorough biography offers a comprehensive history of Steele's life and places her within the larger context of the long eighteenth century. Broome's purpose is to tell the story of Steele's life while also using her and her family as an interesting and illuminating illustration

136. Davies, *From Watts and Wesley to Maurice*, 100.

137. Aalders, *To Express the Ineffable*, 35.

138. Aalders, *To Express the Ineffable*, 36. Lionel Adey's relatively recent social, cultural, and political analyses of the English hymn in his two books *Hymns and the Christian "Myth"* and *Class and Idol in the English Hymn* have not been cited in this section. They will, however, inform the analysis in the chapters below following the recent scholarship on Anne Steele.

139. It is worth noting that neither James nor Aalders had access yet to Broome's magisterial biography of Anne Steele at the time each was completing her research.

of Particular Baptist life in England in the eighteenth century. By basing his narrative on the detailed and spiritually rich journal entries of Steele's stepmother, Anne Cator Steele (1689–1760), Broome presents a lively history of Steele's family and church life. He also uses surviving correspondence between Steele and various family members and friends to shed light on her personality and character, her likes and dislikes, and her comings and goings within the small geographic area within which she resided her entire life. Finally, by examining her hymns he demonstrates where her internal thoughts, desires, and spiritual life intersect with her experience and how she sought to express that to others as a writer and poet.

Broome begins with the birth of Steele's maternal grandfather in 1645 and takes the reader through a detailed study of the family in its religious and cultural context right up to the beginning of the nineteenth century. By taking her life chronologically, Broome traces her personal pilgrimage of faith and her development as a writer within her historical context. He takes one detour within his larger narrative in order to concentrate on her literary output during the prime years of her hymn-writing. He describes the helpers and advisers who encouraged Steele's literary output, the influence of Isaac Watts on her hymn-writing, and the methods of her craft. In analyzing the content of her hymns he notes Steele's prayerfulness, submission to God's will, desire for assurance, experiential faith, and the broad theological themes about which she wrote.

Broome's narrative of Steele's life operates upon the foundation of several presuppositions. One of these presuppositions is that individuals are the products of the historical circumstances and familial structures within which they grow and live throughout their lives.[140] Steele grew up in a family of English Particular Baptist pastors whose history included living through a time of intense persecution that had subsided into relative freedom of worship by the time of her birth and life. Steele's life and hymns reflect this family history. Further, Steele grew up in a family in which practically every member had literary and poetic gifts. Surviving papers demonstrate this fact. Also, Steele's own literary output bears this out. Anne Steele lived in a day when journal-keeping and letter-writing formed a major cultural expression and form of communication. Broome presupposes that these journals and letters, not to

140. Though this presupposition is operative throughout, in the first three chapters (chap. 1, "An Age of Intolerance [1645–1688]," chap. 2, "A Child of Dissenters [1688–1720]," and chap. 3, "A Daughter of Broughton [1720–32]"), he tells the story of the ancestors of Anne Steele up to the time of her youth. Broome illustrates the formative influence the political, social, and spiritual climates within which a family system develops have on that family and thus how the family structure and dynamics (including extended family) interact with and influence the personalities as well as the intellectual and spiritual growth of those living therein.

mention Steele's hymns, offer an accurate glimpse into the life of the day.[141] Another presupposition undergirding Broome's work is that the personal experiences of a hymn-writer—geographic, spiritual, physical, and vocational—have a significant effect on the hymns of that particular writer.[142] Lastly, Broome presupposes that through the thoughtful lyrics of hymns, namely those of Anne Steele, modern readers are offered a wonderful glimpse into a specific aspect of eighteenth-century life in England.[143]

With a book that seeks to cover such a scope as that of Broome he seems to have a number of related theses that he desires to prove throughout his narrative of Anne Steele's life and times. Broome's primary thesis can be simply stated, as he quotes John Sheppard, that while "perhaps the current of her life flowed too smoothly to invite anyone to follow it," yet through writing "a few of the sweetest hymns" and "thus using the poetical talent, which she recognized as divine, . . . her usefulness has far distanced her fame."[144] This statement works as a thesis for Broome's work on Steele and as an important thesis underlying this book because it is the quality of her hymns that attracted Broome to Steele for research interest. A number of subsidiary theses tie Broome's biography of Steele together.

In studying Steele, Broome's work, as well as the others that will be considered below, constantly demonstrates the interplay between observing Steele's life and examining her hymns. After reading her hymns it is hard to separate Steele's hymns from her life. One of Broome's subsidiary theses is that as one studies her hymns it is revealed "that much of her spiritual experience lies embedded in them."[145] One aspect of Steele's hymns is that they put in colorful language what she experienced seen through the lens of what she believed. This experience included her upbringing. In examining the impact of Steele's family upon her, Broome says, "The religion of the Gays, Cators, Steeles, and Froudes is clearly revealed in the hymns and poetry of Anne and never more so than in their deaths."[146] Broome argues that Steele's ability to communicate physical and spiritual experience is part of the brilliance of her

---

141. Broome, *Bruised Reed*, 177. This presupposition is indirectly demonstrated throughout as Broome's primary source for his narrative of the Steele family is surviving letters, journals, and hymns, each written as family members corresponded with either one another or with friends.

142. See chap. 6, "A Natural Talent [1743–60]," in Broome, *Bruised Reed*, 151–75.

143. Broome, *Bruised Reed*, 151–75.

144. Extract from the *Memoir of John Sheppard*, which formed the Preface to the single-volume ed. of *Anne Steele's Works*, published in London by Daniel Sedgwick in 1863, in Broome, *Bruised Reed*, 10.

145. Broome, *Bruised Reed*, 82.

146. Broome, *Bruised Reed*, 101.

hymns. He writes, "While no written record survives of her spiritual experience, yet in her open frank way she reveals much of it indirectly in her hymns, which gives to them a peculiar relevance to succeeding generations of Christians who walk in the same spiritual paths as she did."[147]

Witnessing the deaths of so many family members and friends in her lifetime as well as dealing with her own constant physical pain, especially from malaria, also influenced the subject matter and lyrics of Steele's hymns.[148] Another subsidiary thesis Broome demonstrates is that Anne's own poor health, which affected her from at least her early teen years, and her experience of the death of friends and family members throughout her life also manifested itself in her approach to her faith and hymn-writing. Broome suggests, "Her health was a continual cause of concern to her family, but her writings and especially her hymns show that suffering was sanctified to her and used to enable her to write hymns which manifest feeling and compassion."[149] Steele's hymns therefore served as an expression of her way of enduring pain, suffering, and death with a view to offering others both comfort and resources to do the same.

Broome also argues that some specific theological beliefs formed the center of Steele's skill of lyrical expression through her hymns. He suggests that both her physical and spiritual experiences played out in her hymn-writing through her ability to put a living theology to verse. Broome perceives a sense of pleasure communicated by Steele as she meditated on "the doctrine of the Trinity, the incarnation, redemption, the sufferings and resurrection of Christ. . . . She spoke unaffectedly and with feeling. Her hymns contain truth, experience, and worship."[150] Broome traces these and other themes through Steele's life and takes a specific chapter within which to briefly trace them through her hymns. It is appropriate to note an additional thesis embedded in Broome's analysis of Steele's hymns. In his history of the eighteenth century as he tells it through the greater Steele family he includes the development of hymn-writing and congregational hymn-singing both in the evangelical church generally and among the English Particular Baptists specifically. Broome demonstrates Watts's influence upon Steele's hymn-writing and discusses their similar skills at putting orthodox theology to verse. And while he notes that Watts "had a far greater realization of the majesty and glory of God as he wrote, . . . when, however

---

147. Broome, *Bruised Reed*, 173.

148. For a modern interpretation of the symptoms of Anne Steele's health, see Dixon and Steele-Smith, "Anne Steele's Health," 351–56.

149. Broome, *Bruised Reed*, 118.

150. Broome, *Bruised Reed*, 175.

it came to matters of the soul, then Anne equaled him."[151] In concluding his analysis of Steele's hymns, Broome declares, "No one has excelled Anne Steele in her tender, memorable, sensitive expression of the heart feelings of a tempted, exercised, tried Christian."[152]

Broome's sweeping biography of Anne Steele places her within the geographical, theological, and cultural context of eighteenth-century England. He focuses on Steele's life within her family and Particular Baptist church, her life as a writer of letters, hymns, and poems, and her life of physical suffering and faith. In so doing, he provides essential background material for a detailed study of the theology and piety in her hymns.

Sharon James's *In Trouble and in Joy: Four Women Who Lived for God* offers a more abbreviated look at Steele's life than Broome's work. In many ways, this is its strength. James provides a look at Steele strong in breadth and depth, yet a model of brevity. She also offers extracts of Steele's hymns, poems, and letters that add texture to her analysis. Steele is one of four women that James briefly examines for the purpose of highlighting their spiritual character and faith as found in their writings. The common denominator of the four women she studied—Margaret Baxter (1639–1681), Sarah Edwards (1710–1758), Anne Steele, and Frances Ridley Havergal (1836–1879)—according to James, is "a common perspective."[153] James describes these women, "Their contentment and happiness did not depend on good health, a fulfilling job, or a happy family life. It came from living for God. . . . Each one was genuinely able to praise God through the bad times as well as the good."[154] Like Broome, James moves through a roughly chronological narrative of Steele's life and bases her portrait of Steele on the hymns, poems, and letters of Steele as well as the journals and letters of her family and friends. For Steele, in particular, James depicts her spiritual character traits as seen in one who in the midst of physical suffering yet retained a winsome personality, a spirit of dependence upon God, and a spirit of quiet confidence in God displayed in the lack of a need for the approval of others.

James develops her character study of Steele in three ways. The first two concern Steele's personal experience and how it is displayed in her writing while the third concerns her talent for her craft. James argues that though Steele endured physical suffering and the death of many loved ones, she still showed herself to be a cheerful woman of faith and good humor. Regarding Steele's personality, James even says, "I was astonished to discover

---

151. Broome, *Bruised Reed*, 165.

152. Broome, *Bruised Reed*, 175.

153. James, *In Trouble and in Joy*, 13.

154. James, *In Trouble and in Joy*, 13.

letters and poems by Anne Steele that showed her to have a sparkling sense of humor, and which belied the solemn impression I had of her from her hymns."[155] Yet Steele saw her suffering as a means of God to bring her closer to himself and to cause her to rely on God in prayer. Next, James examines Steele's faith and character as found in her writings. James states, "From the few letters we have, and from her hymns, we can see that Anne's life was characterized by a consistent gratitude for God's goodness, a steady desire to experience his presence, and a realistic sense of the temporary nature of earthly things."[156] Steele's life embodied the Particular Baptist belief in God's sovereign control of all things.

Finally, James demonstrates that Anne's cheerfulness, humility, faith, and contentment were revealed most vividly in her hymns, and coupled with her skill in hymn-writing, allowed her to offer a major contribution to the development of the eighteenth-century hymn. James points out two important aspects of Steele's hymn-writing: its breadth and its depth. Regarding the breadth of subject matter in Steele's hymns, James writes, "Anne's sensitivity to the needs of public worship inspired her to write hymns on the whole range of themes appropriate to different occasions and to fit the range of topics covered in the preaching ministry."[157] And in terms of the spiritual and experiential depth of Steele's hymns, James notes, "The appeal of Anne's hymns and poems is the transparent honesty with which she confessed to struggling as a Christian."[158] Though she struggled, Steele's hymns express a hope of God's presence in Christ with the suffering believer on earth as well as the hope of heaven beyond this life.

James's own summary of her work on Steele is worth quoting:

> Anne Steele lived during the eighteenth century in a small village in the south-west of England. Part of a well-off and closely-knit family, she deliberately remained single in an age that assumed that the ideal for women was marriage and motherhood. Through correspondence, she participated in a lively circle of educated and witty friends. Two volumes of her hymns and poems were published during her lifetime. Anne suffered ill health for most of her life (modern doctors reckon she had a persistent form of malaria). Despite this, she was a cheerful

---

155. James, *In Trouble and in Joy*, 14–15.
156. James, *In Trouble and in Joy*, 137.
157. James, *In Trouble and in Joy*, 129.
158. James, *In Trouble and in Joy*, 142.

woman, whose faith (and sense of humor) kept her positive
even through times of intense pain.[159]

This quote provides both an outline to the work of James and a rough statement of her thesis as well. James finds in Steele a woman of intense devotion: to God, family, the church, friends, and the craft of hymn-writing, and
all this in the midst of physical suffering. This same essay, with a slightly
different arrangement of the information, appears in *The British Particular
Baptists 1638–1910* vol. 3, edited by Michael A. G. Haykin.

In Nancy Cho's unpublished PhD dissertation, "'The Ministry of Song':
Unmarried British Women's Hymn Writing, 1760–1936," Cho examines
the hymns, lives, and writing context for a selection of unmarried British
women, beginning with Anne Steele. Looking at the work of early hym-
nologists, Cho found that "the impressive proportion of recognized women
hymn writers early in the history of British hymnody is extraordinary."[160]
Cho seeks to expand upon the recent brief scholarly treatments of women
hymn-writers in two broader hymn studies: Ian Bradley's *Abide with Me:
The World of Victorian Hymns* and J. R. Watson's *The English Hymn: A Critical and Historical Study*. Cho notes, "These studies assessed the significance
of the hymn from a variety of cultural viewpoints, including history, literature and theology."[161] Cho further states more specifically, "This thesis seeks
to examine British women's hymn writing primarily as a tradition of English literature."[162] Cho notes that her study also intersects with "other disciplines including church history, women's history and nineteenth-century
studies."[163] She describes her main critical method of examination as "the
close reading of individual hymns considered within the socio-historical
context of the time in which they were written."[164] Further, while Cho's dissertation may be considered "gynocritical," she notes that her approach will
not be aligned explicitly with one particular political strand or theory of
feminisms.[165]

---

159. James, *In Trouble and in Joy*, 117.

160. Cho, "Ministry of Song," 1.

161. Cho, "Ministry of Song," 3.

162. Cho, "Ministry of Song," 28.

163. Cho, "Ministry of Song," 28.

164. Cho, "Ministry of Song," 37.

165. Gynocriticism is "[a] branch of feminist literary theory and studies which focuses on women as writers, as distinct from feminist criticism and evaluation of male
writers." Cuddon, *Penguin Dictionary of Literary Terms and Literary Theory*, rev. Preston, 370, cited in Cho, "Ministry of Song," 2.

Cho's dissertation is made up of an introductory section covering literary criticism, historical contextualization, and methodology. There are seven chapters arranged chronologically, each examining a woman hymn-writer along with one chapter adding an additional comparative study, and finally, a conclusion. Cho begins her analysis in 1760 with Anne Steele since that was the date when Steele first published her *Poems on Subjects Chiefly Devotional*, though it was published under the pseudonym, Theodosia. Cho has chosen Steele as her starting point because, according to Cho, she was "the first major woman hymn writer, and a famous cultural figure of the eighteenth century."[166] Cho notes that Steele "was celebrated in a select list of distinguished women in Mary Scott's (1751–1793) *The Female Advocate* (1774)."[167]

In her broad introductory section Cho offers several particular and notable insights concerning Anne Steele. First, she quotes a 1986 essay that calls Steele "one of the brightest stars in the firmament of Baptist hymnody, hailed by the historians as the 'mother' of English women hymn writers."[168] Yet, Cho also uses Steele as an example of one of the problems with the ever-present "story behind the hymn" phenomenon in popular hymn studies. Cho points out that many of the commendations of Steele come in the context of viewing her hymns through the lens of the apocryphal story of her suffering the loss of a fiancé on the day of their wedding.[169] This has caused numerous students of Steele to frame her hymn-writing particularly through the idea, mostly mistaken, of the tragic story of lost love and disappointment. Cho later adds to this a discussion of the over-emphasis that seems to be placed on the suffering of hymn-writers, as if this was the only vantage point from which they wrote hymns. Cho attempts to deconstruct this regrettable tendency. Cho also describes the popularity of hymns and hymnals, noting the heavy representation of Steele's hymns in John Rippon's *Selection of Hymns*. She offers a helpful discussion of "the high purpose of hymn-writing (to express worship and glorify God)"[170] as found generally, while noting Steele's personal belief "that God's gifts must be spent as Christ had taught in his Parable of the Talents."[171] Finally, Cho lists Steele among those whose hymns express both an internal faith and an Evangelical

---

166. Cho, "Ministry of Song," 5.

167. Cho, "Ministry of Song," 5.

168. Maison, "Thine, Only Thine," in Malmgreen, *Religion in the Lives of English Women*, 14 cited in Cho, "Ministry of Song," 6.

169. See Watson and Cho, "Anne Steele's Drowned Fiancé," 117–21 for the research recovering the true story.

170. Cho, "Ministry of Song," 26.

171. Cho, "Ministry of Song," 27.

theology.[172] Steele's life and hymnody are thus well-represented in the Introduction to Cho's dissertation.

Cho entitles her first chapter "The Construction of the First Woman Hymn Writer: Anne Steele (1717–1778)." In this chapter, which includes many sub-theses found within its nine sections, she does build and skillfully argue the case that "the influence of Steele's writing was tremendously significant in setting trends within hymnody which women continued to follow for several generations."[173] Cho observes that the female hymn-writers that followed Steele were measured by and against the prototype developed by Steele through her life and hymn-writing. Throughout the nine sections of the chapter on Steele, Cho develops and argues her thesis by examining specific hymns by Steele while offering a running biographical sketch that interacts with the presentation of her life by her traditional biographers. Among the themes and episodes in Steele's life analyzed by Cho are Steele's full and healthy relationships with members of her family, a revised and updated understanding of the suffering Anne did endure, a more robust understanding of her personality, her network of friends and acquaintances who both offered her intellectual stimulation and helped her to be published, her own self-conscious understanding of her craft, the evangelical themes of her hymns, her death, and a thorough exploration of "the processes by which her work came to be distributed and gained recognition and popularity within the Church."[174] Cho constructs her biographical sketch and analysis both to correct some historical misunderstandings about Steele and her hymn-writing and also to demonstrate how the historical perceptions of Steele for roughly two hundred years after her death influenced her position "as the forerunner who points the way for other literary Christian women to follow in praise of God."[175] Cho's work is a brief but well-rounded examination of Steele's life, hymns, and personal craft of hymn-writing that also highlights her influence on those who followed.

Cynthia Y. Aalders's *To Express the Ineffable: The Hymns and Spirituality of Anne Steele* likewise offers insight into Steele's life and times. For her background research Aalders uses the same primary sources as Broome, James, and Cho, the Broughton Baptist Church records and the Steele Collection. Writing before Broome's manuscript was complete, Aalders offers similar biographical information as well as the intellectual, literary, religious, and cultural contexts within which Steele wrote. Aalders, however, goes on to

172. Cho, "Ministry of Song," 42.
173. Cho, "Ministry of Song," 84.
174. Cho, "Ministry of Song," 43.
175. Cho, "Ministry of Song," 43.

examine Steele's spirituality through a study of her hymns. Aalders tells the reader up front that she has four clear purposes in her study of Anne Steele. First, she desires to "illuminate the life of a significant though, in the last century, largely ignored figure in the history of the church."[176] Second, she believes that Steele's hymns shed light on the spirituality of "eighteenth-century English Christians, and of Baptists more particularly."[177] Next, Aalders rightly claims that as the first notable woman hymn-writer, Steele's work deserves attention. Finally, she wants to "elucidate Steele's unique expression of devotion via an exploration of the particular spiritual themes present in her hymnody."[178] Having offered such a clear statement of the purpose of her work on Steele, the question arises: "Did Aalders accomplish her purpose?" Even a cursory reading of the book will convince the reader that, on one level or another, Aalders's purposes are accomplished. Following a discussion of her presuppositions, Aalders's thesis will be considered.

The primary presupposition undergirding Aalders's work is that an historical and literary analysis of a writer's hymns, corroborated with a study of her extant unpublished poetry and letters, offers a legitimate window through which to view the Christian spirituality of a particular time period. Aalders presupposes that the analysis of Steele's hymns elucidates the spiritual beliefs, experiences, devotional practices, and view of life of Steele and the larger culture within which she lived.[179] The primary source for her study is Steele's 1780 edition of *Poems on Subjects Chiefly Devotional, by Theodosia.*[180] She also considers the entire Steele Collection already mentioned.

Aalders's thesis is that an analysis of Steele's hymns reveals that "the prevalent themes in Steele's hymnody gesture toward two related problems: problems pertaining to language and suffering."[181] Aalders detects in Steele a sense, found in her hymns, that human language is terribly limited, perhaps incapable of articulating meaning about God. Aalders also finds in Steele a search for God in the midst of her suffering. Steele seems to have asked, "Why am I suffering so and where are you, God, in the midst of this?" Steele tackled the classic spiritual theme of the ineffability of God. Aalders demonstrates and explains these themes in Steele's hymns and letters. She does find that Steele's Calvinistic faith and evangelical hope yet resulted in her

176. Aalders, *To Express the Ineffable*, 3.
177. Aalders, *To Express the Ineffable*, 3.
178. Aalders, *To Express the Ineffable*, 3.
179. Aalders, *To Express the Ineffable*, 1–8.
180. Steele, *Poems on Subjects Chiefly Devotional, by Theodosia.*
181. Aalders, *To Express the Ineffable*, 4.

attempt through hymn-writing to articulate praise to this seemingly absent God through the inadequate medium of the human language. Following a statement of her methods, purposes, presuppositions, and thesis, Aalders concludes the introductory chapter, chapter 1, with a brief but thorough biographical sketch of Steele's life.

In the second chapter Aalders situates Steele in the evangelical hymn-writing world during the eighteenth century, the golden age of the English hymn. She describes the English hymn as both literature and theology and demonstrates its cultural and spiritual influence and power as a valuable devotional art form in Steele's day. After considering the relevant contemporary hymn-writers with which to compare Steele—Isaac Watts, Charles Wesley, William Cowper, Elizabeth Singer Rowe (1674–1737), and Anne Dutton (1692–1765)—Aalders then explains Steele's more specific role as the major figure in eighteenth-century Baptist hymnody. Aalders sees hymns as "valuable pointers" to both personal and corporate spirituality in the eighteenth century.[182]

In chapters 3 and 4 Aalders develops the two major strands of her thesis. Aalders clearly states the first aspect of her thesis, Steele's "hymns sound a new note in eighteenth-century hymnody, largely because through them she introduces a self-conscious reflection on the ability of language to offer meaningful praise to God."[183] Aalders finds Steele doubting both her personal ability to articulate praise to God and the ability of "language itself to convey meaning when God is the subject."[184] Aalders argues for her thesis by starting with the broad and general and moving to the specific. Here she begins with a consideration of Steele's own reflections on writing and language and the themes that seem to have emerged as Steele applied her craft. Following a look at the ineffability of God as considered in language and literature, Aalders explains the theme of ineffability in Steele's thought and hymnody. Aalders offers specific examples of these themes in Steele's hymns and declares that though Steele found her own person and words inadequate for the task of offering meaningful praise to God, yet she attempted to do so anyway.

In the fourth chapter Aalders moves to an examination of the relationship between language and understanding. In her own words, Aalders seeks to "explore Steele's efforts to understand God by attending to her experience of loss and suffering, and by considering her subsequent efforts to articulate

---

182. Aalders, *To Express the Ineffable*, 65.
183. Aalders, *To Express the Ineffable*, 66.
184. Aalders, *To Express the Ineffable*, 66.

her experience of the seeming silence or absence of God."[185] This should lead to a better understanding of Steele's thoughts regarding the incomprehensibility of God. Aalders's method for arguing this second strand of her thesis is to first examine Steele's experience of and her writing about her own suffering and the perceived silence of God in the midst of it. This logically leads to Steele's conclusion that God is thus incomprehensible.

Next Aalders traces the theme of incomprehensibility through some specific hymns of Steele. Aalders finds in Steele a lack of confident assertions. This void is apparently filled in Steele's hymns by questions regarding her suffering and God's silence within her experience. Yet Steele attempted to write about God nevertheless: "Writing in private, attempting to make sense of her experience of personal suffering, Steele was made to confront her inability to comprehend fully the nature and ways of God."[186] So Steele asked the hard questions in faith, recognizing that human sin hides God from our understanding for he is certainly not ultimately incomprehensible.

In chapter 5 Aalders seeks to resolve the problems she delineates in the previous two chapters and suggests "how indeed Steele was able to overcome the problems of language and suffering in order to make affirmations about God and the spiritual life, despite her belief that God was both ineffable and incomprehensible."[187] One might say that Aalders spends two chapters clearly demonstrating that Anne Steele did not consider herself or language capable of articulating meaningful praise to a silent, absent, and ineffable God. Then she uses the fifth chapter to show that Anne Steele herself yet uses the English language to construct hymns of praise to an omnipresent God who has clearly revealed himself to his children by his word and Spirit. Aalders finds Steele's understanding of and apprehension of personal resignation to the will of God, a longing for God's presence and blessing, and an eschatological hope, all grounded in the word of God, to be the vehicles allowing her to write hymns in the face of her perceived limitations.

In the concluding chapter, Aalders offers a helpful summary of her project of examining the hymns of Anne Steele. She also specifically applies her findings through a brief exposition of Steele's hymn, "Dear Refuge of my Weary Soul," the hymn with which Aalders introduces her interest in Steele. In *To Express the Ineffable*, Aalders outlines Steele's life, hymnody, and piety based on Steele's "Problem of Language," "Problem of Suffering," and "Faith in an Ineffable God." By examining Steele's hymns within the context of her life, Aalders offers helpful insight into Steele's craft as a poet, her faith as

---

185. Aalders, *To Express the Ineffable*, 102.

186. Aalders, *To Express the Ineffable*, 123.

187. Aalders, *To Express the Ineffable*, 6–7.

a Christian, and how these aspects of her life intersect. Aalders examines Steele's hymns through the lens of Steele's own direct or indirect discussions in her letters, poems, and hymns of the limits of language and the life of suffering. Aalders focuses on these themes particularly as found in a number of hymns found in *Poems on Subjects Chiefly Devotional* plus several unpublished hymns. In her final chapter Aalders restates her thesis, "The real power of [Steele's] hymnody is surely located in her honest, introspective searching for answers to the problems which inhibit her spiritual confidence—problems which . . . are related to her reflections on language and suffering."[188] While Aalders does affirm Steele's ultimate confidence in a sovereign and loving God and some positive aspects of Steele's Calvinistic theology in her hymns, Aalders seems to suggest that the two major themes of Steele's poetry are the problems of language and suffering as considered in light of God's ineffability. An examination of Steele's hymns with their balanced representation in Rippon's *Selection of Hymns*, however, will expand the horizon of theological and experiential themes found in Steele's corpus.

With "'In Melting Grief and Ardent Love': Anne Steele's Contribution to Eighteenth-Century Hymnody," Cynthia Aalders offers her arguments for Anne Steele's contribution to the English hymn in a shorter essay format than that of her monograph on Steele. Aalders begins her essay with a biographical sketch and then reviews the remarkable popularity of Steele's hymns in Britain and America from the time of their publication until the end of the nineteenth century. Next, while acknowledging the reality of Steele's sufferings, she deftly deconstructs the myth of Steele as merely a sensitive and melancholic woman of extreme piety whose verse rose naturally from her experiences of personal loss.[189] Though Steele did write some somber hymns, her letters show her to be a woman of both wit and good humor. Aalders continues by planting Steele firmly within her family and the circle of witty, intelligent, and literary companions within which she developed as a writer. Finally, she moves more formally into the analysis of Steele's hymns and poems that she has already begun in part in the biographical sketch. Aalders describes the purpose and plan of her essay, "I argue that rather than the robust confidence or stately elegance of other, better known eighteenth-century hymn-writers, Steele's hymns introduce an expression of faith that is personal and introspective, and that reveals a compelling depth of honesty regarding the common human experiences of suffering and doubt."[190]

---

188. Aalders, *To Express the Ineffable*, 177.

189. Aalders, "In Melting Grief and Ardent Love," 16–25.

190. Aalders, "In Melting Grief and Ardent Love," 16.

In light of her thesis statement, Aalders builds her case for the power of Steele's hymns around the following characteristics and qualities of her hymn lyrics: sensitivity, hesitation, and introspection. While Aalders describes Steele's hymns as doctrinally sound for her Particular Baptist context, as expressions of a vibrant faith, and as written both intelligently and devotionally, yet Aalders finds Steele's hymns as primarily reflections of an introspective faith expressed more by questions than by declarations. In fact, Aalders finds in Steele's hymns "a certain lack of confident assertions," a plaintive tone, an uncertain approach to God, and an "experience of God as inscrutable or incomprehensible."[191] Aalders describes her own evaluation of Steele, "The result is a powerful and unique contribution to eighteenth-century hymnody."[192] This contribution came alongside those of the well-known hymn-writing giants of the English hymn's golden age.

Aalders conducts her analysis of Steele's hymns by comparing hymns that Aalders believes both Steele and Charles Wesley modeled after the hymn written by Isaac Watts and known today as "When I Survey the Wondrous Cross." These serve as acceptable hymn-writers with which to compare Steele, as Aalders describes Watts's hymns as especially dignified and didactic and Wesley's as confident and even exuberant.[193] How does Steele compare when writing on the same subject? Aalders lists two verses from Watts's hymn:

> When I survey the wondrous Cross
> Where the young Prince of Glory dy'd,
> My riches Gain I count but Loss,
> And pour contempt on all my Pride.
>
> His dying Crimson like a Robe
> Spreads o'er his Body on the Tree,
> Then am I dead to all the Globe,
> And all the Globe is dead to me.[194]

Alders describes Watts's hymn as one in the Augustan vein, that is, a hymn in which "language is controlled and dignified."[195] He surveys the crucifixion with a sense of confidence. And though he writes personally, his verse

191. Aalders, "In Melting Grief and Ardent Love," 18.

192. Aalders, "In Melting Grief and Ardent Love," 18.

193. Aalders, "In Melting Grief and Ardent Love," 18–20.

194. Watts, "Crucifixion to the World by the Cross of Christ," in *Hymns and Spiritual Songs*, 189, cited in Aalders, "In Melting Grief and Ardent Love," 18–19. The second line of the first verse typically reads, "On which the Prince of Glory died."

195. Aalders, "In Melting Grief and Ardent Love," 18.

is "neither emotional nor dramatic."[196] Aalders compares Watts's lines to
Charles Wesley's version:

> For you the purple current flowed,
>   In pardons from his wounded side,
> Languished for you the eternal God,
>   For you the prince of glory died,
> Believe, and all your sin's forgiven,
> Only believe, and yours is heaven![197]

Aalders says, "Wesley's language is confident, his tone exuberant."[198]
Aalders finds in Wesley's verses a confidence that his sins are forgiven, an
evangelistic enthusiasm toward his audience, and even notes that "an abun-
dance of exclamation points punctuate Wesley's verse."[199] Finally, Aalders
lists some verses from Steele to clarify her voice:

> Stretch'd on the cross the Saviour dies;
> Hark! his expiring groans arise!
> See, from his hands, his feet, his side,
> Runs down the sacred crimson tide!
>
> Can I survey this scene of woe,
> Where mingling grief and wonder flow;
> And yet my heart unmov'd remain,
> Insensible to love or pain!
>
> Come, dearest Lord, thy power impart,
> To warm this cold, this stupid heart;
> Till all its powers and passions move,
> In melting grief and ardent love.[200]

Comparing Steele's verses to those of Wesley, Aalders comments that in
contrast to Wesley's hymn that has a "hearkening, rousing way" about it,
we see in "Steele's a more tender, introspective way" as Steele even acknowledges "how her own hard heart wounded her Saviour."[201] Aalders summarizes her analysis of the three writers, "Where Watts surveys the scene of the

196. Aalders, "In Melting Grief and Ardent Love," 19.

197. Wesley, *Collection of Hymns, for the Use of the People Called Methodists*, 34,
cited in Aalders, "In Melting Grief and Ardent Love," 20.

198. Aalders, "In Melting Grief and Ardent Love," 20.

199. Aalders, "In Melting Grief and Ardent Love," 20.

200. Steele, "A Dying Saviour," *Poems on Subjects Chiefly Devotional*, 1:180, cited in
Aalders, "In Melting Grief and Ardent Love," 20.

201. Aalders, "In Melting Grief and Ardent Love," 20.

crucifixion from a thoughtful distance, Steele is emotionally drawn into the drama. . . . We see that Steele's verse is sensitive and introspective, and where Wesley's is marked by exclamation points, Steele's is just as often punctuated by question marks. This is true of Steele's hymnody in general."[202]

Writing during the "Age of Sensibility," that time of transition between the Augustan period and Romantic age, Steele, according to Aalders, wrote personal hymns in which she was free "to express her emotion as she reflected on her own spiritual experiences."[203] While Watts's hymns served the corporately worshipping congregation and Wesley's helped to spark the fires of revival, Steele wrote, as it were, in her private prayer journal. Steele's hymns, argues Aalders, "introduce a powerful and personal voice to eighteenth-century hymnody—a voice that is sometimes hesitant and often sensitive and introspective, a voice that consistently and frankly acknowledges the existence of human loss and limitation."[204]

Ken Manley's *'Redeeming Love Proclaim': John Rippon and the Baptists* provides insight into John Rippon as an Evangelical Baptist leader, pastor, hymn-writer, compiler of hymns, and publisher. The culmination of over thirty years of work on Rippon, Manley devotes a full chapter to John Rippon and Baptist hymnody. Manley's analysis of Rippon's *Selection of Hymns* is thorough and well-organized. He considers Rippon's selection criteria, issues of the theology and piety expressed by the authors he selected, and how the editions evolved over many years and through many reprints. Manley lists tables that show the number of hymns per topic as Rippon saw fit to arrange them, the denominational allegiances of the hymn-writers listed, and the number of hymns by each writer in all the major editions of the *Selection of Hymns*. Manley also offers a good analysis of both evangelical and Baptist life during the first decades in which Steele's hymns were being disseminated and sung by congregations, and thus able to have an impact on the spirituality of the period. Manley's "spade-work" is immensely beneficial research on the *Selection of Hymns*, inviting further analysis of the hymn-writers contained therein.

There have, of course, been other studies on Steele's thought and life. In his book *The English Hymn: A Critical and Historical Study*, J. R. Watson devotes eight pages to Anne Steele and another six pages to her English Particular Baptist contemporaries, Benjamin Beddome and Samuel Stennett. Earlier in the book he spends a chapter profiling Baptist hymn-writers Benjamin Keach, John Bunyan (1628–1688), and Joseph Stennett I. Watson's

202. Aalders, "In Melting Grief and Ardent Love," 20.
203. Aalders, "In Melting Grief and Ardent Love," 21.
204. Aalders, "In Melting Grief and Ardent Love," 21.

relatively recent book is particularly helpful toward further research on the hymns of Anne Steele as he goes beyond the typical book on hymns written strictly in relation to church worship, to the content, to the tunes, or as a study of the "story" of the hymn, or finally as a subjective or psychological study of the hymn or its author. For example, Watson begins his study of Steele by examining the frontispiece engravings of Steele's two volumes before jumping into a comparison of Steele's hymns to those of Watts. He does a literary analysis of selected verses of Steele's hymns, focusing on the theology of her hymns as crafted by her skill with verse. For example, he says, "Anne Steele's excellent craft . . . is extraordinarily good at finding the correct word or phrase for what she wants to say, and contrasting one element of the hymn with another."[205] Explaining his book, Watson writes, "On the whole the texts of hymns have received little critical study from students of English literature. This book . . . is different from most of the others because it is a work of literary criticism, rather than a study of the content and usefulness of hymns in a liturgical setting."[206] Yet it is exactly his literary criticism that helps unlock the theology and attractiveness of Steele's hymns. In his brief treatment Watson offers a model of literary criticism directed at hymns and highlights such doctrines found in Steele's hymns as the atonement, creation, providence, suffering, the problem of evil, human nature, sin, and the doctrines of grace. Watson also directs the reader's attention to Steele's intense and dramatic use of language, her "rhetorical art," her "skillful articulation of ideas," her range of vocabulary, and her piety.[207] Watson's coverage of the entire history of the English hymn from his literary vantage point also offers insight into the period within which Steele wrote and within which Rippon's *Selection of Hymns* received its greatest use.

More recently Watson's chapter, "Eighteenth-Century Hymn Writers," in *The Blackwell Companion to the Bible in English Literature* both updates and condenses his work of literary analysis of the English hymn while also focusing on the hymn-writers' attempts to remain faithful to the biblical text as the foundation of their hymn lyrics. Watson focuses his literary analysis on the major writers of the period, including Steele and Benjamin Beddome. He compares the use of Scripture texts by different authors, highlighting hymns on the Nativity story in Luke 2. Watson's understanding of how hymn-writers' paraphrase and express the theology and content of biblical texts is helpful and illuminating. And his continued personal work on the hymns of Anne Steele is noteworthy as well. Here he concentrates on how the

---

205. Watson, *English Hymn*, 196.
206. Watson, *English Hymn*, vii.
207. Watson, *English Hymn*, 190–98.

disadvantage of Steele's writing as a woman is overcome by her skill as a poet and the fact that "the Bible is of central importance in directing her thoughts. It becomes a comfort and a guide."[208] He also highlights the ways in which Steele's verse reveals an intense devotion that is based on the narratives of the Bible and especially of the Passion of Christ.

Finally, Richard Arnold's 1989 article, "A 'Veil of Interposing Night': The Hymns of Anne Steele (1717–1778)," from *Christian Scholar's Review* offers a literary and speech theory analysis of Steele's hymns. At a time when Broome appeared to be the only Steele scholar of note, Arnold's article served as an important contribution to Steele research and continues to demand review and comment. He locates Steele as the pre-eminent Baptist hymn-writer of the important age within which she wrote, as holding a unique and significant position in the history of English hymnody, and as the only hymn-writer to receive favorable assessments from the critical media of her day.[209] Arnold also briefly traces the popularity of her hymns from the time of their first publication through the next 150 years. Arnold, not unlike the approach of Aalders, zeroes in on Anne Steele's self-conscious process of writing, her comments on language and its inadequacy to express all that she longs to say, and especially her apparent doubts and questions of faith and of God's goodness and love for his creatures. Arnold finds Steele's self-identification as the writer of her hymns and desire to find the right words to be "unprecedented in English hymnody."[210] Further, regarding her use of and thoughts on language, Arnold posits, "Anne Steele is innovative and unprecedented in her application of this linguistic concern to the congregational *hymn*."[211] Arnold's contribution is thorough and helpful as he explores and defends his thesis. Yet, there is a certain lack of understanding of Steele's worldview and inner foundation of faith, in Arnold, that deserves further exploration and explanation.

---

208. Watson, "Eighteenth-Century Hymn Writers," 335.
209. Arnold, "Veil of Interposing Night," 371–72.
210. Arnold, "Veil of Interposing Night," 376.
211. Arnold, "Veil of Interposing Night," 371.

2

A Biography of Anne Steele

IN CONSTRUCTING A BIOGRAPHICAL sketch of the life of Anne Steele[1] as an introduction to a study of her hymns in Rippon's *Selection of Hymns*, a thematic presentation of her life will shed light on the contexts within which she composed hymns. Thus several themes will be considered below as a window into the life of the English Baptists' premier hymn-writer. The first theme to consider is the ecclesiastical and theological tradition within which Steele was born and raised. In what belief system was Steele raised and what was the context within which she developed her convictions? The next theme to consider is her family life, including family relationships as well as the educational, spiritually edifying, and intellectually stimulating aspects of the Steele clan. A deep sense of family love, loyalty, piety, intelligence, and creativity influenced Steele all her life. The third theme to explore is the physical, emotional, and spiritual suffering Steele endured. She often composed her hymns from within the crucible of suffering. She also wrote hymns as she faced the deaths of family members and friends throughout her life. How did that suffering and her regular experience of the deaths of those she loved relate to her approach to her craft? Fourth, throughout her years, Steele was surrounded by a network of friends and advisors that offered both spiritual and intellectual direction to Steele's life and poetry and also contributed to the publishing of her hymns. Somewhat unknown to early students of Steele's life and work, this theme deserves exploration. Finally, the circumstances of the publishing of Steele's hymns both in her lifetime and thereafter deserves

1. The following biographical sketch is based primarily upon research of the Steele Collection at the Angus Library, Regent's Park College, Oxford, by the following four authors: Broome, *Bruised Reed*; James, *In Trouble and in Joy*; Cho, "Ministry of Song"; and Aalders, *To Express the Ineffable*.

consideration. This theme leads into a study of her hymns as published in Rippon's *Selection of Hymns*. The consideration of these themes, offering an initial brief introduction to Anne Steele's life, will re-emerge as particular hymns are analyzed in a later chapter.

Anne Steele was born in 1717 in the quiet village of Broughton, in Hampshire, southern England. She was the daughter of Particular Baptist pastor William Steele (1689–1769) and Anne Froude Steele (1684–1720). William had taken over the pastorate of the Baptist chapel at Broughton from his uncle, Henry Steele (1655–1739), who died in 1739 after serving this church for forty years. From an early age Anne was involved in the life of this Baptist congregation. Henry and William were successful timber merchants who did not take salaries for their roles as ministers.

The Steeles were a family of Particular Baptists. This means Steele was born into the community of Dissenters or Noncomformists. Both her paternal and maternal ancestors had endured years of religious persecution for refusing to conform to the Church of England. In fact, John Rede (d. 1710), the founder of the Steele family's church, was arrested and imprisoned in the Tower of London for a number of years in the early 1660s. J. R. Broome declares, "The forebears of Anne Steele's church were certainly a hardy people made ready, as the Apostle Paul, to endure unto the death for the truth's sake."[2] Though, after the Glorious Revolution of 1688, Dissenters were granted relative freedom to worship, they still had not been given full equality of citizenship. Nonconformists were "still excluded from the universities and from civic and political life."[3] Perhaps Henry and William Steele would have used the abilities that brought them wealth and success in the timber trade in Parliament or in the practice of law had they been Anglicans.[4] The Dissenters did found successful academic institutions to train their own in the face of the restrictions placed upon them. The Bristol Baptist Academy, for example, successfully trained many Particular Baptist pastors, not a few of whom also wrote hymns. They also began to grow churches once they emerged from the shadow of the state.

Life in the Steele household "revolved around the regular meetings of the Baptist chapel."[5] In 1653, prior to the days of religious freedom, John Rede, a member of the Parliamentary Army at the time, founded the chapel initially in Porton. Apparently many Particular Baptist churches were founded by Baptist officers who also happened to be evangelists. In terms of

2. Broome, *Bruised Reed*, 30.
3. James, *In Trouble and in Joy*, 118.
4. See James, *In Trouble and in Joy*, 118.
5. James, *In Trouble and in Joy*, 123.

their theological ancestry, the English Particular Baptists[6] were products of the English Reformation,[7] and more specifically, "they emerged from the womb of English Puritanism in the early to mid-seventeenth century."[8] Following the Toleration Act of 1689, English Particular Baptist leaders William Kiffin (1616–1701), Hanserd Knollys (ca. 1599–1691), and Benjamin Keach together with four other ministers met in London to organize and call forth a General Assembly of representatives from Particular Baptists Churches.[9] Edward Froude (1645–1714), Anne Steele's maternal grandfather and pastor of the Erlestoke congregation in Wiltshire, represented his congregation at that gathering. This assembly republished the *Second London Confession* of 1677, within which the theological convictions of the Particular Baptists had been crystallized.[10] This confession reflected Calvinistic emphases, such as justification, sanctification, the extent of the atonement, predestination, and perseverance of the saints. Tom Nettles says that this document "became the single most formative theological influence on Baptist life in England and America."[11] The Particular Baptists' first generation of leaders, including such men as Knollys, Kiffin, and Keach, were able to balance "conservative Calvinism with a warm and fervent evangelism."[12] J. R. Broome says of Steele's father, William, to whom she was very close all his life, "Doctrinally, in his preaching he followed the

6. From the first quarter of the seventeenth century through the nineteenth century, Baptists in England were divided into two main sections, i.e., *General* and *Particular* Baptists. The former group favored the Arminian view of the Christian atonement and human free-agency, or *General* redemption. The latter and larger group professed the doctrines usually associated with the name of Calvin, including *Particular* redemption.

7. Haykin, "British Particular Baptist Biography," 15.

8. Haykin, "British Particular Baptist Biography," 16.

9. Broome, *Bruised Reed*, 43.

10. The Presbyterians produced the *Westminster Confession of Faith*, written by the Westminster Assembly of divines meeting in London from 1643–1647. The *Westminster Confession of Faith* was copied in large measure by the Independents in their *Savoy Declaration* in 1658. The *Savoy Declaration* was the model for the Particular Baptists' *Second London Confession*. They also drew some inspiration from the First London Confession of Faith of 1644, produced by seven London Particular Baptist congregations during the Civil War. These confessions obviously differ from one another as regards such issues as baptism, the Lord's Supper, and church government. Their common sufferings, however, led the three groups much closer together by this time. See Broome, *Bruised Reed*, 18, 33–35.

11. Nettles, *Baptists*, 1:36.

12. McBeth, *Baptist Heritage*, 171. Cramp says that they "might be called 'the first three' among the Baptist ministers of those days. Their talents and characters gave them influence, which appears to have been wisely exerted for the benefit of the denomination." See Cramp, *Baptist History*, 440. See also *British Particular Baptists*, vol. 1, for individual articles about each of these pious Particular Baptist pioneers.

1689 Confession of Faith."[13] Obviously, Steele would have heard most of her father's sermons, and thus been acquainted with the theology of the *Second London Confession* since her birth.

These Particular Baptist congregations were rather economically diverse in their memberships from their beginnings. Of special note is the fact that their pastors were sometimes quite well-to-do. William Kiffin, for example, "was a wealthy merchant and in 1687 an Alderman of the City of London."[14] John Rede was not only a soldier, but also probably a lawyer, an MP, and "a man of considerable importance in his locality."[15] Further, Edward Froude, farmer and preacher, was of such income, status, and education that not only was he buried in the main nave of the Edington Priory of the Anglican Church, but the inscription on his grave was in Latin.[16] J. R. Broome summarizes it this way,

> If many Particular Baptist ministers were men of the social caliber of John Bunyan, a tinker, a good number of others such as William Kiffin and John Rede were to be numbered among the upper echelons of society. The Broughton/Porton Church was composed of weavers, farmworkers, yeoman farmers, carpenters, house builders and also business and professional men, who would sign their wills as Edward Froude did at Edington, "Gent," and have gravestones with the inscription in Latin. Knowing a little of this political and cultural background among the Particular Baptists helps us understand the type of Particular Baptist society into which Anne Steele was born in 1717.[17]

Anne Steele's father and uncle, who also happened to be her pastors, likewise provided a comfortable life for Anne. The relatively independent life they offered her served to contribute to her development as a writer.

Anne Steele's family was close-knit and affectionate all her life. They were also a learned, witty, and poetically gifted group. Her father, William, married Anne Froude, the daughter of a Particular Baptist pastor. It is possible that they met when William was the guest preacher at her home church in Erlestoke. Surviving correspondence shows that they were a romantic pair.

13. Broome, *Bruised Reed*, 194. Broome lists excerpts from one of his sermons, showing it to be Evangelical, Calvinistic, and gospel-driven. See Broome, *Bruised Reed*, 194–98.

14. Broome, *Bruised Reed*, 27.

15. Broome, *Bruised Reed*, 27.

16. Broome, *Bruised Reed*, 17, 21.

17. Broome, *Bruised Reed*, 27. For more on this issue see Champion, "Social Status of some Eighteenth Century Baptist Ministers," 10–14.

The first surviving letter from William to Anne, likely his first communication with her, was a love-letter written in verse and running more than seventy lines.[18] Barred from university education as a Dissenter, William perhaps attended a Baptist academy. Whether formally educated or not, Broome suggests, "It is likely that, as with Isaac Watts, William Steele was a born poet and that this ability was inherited by his daughter Anne, the hymnwriter."[19] William and Anne were married sometime between December 1713 and February 1714 after a relatively short courtship.

Steele had an older brother, William (1715–1785), born two years before her in 1715. By the time of Steele's birth in 1717, her parents had moved to the old family house in Broughton called "The Grandfathers." Her little brother Thomas was born there three years later in May 1720, but only lived a month and was buried July 1. Steele's mother died suddenly on May 22, apparently while giving birth to Thomas. William Steele, who had lost both parents by the age of nineteen, found himself again in the throes of sorrow, now at the age of thirty-one. He had lost a wife he dearly loved while giving birth to a son who died shortly thereafter, and he was left with William, aged five, and Anne, aged three. And all this occurred in the midst of extensive travel with the family timber business, not to mention regular preaching engagements. Thus little Anne Steele's life of sorrows and bereavements, beginning at the tender age of three, was not unlike that of each of her parents.

William persevered for more than two years as a single father of two, businessman, and preacher. Surviving love-letters, written to Anne Cator at Trowle Common near Trowbridge, signal a new romantic turn in his life. William married this pious Particular Baptist lady in 1723. A certain amount of family wealth also followed her into the Steele family. Anne Cator Steele quickly began to care for the two children as her own and showed early on a concern for their spiritual well-being as well as her step-daughter's health.[20] A baby girl was added to the Steele family in 1724 when Steele was seven. Little Mary (1724–1772) as she was named was always called Molly, while Steele was known as Nanny in the family. Though obviously learned men, there is no surviving information on William the Senior or Junior's education. Nevertheless, letters from boarding school show that Steele was receiving an education in Trowbridge by the age of twelve.

A few examples from family life will demonstrate the spirituality, creativity, and intelligence of the Steele household. William Steele Sr.'s piety and

18. See Broome, *Bruised Reed*, 51–55.

19. Broome, *Bruised Reed*, 52.

20. Much of the biographical information on Steele and the greater Steele family come from the surviving journals of Anne Cator Steele.

affection as expressed through his sermons and love-letters has already been mentioned. Like others of the Puritan tradition, Mrs. Steele kept a journal.[21] Her journal entries reveal her constant concern for the spiritual lives of the three children. Surviving family letters also offer insight into Steele and her family. A letter from twelve-year-old Steele away at school sheds light on a number of aspects of her life. She wrote,

> [I] am sorry to hear of my brother's illness and Aunt's death and doubt not but my cousins are in a great deal of trouble for the death of their mother, but I hope the same God that no doubt for wise ends took her from them, will enable them to bear their affliction with patience. As to my liking the place, I suppose you know my mistress is an odd-tempered woman, but she is as kind to me as to the rest. Our work is most on headcloths and I hope I shall learn very well. . . . I also am through mercy in good health. Cousin Betty is sent for home, which makes me a little dull to be without her. I long to see you all and hope I shall see my father in a little time. . . . This with my duty to my father and to yourself and love to sister Molly is from your dutifull and obedient daughter, Anne Steele.
>
> P.S. I desire you would excuse my bad handwriting being by candle, because we work till it's dark now.[22]

This quote from such a young girl offers more than can be fully considered here, but at least a few comments are in order. First, it shows the obvious influence of loving parents who have raised Steele in an environment of Christian nurture and instruction. It also reveals Steele's love for her parents and siblings. Hints of Steele's developing poetic piety can be seen even in such a short excerpt from her young pen. She also shows a bit of her personality, respectfully admitting the truth of the "odd-tempered" mistress while also soberly offering honor to her parents. The mention of making "headcloths" as the primary application of education has elicited various

21. From this point on, Anne Cator Steele will be called Mrs. Steele to distinguish her from Anne Steele, the subject of this book. Mrs. Steele bequeathed her journals and in doing so staggered the volumes. The volumes which have survived contain entries for the years 1730–1736, 1749–1752, and 1753–1760. These years correspond to Steele at the following ages: thirteen to eighteen, thirty-one to thirty-five, and thirty-six to forty-three.

22. Steele Collection, Angus Library, Regent's Park College, Oxford, England (hereafter STE), 3/7/i, in Broome, *Bruised Reed*, 76. Quotes from Mrs. Steele's journals will be copied directly from the four major biographies being used and thus will contain those authors' corrections of spelling and grammar or lack thereof.

responses from authors.[23] While it may have been an innocuous and perhaps even frustrating pursuit for such a bright young mind, at least two positive things can be said about this education. First, she would have been one of a privileged minority of women to be receiving a formal education at all in her day. And second, Broome points out that the cloth trade "was the most important industry in England at the time."[24] Finally, Broome adds that her handwriting is quite neat and regular with excellent spelling and that this letter shows "that Anne had obviously had some previous education before she came to Trowbridge."[25]

Anne Steele loved her father and step-mother, as well as her siblings. The surviving letter from her youth shows this. And that love was reciprocated. Her love for her father is seen most vividly later in her life when she became his housekeeper and nurse during the last nine years of his life after the death of Mrs. Steele. Early on, however, letters and journal entries of a particularly spiritual nature reveal the care of the family for one another. Mrs. Steele often wrote in a very loving tone of Anne's spiritual sensitivities and her regular struggle with ill health. [26] Following a conversation with Anne about the concerns of the young lady's soul, Mrs. Steele once wrote "that the conversation stirred her up 'to cry earnestly on Anne's account that as God has been pleased to make her sensible of the want and worth of a Saviour, so he would also give her a well-grounded hope that she have an interest in that Saviour that so she might be happy here and forever.'"[27] A few weeks later, continuing to pray for Anne's health, she wrote, "I beg the affliction may be sanctified to her and that her life may be spared."[28] And Mrs. Steele's prayers continue as a few months later she adds, "I have great hope that God have [sic] indeed begun to work upon the souls of our children."[29] Her prayers were answered in the professions of faith and baptisms of William and Anne not long thereafter. Later correspondence between sister and brother confirm the fruit of these experiences. At age nineteen Steele once wrote from Trowbridge to her brother,

23. As a part of her education, Steele was learning to do elegant sewing to make headcloths, often for export, and learning something about the cloth trade.

24. He adds, "Much of the cloth was exported to Europe." Broome, *Bruised Reed*, 77.

25. Broome, *Bruised Reed*, 176.

26. Based on descriptions from Anne Cator Steele's journal entries, a modern pathologist has convincingly argued that what she usually refers as "the ague" and later as consumption is very likely chronic malaria. See Dixon and Steele-Smith, "Anne Steele's Health," 351–56.

27. Broome, *Bruised Reed*, 79.

28. Broome, *Bruised Reed*, 79.

29. Broome, *Bruised Reed*, 79–80.

I really believe your writing to me would be very useful, both to improve my understanding, and to exalt my thoughts more to the solid pleasures of virtue and religion; the most necessary and important subjects. . . . My sister and I join our duty to my Father and Mother and love to yourself, I hope my mother won't be angry for my not writing to her. I designed it but had not time. I beg a long letter from you as soon as possible; I assure you tis very desirable and will be thankfully received by Sir, your affectionate sister, sincere friend, and servant, Anne Steele."[30]

William likewise writes to his sister a few months later, having observed the agonizing death of their cousin in Haycombe,

Dear Sister, Nothing could be more welcome than your moving letter, (which I yesterday received) to revive those tender sentiments of grief and compassion which seemed to languish in my breast. I have indeed, as you observe, been witness, and not only so but have been partaker of the most affecting scene of sorrow and distress. . . . How great, how momentous is a preparation for a future state; it should certainly be the chief concern of life since thereon depends eternal happiness. May my dear sister seek the true means of salvation, which is surely an interest in our Redeemer, and never give over until we have finished our race with Glory. . . . I remain dear sister, Your loving brother and faithful friend, Wm Steele Jun.[31]

Mrs. Steele's journal entries and the correspondence between sister and brother reveal the spiritual core—the Christian and Particular Baptist piety—of this family. Furthermore, they display the sincere love and affection within the family.

Now, these were not perfect people. Mrs. Steele mentions in her journal that Anne had trouble with Molly. And by this time both girls were probably suffering from malaria. Broome suggests in fact that "Molly was also difficult and bad-tempered."[32] He elaborates,

In the previous year Mrs. Steele had mentioned in her diary that there were constant feuds between Anne and Molly and she had reasoned with them. She also said, 'If I am partial I desire the Lord to make me sensible of it.' In April 1735 she said, 'I

30. STE 8/i, Anne Steele to William Steele June 27, 1736, in James, *In Trouble and in Joy*, 137–38.

31. STE 3/8/iii, William Steele to Anne Steele October 5, 1736, in Broome, *Bruised Reed*, 99.

32. Broome, *Bruised Reed*, 93.

observed the stubbornness and crossness of my child [aged eleven] . . . the child is often thrown into anger . . . which grieved me.' All this shows that Anne's life was not easy. She was now ill over long periods with weakness and the ague and was plagued by this young half-sister. Also her father was constantly away from home, either preaching or going out to value timber.[33]

From a young age, Steele's health and her and her family's compassionate response to it was formative in her development as a person. The constant care from her step-mother, whom Steele regularly refers to as her "mother," was also a crucial element in the lives of Steele and her siblings. This is important to consider especially in the midst of the physical absence of their father. With this in mind, it is worth noting that during Steele's last known stay at a boarding school around the age of sixteen, Mrs. Steele was forced to defend her daughters' presence there to Uncle Henry Steele. Mrs. Steele wrote, "'Uncle Steele' . . . took this time to reprove me concerning our daughters going to scool charging it upon me as sin. I defended myself as well as I could in such a doubtful case but my thoughts were pretty much ruffled about it."[34] To her credit Mrs. Steele had recorded, just a few months before, her own concerns "about putting our daughters out to bording scool. I had many doubts about it."[35] Finally, Mrs. Steele's admission of her own weakness and concern for her own spiritual sanctification is also commendable.

William Steele Sr.'s second wife played an important role in Steele's life. Journal entries and letters make this obvious. Her journal entries, in fact, are what make the construction of a well-rounded biography of Anne Steele's life even possible. Mrs. Steele displayed Christian character in seeking the physical and spiritual well-being of both her child and her step-children. Sharon James summarizes the impact of this woman on the lives of her children with an honest assessment:

> She agonized and prayed when Anne and Molly quarreled. She prayed earnestly for the spiritual welfare of each child. She worried about sending them away to boarding school; she fretted over the "secular" books they enjoyed. Each time they left home—whether on a day trip to Weyhill Fair or for longer visits to relations or friends, she prayed earnestly that they would be kept from sin. She was overjoyed when they professed

33. Broome, *Bruised Reed*, 93.

34. STE 2/1/1, Anne Cator Steele diary, June 9, 1733, in Aalders, *To Express the Ineffable*, 18.

35. STE 2/1/1, Anne Cator Steele diary, February 20, 1733, in Aalders, *To Express the Ineffable*, 17–18.

conversion and were baptized. Mrs. Steele was a worrier, and probably irritated her family immensely at times, but she and Anne became close companions, especially after William and Molly left home. Her diary records times of "sweet" or "delightful" conversation about spiritual things with Anne.[36]

Mrs. Steele's influence in Anne Steele's life cannot be underestimated.

Suffering of various sorts—physical, emotional, and spiritual—played a formative role in Anne Steele's life. While this fact has been overstated, sometimes rising to mythical proportions in the literature telling the "stories behind the hymns," it nevertheless must be considered in tracing Steele's development as both a Christian woman and a hymn-writer. Mrs. Steele often comments in her journals that her daughters "have had an ague" or makes statements such as, "Anne is likely to go into consumption."[37] A modern-day consultant pathologist, Michael F. Dixon, was asked to offer a diagnosis of Steele's health based on her step-mother's journal entries and her own extant letters. He concluded, "There is no doubt that Anne Steele suffered from malaria for most of her life. . . . Chronic malaria would have had a progressively debilitating effect on Anne, the major consequence of which would have been anaemia, weakness, lassitude and a proneness to other infections."[38] This liability to infection, in particular, sheds light on such statements from Mrs. Steele as mentioned above. The pathologist also suggests that the various coughs and colds from which Steele suffered were not unlikely to be found in a debilitated girl living near a low-lying and marshy area such as the "water meadows of Wallop Brook."[39]

Establishing chronic malaria, however, as Steele's major physical ailment, still only begins to tell the story of the suffering she endured. She lived during a time when the practice of medicine in Britain was still in its primitive stages. It was prior to the time of the use of effective pain-killers and antiseptics. In fact, doctors still tended to operate under the old assumption that sickness was the caused by an imbalance of "humors" or bodily fluids. Sharon James comments on this situation and how it related to Anne Steele,

> Common remedies were bleeding (by knife or leech), purging, blistering (agonizingly painful, supposed to draw out bad bodily fluids), and inducing vomiting. . . . It is truly pitiful to read of Mrs. Steele's fervent prayers that such "means" would procure relief. Her diaries give a fairly consistent picture of Anne's

36. James, *In Trouble and in Joy*, 122–23.
37. Broome, *Bruised Reed*, 79.
38. Dixon and Steele-Smith, "Anne Steele's Health," 353–54.
39. Dixon and Steele-Smith, "Anne Steele's Health," 353.

recurring fevers, pain, stomachache and toothache. Malaria
sometimes brought on fits caused by extremely high fever, and
eventually resulted in a nervous disorder.[40]

Steele also eventually suffered from shortness of breath and severe head-
aches. Dixon has suggested regarding these symptoms, "The stomach trouble was either caused by peptic ulceration or irritable bowel syndrome, and
the breathlessness by coronary insufficiency or by repeated respiratory tract
infections, chronic bronchitis or recurrent attacks of pleurisy."[41] During
a sustained period of illness when Steele was thirty-two, Mrs. Steele often
wrote of Steele's illnesses and her prayers on behalf of the young woman. She
wrote, for example, "Nanny was extremely bad in her stomach, her groans
seemed to pierce me. I cry therefore to her God and my God that he would
pity, ease and support her and sanctify the stroke."[42] Recurrent illness was a
regular part of Anne Steele's life.

　　Steele wrote her hymns while intermittently suffering from the illnesses mentioned above. Lengthy periods of her life were taken up simply trying
to cope with her physical condition. For example, Steele and her sister-in-
law, Mary Bullock Steele (1713–1762), spent May and June of 1751, Steele's
thirty-fourth year, in Bath. Their hope was that drinking the waters and
bathing in the Roman baths would bring a return to good health. Letters
and poems from their stay reveal that not only did they receive little relief,
but that Steele also longed for the quieter life of Broughton.

　　Steele's poems, prose pieces, and letters often reveal her own thoughts
on dealing with illnesses. She wrote in 1762 to her sister-in-law that "long-
protracted pain and weakness" often brings with it "faintness and dejection of
spirit."[43] But the mind is also affected by such physical pain. In a prose piece
called "Thoughts in Sickness, and on Recovery," Steele wrote, "Of what a feeble
texture is this mortal tabernacle! and how much is the tenant mind (though
of an immortal nature) pained and depressed by its weakness, and hurt by the
storms which shake the tottering frame!"[44] Sharon James lists a chronology of
Steele's health for the last part of her life.[45] James notes that Steele spent much
of her thirty-seventh year ill. She adds that by Steele's fortieth year she began
showing signs of a nervous disorder (which fits the diagnosis of malaria) and

40. James, *In Trouble and in Joy*, 140.

41. Broome, *Bruised Reed*, 79.

42. Anne Cator Steele diary, in James, *In Trouble and in Joy*, 140.

43. STE 3/9, Anne Steele to Mary Bullock Steele March 16, 1762, in Aalders, *To Express the Ineffable*, 109.

44. "Thoughts in Sickness, and on Recovery," in Steele, *Works*, 2:293.

45. James, *In Trouble and in Joy*, 140–41.

that at age forty-three she began suffering from shortness of breath. For the next nine years, until Steele was fifty-four, her health fluctuated between periods of difficulty and relief. Finally, from that time until her death six years later, she was essentially house-bound.

Anne Steele, others in her family, and obviously many other people around her, suffered the common ill-health of those in eighteenth-century England. As a hymn-writer, as well as a writer of prose, poems, and letters, Steele had a natural outlet through which to communicate about these common experiences of her time. And although Steele's health struggles began early in her life, Broome finds "no indication that she was naturally depressive from a child, though obviously her recurrent illnesses would have had an effect on her."[46] James proposes that Steele's "own experience of suffering, and her conscious acceptance of it from the hand of God, meant that her poems and hymns on this theme struck a real chord with other sufferers."[47] Looking back over her life and hymns, Broome observes, "Her ill-health over many years had been sanctified to her and out of it she had learnt that faith in the Son of God was the only source of help, happiness and hope."[48]

A good vantage point from which to view Steele's response to physical and emotional trials is found in a letter Steele wrote to her suffering sister-in-law, Mary Bullock Steele, in 1762, just over two months before the latter passed away. Displaying a sense of calm and resigned contentment at the age of forty-five, Steele wrote,

> Past experience affords great encouragement to look up with humble hope and trust to the kind Hand which hitherto hath helped us. I know that faintness and dejection of Spirit often attends long-protracted pain and weakness, but while the Eternal God is our Refuge, and underneath are the Everlasting Arms, we can never be utterly cast down. It was a good saying of Dr. Watts in his sickness "The Business of a Christian is to bear the will of God as well as to do it" but in this part of the Christian's duty as well as in all others we have need (in a conscious sense of our own weakness) to pray for a firm and constant assurance in Almighty power and goodness. . . . Perhaps if our path were always smooth and easy and we met with no cold storms or distressing accidents we should be ready to sit down or at least loiter by the way, and be forgetful of our journey's end.[49]

46. Broome, *Bruised Reed*, 79.

47. James, *In Trouble and in Joy*, 141.

48. Broome, *Bruised Reed*, 165.

49. STE 3/9, Anne Steele to Mary Bullock Steele, March 4, 1762, in James, *In Trouble and in Joy*, 139–40.

When Mary Bullock Steele did pass away thereafter, Steele immediately stepped in to mother her own bereaved niece, Polly Steele (1753–1813), who was only eight at the time of her mother's death.[50] Following Steele's death in 1778, Polly expressed in verse her reflection on the care she had received from her aunt during those formative years, especially the six years before her father William married again:

> Aunt and friend in one, whose anxious care
> Watched o'er my helpless childhood . . .
>
> Ah where is now that friend, to whom my heart
> In every past distress was wont to fly,
> While the dear sufferer, her own pains forget,
> Would gently sooth my passions into peace?
> Where that maternal friend, whose watchful care,
> Whose fond, assiduous tenderness sustained
> My helpless childhood? . . .
>
> My dearest pleasures, my most loved employments,
> She taught me first to relish, first awaked
> The wish for knowledge.[51]

It seems that Steele followed her own advice "to bear the will of God as well as to do it." She lovingly fulfilled her Christian duty to her brother and his daughter Polly. Steele's journey definitely included her share of physical pain and suffering to which it appears she responded with self-giving grace and dignity.

Two incidents in Steele's life that have been highlighted often in short "hymn story" biographical sketches, but typically with inaccuracy or hyperbole, must be addressed. First is what may be called "The Strange Case of James Elcomb of Ringwood." Joseph Ivimey (1773–1830) included in his *History of the English Baptists* a sad incident that took place in the life of Anne Steele on May 23, 1737. He referred to Caleb Evans's (1737–1791) preface to the second edition of Anne Steele's hymns in 1780. He wrote,

> Dr. Evans has not mentioned an incident in the life of the "pious Theodosia" [Steele's pen name] which must have been most painful to her heart. She had consented to give her hand in marriage to a young gentlemen, James Elcomb, who resided in Ringwood, and the day of the marriage was fixed. The day

---

50. Mary was Polly's given name, but she was always known as Polly. For a recent study of Polly, see Holmes, "Resurrecting the Anonymous."

51. *Poems on Subjects Chiefly Devotional*, 3:xii–xvii, in Broome, *Bruised Reed*, 179.

preceding it he went to bathe in the river [the Avon] below the town at a place called South-Mead, and was drowned. A tradition which the writer, who is native, recollects, was that his shrieks were heard in the town, and the place is still called on account of the circumstance, "Elcomb's Hole."[52]

If this account be true, it is surprisingly absent from Evans's sketch. Later biographers, however, repeat the account, sometimes with further embellishment. In fact, some list his drowning as on the day on which the wedding was planned. Primary sources, however, disprove some of the sensational details of the story as it has been handed down.[53] A letter dated May 25, 1737, was discovered among the Steele family papers written by John James Manfield, a lawyer and first cousin of Steele by marriage, who lived in Ringwood.[54] The letter details the drowning incident and says, "Not knowing how far he [Mr. Elcomb] may have prevailed on the affections of Miss Steele, I send my man on purpose to prevent any shock that may attend her hearing it in too sudden a manner."[55] Thus Mr. Elcomb obviously did not drown the day of or before a scheduled wedding, nor does it appear the couple was even engaged. And yet several hymns which Steele gave such titles as "Desiring Resignation and Thankfulness," "Searching after Happiness," "Submission to God in Affliction," and "Complaining at the Throne of God" are said to have been written in response to this experience that happened when Steele was twenty years old. Yet the apocryphal story endures.

Second, some accounts report Steele to have taken a fall from a horse that left her a lifelong invalid.[56] In point of fact, Mrs. Steele records in her diary falls from a horse for Steele in both 1735 and 1753, both of which brought physical pain, but which certainly did not leave her permanently disabled.[57] Therefore, it is much too simplistic to say that Anne Steele's entire corpus of hymnody was somehow significantly influenced by two events of such dubious record. Yet, suffer Anne Steele did. And her suffering included the experience of the death and loss of others.

While the symptoms of debilitating physical illnesses plagued Anne Steele throughout her life, she also witnessed the deaths of those nearest

52. Ivimey, *History of the English Baptists*, 4:312.

53. See especially Watson and Cho, "Anne Steele's Drowned Fiancé," 117–21.

54. STE 1/5/I, James Manfield to William Steele, May 25, 1737, in Broome, *Bruised Reed*, 102.

55. STE 1/5/I, James Manfield to William Steele, May 25, 1737, in Broome, *Bruised Reed*, 102.

56. See Bailey, *Gospel in Hymns*, 70.

57. STE 2/1/1, Anne Cator Steele diary, August 6, 1735, and STE 2/1/2, Anne Cator Steele diary, July 11, 1752, in Aalders, *To Express the Ineffable*, 105.

and dearest to her and in addition distant family and friends as well. Death was more of a clear and present danger to those living in eighteenth-century England than modern people tend to think of it for themselves. Besides witnessing the deaths of aunts, uncles, cousins, nieces, and nephews throughout her life, not to mention the death of her own mother and infant brother at an early age, the deaths of those closest to her left an indelible imprint on her in the years that followed.

Many of Steele's family members died within several years of one another. Steele's dear step-mother, Anne Cator Steele, died in 1760, the year Steele's first book of hymns was published. Three days before her own death, even as her health was rapidly deteriorating, Mrs. Steele wrote in her journal, "Nanny is very ill and I am thoughtful about her. I want to be in a more spiritual frame, but I can make no progress in the ways and things of God and yet sometimes I can hope I am a child of God."[58] The day before her death her final entry said, "My weakness and depravity is exceeding great and my whole dependence is on the merits and righteousness of the Lord Jesus Christ."[59] A steady influence on the forty-three-year-old, unmarried hymn-writer was now gone and her loss would have certainly been felt. However, Steele's constant love for her father resulted in her committing herself to care for him for the rest of his life. Next, Steele's brother William's wife died in 1762. Sharon James writes, "Anne had been a constant visitor to their nearby home. Mary had been a friend as well as a sister-in-law, and, of course, Anne was devastated on William's behalf as well as her own."[60] Even after William remarried, Steele remained a mother-figure to his daughter Polly. But Steele's most bitter loss came when her father passed from this earth in 1769, one month before his eightieth birthday. When William Steele Sr. died, Steele lost a father, pastor, friend, and confidant.

Steele thus wrote poems and hymns as a way of mourning and reflecting upon the lives and deaths of those she loved. These products of her pen, especially those relating to young people who died prematurely, brought sobering reminders of the brevity of life on this earth. Suffering and death were strong factors in giving shape to Steele's life and hymn-writing.

Brighter influences, however, also made an indelible mark upon Steele—and much to her delight. Throughout those same years of personal physical suffering and witnessing the deaths of friends and loved ones, Steele was also surrounded by a network of friends and advisors that brought much joy to her life. These companions and acquaintances offered both spiritual

58. Quoted in Broome, *Bruised Reed*, 147.

59. Quoted in Broome, *Bruised Reed*, 147.

60. James, *In Trouble and in Joy*, 144.

and intellectual direction to Steele's life and poetry and also contributed to the publishing of her hymns. So, although Steele wrote in both letters and poems of her enjoyment of a quiet and contemplative life, she also enjoyed both going to visit and receiving for visits family, friends, and other guests, who provided rich intellectual stimulation. Such guests were often men, typically Dissenting pastors, a good number of whom were vitally interested in hymnody and poetry, and eager to facilitate the publishing of such compositions. It is appropriate to note here that, though Steele accumulated a number of male friends throughout her life, she made a conscious decision to remain single. It appears in fact that Steele refused an offer of engagement more than once. Because of the surviving letter of his proposal and of her refusal to comply with his wish, it is often noted that, Benjamin Beddome, a Particular Baptist pastor, offered a fervent request of Steele's hand in marriage to no avail.[61] Surviving letters between Steele and her sister Molly following Molly's marriage contain sisterly jousting as the former declares the freedom and simplicity of singleness in response to the latter's cajoling her older half-sister to marry while she still has opportunity. Molly also wrote to Steele of the restrictions and difficulties of marriage and parenting while still commending it to her as better than being alone.

The cultured and witty group of men with which Steele became acquainted included, among others, Particular Baptist pastors James Fanch (1704–1767) from Romsey, Daniel Turner (1710–1798) of Abingdon, Caleb Evans of Bristol, and John Ash (ca. 1724–1779) from Pershore; Presbyterian turned Independent pastor Philip Furneaux (1726–1783) from London; and Presbyterian pastor John Lavington (1690–1759) from Exeter.[62] It appears from letters that Fanch, Turner, and Furneaux each advised Steele regarding the craft of hymn-writing, may have helped her edit hymns she had already written, and contributed to Steele's publishing efforts. This help came both during visits to Broughton and through written correspondence. James notes that "Furneaux helped get her work published in 1760, and Evans and Ash collaborated on a further edition of her poems after her death."[63] When this influence is coupled with the family dynamic of writing within the Steele household, it is quite obvious that Anne Steele did not compose her hymns in a solitary vacuum.

Steele's friends and writing companions also included a group of literary women in which Steele was clearly the central figure. Those in this

---

61. Broome, *Bruised Reed*, 110–13.

62. See Aalders, *To Express the Ineffable*, 20; Broome, *Bruised Reed*, 155–58; Cho, "Ministry of Song," 50; and James, *In Trouble and in Joy*, 135.

63. James, *In Trouble and in Joy*, 135.

writing circle often corresponded under romantic, classical pseudonyms. Steele, for example, was "Silvania," her sister Molly was "Amira," her niece Mary was "Silvia," and her friend Mary Scot was "Myra." One of the more famous authors, the bluestocking Hannah More (1745–1833), was also included in this circle. Scott and More were well-known for their writing efforts. These women wrote poems to one another that considered the craft of writing and also covered themes that ranged over the entirety of human emotion. Men also were to be found sometimes within Steele's literary circle, using pseudonyms as well: Furneaux was "Lucius," and Lavington was "Lysander." Her brother William was known as "Philander" and her brother-in-law Joseph Wakeford (1719–1785) as "Potius." There is no doubt Steele cherished these writing friendships and they were vital to her Christian pilgrimage. Aalders observes, "While Steele chose a life of limited social stimulus, the friendships she did nurture were particularly supportive of her writing efforts."[64] In a poem about friendship's influence on her writing and publishing efforts, Steele herself once mused,

> Indulgent Friendship, list'ning, caught the strain,
>   And fondly fancy'd it was tun'd to move;
> Then, smiling, bore it to the distant plain,
>   Far, ah how far beyond its native grove!
> But say, Lysander, can such notes as these
> Amid politer scenes expect to please? . . .
>
> Yet friendship dwells with piety sincere,
>   Or in the cottage, or the stately dome,
> Whether detain'd in crouded scenes of care,
>   Or on the village fix'd, her peaceful home:
> Where these reside, though artless be her strain,
> O may the muse a kind admission gain.
>
> If minds, where piety and friendship glow,
>   Approving smile, and own the kindred theme;
> That smile a nobler pleasure will bestow,
>   Than all the laurell'd wreaths of boasting fame:
> Blest minds! to these the Muse devotes her lays;
> If these approve, she seeks no other praise.[65]

Displaying the same humility of the twelve-year-old girl writing home from school earlier in life, Steele expressed that the approbation of the same friends who sought publication of her work and "bore it to the distant plain" of

64. Aalders, *To Express the Ineffable*, 21.

65. "To Lysander," in Steele, *Works*, 1:180.

London is all she could desire. Further, both Aalders and Cho suggest that Steele in particular offered encouragement and inspiration to younger writers in her own day, and also posthumously through her writings.[66]

In sum, Anne Steele was a poet from a family of poets. She found herself corresponding with a circle of witty and gifted writers that included both men and women. Though she never married, suffered from debilitating physical symptoms for much of her life, and seems to have received little formal education, yet she lived a full life in which she sought to glorify, know, enjoy, and serve the sovereign Lord in whom she believed. She sought and relished intellectual stimulation, and she loved to spend her evenings in social gatherings in her home with family and friends. She once wrote of such an evening and how they shortened "the dull wintry nights":

> A Candle is lighted and cheerful we sit
> Close round a good fire of odiferous Peat . . .
> Our Needles employ us and chat miscellaneous
> Or serious or trifling or News entertain us . . .
> When one of the company reads to the rest
> Grave author or Poet or what we like best
> All soft and harmonious the hours glide along
> Conversing with Pope or with Thompson or Young . . .
> But to the sublime we can't always attend
> I mean Polly and I for we sometimes descend
> To capping of verses for Vanity's sake
> And laugh at the whimsical Mixture we make.[67]

She also used her gift of verse to write poems and hymns for obvious devotional purposes that covered all the basic theological loci of the Christian life. Some of these hymns she offered to her father's Particular Baptist congregation to supplement their collection of the hymns of Isaac Watts. In time, her circle of writing friends, including her family, saw poetic beauty, theological robustness, and experiential depth in these hymns. So they sought to have them published. In a letter from Steele's brother William to his daughter, however, he suggests that the bookseller did not share their zeal, noting, "He talks Poetry like a Man of Trade that knows no more of it than belongs to his business."[68] So it was Steele's family, using the proceeds from their successful

---

66. Aalders, *To Express the Ineffable*, 22; and Cho, "Ministry of Song," 49.

67. STE 3/3/1, 3–4 in Reeves, *Pursuing the Muses*, 66 quoted in James, *In Trouble and in Joy*, 152–53.

68. STE 4/5, William Steele to Mary Steele Dunscombe, August 14, 1777, in Aalders, *To Express the Ineffable*, 26.

timber business, which financed the publishing of her poems and hymns.[69] For Steele's family and friends, the publishing endeavor was worth their money and time, as they believed the publication of her work would benefit not only individual Christians, but also the church catholic.

Poems on Subjects Chiefly Devotional, by Theodosia, a two-volume set of Anne Steele's hymns and poems, was published in 1760. She was 43. Her choice to publish under a pseudonym was certainly not outside eighteenth-century feminine ideals. It may have also been both an expression of self-protection, but also of a sense of humility. Caleb Evans notes in his "Advertisement" in the 1780 edition of Steele's works, "It was not without extreme reluctance she was prevailed on to submit any of them to the public eye."[70] Early on it was friends such as Philip Furneaux and her brother-in-law, Joseph Wakeford, who directly influenced her decision to seek publication. She once wrote to her brother, "Mr. Furneaux came yesterday a little before noon, preach'd in the evening & return'd to Andover this morning. We had a great deal of chatt intermingled with reading my papers & canvassing the printing affair in which his opinion corresponds to yours."[71] James Fanch was also eager to see her publish. As Broome describes Steele's relationship to Fanch, he "was her immediate advisor, an able scholarly, gifted man who was well able to suggest variations and improvements to her verse."[72] Broome further notes that Daniel Turner, Fanch's brother-in-law, once visited the Steele household for two nights, the purpose of which appears to have been the preparation of Steele's hymns and poems for publication.[73] The process of preparing the hymns for publication took several years, the fruit of which was revealed in 1760.

The first publication of Steele's hymns and poems, however, was just the beginning. Nine years later, Ash and Evans included sixty-two of Theodosia's [Steele's] hymns in their popular hymn book that came to be known as the *Bristol Collection*. In 1780, her work was reissued with a third volume of poems and prose, including an introduction by one of her long-time friends and correspondents, Caleb Evans. In 1787, the London Baptist minister John Rippon included forty-five of her hymns in the first edition of his *Selection of Hymns*. This number grew to fifty-two in later editions of this most widely distributed of Baptist hymnals. Her three volumes

---

69. Aalders, *To Express the Ineffable*, 23–28; and Broome, *Bruised Reed*, 158.

70. Evans, "Advertisement," in Steele, *Works*, 1:5.

71. STE 3/8/vi, Steele to William Steele, May 16, 1755, in Aalders, *To Express the Ineffable*, 23, n. 59.

72. Broome, *Bruised Reed*, 157.

73. Broome, *Bruised Reed*, 157.

were published as two, entitled *The Works of Mrs. Anne Steele*, in Boston in 1808, followed by another reprint in England in 1863 with a memoir by John Sheppard. It is noteworthy that Steele's hymns once made up one-third of the selections contained in the hymnal of Trinity Church, an Episcopal church in Boston.[74] There is no doubt that Steele's hymns were extremely popular in the century or so following their publication.

Anne Steele lived for eighteen years after her hymns and poems were first published. Following the death of her beloved father in 1769, she moved in with her brother's family at "Broughton House." Though she loved the beauty of the gardens and terrace and the company of family, her health began to decline severely within two years. Her various physical ailments came to a head in 1771 and she was virtually bedridden for the final six or seven years of her life. Her niece Polly, for whom she had served as a surrogate mother for a number of years, was her nurse for the final years of Steele's life. By the first months of 1778 it became clear that Steele's life on this earth was drawing toward a close. An entry from the diary of a visitor to Steele at this time "reveals that both Dr. Samuel Stennett and Caleb Evans had travelled long distances from London and Bristol to come to Broughton to visit Anne on her death bed."[75] Steele was obviously a beloved daughter of the Particular Baptist community. Evans later recorded the scene:

> When the interesting hour came, she welcomed its arrival, and though her feeble body was excruciated with pain, her mind was perfectly serene. She uttered not a murmuring word, but was all resignation, peace, and holy joy. She took the most affection-ate leave of her weeping friends around her, and at length, the happy moment of her dismission arriving, she closed her eyes, and with these animating words on her dying lips, "I know that my Redeemer liveth," gently she fell asleep in Jesus.[76]

And he adds, "Her excellent writings, by which though dead, she still speaketh, and which are the faithful counterpart of her amiable mind, exhibit to us the fairest picture of the original."[77] This book includes an examination of those writings as chosen by John Rippon for his *Selection of Hymns*.

74. See Benson, *English Hymn*, 214; and Aalders, *To Express the Ineffable*, 62–63n112.
75. Broome, *Bruised Reed*, 216.
76. Evans, "Advertisement," in Steele, *Works*, 1:8.
77. Evans, "Advertisement," in Steele, *Works*, 1:8.

3

The Setting of Anne Steele's Hymns and John Rippon's *Selection of Hymns*

Background of the Particular Baptist Community

IN TERMS OF THEIR theological ancestry, the English Particular Baptists[1] were products of the English Reformation,[2] and more specifically, "they emerged from the womb of English Puritanism in the early to mid-seventeenth century."[3] Early in their history, and true to their Puritan heritage, the Particular Baptists' theological convictions came to be crystallized in written confessions of faith.[4] Two such notable documents were the *First London Confession* of 1644 and the *Second London Confession* of 1677 and 1688/89.[5]

---

1. From the first quarter of the seventeenth century through the nineteenth century, Baptists in England had been divided into two main sections. The General Baptist churches adhered to the Arminian doctrine of a general atonement which claims that Christ died for all human beings. This group was founded by John Smyth and the separatists who followed him into exile in Amsterdam in 1608/09. The Particular Baptists were Calvinistic Baptists who believed that Christ's atonement is limited to the elect. See Kurian, *Nelson's Dictionary of Christianity*, 291 and 530.

2. Haykin, "British Particular Baptist Biography," 15.

3. Haykin, "British Particular Baptist Biography," 16.

4. Also like their Puritan forebears, for the Particular Baptists, "the sermon was the crucial point of the service." Watts, *Dissenters*, 306. This contributed to the durability of their movement. Based on Scripture, these sermons would have lined up with their confessions of faith. The hymns written by Particular Baptists also line up with their *Confessions*.

5. The theology of the General Baptists, on the other hand, is based on the *Standard Confession* of 1660 and the *Orthodox Confession* of 1678.

These confessions of faith each reflected Calvinistic emphases such as atonement limited to the elect, perseverance of the saints, and predestination.[6]

Pope A. Duncan suggests that "the period of the Civil War, Commonwealth, and Protectorate (1642–1660) was one of relative freedom for Baptists."[7] "Ecclesiastical tyranny" had been temporarily dethroned.[8] The Particular Baptist community began to form its specific identity at least as early as this period that began with the first English civil war in 1642 and continued their ecclesiastical development during the period of political turmoil that followed. Roger Hayden notes that William Kiffin (1616–1701), an early leader of the denomination, had become a Baptist by October 1642.[9] Kiffin was one of fifteen men representing seven churches in London who signed the *First London Confession* of 1644. This confession of faith served both "to distinguish [the Particular Baptists] from both the General Baptists and the Anabaptists" and to signal their broad theological unity with like-minded Calvinistic groups such as the Independents or Congregationalists and Presbyterians.[10] A comparison of this document with the *Westminster Confession of Faith*, which appeared in 1646, demonstrates "that Baptists indeed belonged to the mainstream of Reformed life."[11] But the *First London Confession* also established the specifically Baptist view that the church is made up only of professed believers and it was "the first Baptist Confession to pronounce in favor of immersion as the proper mode of Baptism."[12] One way the denomination grew in its early years in the midst of England's

6. McBeth, *Baptist Heritage*, 66.

7. Duncan, *Hanserd Knollys*, 11.

8. Lumpkin, *Baptist Confessions of Faith*, 144.

9. Hayden, *English Baptist History and Heritage*, 45.

10. Lumpkin, *Baptist Confessions of Faith*, 145. Michael Haykin observes, "The General Baptists, apart from a few congregations, generally died out in the late eighteenth century in the wasteland of Unitarianism." Haykin, *Kiffin, Knollys and Keach*, 26. For more on the General Baptists, see n1. The Anabaptists (an epithet meaning "rebaptizers") were a continental sect that refused to baptize their infants and reinstituted the baptism of believers alone. Their name was applied to several different groups with slightly different emphases, initially seen as having a revolutionary zeal for changing the world. The Münster Rebellion of 1534 essentially discredited the movement. Persecuted severely, they later accepted the role of a pacifist minority, separate from the world. See Kurian, *Nelson's Dictionary of Christianity*, 25.

11. Lumpkin, *Baptist Confessions of Faith*, 150. See chap. 2, n10 above for a brief comparison of these groups' confessions of faith.

12. Lumpkin, *Baptist Confessions of Faith*, 146, 167. Further, sections 33 and 34 of the 1644 edition and an additional phrase in section 39 of the 1646 reprint seem to indicate the practice of communion, or the Lord's Supper, restricted to those properly baptized members of the church.

political turmoil was by way of the Army.[13] J. R. Broome says, "It seems that as the Parliamentary Army moved about the country with its Baptist officers, many Particular Baptist Churches sprang up in its wake."[14] And he adds, "The officers were obviously evangelists."[15] The Baptists found themselves both supporting and benefiting from the Cromwellian government during this period.[16] As the denomination multiplied, even as far away as Scotland, the formative and influential *First London Confession* was a theological and ecclesiastical tie that bound the churches of this fledgling denomination together. Haykin suggests that it was the *First London Confession* "which laid the foundation upon which the Baptists evangelized and built churches during the tumultuous 1640s and 1650s."[17] Duncan adds that in the period from Cromwell's victory at Preston in 1648 until the Restoration in 1660 the Baptists "flourished as never before."[18]

While life should not be characterized as easy for the Particular Baptists beforehand, with the restoration of Charles II to the throne in 1660 "a dark shadow was cast over the cause of Dissent."[19] Peter Naylor puts it starkly, "After 1660, nonconformist suffering was intense."[20] Michael Watts says, "The period of persecution is usually associated with the name of Charles' Lord Chancellor, the Earl of Clarendon, and with the series of enactments passed by the Cavalier Parliament and known as the Clarendon Code."[21] The Clarendon Code included four laws passed successively between 1661 and 1665 that set the stage for this persecution of Dissenters.

13. See Lumpkin, *Baptist Confessions of Faith*, 151.

14. Broome, *Bruised Reed*, 27.

15. Broome, *Bruised Reed*, 30. It has already been mentioned above that one such evangelist founded the church to which Anne Steele's family belonged.

16. Haykin, *Kiffin, Knollys and Keach*, 46.

17. Haykin, *Kiffin, Knollys and Keach*, 11.

18. Duncan, *Hanserd Knollys*, 11.

19. Walker, "Benjamin Keach," 27.

20. Naylor, *Calvinism, Communion and the Baptists*, 26. In another place he says, "The sufferings of the nonconformists were unspeakable." Naylor, *Picking up a Pin for the Lord*, 31. In seventeenth-century England, a Dissenter was a Puritan, Presbyterian, or a non-Anglican Protestant. Following the Act of Uniformity in 1662, the term Nonconformist came to be used of any group who did not belong to the national Church of England. See Kurian, *Nelson's Dictionary of Christianity*, 217 and 502.

21. Watts, *Dissenters*, 223. See 223–38 for an elaboration of this code and its results on Nonconformists. Thanks to men such as William Kiffin, the Particular Baptists and other like-minded Nonconformists were not involved with such revolutionary uprisings as those of the fifty Fifth Monarchy men who, led by Thomas Venner, terrorized the city of London, killing twenty-two people in January 1661. They did, however, suffer the consequences of such radical dissenting activities. See Haykin, *Kiffin, Knollys and Keach*, 46–47; and Watts, *Dissenters*, 222–23.

The Corporation Act of 1661 required all municipal officials to take Anglican Communion and swear loyalty to the king, thus denying membership of any municipal body to any conscientious Dissenters. Next, the Act of Uniformity of 1662 required submission to the Thirty-nine Articles and to the *Book of Common Prayer*. Nineteen Baptists were among the over two thousand clergymen who refused to comply with this act and were forced to resign their livings.[22] Third, the Conventicle Act of 1664 prohibited the meeting of five or more people together for worship or religious purposes except in accordance with the liturgy of the Church of England.[23] This made Dissenting worship a crime. The penalties for breaking this law were expensive fines or imprisonments. Finally, the Five Mile Act of 1665 forbade Nonconformist ministers from coming within five miles of incorporated towns or the place of their former livings. This act was passed following the "impudence" of Dissenting ministers in assuming the responsibility of the sick and frightened flocks of the Church of England whose clergymen had abandoned their congregations in London during the Great Plague in the summer of 1665.[24] Haykin summarizes the situation, "This legislation made it illegal for worship or evangelism to be carried on outside of the bounds of the Church of England."[25] And Walker observes that for the next three decades "varying degrees of persecution rapidly became the common experience of many dissenting congregations and preachers."[26]

Watts notes that following the passage of the Clarendon Code, "the severity of the persecution depended on the extent to which Dissenters were prepared to abide by the law and compromise with the state."[27] But Duncan adds that generally speaking, "Baptists and others became the objects of harassment and persecution." A few examples from the lives of early English Baptists William Kiffin, Hanserd Knollys (ca. 1598–1691), and Benjamin Keach will illustrate the impact of these laws on the Particular Baptists. Kiffin experienced the trials of such a political situation within his own family. Having dealt with deaths of his wife and two eldest sons, the second of whom was "poisoned by 'a Popish priest' while he visited Venice," he also lost a son-in-in law, Benjamin Hewling.[28] Having taken Hewling's two sons

22. Watts, *Dissenters*, 219.

23. See Watts, *Dissenters*, 225; and Naylor, *Calvinism, Communion and the Baptists*, 23–24.

24. Watts, *Dissenters*, 225–26.

25. Haykin, *One Heart and One Soul*, 15.

26. Walker, "Benjamin Keach," 27.

27. Watts, *Dissenters*, 227.

28. Wilson, "William Kiffin," 1:68–69.

as his own—Benjamin, age 22, and William, age 19—they proceeded to take up arms in the Duke of Monmouth's bid in the summer of 1685 to remove the recently ascended Roman Catholic James II from the throne.[29] Captured after defeat, they were executed in September of 1685 even though Kiffin had "offered the large sum of £3,000 in exchange for his grandsons' freedom."[30] Concerning Hanserd Knollys, Duncan says, "Knollys' sufferings were great."[31] Having fled to both Holland and Germany "to escape the pressures he was under as a nonconformist," he later returned to England and taught school to provide for his family.[32] Following the passage of the Second Conventicle Act in 1670, which renewed the restrictions of the first act after it had expired, Knollys was twice imprisoned, the second time when he was eighty-six years old and for a period of sixteen months. But as a testimony to these Baptists' courage and perseverance under persecution, Duncan notes, "He used the [Newgate] prison as a pulpit, preaching daily to his fellow prisoners of 'the things that concern the kingdom of God.'"[33] Finally, regarding Benjamin Keach, Tom Nettles describes his life after the passage of the Clarendon Code: "Keach, under siege for being a preacher in a dissenting congregation, was almost killed when troopers threatened to trample him with their horses. Being rescued from that, he nevertheless was thrown into a tortuous confinement."[34] Keach endured fines, imprisonment, and, during one period of punishment, a daily two-hour stay in the village square in the pillory, "a wooden framework that had holes for the head and hands of the person being punished."[35] Due to his writings, Keach was "charged with the crime of being a 'seditious, heretical, and schismatical person.'"[36] Courage and steadfastness were required of the Particular Baptists during such dangerous times. And such times of persecution and harassment by the civil authorities obviously led to long-term distrust, antipathy, and ecclesiastical disagreement between Nonconformists and the state and its church.[37]

29. Wilson, "William Kiffin," 69–70.

30. Wilson, "William Kiffin," 69–70.

31. Duncan, *Hanserd Knollys*, 12.

32. Duncan, *Hanserd Knollys*, 12.

33. Duncan, *Hanserd Knollys*, 13.

34. Nettles, "Benjamin Keach," 96.

35. Haykin, *Kiffin, Knollys and Keach*, 85.

36. Walker, "Benjamin Keach," 27.

37. Though it is debatable as to whether he was a Particular Baptsist in the strict sense of the word, John Bunyan (1628–1688) was a notable Nonconformist often claimed by Baptists as one of their own. Isabel Rivers summarizes his afflictions: "The most famous victim of Restoration church policy, Bunyan was arrested in 1660 under a revived Elizabethan Act and tried in 1661 for keeping a conventicle, well before the

One way the Particular Baptists responded to the trials of persecution was with the publication of another confession, the *Second London Confession* of 1677. Basing this second confession of faith on the Presbyterians' *Westminster Confession of Faith* as it had been modified by the Independents in their *Savoy Declaration* solidified a "united Calvinist front in the face of persecution" for these three Nonconformist groups.[38] In terms of following the theological trajectory of the Particular Baptist movement into the following century, it is important to recognize that the *Second London Confession* places the Baptists in the stream of evangelical theology that flowed from the Westminster Assembly.[39] Further, these early English Particular Baptists used such confessional statements as a way of emphasizing "the vital importance of the orthodox doctrine for the Christian life."[40] In times of persecution, both solidarity with like-minded believers and a well-grounded theology were essential not only for spiritual vitality, but even for the survival of the Particular Baptists and other Nonconformists.

The Particular Baptists' first generation of leaders, including such men as Kiffin, Knollys, and Keach, were able to balance "conservative Calvinism with a warm and fervent evangelism."[41] In fact, Haykin notes, "The Calvinistic Baptist cause expanded from the seven churches in London in the mid-1640s to around 130 throughout England, Wales and Ireland by the late 1650s."[42] And the denomination remained steadfast during the subsequent years of persecution. In 1689, however, the year after the Glorious Revolution of 1688, William III authorized "the passing of the Act of

---

passing of the Act of Uniformity. He consistently refused to undertake not to preach, just as he had refused to avoid arrest, and as a result was imprisoned for twelve years until released in 1672 under the terms of the Declaration of Indulgence." Rivers, *Reason, Grace, and Sentiment*, 1:105. For more on Bunyan see Jeffrey, "John Bunyan," 98–102.

38. Haykin, *Kiffin, Knollys and Keach*, 63. Just as its predecessor, the *First London Confession*, distinguished the Particular Baptists from the Anabaptist sect, so this confession of faith distinguished them from the Quakers. The Quakers, also known as the Society of Friends, rejected all sacraments and emphasized the universal Inward Light as sufficient for spiritual enlightenment. They believed the true church worships in silence and waits for the Holy Spirit to inspire ex tempore prayers, sermons, and testimonies. The name Quaker refers to trembling or "quaking" at the Word of God. See Kurian, *Nelson's Dictionary of Christianity*, 577.

39. See Haykin, *Kiffin, Knollys and Keach*, 62–81.

40. Haykin, *Kiffin, Knollys and Keach*, 100.

41. McBeth, *Baptist Heritage*, 171. J. M. Cramp says that they "might be called 'the first three' among the Baptist ministers of those days. Their talents and characters gave them influence, which appears to have been wisely exerted for the benefit of the denomination." See Cramp, *Baptist History*, 440. See also *British Particular Baptists*, vol. 1, for individual articles about each of these Particular Baptist pioneers.

42. Haykin, *Kiffin, Knollys and Keach*, 40.

Toleration, which gave Dissenters both freedom of worship and immunity from persecution, although certain civil restrictions against them remained in force."[43] Time would reveal that the Particular Baptist community did not respond to new freedoms with the same spiritual resolve with which it had responded to adversity. Peter Naylor proposes, "Notwithstanding the Evangelical awakening, the 1700s were twilight years for the Baptists, then free to meet in their churches, yet effectively second-class citizens because of their faith. But the Lord blessed many of them; with other Dissenters they were steadily gaining in numbers, confidence and influence."[44]

The Religious and Cultural Climate of Eighteenth-Century England

A few aspects of general life in England, particularly regarding public morality and the Church of England, must be considered since this was the larger society within which the Particular Baptists emerged and lived. Though at the time of the Glorious Revolution, toleration was granted to Dissenters, the typical British citizen was still born into membership in the Church of England. And though the traditional understanding of the church and state were challenged during the Enlightenment,[45] which roughly coincided with this current period of religious toleration, Mark Noll suggests two prevailing beliefs throughout the eighteenth century: "State churches were institutions ordained by God and . . . the basis of state-church religion should be the historic Christian faith," especially the Trinitarian faith of "classical Christian theology."[46] History, however,

43. Haykin, *Kiffin, Knollys and Keach*, 48.

44. Naylor, *Picking up a Pin for the Lord*, 15. The apparent contradiction of Naylor's statements that at the same time the Particular Baptists experienced both their twilight and gain in many ways is one of the subcurrents this study will address.

45. The Enlightenment, also known as the Age of Reason, was a period during which human reason was elevated to a place of supremacy over supernatural, or biblical, revelation by its prominent thinkers. In fact, traditional Christianity and its theology came under hostile attack as they were gradually displaced among the "enlightened" by modern science and historical criticism. The Creator God was at best relegated to being a remote caretaker as human autonomy became the rule of the day. Regarding the current study, the Enlightenment can be said to have begun with Isaac Newton's *Principia* in 1687 and the Glorious Revolution the next year and to have lasted through the Napoleonic Wars (1804–1815). Some scholars trace its origins to the publication of Descartes's *Discourse on Method* in 1637. Some have it concluding with the French Revolution of 1789. See Ferguson et al., *New Dictionary of Theology*, 223–24.

46. Noll, *Rise of Evangelicalism*, 49.

showed that "neither active personal piety nor conscientious living were necessarily the consequence of holding these assumptions."[47]

As the Enlightenment dawned and as a more tolerant view of religion prevailed, there was a noticeable moral and social declension in Great Britain. Roy Porter notes that some of this was caused by the Enlightenment's influence on the church. And the established church's declension in turn affected the culture. Regarding religion he says, "Protestant scripturalism–the belief that every word of the Bible had been dictated by the Holy Ghost–was refined into a new rational faith, attended by more optimistic models of man's lot under [God]. . . . Biblicism and providentialism were being challenged by naturalism; custom was elbowed aside . . . tradition was spurned."[48] The result of this shift in thinking was a period of spiritual decay by the early decades of eighteenth century. This manifested itself through the Latitudinarian movement within the established church.[49] And these events did affect the ordinary Christian in the Anglican pew. Considering the entire religious landscape as it had developed at the time, David Pailin lays out the Christian's plight:

> Reflective believers thus found themselves faced with disturbing challenges from fanatics with more zeal than apparent sense, from skeptics whose doubts threatened sensible belief, and from believers whose appeals to the traditional authorities were found to provide no satisfactory way of settling disagreements about faith and practice. The result was a growing conviction that it is to "reason" that people must turn as a final court of appeal. . . . [So] reflective believers in England engaged in a prolonged debate about the nature and contents of what might be justifiable as "reasonable belief" – and about whether or not it is justifiable to judge belief by the canon of reason.[50]

There was thus confusion over the nature of the authority that governed one's life.

Such confusion was bound to influence the morality of everyday life in England. Among the variety of new ways of thinking that came into

47. Noll, *Rise of Evangelicalism*, 49.

48. Porter, *Creation of the Modern World*, 12–13.

49. The Latitudinarians were English churchmen in the seventeenth and eighteenth centuries who pleaded for greater tolerance or latitude in matters of doctrine and who expressed willingness to give up adiaphora or nonessentials not specified or prohibited in the Bible. Products of the Enlightenment, they generally appealed to reason as a source of religious authority besides the Bible and ecclesiastical approval. See Kurian, *Nelson's Dictionary of Christianity*, 402.

50. Pailin, "Rational Religion in England," 213–14.

mainstream life and morality at this time, Porter suggests, "The Enlightenment's great historical watershed lay in the validation of pleasure."[51] This resulted in the gradual acceptance that self-fulfillment is more beneficial than self-denial. And with a lack of biblical authority informing social morals and an erosion of the doctrine of depravity in favor of the power of the will, virtue transitioned from the objective to what was relative. Porter also notes a corollary to this new societal doctrine: "The right to pursue one's own interests became an Enlightenment commonplace."[52] As this hedonistic way of life developed, it resulted in a more anthropocentric view of reality and in a relaxing of moral standards. S. M. Houghton describes the situation, "As for the people at large, drunkenness, immorality, cruel and pernicious sports, unbelief, and complete indifference to the divine message, were their most obvious features."[53] Traditional English society was in a decline. Having addressed the impiety of its magistrates, the loss of reverence for Christian instruction, and the general decline in public morality, the Irish Bishop George Berkeley declared,

> Men's behaviour is the consequence of their principles. Hence it follows that in order to make a state thrive and flourish, care must be taken that good principles be propagated in the minds of those who compose it. . . . Our prospect is very terrible; and the symptoms grow stronger every day. . . . The youth born and brought up in wicked times, without any bias to good from early principle or instilled opinion, when they grow ripe must be monsters indeed. And it is to be feared, that age of monsters is not far off.[54]

Berkeley also noted that the Christian religion produces not only virtuous people, but also good citizens. Yet he saw atheistic principles multiplying before him.

The Anglican Church was expected to respond to this culture shift. Ian Green observes that "from the Restoration to the reign of Anne there was a growing concern, especially in London, to curb immorality and defeat religious apathy, by preaching and setting up societies and schools."[55] The achievement of this objective was sidetracked by at least two characteristics of some Anglican clergy at the time. First, as Anglican intellectuals,

51. Porter, *Creation of the Modern World*, 258.

52. Porter, *Creation of the Modern World*, 262.

53. Houghton, *Sketches from Church History*, 187.

54. Berkeley, "Discourse Addressed to Magistrates and Men in Authority," 4:483–506.

55. Green, "Anglicanism under Stuart and Hanoverian England," 180.

conditioned by the ethos of Enlightenment, reacted to "what they regarded as the overzealous enthusiasm of Puritanism and the coercive tyranny of Roman Catholicism," they proposed a "calmer, more self-controlled, more reasonable religion."[56] In some cases this Latitudinarian impulse even gave way to Deism.[57] Porter also suggests that hedonism made its mark among Latitudinarians in their presentation of "a benevolent God as author of a harmonious universe in which earthly joys presaged heavenly rewards."[58] While not totally unorthodox, if this doctrine was worked out according to the reason and will of man, it could lead to a less than robust understanding of the idea of biblical "joy." Houghton offers an assessment of Anglican clergy at this time: "In the Church of England bishops and parish clergy alike were often given up to worldliness. Sports, politics, entertainments, held their chief interest. Ease rather than labor characterized them."[59] Noll points out a second problem with the Anglican pastorate: "The widespread practices of pluralism and non-residence did undercut Anglican effectiveness."[60] An absentee priest could obviously not instruct his parishioners in the doctrines and applications of the Christian faith. Church and society were in need of reform and revival indeed.[61]

56. Noll, *Rise of Evangelicalism*, 40.

57. Deism had its heyday in the eighteenth century. It was an often anti-Christian philosophy substituting natural religion for revealed religion and disbelieving all miracles and supernatural events in the Bible. Deists believe that God created the world but does not actively participate in its running or in human affairs, as man's reason is sufficient for all moral decision-making. See Kurian, *Nelson's Dictionary of Christianity*, 210.

58. Porter, *Creation of the Modern World*, 260.

59. Houghton, *Sketches from Church History*, 186. Noll comments that even if more impartial judges find the state of religion less decrepit than how it is often characterized, "still, even objective evaluators have recognized that confident religious life, persuasive preaching of the gospel and effective Christian pastoring were in relatively short supply during the first decades of the eighteenth century." Noll, *Rise of Evangelicalism*, 39.

60. Noll, *Rise of Evangelicalism*, 39. Noll explains: "Nonresidence was linked to pluralism, because when a minister secured the rights to another parish—or to a post in a cathedral or university—the holder of plural benefices could not be in more than one place at a time." Noll, *Rise of Evangelicalism*, 39.

61. Two caveats must be raised concerning the influence of the Enlightenment on the culture and the dilemma of social and moral declension. First, not all of the "enlightened" sought after a full-fledged doctrine of hedonism. In a number of chapters in Porter's *Creation of the Modern World*, the author points out that moralism was just as much a response to the Enlightenment as was licentiousness by elite thinkers. They simply had a more humanistic basis for morality and virtue. Second, the Anglican clergy and parishioners were obviously not all affected equally by the new social climate. Some pastors and parishioners remained orthodox. See Green's "Anglicanism under Stuart and Hanoverian England" for a thorough description of the Anglican Church during this period.

The Toleration of Dissent

RETURNING TO THE CAUSE of Dissent, Michael Watts skillfully compares the period between the toleration of dissent that begin in 1689 and the Evangelical Revival that commenced in the 1730s and describes the climate of the period regarding the Dissenters by referring to the literary work of the most famous Baptist of the previous era:

> In Bunyan's vision of *The Pilgrim's Progress* the way to the Celestial City lay through Vanity Fair. It was a place where Christian and his companion Faithful were subjected to violent abuse, beaten up by the mob, chained in irons, and thrown into a cage as a public spectacle. Faithful was charged with denying the validity of the town's religion, inciting disloyalty to its rulers, and speaking contemptuously of its nobility. He was sentenced to be scourged and burnt at the stake. But Christian escaped from Vanity Fair and "came to a delicate plain, called Ease" where he traveled "with much content". This was not, though, the end of his trials: "at the farthest side of the plain was a little hill called Lucre, and in that hill a silver mine". And beyond the hill lay Doubting Castle.[62]

John Bunyan's insight proved prophetic as Watts applies it, "Such, in epitome, was the history of Dissent from the persecution of the Restoration period, through the relief of toleration, to the material prosperity yet spiritual decline of the early eighteenth century."[63] During the first decades of their period of religious freedom, the Nonconformists were faced with spiritual decay within their own various movements. The historic connection between orthodox doctrine and a robust Christian life played itself out among Dissenters during this period. Dissension between and within dissenting groups also posed problems for the movements. Noll states, "Nonconformity was declining as a movement and weakening as a theological force."[64] Examples from the major strands of dissent illustrate this issue. Just after their religious freedom was granted, the Presbyterians, and Congregationalists' relatively loose ecclesiastical structures allowed for them to cooperate financially in the sharing of pastors and financial resources for the purpose expanding their movements.

---

62. Watts, *Dissenters*, 263. In his biography of Anne Steele, J. R. Broome argues that Steele's Particular Baptist ancestors faithfully endured the years under the Clarendon Code. Her parents grew up during the first decades of relative religious freedom. Her uncle and then father faithfully pastored the Particular Baptist church within which she grew up while earning a living as timber merchants. See Broome, *Bruised Reed*.

63. Watts, *Dissenters*, 263.

64. Noll, *Rise of Evangelicalism*, 43.

Within months of this union, however, the two groups were quarreling: the Presbyterians accused the Congregationalists of Antinomianism;[65] the later accused the former of Arminianism.[66] While there may have been some truth to the accusations, the division it caused these dissenting brethren was detrimental to the dissenting cause.

An even more critical issue was the "worrying development among Dissenters [concerning] . . . the creeping advance of Arian views."[67] As a result over one hundred leading Baptist, Congregational, and Presbyterian ministers met in Salters' Hall in London in February 1719 to deliberate on what can be boiled down to two crucial issues.[68] First, was it enough for ministers to follow the Scriptures without subscribing to historic orthodox creeds or confessions of faith, as Trinitarian congregations had tradition-ally expected of them? Second, was there room in traditional Trinitarian denominations "for Arians, who regarded Christ as more than man but also as distinctly less than fully God?"[69] The confessional Trinitarians lost the vote by a margin of fifty-seven to fifty-three.[70] From this point forward Arian views advanced rapidly among the General Baptists and the English Presbyterians, with many among them falling eventually into full-orbed Unitarianism.[71]

While the Independents or Congregationalists escaped from Salters' Hall intact, this was not the end of the story for them. By the end of their distinguished careers, two prominent Independent ministers, Isaac Watts and Philip Doddridge, found themselves doubting the adequacy of the

65. "Antinomianism so stresses Christian freedom from the condemnation of the law that it underemphasizes the need of the believer to confess sins daily and to pur-sue sanctification [that is, growth in holiness and conformity to the image of Christ] earnestly. It may even fail to teach that sanctification inevitably follows justification." Ferguson et al., *New Dictionary of Theology*, 379.

66. Watts, *Dissenters*, 289–97. Arminianism is the theological system, so-called due to its basis on the five points of the Remonstrants who carried on the teachings of Jaco-bus Arminius (1560–1609), which says that election is conditional on man's response, dependent on God's foreknowledge of his faith and perseverance. Arminianism inverts the Reformed orthodox order of election and grace. See Ferguson et al., *New Dictionary of Theology*, 45.

67. Noll, *Rise of Evangelicalism*, 43.

68. See Watts, *Dissenters*, 374–77; and Noll, *Rise of Evangelicalism*, 43. Nuttall traces some strands of the history of the Dissenting movement following Salters' Hall in "Cal-vinism in Free Church History," 418–28.

69. Noll, *Rise of Evangelicalism*, 43.

70. Watts, *Dissenters*, 375.

71. Noll, *Rise of Evangelicalism*, 43. Unitarianism is the "heretical Christian tradi-tion that affirms monotheism but rejects both the Trinity and the divinity of Christ." Kurian, *Nelson's Dictionary of Christianity*, 690.

traditional Trinitarian formulas.[72] Michael Mullett adds further that the doctrinal crisis in English Dissent was the product not only of this weakening Christology, but also of a retreat from Calvinism—the intellectual foundation of English religious Dissent—and "even a perceptible decline in Christianity itself, with ancient features, such as belief in hell, under attack from the newly fashionable rationalism and humanitarianism."[73] Though some of their own internal disputes regarding the proper subjects of membership and Communion as well as the beginnings of their troubles with High or Hyper-Calvinism[74] did surface during this period, the Particular Baptists weathered the first few decades of religious freedom with their fundamental theological and ecclesiastical principles still intact.[75] The same cannot be said of all Nonconformists. A stir was caused among Dissenters with the 1730 publication of an anonymous pamphlet, *An Enquiry into the Causes of the Decay of the Dissenting Interest*.[76] "The title of [the] pamphlet, if not its contents," says Watts, "gave expression to the growing uneasiness with which many Dissenters regarded the state of their churches, their principles, and their religion."[77]

The Evangelical Revival

Facing social, moral, religious, and ecclesiastical decline, England and the dissenting interest were ripe for renewal by the 1730s. A people were raised up through whom revival came, but Watts notes the irony of the source,

> They came not from the ranks of the Friends, basking in their newly won respectability [by 1731], nor from the Presbyterians or General Baptists racked by theological dissension, nor from the Congregationalists or Particular Baptists, whose independent polity and Calvinist theology prevented, at least initially, much in the way of evangelism. The revival of religion

72. See Watts, *Dissenters*, 380–81; and Noll, *Rise of Evangelicalism*, 42–43.

73. Mullet, "Radical Sects and Dissenting Churches, 1600–1750," 210.

74. Hyper-Calvinism is an exaggerated form of Calvinism that emphasizes the sovereignty of God so completely that it leaves only limited responsibility to human beings. Making no real distinction between the secret and revealed will of God, it obviates the need to evangelize. John Gill (1697–1771) is often listed as the greatest theologian of this school. See Kurian, *Nelson's Dictionary of Christianity*, 347.

75. Due to these in-house issues as well as their relative isolation from mainstream society, however, it is debatable how much they grew and how healthy the denomination actually was during this period.

76. Mullet, "Radical Sects and Dissenting Churches, 1600–1750," 210.

77. Watts, *Dissenters*, 382.

in England and Wales, and ultimately of Dissent itself, was to come, paradoxically, from the ranks of the established church.[78]

Watts also suggests that it was the confluence of three revivalist movements[79] in the lives of George Whitefield (1714–1770) and John (1703–1791) and Charles Wesley that resulted in the Eighteenth-Century Revival in England and America.[80] These men were members of a group of Oxford graduates and students who, "from 1729, had been in the habit of meeting together for study, prayer, and good works."[81] Their contemporaries scornfully labeled them Methodists and their group the Holy Club due to the rigid daily discipline of their lives. When brought to true conversion on separate occasions a few years later, Whitefield and John Wesley—ministers from within the Church of England—began itinerant preaching tours that ultimately resulted in revival in England and America. Though Whitefield and the Wesleys eventually parted ways due to Whitefield's Calvinism and the Wesleys' Arminianism, the influence of their evangelical preaching and encouragement to good works flowing from faith, cannot be underestimated. Further, the evangelical hymns of the Independent Isaac Watts and the Anglican Charles Wesley, the two greatest writers of the golden age of hymnody that coincided with these revivals, contributed to personal and corporate spirituality during this period. David Bebbington states emphatically that in this period of revivals based on the Reformation message of justification by faith, the English-speaking world witnessed "a more important development than any other, before or after, in the history of Protestant Christianity: the emergence of the movement that became Evangelicalism."[82] He further notes that this revival was "a quickening of the spiritual tempo in Britain and beyond," but that it "made much less

---

78. Watts, *Dissenters*, 393.

79. Around the late 1720s and early 1730s, evangelical Calvinistic preaching by such as the Dutch Reformed Theodorus Frelinghuysen (1692–ca. 1747), the Presbyterian Gilbert Tennent (1703–1764), and Congregationalist Jonathan Edwards (1703–1758) in the American colonies was gaining converts to an evangelical Christianity. At roughly the same time in Germany the Pietists (a group dedicated to living a "pious" Christian life based on the teachings of the Bible) emerged through the influences of Hermann Francke (1663–1727) and Nicholas Ludwig, Count von Zinzendorf (1700–1760), bringing missionary enthusiasm through the New Moravian Church. Meanwhile, two Welsh Anglicans, Howell Harris (1714–1773) and Daniel Rowland (1713–1790), having each been evangelically converted, agreed to work together for the conversion of Wales. These three movements were all independent of each other. See Watts, *Dissenters*, 394–97; and Houghton, *Sketches from Church History*, 174–85.

80. See Watts, *Dissenters*, 393–406.

81. Watts, *Dissenters*, 397.

82. Bebbington, *Evangelicalism in Modern Britain*, 20–21.

impact on the Established Church than among Dissenters."[83] Two questions then must be asked: What was the spiritual state of the Particular Baptist denomination at the time of the Evangelical Revival and what was the relationship of this revival to the Particular Baptist Community?

The Particular Baptist Community and the Evangelical Revival

Although the Particular Baptists arrived at the time of the revivals in the 1730s with their basic theological principles still intact, it is nevertheless a difficult task to assign a grade to their overall spiritual health. One reason is that even though it has been argued that they flourished during the time of the oppression of the Clarendon Code, the introductory words to the reader of the *Second London Confession* in both its original edition in 1677 and its 1688/89 reprint declare them to be living "in this backsliding day."[84] Therefore, they should "begin at home, to reform in the first place our own hearts and wayes; and then to quicken all that we may have influence upon, to the same work."[85] It goes on to say they desire not to "deceive themselves, by resting in, and trusting to a form of Godliness, without the power of it, and inward experience of the efficacy of those truths that are professed by them."[86] These words reveal several things about the leading ministers of this denomination. First, they believe they need spiritual renewal. Yet the simple fact that a cross-section of Particular Baptist pastors would meet in 1689 means that they still had congregations who were alive even if not at their healthiest. Second, as Dissenters, who would be tempted to think themselves better than their Anglican neighbors who toed the party line in terms of religion, these Particular Baptist pastors did not want to be spiritual hypocrites. Third, though Calvinists, who would come to be perceived as less than evangelistic, they described a desire to influence others through both doctrine and the personal spiritual experience thereof. They also finally note that the "decay of religion" is due to "the neglect of the worship of God in Families, by those to whom the charge and conduct of them is committed."[87] Thus, they should use the *Confession* to "catechise and instruct" their young "with the knowledge of the truth of God as revealed in the Scriptures" as

---

83. Bebbington, *Evangelicalism in Modern Britain*, 21.

84. Lumpkin, *Baptist Confessions of Faith*, 247.

85. Lumpkin, *Baptist Confessions of Faith*, 247.

86. Lumpkin, *Baptist Confessions of Faith*, 247.

87. Lumpkin, *Baptist Confessions of Faith*, 247.

they recommit themselves to prayer and other "duties of Religion in their families."[88] These pastors had not only noble but also spiritually renewing and reviving pursuits in mind for their *Confession.*[89]

For a while at least, the hopes of the ministers who composed and published, and then later the ones who republished, the *Second London Confession*, were fulfilled. Following the Glorious Revolution and the re-printing of the *Second London Confession*, Haykin notes, "After a considerable degree of vitality during the reigns of William III and Anne, who was queen from 1702 to 1714, the Calvinistic Baptist cause began to decline."[90] So Naylor's paradoxical comment above begins to make sense: just after the Glorious Revolution, the Particular Baptists used their newfound freedom to advance their cause, but only for a couple of decades. In another place, Haykin speaks of the particular Baptists in terms of numbers: "The Baptist Zion was 'drooping'. From possibly as many as 300 congregations in 1689, the denomination had shrunk to around 220 Calvinistic Baptist churches in 1715. By the 1750s, probably the nadir of the decline, there were only about 150 churches."[91]

Thus, during the very time in which a revival was taking hold in England through the preaching of ministers of the established church, the Particular Baptists found themselves in a state of declension. Further, the Evangelical Revival seems to have had a less than robust relationship to the Particular Baptist denomination either in influence or participation. Haykin identifies a number of "political, social and geographical, as well as theological" factors to which "the decline of the Baptists during the early and mid-eighteenth century" and their reluctance to participate within the Evangelical Revival may be attributed.[92]

Haykin notes first that Baptist writers and historians have traditionally fixed the blame for the declension of the Particular Baptist movement through the first three quarters of the eighteenth century "on the High Calvinism, or Hyper-Calvinism, of such influential Baptist theologians as John Gill (1697–1771) and John Brine (1703–1765), both of whom pastored

88. Lumpkin, *Baptist Confessions of Faith*, 247.

89. It could also be argued that with the threat of hyper-Calvinism having appeared in the southwest of England, the new confession's emphasizing "the obligation to preach the Gospel in all ages and all nations" essentially addressed the hyper-Calvinist questions from the earliest days of the Particular Baptist movement. See *Second London Confession* chap. XX, sec. 3; Haykin, *Kiffin, Knollys and Keach*, 64; and Lumpkin, *Baptist Confessions of Faith*, 237–38.

90. Haykin, *One Heart and One Soul*, 17.

91. Haykin, "Benjamin Beddome," 109.

92. Haykin, *One Heart and One Soul*, 24.

congregations in London."[93] P. J. Morden says that fundamental to High Calvinism "was the belief that the unconverted were under no moral obligation to repent and believe the gospel, because total depravity rendered them incapable of doing so, and they could not justly be held accountable for doing what in reality they were completely unable to do."[94] As key sections of the Particular Baptist movement indeed fell into a hardened hyper-Calvinism over the years, it tended to bring with it the loss of a sense of warm piety as well as a neglect to offer the gospel to the lost.[95] Quoting a notable evangelical Calvinist of the period, Haykin reveals the core problem with High Calvinism: "John Ryland, Jr., the pastor of Broadmead Church, Bristol and the principal of Bristol Baptist Academy writing in 1816, stated that through the influence of both Gill and Brine the opinion 'spread pretty much among ministers of the Baptist denomination' that 'It is not the duty of the unregenerate to believe in Christ.'"[96] Historian J. M. Cramp says that the men infected with High Calvinism made only feeble efforts at urging holiness upon believers and that though they would state men's danger, "they did not call upon them to 'repent and believe the gospel.' They did not entreat them to be 'reconciled unto God.'"[97] Noll agrees with Cramp, suggesting that the Particular Baptists "had remained doctrinally orthodox, but often in an extreme Calvinist form that discouraged active evangelism and that placed more stress on correct doctrinal formulas than on active piety."[98]

Watts offers a brief history of how this movement eventually spread throughout the Particular Baptist community:

> By the middle of the eighteenth century Particular Baptists were being widely influenced by the High Calvinism of Joseph Hussey [1660–1726] and John Gill. . . . Hussey took his Calvinism so seriously that he denied that God's grace should be offered to the non-elect; his teaching had a profound effect on a

---

93. Haykin, *One Heart and One Soul*, 17. John Skepp (1675–1721), who also pastored in London, is also known as an influential High Calvinist of the period.

94. Morden, "Andrew Fuller and *The Gospel Worthy of All Acceptation*," 129.

95. McBeth, *Baptist Heritage*, 171–78. Tom Nettles adds, "Some Particular Baptists became infected with hyper-Calvinism and seldom, if ever, called the unregenerate to repent of sin and believe in Jesus." Nettles, *Baptists*, 1:318–19.

96. Haykin, *One Heart and One Soul*, 17.

97. Cramp, *Baptist History*, 499. He adds, "And the churches did not, could not, under their instruction, engage in efforts for the conversion of souls. They were so afraid of intruding on God's work that they neglected to do what he had commanded them. They seem to have supposed that *preservation* was all they should aim at; they had not heart enough to seek *extension*. No wonder that the cause declined." Cramp, *Baptist History*, 499–500.

98. Noll, *Rise of Evangelicalism*, 163.

member of his [Congregational] church, John Skepp, who sub-
sequently became a Baptist pastor; and Skepp in his turn relayed
Hussey's views to John Gill, who for more than half a century,
from 1719–1771, was minister to the Particular Baptist church
at Horselydown, Southwark, and one of the most influential
men in the denomination.[99]

At the places in which it took root, this High Calvinism persisted for decades to the detriment of the Particular Baptist cause. For example, Watts
notes that Andrew Fuller wrote of the Particular Baptist preaching to which
he listened in the late 1760s and early 1770s "that nothing was said to the
'unregenerate' 'in the way of warning them to flee from the wrath to come,
or inviting them to apply to Christ for salvation.'"[100] Fuller, who eventually
helped to spark a revival among Particular Baptists in the last quarter of the
eighteenth century, once reflected upon his denomination, "The Christian
profession had sunk into contempt amongst us; inasmuch, that had matters
gone on but a few years longer, the Baptists would have become a perfect
dunghill in society."[101] The issue of High Calvinism was obviously a serious
matter for the Particular Baptists.

   While there is no consensus among current historians as to John
Gill's exact relationship to High Calvinism as a full-orbed movement, and
though it can even be said that "from time to time his writings display a
commitment to evangelical Calvinism rather than High Calvinism," yet
Haykin says, "When Gill's thinking about faith and evangelism was pon-
dered and acted upon by his fellow Baptist preachers, it was invariably his
High Calvinism that was their lodestar. These preachers thus refrained from
urging upon the lost their responsibility to embrace Christ and to trust in
him alone for their salvation."[102] For example, succeeding his mentor, John
Eve, as the pastor at Soham, Andrew Fuller said of his predecessor, who

---

99. Watts, *Dissenters*, 456–57. The specific issue from which this movement arose
was the Modern Question, which was first asked formally by Hussey, a Congregationalist minister, in 1706. Nettles lists the two parts to the question: "Is unregenerate man
under spiritual obligation to repent of sin and believe in Christ upon hearing the gospel, and, parallel to that, is the gospel minister to call upon such sinners for evangelical
faith and repentance?" Nettles notes that this question "greatly affected the Congregationalists and Presbyterians, and made its way into Baptist life through John Brine's
influence." He also points out that "though he never wrote on the subject itself, some
claim that John Gill held the 'negative' side of the question." Nettles, *Baptists*, 1:247–49.

100. Ryland, *Life and Death of the Rev. Andrew Fuller* (1833), 51, cited in Watts, *Dissenters*, 458.

101. Cited by J. W. Morris, *Memoirs of the Life and Death of the Rev. Andrew Fuller*
(London: High Wycombe, 1816), 267, quoted in Haykin, *One Heart and One Soul*, 15.

102. Haykin, *One Heart and One Soul*, 19.

was an avid reader of Gill, that he was "'tinged with false Calvinism,' having 'little to nothing to say to the unconverted.'"[103] Gill's influence, through his voluminous and influential writings, whether intended or not, thus contributed to his denomination's decline. While it will be discussed below that this High Calvinism was not pervasive throughout every region of the Particular Baptist community, it is not hard to surmise its detrimental effect on the spiritual health and growth of the denomination. Morden notes further destructive tendencies of High Calvinism illustrated by Eve and the congregation at Soham, namely, the accompanying features of "an insular ecclesiology, antinomianism and theological hairsplitting."[104] Further, any Particular Baptists who followed a consistent High Calvinism, which would include a reluctance to offer the gospel freely to the unregenerate, would by this fact be impeded, if not completely restricted, from having a positive relationship to the Evangelical Revival.

Another factor that Haykin suggests contributed to the decline of the Particular Baptists was "isolation and lack of communication."[105] The isolation was both geographical and ecclesiastical. This factor would have also worked against the Baptists taking part in the Evangelical Revival. "Many of the congregations were in small market-towns, villages and hamlets."[106] This natural geographic isolation when coupled with rough weather, winter conditions, or poorly maintained roads did not lend itself to numerical growth or positive interdenominational communication. But there was also an ecclesiastical isolation inherent in the Baptist system of polity. The *Second London Confession* says of the local congregation that Christ, in his word, "hath given all that power and authority, which is in any way needful, for their carrying on that order in worship, and discipline, which he hath instituted for them to observe."[107] There would therefore not have been any formal reason to seek counsel or cooperation in church-related pursuits beyond one's local congregation. Although their forefathers, who had written their confessions of faith, had chosen to meet in voluntary associations for mutual edification and benefit of the church and its ministers, during the middle

---

103. John Ryland Jr., *The Work of Faith, the Labour of Love, and the Patience of Hope Illustrated in the Life and Death of the Late Rev. Andrew Fuller*, 2nd ed. (London: Button and Son, 1818), 11, cited in Morden, "Andrew Fuller and *The Gospel Worthy of All Acceptation*," 130.

104. Morden, "Andrew Fuller and *The Gospel Worthy of All Acceptation*," 130.

105. Haykin, *One Heart and One Soul*, 23.

106. Haykin, *One Heart and One Soul*, 23.

107. Lumpkin, *Baptist Confessions of Faith*, 287. See also Haykin, *One Heart and One Soul*, 23.

half of the eighteenth-century Particular Baptist association life was mostly "moribund."[108] Deryck W. Lovegrove succinctly summarizes the situation, "The very strength of independency, the internal cohesion of the gathered church, became its weakness as geographical remoteness conspired with autonomy and lack of common purpose to foster numerical decline."[109]

Their distance from the Evangelical Revival during the middle of the eighteenth century, and perhaps a perception as less than attractive to evangelicals in general, may also be attributed to the theology of the Particular Baptist community, especially as applying to their ecclesiology and regarding points of dispute or controversy. The Particular Baptists were a minority denomination within a minority dissenting movement when it came to their membership practices. Though they shared the self-governing "gathered Church" idea and the need for a testimony of an inward conversion experience for communing membership of a church with their Congregational brethren,[110] their membership practices contained a particular distinction. The Baptists did not practice infant baptism, but only believer's baptism by immersion at the time the prospective member offered some proof of inward regeneration by the Holy Spirit. While it must be said that a Baptist would obviously not cite the Baptist belief and practice of believer's baptism by immersion as an impediment to growth or reason for decline,[111] the common practice of holding baptisms in streams or creeks could open them to criticism.[112] Further, at least after the time of the 1688/89 reprint of the *Second London Confession*, the typical congregation also practiced closed communion. This means that only Christians who had been baptized by

108. Haykin, *One Heart and One Soul*, 24.

109. Lovegrove, *Established Church, Sectarian People*, 7.

110. Watts, *Dissenters*, 291.

111. Their distinctive practice is mentioned here as an observation of the Particular Baptist community in comparison to fellow Dissenters and Evangelicals. It is worth noting, however, that the practice may have impeded numerical, even if not spiritual, growth. Haykin notes that even at the end of his life, Benjamin Beddome, in the sleepy hamlet of Bourton on the Water, could boast of a church attendance of 500–600, though actual membership had dwindled to 123. Haykin, "Benjamin Beddome," 104.

112. Regarding the "many degrading circumstances attending" the ordinance of baptism in an area of Yorkshire, Baptist pastor William Steadman once commented that certain ministers "from a foolish scrupulosity, . . . objected to baptistries in their places of worship, and administer the ordinance in rivers, to whatever disadvantage it may subject them. At Bradford they have baptised in a small stream, the only one near them, scarcely deep enough, muddy at the bottom, and from which the minister and the persons baptised have at least a quarter of a mile to walk along a dirty lane in their wet clothes before they can change. The place, likewise, is quite unfavourable for seeing or hearing, and by that means the benefits of the ordinance are lost to the congregation, few of whom ever attend it." Steadman, *Memoir of the Rev. William Steadman, D.D.*, 234–35.

immersion in a recognized congregation would be received to the Lord's Table or for a transfer of membership to a Particular Baptist church. These factors placed the Particular Baptist community not only outside the mainstream ecclesiastical life of England, but even beyond the religious life of their fellow Dissenters. John Wesley's views of the Baptists offers an example of the kind of ire Baptist distinctives could provoke among those with Anglican proclivities: "When a sinner is just awakened to see his state as a sinner, the people called Anabaptists [i.e. Baptists], begin to trouble him about outward forms and modes of worship, and that of baptism; but they had better cut his throat, for it is sending . . . him to hell and perdition."[113]

As Calvinistic heirs taking their cue from their Puritan forebears, Particular Baptists were serious about their theology and ecclesiology. So it is not surprising that theological controversy erupted at times.[114] The views of closed membership and closed communion held by the majority of Particular Baptist churches offered such opportunity for points of dispute for their churches and their witness. Though the majority of Particular Baptist congregations always held to closed membership and closed communion, since the days of Bunyan, there was typically a minority that sought to show "charity" to fellow evangelical believers on these issues. Regarding the refusal of Baptist churches to receive into membership those who had only been baptized as infants (which according to the definition of baptism held by most Baptists would have been no baptism at all), Daniel Turner[115] pleads for his brethren to display a "'true *Protestant Catholic* spirit.'"[116] In that vein, Paul S. Fiddes describes Turner's argument, "Churches ought to recognize each other as true churches of Christ, seek advice from one another, receive members from one another when recommended, and transfer their members into membership with each other."[117] Concerning paedobaptists, Turner

---

113. Cited by Robison, "Particular Baptists," in Haykin, *One Heart and One Soul*, 28. Of course, many Baptists thought no better of Wesley. Baptist pastor James Turner (d. 1780) once told John Sutcliff Wesley was "a *nothing*, both in politics and religion." James Turner, letter to John Sutcliff, January 13, 1776 (Sutcliff Papers, Angus Library, Regent's Park College, Oxford University), in Haykin, *One Heart and One Soul*, 28.

114. For a recent discussion of two such issues, see Haykin and Robinson, "Particular Baptist Debates about Communion and Hymn-Singing," 284–308.

115. John Briggs lists Turner and Abraham Atkins as having "the most principled arguments for open membership." Briggs, "Changing Pattern of Baptist Life," 15.

116. Daniel Turner, *Charity the Bond of Perfection. A Sermon, The Substance of which was Preached at Oxford, November 16, 1780, On Occasion of the Re-establishment of a Christian Church of Protestant Dissenters in that City; with a Brief Account of the State of the Society, and the Plan and Manner of their Settlement* (Oxford: 1780), i–viii, cited in Fiddes, "Daniel Turner and a Theology of the Church Universal," 113.

117. Daniel Turner, *A Compendium of Social Religion, or the Nature and*

bases his argument on the principle that the paedobaptist sincerely believes he is rightly baptized and thus his Christian brethren ought to respect his "sacred right of private judgment" or conscience.[118] While the majority of Turner's fellow Particular Baptist ministers disagreed, the question still regularly affected both the relationship of the Particular Baptist congregations to one another and to other Dissenters. Views of communion, or the Lord's Supper, added further points of conflict.

Particular Baptist advocates of open communion, or the admission of non-immersed persons to the Lord's Table, included Daniel Turner, John Collett Ryland Sr. (1723–1792), John Brown (d. 1800) of Kettering, and Robert Robinson (1735–1790) of Cambridge.[119] Naylor lists this as a controversy among the Particular Baptists that included outbreaks throughout the entire long eighteenth century.[120] While there were a number of arguments relating to the definitions of church membership, baptism, and communion, the controversy centered around the desire by those in favor of open communion for unity and charity with fellow Christians and the desire by those favoring closed communion for a more consistently biblical (and thus, Baptist) ecclesiology. Turner, for example, based his desire for open communion on a "catholic ecclesiology with the clear concept of the relation of the local church to the whole body of Christ."[121] For him the sacrament, or ordinance, was "a visible bond of unity between societies of believers, not only between individual believers."[122] Turner believed sharing in the Lord's Supper to be a necessary demonstration of the "visible 'unity' of the whole church of Christ 'in the bonds of peace and love.'"[123] In his later years, perhaps influenced by his friendship with the Anglican

---

Constitution of Christian Churches, with the Respective Qualifications and Duties of their Officers and Members . . . Designed as an Essay towards reviving the primitive Spirit of Evangelical Purity, Liberty, and Charity, in the Churches of the Present Times (London: John Ward, 1758), 116–17, cited in Fiddes, "Daniel Turner and a Theology of the Church Universal," 117.

118. Fiddes, "Daniel Turner and a Theology of the Church Universal," 122. Fiddes adds, "Similarly, Turner speaks of the Paedobaptist Brother as 'having an equally just Right' to the Lord's Table because he is 'a Believer in CHRIST, answering in a good conscience to what HE thinks true baptism.'" Fiddes, "Daniel Turner and a Theology of the Church Universal," 123.

119. See Fiddes, "Daniel Turner and a Theology of the Church Universal," 122; and Naylor, *Picking up a Pin for the Lord*, 103.

120. See Naylor, *Picking up a Pin for the Lord*, 87–143.

121. Fiddes, "Daniel Turner and a Theology of the Church Universal," 121.

122. Fiddes, "Daniel Turner and a Theology of the Church Universal," 121.

123. Turner, *Compendium*, 119, cited in Fiddes, "Daniel Turner and a Theology of the Church Universal," 120.

James Hervey (1714–1758), John Collett Ryland sought forbearance on the issue for the sake of peace.[124] John Brown equally maintained that "'strict Baptists' failed to show the fruits of the Spirit; they 'set at naught' other Christians and 'walk uncharitably' with those with whom they disagreed on this matter."[125] Abraham Booth (1734–1806), on the other hand, sharing the majority sentiment, simply stated that if they were going to be true to their principles as Baptists, they must "admit baptized believers only to the Lord's table" because "restricted communion was an essential hall-mark of a strictly Baptist church."[126] Naylor notes that "the glare of the Evangelical Awakening" contributed to the intensity of the controversy.[127] As the Baptists became involved in their own awakening later in the century, which included new Baptist growth that "was in part the fruit of united evangelical witness, Robert Hall, Jr. (1764–1831) began to ponder how it could be right for Christians to be united under the Spirit in mission but separate at the Lord's Table, hence his advocacy for open communion, which was fiercely resisted by others."[128] So while Hall's contemporaries Andrew Fuller (1754–1815), Booth, and Joseph Kinghorn (1766–1832) "all believed that 'closed' or 'strict' communion was necessary for protecting the distinctiveness of Baptist beliefs and ecclesiology,"[129] Briggs notes that there was nevertheless "much agonizing discussion around the rival claims of pan-Evangelical mission and distinctive Baptist ecclesiology and practice."[130]

In describing life in the eighteenth century, Briggs bluntly states that "part of the experience of the people called Baptists" was that they were "prone to division and schism."[131] One final controversy that plagued the Particular Baptists for many years to the point of division in some cases was over congregational hymn-singing. Since this is germane to this study, it merits consideration at this point. Looking as far back as 1658, Naylor

---

124. Naylor, *Picking up a Pin for the Lord*, 104. See also Naylor, "John Collett Ryland (1723–1792)," 1:195–97.

125. John Brown, *The House of God Opened and His Table Free for Baptists and Paedo-baptists, who are Saints Faithful in Christ* (1777), cited in Naylor, *Picking up a Pin for the Lord*, 107. The designation "strict Baptist" refers essentially to the issue of closed, or restricted, communion.

126. Naylor, *Picking up a Pin for the Lord*, 112.

127. Naylor, *Picking up a Pin for the Lord*, 103.

128. Briggs, "Changing Pattern of Baptist Life," 15.

129. Considering these men and their views, W. R. Ward comments, "Open communion would leave the Baptist denomination with nothing to stand for." Ward, "Baptists and the Transformation of the Church, 1780–1830," 176.

130. Briggs, "Changing Pattern of Baptist Life," 15–16.

131. Briggs, "Changing Pattern of Baptist Life," 1.

says, "Congregational singing with musical accompaniment had long been a point of contention."[132] Though the *Second London Confession* commends "teaching and admonishing one another in Psalms, Hymns and Spiritual songs, singing with grace in our Hearts to the Lord,"[133] it is yet sobering to consider that two of the "big three" of the Particular Baptist forefathers, Kiffin and Knollys, found themselves on opposing sides of the debate.[134] Regarding Kiffin's fear of singing, Naylor points out, "He might have thought that it would prejudice restricted communion."[135] Haykin suggests that during the period of persecution, this issue had been quiescent, but once toleration came, a "bitter controversy" over hymn-singing ensued in the 1690s. It was especially contentious in London.[136] Of course, Keach and Joseph Stennett I were early writers of hymns, especially to be sung after communion, and promoters of hymn-singing. As has already been mentioned, many others followed them in such pursuits. Keach even mentions among the articles of faith for the Horsleydown church, like-minded churches that did not agree concerning the "singing of God's praise", yet indicates that Horsleydown should "not refuse Communion with them."[137] Keach is well-known for his seminal work on the subject, *The Breach repaired in God's Worship or Singing of Psalms, Hymns and Spiritual Songs.* And yet Baptists remained "sharply divided" over the issue for decades.[138] Such division did not commend the Particular Baptist community to others nor to the spirit of the Evangelical Revival.

Political and social factors also contributed to the Particular Baptists' malaise during the eighteenth century. Haykin describes their situation as one of "legal and social discrimination."[139] Politically, as Briggs notes, there was only a "very prescribed form of toleration [that was] secured in 1689."[140] In fact, Briggs adds, "The Act of Toleration did not give dissenters equal rights under the law with churchmen."[141] For example, dissenters

---

132. Naylor, *Calvinism, Communion and the Baptists*, 50.

133. Lumpkin, *Baptist Confessions of Faith*, 281.

134. Haykin, *One Heart and One Soul*, 22.

135. Naylor, *Calvinism, Communion and the Baptists*, 51.

136. Haykin, *One Heart and One Soul*, 22.

137. Benjamin Keach, *The Articles of Faith of the Church of Christ, or Congregation meeting at Horsley-down, Benjamin Keach, Pastor, As Asserted this 10th of the 6th Month, 1697* (London, 1697), Dedicatory Epistle cited in Naylor, *Calvinism, Communion and the Baptists*, 52.

138. Haykin, "Benjamin Beddome," 96.

139. Haykin, *One Heart and One Soul*, 20.

140. Briggs, "Changing Pattern of Baptist Life," 2.

141. Briggs, "Changing Pattern of Baptist Life," 16.

could only worship in lawfully registered and licensed meeting-houses, and then only with the door propped open so that should the constable pass by he could hear from the outside whether revolutionary activities were occurring inside.[142] Dissenting baptisms were not recognized, thus disqualifying dissenters from burial in the parish churchyards.[143] Further, Lord Hardwicke's Marriage Act of 1753 made all weddings illegal except those celebrated by the Church of England. This situation existed until 1836.[144] Dissenters were still required to take the oath of allegiance and to subscribe to most of the articles of the Church of England, and were effectively disqualified from political office.[145] Finally, Briggs suggests, "Baptists remained second-class citizens suffering penal legislation until 1828 when the Test and Corporation Acts, limiting their ability to take civil offices, were repealed."[146] Though some Particular Baptist congregations and ministers weathered these restrictions with dignity and success, "notwithstanding such exceptions, the limitation of toleration was keenly felt with local oppression fostering resentment in many places."[147]

Although the Act of Toleration forced the Anglican majority "to concede religious liberty to Dissenters, rigid Anglicans were most reluctant to extend to them civil equality."[148] Tolerated by the law of the land, Dissenters were nevertheless highly disliked by most Churchmen, often being described as schismatics.[149] Haykin sums up the legal and social plight of the Particular Baptists during the eighteenth century and its effect on the growth of their movement:

> Certain legal restrictions enacted during the reign of Charles II, which were designed to curtail Nonconformist participation in the mainstream of English society, remained unrescinded. Significant obstacles, for instance, continued to lie in the path of those Dissenters who sought to study at either Oxford or Cambridge University, or who wanted to pursue a career in the government at either the national or civic level. Nonconformists, Baptists included, were clearly in a position of social inferiority throughout the eighteenth century. This legal and social

142. Haykin, *One Heart and One Soul*, 20.

143. Briggs, "Changing Pattern of Baptist Life," 16.

144. Briggs, "Changing Pattern of Baptist Life," 16.

145. Naylor, *Picking up a Pin for the Lord*, 34.

146. Briggs, "Changing Pattern of Baptist Life," 16.

147. Briggs, "Changing Pattern of Baptist Life," 16.

148. Watts, *Dissenters*, 264–65.

149. Naylor, *Picking up a Pin for the Lord*, 33.

discrimination undoubtedly cast the Baptists in a poor light and helped to contribute to their failure to attract new members.[150]

How these second-class citizens handled this aspect of their lives is another issue to consider.

For some sections of the Particular Baptist denomination, these legal and social restrictions placed upon them seem to have exacerbated the insular nature from which they already suffered. First, Haykin suggests that for most of the eighteenth century they accepted the restrictions placed upon them and "limited their horizons to the maintenance of congregational life."[151] Using the imagery from Song of Solomon 4:12 of "a garden enclosed," John Gill said that the church is protected and "'encompassed with the power of God, as a wall about it', and is 'so closely surrounded, that it is not to be seen nor known by the world; and indeed is not accessible to any but believers in Christ.'"[152] Haykin observes, "Gill's language here well reflects the inward-looking attitudes of many Calvinistic Baptists during the early years of the eighteenth century, when they were largely content to enjoy the fruits of toleration and to rest secure behind the walls of their meeting-houses."[153] Second, the "spatial 'settledness'" that seems to have set in upon the Particular Baptists resulted in both a lack of vigorous desire for Christian growth and evangelistic effort previous generations had displayed.[154] In this point, the Particular Baptists proved they were not yet in line with that characteristic of Evangelicalism as described by Bebbington: they were woefully deficient in activism. Haykin describes the problem this created, "Far too many of the Nonconformist pastors . . . and this would have included Calvinistic Baptists—were content to live on their past experience of conversion and displayed little hunger for the presence and power of God in their lives."[155] Such an atmosphere certainly did not lend itself either to spiritual health or to participation in an evangelical awakening.

Further theological and ecclesiological, as well as experiential, factors gave pause to the Baptists concerning the Evangelical Revival as they observed it. While the Particular Baptists obviously concurred with the revival's emphasis on justification by faith, they were not happy with other elements. First, by functioning as itinerant evangelists, some of the revival preachers

150. Haykin, *One Heart and One Soul*, 20.

151. Haykin, *One Heart and One Soul*, 20.

152. John Gill, *An Exposition of the Old Testament* (London: Matthews and Leigh, 1810), 4:662, cited in Haykin, *One Heart and One Soul*, 20.

153. Haykin, *One Heart and One Soul*, 20.

154. See Haykin, *One Heart and One Soul*, 20–21.

155. Haykin, *One Heart and One Soul*, 21.

betrayed a weak understanding of the local church. Daniel Turner, for example, making a distinction between the village preaching of Baptists and the itinerant evangelism associated with the revival, stressed the importance for Baptist congregations to have "a constant and settled ministry amongst them."[156] Second, the revival preachers appeared to have little if any "convictions regarding church government and the proper subjects of baptism," two vital issues for Baptists.[157] Speaking of most Calvinistic Baptists of the period, Naylor notes that, unlike many advocates of the revival, they discerned the proper relationship between evangelism and churchmanship.[158] Baptists recognized that the New Testament teaches that new converts need the spiritual home provided by the local church. Next, the early key leaders of the revival movement were ministers in the Church of England, "which most Baptists regarded as an apostate institution."[159] Horton Davies suggests that it had even become a "point of honour" for Baptists and their fellow Puritan descendants of the eighteenth century "to refuse all compromise with the Anglican way of worship."[160] Reflecting on the thought and ministry of Benjamin Wallin, whose congregation actually grew during the time of denominational decline, Haykin offers an illustration of these factors: "Wallin, for instance, was insistent that as long as there was a neglect of believer's baptism and the principles of congregational church government, any attempt to revive the churches of Christ was 'essentially deficient.'"[161] Finally, the Arminianism that was preached, at least from the Wesley brothers' side of the revival, was anathema to the Calvinistic Baptists. The two groups often took jabs at one another both in print and verbally.[162] Regarding this aversion to Arminianism, Watts recounts that when Dan Taylor, a former Wesleyan preacher and soon-to-be leader of the New Connexion of General Baptists, came to see the necessity of believers' baptism, "the local Particular Baptist ministers refused to baptize Taylor as he was an Arminian."[163] Dif-

---

156. Daniel Turner, *A Brief and Faithful Narrative of the Extraordinary Rise and Present State of a Protestant Dissenting Congregation of the Baptist Denomination; at Lockerley, a small village near Romsey in Hampshire* (London: 1758), 15, cited in Smith, "James Fanch," 15.

157. Haykin, *One Heart and One Soul*, 26.

158. Naylor, *Picking up a Pin for the Lord*, 204.

159. Haykin, *One Heart and One Soul*, 27.

160. Davies, *From Watts and Wesley to Maurice, 1690–1850*, 23.

161. Benjamin Wallin, *The Folly of Neglecting Divine Institutions* (London: 1758), iv, v, cited in Haykin, *One Heart and One Soul*, 26.

162. See Haykin, *One Heart and One Soul*, 28.

163. Watts, *Dissenters*, 455.

fering views of, or at least applications of, theology and ecclesiology hindered the Particular Baptist involvement in the revival.

From the standpoint of "experimental divinity," the Particular Baptists saw another reason to doubt the orthodoxy of the revival movement. The Evangelical Revival appeared to be saturated with a characteristic dreaded by many thoughtful people of the eighteenth century and the Enlightenment: enthusiasm. Defined in Johnson's *Dictionary* as "a vain belief of private revelation; a vain confidence of divine favour or communication,"[164] enthusiasm was a bugbear of the enlightened mindset. Though both Whitefield and John Wesley recoiled at enthusiasm so defined, the movement of which they were key leaders was often linked to those who claimed the ability to heal the sick, prophesy new revelation, and exorcize demons, among other quasi-apostolic powers.[165] The Particular Baptists found this distasteful and unorthodox. Beyond these phenomena, the Baptists not only did not appreciate the overly emotional aspects of crying and weeping often associated with the revival, but neither did they appreciate the demands made by even respectable evangelists that the workings of the Holy Spirit must be "felt" or "experienced" to be considered valid.[166] Some Particular Baptist congregations took these issues so seriously as to forbid members from attending such meetings or even to excommunicate those who did.[167] Of course, these attitudes would lead to the charge that the orthodoxy of Particular Baptists "was sometimes a form of rigid dogmatism rather than the experiential faith so characteristic of the revival movement."[168] All in all, for many pockets of the Particular Baptist community their relationship to the Evangelical Revival was strained at best and downright antithetical at worst.

The Renewal and Revival of the Particular Baptists

So the Particular Baptists survived as a denomination, yet they were sore in need of revival. Reviewing these issues, Briggs notes, "Not only were there weakening theological disputes which robbed them of both relevance and attractiveness, but small congregations had become increasingly

---

164. Samuel Johnson, *A Dictionary of the English Language* (London, 1755), s.v. "Enthusiasm," cited in Haykin, *One Heart and One Soul*, 29.

165. See Haykin, *One Heart and One Soul*, 30.

166. See Haykin, *One Heart and One Soul*, 30–32.

167. See Haykin, *One Heart and One Soul*, 26–33.

168. Noll, *Rise of Evangelicalism*, 161.

inward-looking and defensive."[169] This decline concerned those on both sides of the Calvinist camp. For example, Briggs cites John Gill, whose life and ministry coincided with the days of declension, as speaking "of both a lack of zeal and a widespread diffusion of error, together, with rare exception, of an absence of able young leaders to take the place of older men."[170] And Morden cites Gill's slightly younger contemporary and an evangelical Calvinist, Benjamin Wallin, as mentioning in 1746 "the universal complaints of the decay of practical and vital godliness" as well as observing in 1752 the "melancholy day" and "present declensions" among Baptists.[171] Finally, Naylor recounts that in general the "Particular Baptists maintained a stubbornly negative attitude towards the Evangelical Awakening; in addition to their views about the Church of England, they would not digest the Arminianism of the Wesleys."[172] But this was not the only story to be told of the Particular Baptists during the eighteenth century.

Even while the pastors and theologians most identified with the religious declension of the movement seemed to be leading the denomination away from the Evangelical Calvinism of its forbears,[173] there were other groups of Particular Baptists who maintained an evangelical Calvinistic theology. It must not be forgotten that earlier Calvinistic Preachers such as Keach, who died in 1704, "believed in what is called the 'free offer of the gospel': that preachers had a biblical warrant freely to offer salvation to all and to urge unbelievers to come to Christ, pointing out their responsibility to repent of their sins and believe on Christ."[174] That was not High or Hyper-Calvinism! Some pastors and their congregations over the next decades followed Keach in his evangelical ways. Other men who also eventually became Particular Baptist pastors, such as John Fawcett and Abraham Booth, were converted through the preaching of Whitefield or others involved with the Evangelical Revival, and thus expressed a moderate or evangelical Calvinism.[175] And then consideration must be given to

169. Briggs, "Changing Pattern of Baptist Life," 6.

170. Briggs, "Changing Pattern of Baptist Life," 6.

171. Bemjamin Wallin, *The Christian Life, In Divers of its Branches, Described and Recommended*, vol. 2 (London: Aaron Ward, 1746), ix, and *Exhortations, Relating to Prayer and the Lord's Supper* (London, 1752), 8, 10, cited in Morden, "Andrew Fuller and *The Gospel Worthy of All Acceptation*," 132.

172. Naylor, *Picking up a Pin for the Lord*, 66.

173. Cramp, *Baptist History*, 499. See also Oliver, "John Gill," 160–64.

174. Walker, "Benjamin Keach," 36–37.

175. See Haykin, *One Heart and One Soul*, 40–41; and Roberts, *Continuity and Change*, 100–101. For more on Whitefield and Baptists see Whitley, "Influence of Whitefield on Baptists," 30–36.

the strand of Calvinistic Baptist witness associated with the Western Association and its training institution, Bristol Baptist College. Going against common opinion that hyper-Calvinism, accompanied by its deteriorating effects, was the rule for the eighteenth-century Particular Baptist denomination, Roger Hayden has argued,

> From the very beginning Particular Baptists had been evangelical in their Calvinism. In the seventeenth century this was true of all Particular Baptists who shared the *1644 Confession of Faith* and sought to promulgate it in various parts of the country. At the end of the century this Evangelical Calvinism still gripped the minds and hearts of many Particular Baptists in the Western Association, based upon Bristol; and under the leadership of Bernard Foskett in the next century Evangelical Calvinism was vigorously continued by those who came into contact with him and the students he trained at the Bristol Academy.[176]

Hayden further argues that "West Country Baptist ministers like Andrew Gifford (1700–1784), John Ash, John (1674–1757) and Benjamin Beddome, Benjamin Francis, the younger Robert Hall (1764–1831), John Sutcliff (1752–1814), Joshua Thomas (1719–1797), and John Rippon are far more representative of Particular Baptists in this period than the London Johns, Brine, Skepp and Gill."[177] Ken Manley also cites Hayden's demonstration that part of the successful influence of Bristol and the college was their consistent maintenance of the *Second London Confession* within a vigorous association life.[178] Philip Roberts further maintains that only one third of the Calvinistic Baptist churches in London, usually seen as the bastion of High Calvinism, "in the period 1727–1760 may have ever become consistently high Calvinist."[179] "But," says Manley, "after all this necessary balance has been drawn . . . the common witness was undoubtedly that by about 1760 Particular Baptists in London and many regions, for whatever reason (and Gill's theology is most commonly cited), evidenced little spiritual vigour."[180] Reflecting on their relationship to the Evangelical Revival as the final decades of the century dawned, Haykin adds, "When George Whitefield died

---

176. Hayden, *Continuity and Change*, xi.

177. Hayden, *Continuity and Change*, xii. See also Roberts, *Continuity and Change*, 127–28.

178. Manley, *Redeeming Love Proclaim*, 2.

179. Roberts, *Continuity and Change*, 42.

180. Manley, *Redeeming Love Proclaim*, 2.

at Newburyport, Massachusetts, in 1770, the Calvinistic Baptists were still largely dormant and unaffected by the revival."[181]

Revival, however, was coming to the Particular Baptist movement and the days of declension began to draw to a close. Describing the slow growth among the Baptists during the period of the Evangelical Revival, Noll surmises that it was not until 1770 that the Particular Baptists began to respond to the evangelical appeal.[182] Among the various means to and manifestations of revival among the Particular Baptists that revealed the reversal of their decline were the preaching and publishing of gospel-focused sermons; the influence of the Bristol Baptist Academy's graduates; a renewed association life; the theological influence of Jonathan Edwards (1703–1758) regarding the importance of intentional corporate prayer, revival, and the free offer of the gospel; a new vision of foreign missions; and the vigorous corporate praise assisted by the distribution of hymn-books.[183] Some illustrations of these phenomena are important in setting the stage for a consideration of Anne Steele's hymns as they appeared in Rippon's *Selection of Hymns*.

Biblical and evangelistic preaching set the stage for a revival among the Particular Baptists. Two sermons deserve special comment. First, Abraham Booth's *Reign of Grace* was first published in 1768. This exposition of his newly discovered evangelical Calvinism resulted in his call the next year to the Prescott Street Church in London where he engaged in a fruitful pastorate of more than thirty years. Booth's influence from his London pulpit included his defense of the church against Antinomianism and Socinianism, his sermons preached against the slave trade, and his support of the Particular Baptist Missionary society, something his fellow London Baptists were slower to support. His controversies with Andrew Fuller over the warrant of faith and the nature of the atonement, notwithstanding, of Booth it has been said, "Humble and unassuming [the 'venerable Mr. Booth'] stood firmly for the Calvinistic theology which the Particular Baptists had inherited from their Puritan forbears."[184]

---

181. Haykin, *One Heart and One Soul*, 33.

182. Noll, *Rise of Evangelicalism*, 164. In his analysis, however, Noll neglects to account for the influence of the Western Association and Bristol Academy in Particular Baptist life.

183. For an analysis of the Baptist revival from the standpoint of eschatological, sociological, and institutional factors, see Ward, "Baptists and the Transformation of the Church," 167–84. For a theological analysis with application for the present, see Champion, "Evangelical Calvinism," 196–208.

184. Oliver, "Abraham Booth," 53. See also Oliver, "Abraham Booth," 31–53; and Briggs, "Changing Pattern of Baptist Life," 7, 13. Regarding the differences of opinion between Booth and Fuller, Oliver says, "The controversy was somewhat confused and it did not emerge as an open debate between Booth and Fuller." Oliver, "Abraham Booth," 48.

Second, Robert Hall Sr.'s *Help to Zion's Travellers*, was preached in 1779 and published in 1781.[185] So influential did this become that, according to Joseph Ivimey, the Baptist historian of the next century, Hall's delivery of the sermon "was . . . the commencement of a new era in the history of our denomination."[186] The work covered such doctrines as the deity of Christ, the nature of God's love, election, atonement, and experiential matters while also vindicating the doctrines of the gospel against Antinomians, Arminians, Socinians, and Sabellians.[187] Ivimey declared its greatest impact was that "the principles of the admirable little work were those of modern Calvinism in opposition to the system of high or hyper-calvinism, which had so generally prevailed in our churches, chiefly in consequence of the preaching and writings of Messrs. Brine and Gill."[188] William Carey (1761–1834), who often walked from Olney to Arnsby to hear Hall preach, described his first encounter with the book: "I do not remember ever to have read any book with such raptures."[189] Briggs notes the genius of such sermons, "The preaching of eighteenth-century evangelical dissent majored on well thought-out argument. . . . At its best the Baptist pulpit was both rational and evangelical, able to relate to the changing cultural context whilst demonstrating that the exploration of revelation required hard intellectual analysis."[190] Such hard work contributed to the renewal of the denomination.

The early vision for what eventually became the Bristol Baptist Academy came from the deed of a gift Edward Terrill signed in favor of the Broadmead church in Bristol to be used after his death "for the support of a minister at Broadmead who was skilled in the Biblical languages and whose task would be to prepare young men for ministry among Baptist churches."[191] While it took a number of years for this to come to fruition, the academy did begin to take shape during the pastorate of Bernard Foskett (1685–1758). After the Western Association re-formed in 1734 under Foskett's leadership the academy trained more than seventy students from both England and Wales over the next twenty-five years.[192] Foskett was succeeded by Hugh Evans (1713–1781) in 1758 who, in turn, "was joined by his son Caleb at the Broadmead

---

185. Hall's work was recently reprinted. See Hall, *Help to Zion's Travellers*.

186. Ivimey, *History of the English Baptists*, 4:41.

187. Haykin, "Robert Hall, Sr.," 206; and Ivimey, *History of the English Baptists*, 4:41.

188. Ivimey, *History of the English Baptists*, 4:41.

189. Brown, *English Baptists of the Eighteenth Century*, 116, in Haykin, "Robert Hall, Sr.," 207.

190. Briggs, "Changing Pattern of Baptist Life," 13.

191. Hayden, *Continuity and Change*, 21. See also Clements, "Significance of 1679," 2–6.

192. See Hayden, *Continuity and Change*, 21–36.

Church and the Baptist Academy in 1759."[193] Hugh Evans's prayers, preaching, teaching, and personal interest in each student, not to mention his moderate Calvinism, influenced scores of Bristol students.[194] Finally, with both the forming of the Bristol Education Society[195] as a fundraising wing of the institution and a restructuring of the Academy in 1770, the "adequate" education of its earliest years was succeeded by an intellectually stimulating curriculum informed by a "vigorous gospel vision" through which "the head and the heart" would be trained together for pastoral ministry and missions.[196] John Ash's 1778 sermon for the Bristol Education Society displays such a vision. Ash concluded his sermon,

> If we have not our commission and our qualification from Christ, and if he be not with us in the discharge of our ministry, alas! our learning, our labour, our preaching is in vain. But enlivened by his grace, qualified by his Spirit, directed by his providence and blessed with his presence, wherever we go, wherever we are stationed . . . we shall be glorious in the eyes of the Lord and our God shall be our strength.[197]

The Bristol Academy, which was secured doctrinally to the *Second London Confession*, became a conduit for a Calvinism that was joined with the spirit of the Evangelical Revival. Hayden notes that by the 1750s the influence of the revival was evident through both the writings of the New England divine Jonathan Edwards and "also by the presence of those who had experienced it for themselves."[198] As these men took pastorates from which they would shepherd God's people and disseminate a biblical and evangelical Calvinism, fruitful ministry followed. Roberts describes Bristol's impact in London, "In the course of the period 1760–1820 several Bristol Academy graduates [including John Rippon at Carter Lane in 1772] filled London Calvinistic pulpits and represented perhaps the most vibrant force for change on behalf of evangelical Calvinism and the new evangelicalism."[199] Raymond Brown singles out several students who studied at Bristol, but labored outside the larger cities:

193. Wellum, "Caleb Evans," 216.

194. Manley, "Making of an Evangelical Baptist Leader," 262, 267.

195. See Moon, "Caleb Evans, Founder of the Bristol Education Society," 175–90.

196. Wellum, "Caleb Evans," 216, 218.

197. John Ash, *The Perfecting of the Saints for the work of the Ministry* (Bristol, 1778), 7, cited in Hayden, *Continuity and Change*, 134.

198. Hayden, *Continuity and Change*, 101.

199. Roberts, *Continuity and Change*, 128.

> Many of . . . [the] Bristol students brought an outstanding
> contribution to the life of the churches in the second half of
> the eighteenth century. Men like John Ash (1724–79) of Per-
> shore, Benjamin Beddome (1717–95) of Burton-on-the-Water
> and Benjamin Francis of Horsley were content to serve their
> respective churches for between forty and fifty years, pouring
> their entire working ministry into the pastoral care of rural
> congregations, faithful biblical preaching, the development of
> association life, the establishment of new causes and, in each
> case, the composition or publication of hymns. Their devo-
> tional hymnology, passion for associating, and evangelistic ini-
> tiatives helped divert many churches from high Calvinism and
> introduced them to these influences which were powerfully at
> work in the Evangelical Revival.[200]

The evangelical Calvinistic legacy of the Bristol Academy thus bore fruit and
helped the larger denomination experience revival. Briggs also explicitly
connects the revival and association life thus, "As the revival renewed Baptist life and spawned more adventurous mission so the need for churches to
co-operate with one another was underlined, and so the idea of association
was revived."[201] And the associations further encouraged renewal through
the relationships developed between the ministers in the associations. It
was during the 1776 meeting of the Northampton Association, for example,
that Sutcliff and Fuller first met and discovered that they were kindred spir-
its.[202] As an illustration of the spiritual vitality fostered by the associations
consider this excerpt from the circular letter of 1778 for the Western Association written by Benjamin Francis. It offers instruction for the Christian
regarding assurance and faith:

> Place then your entire confidence in Christ for the whole of sal-
> vation: Let the declarations and promises of the gospel be your
> only warrant for believing in him: and consider your purest
> principles, happiest frames, and holiest duties, not as the foun-
> dation, but the superstructure of faith: Let not your sweetest
> experiences, which are at best but shallow cisterns, but Christ

200. Raymond Brown, *The English Baptists of the Eighteenth Century* (London: The
Baptist Historical Society, 1986), 94, cited in Haykin, "Benjamin Francis," 19.

201. Briggs, "Changing Pattern of Baptist Life," 11. Particular Baptist pastors would
also develop relationships and correspond with other evangelicals outside their own denomination. For example, fifty-eight letters of heartfelt correspondence between John
Newton and John Ryland Jr. written between 1774 and 1803 are housed at the Bristol
Baptist College. See Champion, "Letters of John Ryland to John Newton," 157–63.

202. Haykin, "John Sutcliff," 25.

> alone be the source of your comfort, and constantly live upon
> that inexhaustible fountain.[203]

The circular letters of the associations provide a rich resource for getting a sense of the robust Christian piety of many Particular Baptist pastors and congregations.

Haykin suggests that in Jonathan Edwards, a number of like-minded and considerably influential Baptists found their "theological mentor."[204] For example, Hayden finds in Sutcliff, who received his training for ministry at Bristol Academy and was introduced to Edwards's writings by his tutor Caleb Evans, a connecting point between Bristol and the missionary spirit that eventually emerged in the Northampton Association.[205] Haykin describes the influence of Edwards on the leading Baptists at the end of the eighteenth century: "More than any other eighteenth century author, Edwards showed Sutcliff, and fellow Baptists like Fawcett, Evans, and Fuller, how to combine a commitment to Calvinistic theology with a passion for revival, fervent evangelism and experimental religion."[206] Watts states it forcefully, "The most decisive Evangelical influence on the Particular Baptists was that of Jonathan Edwards."[207] And commenting on the larger theological community of which the Baptists were a part, Bebbington says, "There can be no doubt that Edwards was the chief architect of the theological structures erected by Evangelicals in the Reformed tradition."[208]

At least three areas of Edwards's influence on the Particular Baptists must be considered. He gave the Particular Baptists a vision for corporate prayer, a biblical and experiential lens through which to view the Evangelical Revival, and he offered them a biblical and theological rationale for the free offer of the gospel to the general public. In 1784, Sutcliff read Edwards' treatise, *An Humble Attempt to Promote Explicit Agreement and Visible Union of God's People in Extraordinary Prayer, For the Revival of Religion and the Advancements of Christ's Kingdom on Earth* (1748).[209] So struck was he by Edwards's call for fervent prayer that God would "pour out his Spirit, revive his work, and advance his spiritual kingdom in the world,"[210] that

---

203. Benjamin Francis, *Circular Letter of the Western Association* (1778), 3, cited in Haykin, "Benjamin Francis," 26–27.

204. Haykin, *One Heart and One Soul*, 13.

205. Hayden, *Continuity and Change*, xii–xiii and 198–99.

206. Haykin, "John Sutcliff," 24–25.

207. Watts, *Dissenters*, 456.

208. Bebbington, *Evangelicalism in Modern Britain*, 65.

209. Haykin, "John Sutcliff," 27–28.

210. *An Humble Attempt to Promote Explicit Agreement and Visible Union of God's*

later in the year Sutcliff suggested what has become known as the Prayer Call of 1784.[211] Writing a preface to a reprint of Edwards's treatise five years later, Sutcliff describes the genesis of this call to prayer:

> At an association of the ministers and messengers of the Baptist Churches in the counties of Northampton, Leicester, &c. held at Nottingham, in the year 1784, a resolution was formed to establish through the association, *a meeting of prayer for the general revival and spread of religion.* This was to be observed the first Monday evening in every calendar month, by all the churches. It still continues. . . . Many other churches . . . have adopted, and now follow, the above practice. We have the pleasure also to find, that several *Paedobaptist* churches statedly meet on those evenings for the same purpose.[212]

This renewed spirituality through the discipline of prayer included both a vision of winning the world for Christ and doing so through a cooperative effort that crossed denominational boundaries.

Through such works as *A Faithful Narrative of the Surprising Work of God in the Conversion of Many Hundred Souls in Northampton and the Neighbouring Towns and Villages* (1736), *The Distinguishing Marks of a Work of the Spirit of God* (1741), and *A Treatise Concerning Religious Affections* (1746), Edwards also offered "a marvelous foundation for thinking about and labouring for revival."[213] Beddome, for example, seems to have read, or at least purchased, the first two of these books by April 1742.[214] Edwards's reflections helped Beddome respond to the revival in Bourton-on-the-Water that had occurred under his ministry during the early months of 1741.[215] Bebbington says, "Edwards created an Evangelical framework for interpreting Christian experience."[216] Hayden suggests that it was their interest in Jonathan Edwards's account of the revival in New England as well as their commitment to

---

People in Extraordinary Prayer, For the Revival of Religion and the Advancements of Christ's Kingdom on Earth, in Edwards, *Works* 2:281.

211. See Briggs, "Changing Pattern of Baptist Life," 7.

212. Sutcliff, *An Humble Attempt*, Preface, in Edwards, *Works*, 2:278.

213. Haykin, "Benjamin Beddome," 99–100.

214. Hayden, *Continuity and Change*, 196L and Haykin, "Benjamin Beddome," 99–100. Haykin notes: "Beddome's own copy of [*The Distinguishing Marks of a Work of the Spirit of God* (1741)] may be seen in the Angus Library, Regent's Park College, University of Oxford. On the title page Beddome has written the date 'Apr. 1742,' which would indicate either the date that he purchased the book or the date by which he had read it." Haykin, "Benjamin Beddome," 100n28.

215. Haykin, "Benjamin Beddome," 99.

216. Bebbington, *Evangelicalism in Modern Britain*, 47.

monthly prayer for the revival of religion that "was the Baptists' affirmation of the necessity for the Holy Spirit to blow over the walled garden of their Calvinistic faith so that evangelical activity might follow."[217]

Edwards also provided them with a biblical and theological rationale for the free offer of the gospel to the unconverted. In his book, *The Freedom of the Will* (1754), Edwards distinguishes between humankind's "moral ability" (the desire to turn to God) and "natural ability" (the capacity to turn to God). Noll suggests that through this book, "with Edwards, Fuller came to embrace the conviction that all people should and could turn to God if they would do so—thus justifying free and full gospel preaching."[218] So the turning of the tide in terms of the spiritual vitality of the Particular Baptists came with the publication in 1785 of Andrew Fuller's *The Gospel of Christ Worthy of All Acceptation*, a book Bebbington describes as "the classic statement of eighteenth-century Evangelical Calvinism."[219] Hayden notes that it was through Fuller's forty-year friendship with Sutcliff that Edwards became "Fuller's powerful instructor . . . [and] presented to Fuller the possibility of an Evangelical Calvinism which provided him an appropriate philosophical basis in Baptist life for the doctrines of justification by faith, the atoning death of Christ, and an eschatology which could be preached with proper evangelical concern to all who would hear it."[220] Fuller expressed his new understanding in his incredibly influential book. Tom Nettles notes that with this book Fuller "fired the shot that provoked the army onto the field of battle" for a revolution that "opened a door for Baptists and others onto the vast world of gospel-preaching to the nations."[221] Noll echoes Nettles's sentiments. In a listing of key dates charting the expansion of evangelicalism, he suggests that the 1785 publication of Fuller's book marked "the triumph of evangelicalism among England's Particular Baptists."[222] Naylor, in fact, describes Fuller as the "man who perhaps more than anyone else led the Particular Baptist reaction against High Calvinism."[223]

In 1792, William Carey, having been influenced by Sutcliff, Hall, and Fuller, preached a moving sermon to the Northampton Baptist Association and also published a tract which he titled, *An Enquiry Into the Obligations*

217. Hayden, *Continuity and Change*, 178.

218. Noll, *Rise of Evangelicalism*, 208.

219. Bebbington, *Evangelicalism in Modern Britain*, 64–65.

220. Hayden, *Continuity and Change*, xiii.

221. Nettles, "Andrew Fuller," 97. See also Morden, "Andrew Fuller and *The Gospel Worthy of All Acceptation*."

222. Noll, *Rise of Evangelicalism*, 193.

223. Naylor, *Picking up a Pin for the Lord*, 193.

of Christians, to Use Means for the Conversion of the Heathens. In Which the Religious State of the Different Nations of the World, the Success of Former Undertakings, and the Practicability of Further Undertakings are Considered. Timothy George calls Carey's tract, his "masterpiece, the manifesto of the modern missionary movement."[224] Carey's vision, along with Edwards's *An Humble Attempt*, and Fuller's book served to give a "stimulus towards a growing missionary endeavor in the Northamptonshire Baptist Association and the formation of the Baptist Missionary Society in 1792."[225] This same society, with friends Fuller, Sutcliff, and the younger Ryland staying home to "hold the ropes" sent Carey down into the "gold-mine in India" in 1793 to share the gospel.[226]

Without exaggeration, Watts can conclude, "Thus did the writings of the Congregational pastor of Northampton, Massachusetts, lead to religious revival among the Particular Baptists of Northamptonshire, England, and set in train the dispersion of the principles of English Dissent to the four corners of the world."[227] Bernard Manning describes it this way, "The confluence of Calvinism and the evangelical revival produced at the end of the century the modern missionary enthusiasm of our churches."[228] Considering things at home Haykin declares, "During the final three decades of the century the Baptists became a dynamic force in England and Wales, outward-looking and seeking to recruit new members for their congregations."[229] And so with the influence of such visionary pastors as Fuller and Rippon, and the writings of Edwards, it can be said that "as the eighteenth century drew to its close many among the English Particular Baptists reverted gradually to the original Calvinism of their seventeenth-century forefathers."[230]

---

224. George, "William Carey," 153.

225. Hayden, *Continuity and Change*, 197.

226. Morris, *Memoirs of the Life and Death of the Rev. Andrew Fuller*, 101, cited in Haykin, *One Heart and One Soul*, 12. William H. Brackney argues that the Baptist Missionary Society, its founders, and William Carey had patterns to draw upon and a century and a half of experience in other English Christian traditions of voluntary association as they began their venture. He also notes that Carey, a keen student of organizational strategies, studied mission from the time of the apostle Paul up to John Wesley. See Brackney, "Baptist Missionary Society in Proper Context," 364–77.

227. Watts, *Dissenters*, 461.

228. Manning, "Congregationalism in the Eighteenth Century," 194.

229. Haykin, *One Heart and One Soul*, 33.

230. Naylor, *Picking up a Pin for the Lord*, 215.

Anne Steele, John Rippon, Hymns, and Hymn-books

One can argue, however, that currents of evangelical revival were already emerging among Particular Baptist hymn-writers more than thirty years before Fuller's book. The English Particular Baptists were some of the early pioneers of the English hymn, with Anne Steele leading the way.[231] This current was eventually channeled into the warp and woof of Baptist spiritual life through the dissemination of the best of these hymns in Rippon's *Selection of Hymns*, first published in 1787.[232] Manley observes, "English Nonconformity underwent a radical transformation during the long life of John Rippon (1751–1836)."[233] Besides the evangelical Calvinistic preaching he offered from his London pulpit—which had been that of John Gill no less!—Rippon contributed to the Baptist cause in other ways as well. Manley explains, "Rippon's influence on the thought and denominational patterns of the Baptists was unique."[234] Leading a notable London congregation in the midst of the spiritual renewal of his denomination, Rippon offered two novel contributions to the reviving of the Particular Baptist community: a denominational hymn-book that supplemented Watts to "provide a comprehensive resource for the homiletical bias of Baptist worship" and the publication of his *Baptist Annual Register* (1790–1802), which "not only provided a unique expression of the denomination's new maturity and confidence but also promoted a deeper mutual awareness among Baptists."[235] During the five decades following these two ventures by Rippon, the Particular Baptist denomination grew from about 17,000 members in 1790 to 86,000 by 1838, an increase exceeding population growth.[236] Rippon's positive and innovative involvement in Baptist renewal cannot be denied.

As a major Baptist contributor to the *Selection of Hymns* and the revival to which it contributed and illustrated, perhaps the most notable Baptist hymn-writer of the period, and the only woman of her generation to achieve

231. See Stevenson, "Baptist Hymnody, English," 110–12. Discussing hymn-singing in the seventeenth century, Stevenson lists John Bunyan and Benjamin Keach as Particular Baptist advocates for congregational hymn-singing and notes that Baptist pastor Hercules Collins asserted "that singing was a public duty," 110–11. Stevenson also notes that "during the first half of the 18th century the *General Baptists* for the most part retained their prejudices against congregational singing," 111.

232. For a discussion of Rippon's selection criteria for his hymnal see 9–13 above.

233. Manley, "Making of an Evangelical Baptist Leader," 254.

234. Manley, '*Redeeming Love Proclaim*', 7.

235. Manley, '*Redeeming Love Proclaim*', 7.

236. Manley, '*Redeeming Love Proclaim*', 7.

such success, Anne Steele's hymns prove to be a valuable illustration of the fact that hymns are related to both "the head and the heart" of Christianity. In other words, hymns reveal and relate Christian experience and doctrine, or said another way, spirituality and theology. So hymns can both illustrate and encourage revival, spiritual renewal, and evangelical theology and experience. Writing self-consciously as a Particular Baptist, Steele's hymns also preserved the orthodoxy of another theologically unifying force in Particular Baptist life during the period, the *Second London Confession* of 1688/89. Michael Haykin explains the importance of these characteristics and the *Second London Confession*: "Like the Puritan movement out of which they emerged, the Calvinistic Baptists . . . were aware of the fact that the coals of orthodoxy are ever necessary for the fire of spirituality. Where orthodox doctrine is regarded as unimportant, the fire of Christian piety will inevitably be quenched."[237] This strong doctrinal foundation served both to solidify and expand the influence of the *Selection of Hymns*. Steele's hymns offer expressions of this theology in many ways.

Rippon knew the power of hymns to inculcate the faith through poetry. In noting how "[D. H.] Lawrence's art seems at times to carry a message with a preacher's anxiety," William York Tindall observed, "In spite of the recent prejudice against the didactic, however, history proves that a work may teach while pleasing. A persuasive element may get along comfortably with the contemplative and visionary. It may even serve to intensify them."[238] Cynthia Aalders suggests the usefulness of examining hymns in cultural context: "Eighteenth-century hymns reveal something of the religious climate of their time, elucidating the theology and spirituality of their writers and singers."[239] Madeleine Marshall and Janet Todd elaborate on this theme:

> The convictions found in the hymns of the past thus provide an index to the acceptable, approved, and recommended doctrine and spiritual response at a particular time within a given Protestant tradition, yielding a great quantity of information about popular religious feeling that is inaccessible elsewhere.[240]

Watson relates this fact to the culture at large, noting that hymns "are a part of popular culture, and yet also part of a religious and literary culture."[241] Rippon's *Selection of Hymns* illustrates all of these phenomena.

---

237. Haykin, *Kiffin, Knollys and Keach*, 100.
238. Tindall, "Introduction," vi.
239. Aalders, *To Express the Ineffable*, 33.
240. Marshall and Todd, *English Congregational Hymns in the Eighteenth Century*, 2.
241. Watson, *English Hymn*, 5.

4

Anne Steele as a Hymn-writer

ANNE STEELE CAME OF age within a family filled with creative people. Each member of her immediate family appears to have been skilled in various aspects of literature, particularly poetry, and for edification and entertainment they shared their writings within the family circle many a night around a peat fire. The evidence shows that Steele both inherited her gift of poetry and cultivated it through constant interaction with those whom she loved. She was also involved in a literary circle with friends and family in which constant mutual sharpening of literary talents was the norm. Further, as a woman—the first notable female hymn-writer of the golden age of the English hymn—she brought to her compositions her own feminine sensibilities. But any discussion of Steele's approach to her craft and those influences upon her must begin with a discussion of the one about whom she said, "O could I write like Watts."[1] Isaac Watts's influence upon Steele is crucial to consider in any discussion of her growth and development as a hymn-writer.

In an "occasional poem" that Steele entitled "Christ the Christian's Life,"[2] she wrote of Watts,

> O for the animating fire
> That tun'd harmonious Watts's lyre
>   To sweet seraphic strains!
> Celestial fire, that bore his mind
> (Earth's vain amusements left behind)
>   To yonder blissful plains.

1. Steele, in Broome, *Bruised Reed*, 163.
2. Steele, *Works*, 1:314–15.

There Jesus lives, (transporting name!)
Jesus inspir'd the sacred flame,
   And gave devotion wings;
With heaven-attracted flight she soar'd,
The realms of happiness explor'd,
   And smil'd, and pitied kings.

Contemplating Watts's life, work, and death, Steele sees a divine inspiration, namely the person of Jesus, behind Watts's successful hymnody. She views Watts's happiness as that of one inspired by Jesus and with a gaze set toward heaven. With the third stanza—"Come, sacred flame, and warm my heart, / Thy animating power impart, / Sweet dawn of life divine!"—Steele pleads with the Lord to give her the same inspiration he gave to Watts. She then proceeds to write five and a half more stanzas that apply this divine inspiration to a well-lived Christian life of faith. Like Watts before her, and even in her tribute to him, Steele writes biblical and theological verse for the sake of very practical spiritual concerns.

Steele was one of several notable members of her generation who can be considered part of the "school of Watts." Born forty-three years before Steele, Watts had already written the eighteenth-century "hymns that we may regard as belonging to the continuous English tradition"[3] by the time "we first begin to hear about hymns being composed in the Steele family" in 1733.[4] Moreover, J. R. Broome notes that Steele grew up from childhood singing out of Watts's hymn-book in the Particular Baptist congregation at Broughton. He says, "It is clear that Watts's *Psalms and Hymns*, published in two parts, as *Hymns and Spiritual Songs* (1707) and as *Psalms of David* (1719) was the primary influence in her hymns and paraphrases of the Psalms."[5] J. R. Watson also declares Watts's influence upon Steele "considerable."[6]

Consider a few of the ways in which Watts's influence can be seen in the hymns of Steele. Steele followed Watts in using only a few standard meters in her hymns.[7] An examination of Steele's hymns reveals her regular use of Long, Common, and Short Meter.[8] Because Steele focused her writing within these three primary poetic meters of her day, it is worth briefly

3. Marshall and Todd, *English Congregational Hymns in the Eighteenth Century*, 2.

4. Broome, *Bruised Reed*, 86.

5. Broome, *Bruised Reed*, 153.

6. Watson, *English Hymn*, 191.

7. Watson notes that Watts, in deliberately keeping things simple, used only four meters. Watson, *English Hymn*, 148.

8. Aalders notes, "Of the 105 hymns in *Poems on Subjects Chiefly Devotional*, Steele used Common Meter 51 times, Long Meter 48 times, and Short Meter 5 times." Aalders, *To Express the Ineffable*, 91.

explaining these. Watson deftly discusses the subject: Short Meter (S.M.), or 66.86, "specializes in the sharp, neat, well-focused use of biblical texts." Common Meter (C.M.), or 86.86, "allows a much more flexible and expansive pattern" than Short Meter. Long Meter (L.M.), or 88.88, with its longer lines "changes the whole range of possibilities. . . . The chief glory of L.M. is its ability to carry sustained units of speech, so that the verses can develop and amplify ideas."[9] Steele emulated Watt's skilled use of these basic meters: Short, Common, and Long.

Watson makes the point that the "careful observation of the ways in which words behave was the foundation of Watts's skill as a hymn-writer."[10] Watts sought clarity, order, and simplicity in his methodical use of language.[11] He used repetition in pairing lines as well as within lines and he used basic metaphors to illuminate his theological concerns. Watts can also be considered adventurous in his choice of words. Steele sought to use words along the same lines. For example, Watson cites Steele's hymn "On a Stormy Night" to illustrate her skillful use of words. Through its six stanzas this hymn takes the singer from "At thy command the tempests rise," to "With terror would o'erwhelm our souls;" to "Then safe beneath thy guardian care, . . . In thee, my God, my refuge, blest."[12] As Watson observes, "The skillful articulation of ideas in this hymn, its progression from storm to calm, from spectacular oxymoron to the expected 'blest', is characteristic of Anne Steele's excellent craft, which is extraordinarily good at finding the correct word or phrase for what she wants to say, and contrasting one element of the hymn with another."[13]

An example of each of their uses of repetition illustrates their similar use of words. In "When I survey the wondrous cross," Watts wrote, "Sorrow and love flow mingled down; / Did e're such love and sorrow meet."[14] Steele likewise used repetition: "Here may the wretched sons of want / exhaustless riches find: / Riches, above what earth can grant, / And lasting as the mind."[15] Steele consistently used rhyme in her hymns, typically rhyming lines one and three and lines two and four, but like Watts she allowed the

---

9. Watson, *English Hymn*, 32–33. See also Aalders, *To Express the Ineffable*, 31n5. For a comprehensive examination and explanation of meter, see Lovelace, *Anatomy of Hymnody*.

10. Watson, *English Hymn*, 139.

11. Watson, *English Hymn*, 143.

12. Steele, *Works*, 1:44–45.

13. Watson, *English Hymn*, 196.

14. Watts, in Broome, *Bruised Reed*, 162.

15. Steele, "The Excellency and Sufficiency of the Holy Scriptures," in Rippon, *Selection of Hymns*, 48–49.

rhyme to assist in the expression of the thought. They both usually succeeded in their use of rhyme according to the standard of composer Austin Lovelace: "The good hymn writer succeeds in making the rhymes sound and feel natural, not forced and obvious."[16] Though certainly much less educated than Dr. Watts, Steele nevertheless "clearly spent time on writing drafts and improving her verse, sending copies for comment to such people as James Fanch the classical scholar, Baptist minister and poet."[17] Karen E. Smith notes in her essay on James Fanch,

> Writing to his brother-in-law, Daniel Turner, several years before her poems were published, Fanch claimed of Anne Steele: "Her poetical compositions, both of the serious and amusing kind are almost inimitable, much beyond anything I have yet seen since those of Dr. Watts. She aims not at the sublime or any high flights of imagination but her productions are admirably correct and delicate. I have several of them in my hands which she desired me to review, all of which are truly delightful."[18]

And so like the master, one could describe the writing of Steele "as polished and carefully worked out."[19]

But Steele also followed Watts in the interplay of observation and internal conviction, of theology and experience, of orthodoxy and practice in her hymns. For example, both hymn-writers saw the handiwork of a Creator in the natural order. But these observations of general revelation led them each to consider their own and humankind's standing before God as found in the special revelation of Holy Scripture. Watson says of Watts, "His joy in the created world, which is found so impressively in his hymns, . . . becomes an important part of his theology."[20] Joy in the created world could also give way to a sense of the awe and power of the creator of such a world. In this vein, Broome finds that Watts "reaches great heights of grandeur, such as 'God of the seas! Thy thundering voice / Makes all the roaring waves rejoice, / And one soft word of thy command, / Can sink them silent in the sand.'"[21] Steele, likewise, seeks to ascend such heights as in "Praise for National Peace,

16. Lovelace, *Anatomy of Hymnody*, 16.

17. Broome, *Bruised Reed*, 164–65.

18. Smith, "James Fanch" 58–59n3, quoted from Daniel Turner, *A Brief and Faithful Narrative of the Extraordinary Rise and Present State of a Protestant Dissenting Congregation; at Lockerley, a small village near Romsey in Hampshire* (London, 1758), 29–30.

19. Broome, *Bruised Reed*, 165.

20. Watson, *English Hymn*, 134.

21. Broome, *Bruised Reed*, 162.

Psalm xlvi:9,"[22] which appeared in Rippon's hymnal: "Great Ruler of the earth and skies, / A word of thy Almighty breath / Can sink the world, or bid it rise; / Thy smile is life, thy frown is death." But while Broome still finds in Watts a "greater realization of the majesty and glory of God" than in Steele, he does propose that "when however it came to matters of the soul, then Anne equaled him."[23] And Broome, echoing Watson, suggests that "her best hymns . . . are those which testify of her love for Christ."[24] And of course, that is exactly what Steele saw in Watts's compositions.

It was both a profound sense of awe with regard to Christ's person and work and a sincere desire to be with him, two somewhat inseparable themes, that contributed to Watts's desire to paraphrase the psalms from the vantage point of their fulfillment in Christ and also formed the theological and experiential foundation of the hymns of his follower, Steele. A consideration of each poet's reflection on Christ's role as Redeemer, set against the backdrop of a desire to be with him in heaven, will illustrate. In a piece of prose, as he dreams of Christ's return, Watts offers a glimpse into the inspiration behind his Christ-focused hymns: "O happy day and happy hour indeed, that shall finish the long absence of my beloved, and place me within sight of my adored Jesus! When shall I see that lovely, that illustrious Friend, who laid down his own life to rescue mine, his own valuable life to rescue a worm, a rebel that deserved to die?"[25] Watson says of him in this regard, "There is only one thing which Watts insists upon as greater [than the idea of God as Creator], and that is God as Redeemer."[26] Steele followed suit. She wrote of heaven, "Dear Saviour! let thy Spirit seal / Our int'rest in that blissful place; / Till death remove this mortal veil, / And we behold thy lovely face."[27] And in "The Wonders of Redemption," one of her many hymns detailing the work of Christ on behalf of sinners, Steele declared, "Yes! the Redeemer left his throne, / His radiant throne on high, / (Surprising mercy! love unknown) / To suffer, bleed, and die."[28] Like Watts before her, Steele constantly explored Christ's works accomplished in the place of and for his own sinful, but redeemed, people.

22. Steele, "Praise for National Peace, Psalm xlvi. 9," in Rippon, *Selection of Hymns*, 684, 686.

23. Broome, *Bruised Reed*, 165.

24. Broome, *Bruised Reed*, 169.

25. George Burder, ed., *The Works of the Reverend and Learned Isaac Watts, D.D.* (London, 1810), i. 394, cited in Watson, *English Hymn*, 136.

26. Watson, *English Hymn*, 146.

27. Steele, "The Worship of Heaven, John xvii. 24," in Rippon, *Selection of Hymns*, 762–63.

28. Steele, "The Wonders of Redemption," in Rippon, *Selection of Hymns*, 631–32.

Further brief consideration of "The Wonders of Redemption" will offer an opportunity to conclude the discussion of Watts's influence on Steele while also pointing forward to some of her own personal elements of the craft of hymn-writing. While this hymn will be examined more closely in the following chapter as one of Steele's hymns found in Rippon's hymnal, the first four stanzas are listed below for the purpose of the current discussion:

> And did the holy and the just,
>   The sovereign of the skies,
> Stoop down to wretchedness and dust,
>   That guilty worms might rise?
>
> Yes! the Redeemer left his throne,
>   His radiant throne on high,
> (Surprising mercy! love unknown)
>   To suffer, bleed, and die.
>
> He took the dying traitor's place,
>   And suffer'd in his stead;
> For man, (O miracle of grace!)
>   For man the Saviour bled!
>
> Dear Lord! what heav'nly wonders dwell
>   In thy atoning blood!
> By this are sinners snatch'd from hell,
>   And rebels brought to God.[29]

These lines reveal an intersection of the poet, the theologian, and the worshiper in the pew. Such a meeting within a hymn is one of the characteristics Steele found worth emulating in Watts. A few points of many that could be assessed need mentioning. First, Steele, like Watts, found at the center of her assurance and praise "the grace of God and the person of Christ, and his redemptive action."[30] They both shared an evangelical vision of sinners saved by grace through faith in Christ alone. This hymn is one of many of Steele's testimonies to such a vision.

Second, specific words that sometimes sound strange to modern ears were used by Steele, following Watts, to establish a proper theological understanding of man's fallen nature before God—"wretchedness," "guilty worms," "dying traitor," "sinners," and "rebels." Cynthia Aalders states rightly and matter-of-factly that these words are simply Steele's way of expressing

---

29. Steele, "The Wonders of Redemption," in Rippon, *Selection of Hymns*, 631–32.

30. Watson, *English Hymn*, 152.

that "as with other eighteenth-century Calvinistic Baptists, Steele had a large view of her own sinfulness."[31] Watts held the same view. These words are not meant to leave singers (and sinners) in the depths but to elicit joy at the consideration of such divine love as shown by the Redeemer. This aspect of the hymn further positions Steele in the line of the Augustan tradition of Watts with its clear expression of the truth it intends to convey while also offering a didactic purpose, in this case, teaching the doctrines of redemption and substitutionary atonement. Watson says that for Isaac Watts, "Hymns show the mind of a poet applied with skill and dedication to the expression of his belief."[32] Steele's hymns do this as well. As Aalders notes, "The ability to convey clear meaning is of especial importance to the hymn-writer, as congregations are meant to sing and understand what they are singing without the benefit of time to reflect at length on the hymn-writer's words."[33] Simplicity and clarity were marks of both Watts and Steele.

But this hymn also reflects some aspects of Steele's style that take her beyond Watts. For example, it illustrates her use of the question, the exclamation, and the parenthetical remark. These are each aspects of Steele's writing style, revealing something of her personality and her approach to God and the art of writing about him. Watson finds her to be at her best when not only making statements, but also asking questions and making exclamations: "She employs them to probe further than the statements themselves can do, because they gesture towards the unanswered, the mysterious, and the unknown."[34] The final two stanzas of the hymn allow for further reflection on this characteristic of Steele's writing:

> Jesus! My soul adoring bends
>   To love so full, so free;
> And may I hope *that* love extends
>   Its sacred power to me!

> What glad return can I impart
>   For favours so divine?
> O take my all—this worthless heart,
>   And make it only thine.[35]

In the first of these last two stanzas Steele uses two exclamations. The first contrasts her sturdy approach to her Savior, "Jesus!" with the second,

---

31. Aalders, *To Express the Ineffable*, 84.

32. Watson, *Annotated Anthology of Hymns*, 121.

33. Aalders, *To Express the Ineffable*, 90.

34. Watson, *English Hymn*, 198.

35. Steele, "The Wonders of Redemption," in Rippon, *Selection of Hymns*, 632.

which she uses to turn her slight doubt as to whether he will extend his love to her into confidence by placing an exclamation point where a question mark might have been expected. The question in the final stanza offers an application of her faith in response to the love of Jesus toward her. And as in the earlier verses, so it is in these final stanzas, the parenthetical remarks demonstrate the wonder and mystery of a holy God giving himself, in Christ, to sinners. So Steele uses grammar and punctuation to generate questions and exclamations for specific purposes, as "through them her hymnody celebrates not just the doctrine of grace, but the application of that grace to human experience." It is her ability to share her own experience with her readers and singers that is another exemplary characteristic of Steele as a hymn-writer. Sharing her experience of suffering, in particular, and the faith through which she faced it was a hallmark of Steele's hymns.

So, it can be said that writing her hymns self-consciously to express both theological truth and personal experience, Steele first sought to pattern her compositions after Isaac Watts, both valuing his example and longing to write like him.[36] However, if Watts's influence is of the first order of importance in an examination of Steele as a hymn-writer, then her experience of suffering comes next in order. In considering the lyrical content, the theology, and the experiential elements in Anne Steele's hymns, one must acknowledge that Steele's physical and emotional suffering was the crucible from within which she composed many of her hymns. While the popularizing of "hymn stories" over time has caused a sentimentalizing and inaccurate reporting of the range of Steele's sufferings,[37] there is no doubt that she lived through much physical and emotional pain in her life. From her childhood she endured high fever and fits caused by malaria (eventually leading to a nervous disorder) as well as severe toothaches, stomach problems and other bodily afflictions.[38] She wrote hymns from the experience of faith in God as it was tested through life's "dark providences." Broome posits, "Her ill-health over many years had been sanctified to her and out of it she had learnt that faith in the Son of God was the only source of help, happiness and hope."[39] Aalders finds in Steele's writings a "persisting sensitivity

---

36. Broome, *Bruised Reed*, 163.

37. For example, as noted in chapter 2 above, surviving letters regarding the story of the drowning incident of her fiancé before their wedding show this story to be of questionable veracity. In fact, not only did her potential suitor not drown the day of or before a scheduled wedding, it does not appear the couple was even engaged. See Watson and Cho, "Anne Steele's Drowned Fiancé," 117–21.

38. James, *In Trouble and in Joy*, 140.

39. Broome, *Bruised Reed*, 165.

to God's response to the suffering she witnessed and experienced in the world."[40] And Nancy Cho notes that Steele's step-mother, Anne Cator Steele, identified Steele's patient endurance of suffering as giving "her authority to speak of and for [Christ]."[41] Thus her experience of suffering allowed Steele's hymns to be suffused with a sense of the reality of life in a fallen world. This added credibility to her role as a hymn-writer.

Further, as it was for many in her day, "death was a very near threat which claimed [many of] those nearest and dearest" to Steele throughout her life.[42] She saw her mother die while giving birth followed quickly by the death of her infant brother. She experienced the deaths of aunts, uncles, and cousins during her youth. She lived through the deaths of her beloved uncle, father, and step-mother. And she observed the death of other infant relatives during her adult years.[43] Steele's response was to compose a number of hymns and poems discussing this theme, sometimes commemorating the death of a beloved family member or friend.[44] Aalders suggests that "the losses she endured surely would come to bear on her hymnody, even as they shaped her mind and spirit."[45] Rippon's hymnal included six of Steele's hymns concerning death, resurrection, and heaven. Additionally, Steele lived through decades of British involvement in war and its harsh conditions and grave realities within a family that sold timber to the Navy for the making of warships. Such "a lived experience" led to Steele writing about these historic events. Rippon included four such hymns in his hymnal.

Steele wrote theologically rich hymns from the vein of personal experience. And though she wrote of her experience of suffering, it was not the only subject that inspired her pen. Comparing and contrasting Steele to other immediate followers of Watts (both chronologically and through influence), Watson observes that while Philip Doddridge, like a preacher, "versifies a biblical text," "she more frequently begins with experience."[46] Since Steele gave each of her poems and hymns her own title, the experience about which she is writing can often be seen there. For example, Steele gave her compositions such titles as "Life a Journey," "The Comforts of Religion," "An Evening Walk," "The Sickly Mind," and "Rest and Comfort in Christ

---

40. Aalders, *To Express the Ineffable*, 112.

41. Anne Cator Steele, Diary, STE 2/1/3 in Cho, "Ministry of Song," 64.

42. Aalders, *To Express the Ineffable*, 111.

43. See Aalders, *To Express the Ineffable*, 13.

44. See Broome, *Bruised Reed*, 164–73.

45. Aalders, *To Express the Ineffable*, 112.

46. Watson, *English Hymn*, 195.

Alone."[47] And for one who suffered much physical pain, she has a number of hymns that express the experience of happiness.[48] Further, Steele had a particular affinity for the beauty of creation and the simple pleasures of the rural life. Her hymns often reflect such themes. Rippon included in his hymnal not only Steele's hymns that were more strictly about an aspect of theology or Christian experience, but also hymns about daily life and life in England at the time. But Steele shared of her experiences not simply for her own sake, but for the sake of sharing with others. The pseudonym she took upon publishing her works for the first time in 1760 was Theodosia, a feminine name that means "gift from God."[49] Cho suggests that "rather than highlighting her own literary talents or accomplishments, Steele is declaring that she is God's instrument through which his words flow."[50] A close reading of her hymns reveals such a tone, that of offering a contribution for the benefit of others who find themselves upon the same journey.

While Steele did contribute to the experiential nature of eighteenth-century hymnody, she wrote from the standpoint of theological convictions. Because the following chapter will cover the basic range of theological themes about which Steele wrote, here two other points will be considered about the doctrinal nature of her hymns. First, the Scriptures were the foundation from which Steele composed her hymns. Steele gave her hymns individual titles and often included a Scripture reference to go with it.[51] Commenting on the depth of this characteristic in Steele's hymnody, Aalders says, "This scriptural element becomes part of the formal nature of her hymnody, so that a great deal of her meaning is directed by her consistently biblical approach."[52] Bringing to mind Bebbington's work on Evangelicalism, Cho adds, "Steele's hymns are resolutely Evangelical: word-centred, crucicentric and encouraging a personal relationship with Christ."[53] This book will argue for the truth of the claims of both Aalders and Cho concerning the biblical content of Steele's hymns found in Rippon's hymnal.

Steele's hymns were not only biblical, however. There was also a confessional nature to them. Because the Particular Baptist community operated according to the congregational system of government, no individual

47. Steele, *Works*, 1:105, 238, and 256, 2:126 and 216.

48. For example, "Searching after Happiness," "True Happiness to Be Found only in God," and "Lasting Happiness," in Steele, *Works*, 1:45, 107, and 108.

49. Cho, "Ministry of Song," 53.

50. Cho, "Ministry of Song," 54.

51. Rippon includes Steele's biblical references, but sometimes modifies the titles of Steele's hymns in his hymnal.

52. Aalders, *To Express the Ineffable*, 92.

53. Cho, "Ministry of Song," 71.

congregation was obligated to abide by or align itself with the teaching of any specific confession of faith. But this did not stop them from supporting and teaching a confessional theology based on their theological beliefs. Concerning Steele's theological background, J. R. Broome says of her father, William, to whom Anne was very close all his life and under whose preaching she sat much of her life, that his preaching lined up doctrinally with the *Second London Confession*.[54] This document has been called "the classic expression of Calvinistic Baptist doctrine."[55] Interestingly, the framers of the *Second London Confession* made a subtle but significant change to the *Westminster Confession of Faith*. Regarding the religious worship of God, the *Second London Confession* adds that not only "Psalms," but also "Hymns and Spiritual Songs" are appropriate in the religious worship of God.[56] The composition of theologically robust and experientially rich hymns, endorsed by this reissued confession of faith, became a treasured resource for expressions of "the doctrines of our faith and practice," just as the framers declared of the confession.[57] Congregational hymn-singing, as a result, also became a more prominent and permanent element of the typical Particular Baptist worship service. Anne Steele serves as both a beneficiary of and an exponent of this hymn-writing movement.

Steele obviously did not write her hymns with a copy of the *Second London Confession* at her side. But an examination of her hymns in Rippon's *Selection of Hymns* will demonstrate that its theology was part and parcel of Steele's poetic output. As Steele's hymns are so well-distributed throughout Rippon's theologically organized hymnal, this book will examine them under the headings: God and Creation, Revelation, Christ and His Work, the Holy Spirit and His Work, the Church and Its Life, and Final Events. As the particular doctrinal beliefs under these broad theological concepts are revealed in the hymns of Steele sung by so many churchgoers in the late eighteenth and early nineteenth centuries, her evangelical and Particular Baptist beliefs will be highlighted.

Considering both the literary and theological elements of the hymn as well its dual role in both personal devotion and corporate worship, Aalders sheds light on why it is helpful to focus on a particular hymn-writer's approach to writing: "As a work of literature by which, in its singing the faithful are made to rehearse a particular theology, it is instructive to consider how

54. Broome, *Bruised Reed*, 194. Broome lists excerpts from one of his sermons, showing it to be Evangelical, Calvinistic, and gospel-driven. See 194–98.

55. Haykin, *Kiffin, Knollys and Keach*, 62.

56. *Second London Confession* (1677, 1688/89) XXII:5, cited in Lumpkin, *Baptist Confessions of Faith*, 281.

57. Lumpkin, *Baptist Confessions of Faith*, 239.

hymns are composed and made to convey and enable religious experience."[58] In examining the work of D. H. Lawrence, William York Tindall suggests a rule to keep in mind in analyzing someone's art: "The ideas that an artist persuades us to accept must function in his aesthetic organizations. To know these we must consider those."[59] This advice rings true with the poetry of Anne Steele. Within her hymns one indeed finds her heart, especially if one sees the heart as the biblical poets did—the spiritual, emotional, physical, and intellectual center of one's being.[60] In her examination of Steele's hymns, Aalders notes that "words, meaning, and religious expression are united in the singing of a hymn."[61] And obviously expressing a characteristic of Steele's poetry as it functions within the context of the English hymn, she says, "Literature and theology, the form and the content of the hymn, together become a conduit for devotional experience, the mysterious meeting of God and the human person."[62] An examination of Steele's hymns in Rippon's hymnal, sung by so many worshipers, offers an illustration of this "mysterious meeting."

As the only female hymn-writer from her generation whose hymns have stood the test of time,[63] Steele's gender has been one issue regarding the style and content of her hymn-writing often addressed by those who have studied her work. Hymnologist Louis F. Benson, for example, ranked Steele as a close second to Doddridge in terms of her place as a follower of Watts. But Benson, who otherwise speaks of Steele as the foremost of Baptist hymn-writers, yet in describing her elevated position in the school of Watts, says, "Her truly feminine emotionalism for a time deceived the elect into believing she was founding a school of her own."[64] He says this in the context of relating Watts's moving of the English hymn beyond the realm of literature and into the realm of religious and experiential poetry. Benson's critique seems to be a negative one toward the experiential element of Watts and his followers: "The whole body of Watts' work earns a place in the literature of power; the literature that leaves esthetic critics cold but moves men."[65] As a woman, Steele is seen as taking the hymn even further down

---

58. Aalders, *To Express the Ineffable*, 36.

59. Tindall, "Introduction," vi.

60. See Watson, *English Hymn*, 4, for a discussion of hymns and the heart according to these categories.

61. Aalders, *To Express the Ineffable*, 35.

62. Aalders, *To Express the Ineffable*, 35.

63. Broome, *Bruised Reed*, 151.

64. Benson, *Hymnody of the Christian Church*, 114.

65. Benson, *Hymnody of the Christian Church*, 113.

such a path. His assessment has been tempered, however, by more recent considerations of how Steele's feminine sensibilities affected her approach to writing. Aalders responds to Benson's assessment of Steele in his monumental work, *The English Hymn*, published twelve years before his lectures just cited. She says, "Steele's emotional expression cannot be attributed solely to her identity as a woman, despite Louis Benson's claim that the intensely emotional tone, the 'plaintive, sentimental note,' in Steele's hymns was due to her introducing a 'feminine standpoint' to the eighteenth-century English hymn."[66] Aalders sees Steele tapping into "the developing values of the evangelical movement" such as "heartfelt religious devotion and the honest expression of personal piety" which would not have been at odds with the "feminine virtue of emotion."[67] So, if Steele's femininity affected her writing in this regard, it actually helped give voice to a spiritual emotion that provided a resource for advancing the English hymn in one of its purposes, "to give voice to both doctrine and personal devotion."[68]

Cho points out that Steele influenced later women writers in the use of the language of love.[69] She comments on a verse from Steele's hymn, "Redeeming Love": "I yield, to thy dear conqu'ring arms / I yield my captive soul: / O let my all-subduing charms / My inmost pow'rs control!"[70] Cho says, "Although on one level, Steele is using her own position as a woman to envisage a relationship of love with her Saviour, this verse also successfully articulates the relationship of the Church, the Bride (regardless of the gender make-up of the congregation) to Christ, the Groom."[71] Male writers also wrote of Christ as the groom and the church as his bride using a language of love. And so Cho concludes, "Any male singers also take on the subjectivity of the passive female" in this case.[72] Cho finally suggests that rather than following a distinctly feminine pattern in her writing, she follows "an established devotional convention of her times in her

---

66. Aalders, *To Express the Ineffable*, 122. She quotes from Benson, *English Hymn*, 214.

67. Aalders, *To Express the Ineffable*, 122.

68. Aalders, *To Express the Ineffable*, 122.

69. Cho, "Ministry of Song," 76. See also Watson, *English Hymn*, 191. Cho also observes that "the privileging of sympathy was a feature of Steele's hymns which was continued by later women hymn writers." Cho suggests that "empathetic feeling may have appealed to women because it was a power available to them when more active responses to the world were not." Cho, "Ministry of Song," 74.

70. "Redeeming Love," in Steele, *Works*, 1:36.

71. Cho, "Ministry of Song," 76.

72. Cho, "Ministry of Song," 76.

hymns."[73] And regarding at least one gender theory of spirituality, "Steele's hymns conform more to a masculine pattern."[74] But this is not surprising. Though Steele chose to remain unmarried, she would not have seen herself as competing with men in her work. On the contrary, she was positively influenced by a number of educated men, many of whom were religious leaders who "encouraged the use of her poetic gifts in a religious culture that did not normally welcome the voices of women on sacred subjects, thus facilitating her development as a hymn-writer."[75] So Steele writes from the standpoint of who she is, a woman from a specific family raised in a particular religious tradition at a certain place and time.

It should be pointed out that in Aalders's analysis of Steele, she finds Steele struggling with the "ability of language to offer meaningful praise to God."[76] This problem, she finds, is further exacerbated by Steele's sense of the incomprehensibility and the ineffability of God, especially in the face of human suffering.[77] Thus Aalders finds in a Steele a note of uncertainty and hesitancy in her writing style.[78] While this could be related to gender, it would also be a part of her personality, experience, and cultural context. Steele wrote as a kind of transitional figure between an Augustan era of literature and the Romantic period. Steele wrote both from a sense of sobriety in the face of life in a fallen world and with a sense of delight in the simple pleasures of life in the present and the hope of a life everlasting. It has already been mentioned that Steele wrote about the beauties of the created world. Sharon James finds that Steele and her friends advanced the rhetoric of the Romantic Movement by seeing the rural delights of village life "as facilitating worship to the creator."[79] Additionally, noting that Steele admired and emulated contemporary poetry, Cho finds a "language of sensibility," for example, in Steele's lyrics that "encourage sympathy toward the suffering

---

73. Cho, "Ministry of Song," 60.

74. Cho, "Ministry of Song," 61. The theory is that males see life as a linear journey, with a definite destination in mind, while females see life as more of a cyclical walk, where the journey is more important than the destination. This distinction is thus expressed in their respective approaches to hymn-writing. See Och, *Women and Spirituality*.

75. Aalders, *To Express the Ineffable*, 20.

76. Aalders, *To Express the Ineffable*, 66.

77. See Aalders, *To Express the Ineffable*, 102–71 for her discussion on these topics.

78. In the next chapter it will be argued that Steele's original audience, based on the balanced selection of her hymns they received through Rippon's *Selection of Hymns*, would have seen in Steele a more confident hymn-writer than Aalders finds.

79. James, *In Trouble and in Joy*, 136.

figure of Christ" and sorrow at his rejection.[80] So Steele's understanding of language and literature, of suffering and spiritual redemption, and of private devotion and corporate worship were not cultivated in a vacuum, but within a complex cultural moment. And so, at the conclusion of her analysis Aalders still can say, "Despite being troubled by an inability to understand God's nature and ways, Steele continued to attempt expression. . . . [And] she approached her task with hope."[81] Thus Steele expressed Romantic literature's "sense of aspiration and longing for the infinite" through her—ultimately—hopeful hymnody.[82]

Like Watts before her and Wesley her contemporary, Steele saw hymns as both theology and poetry written for the purpose of piety. She once wrote in a letter that "sacred Poesy" found its purpose "in the service of Religion."[83] Writing "during a time when the prevailing aesthetic sensibility held that art could both edify and delight," Steele's compositions should be viewed as works of both theology and literature.[84] The following chapter will examine Steele's hymns included by Rippon in his *Selection of Hymns* as such.

80. Cho, "Ministry of Song," 60. For example, Steele wrote, "What pain, what soul-oppressing pain, / The great Redeemer bore; / While bloody sweat, like drops of rain, / Distill'd from ev'ry pore! / And ere the dreadful storm descends / Full on his guiltless head, / See him by his familiar friends/Deserted and betray'd!" "Redeeming Love," in Steele, *Works*, 1:32.

81. Aalders, *To Express the Ineffable*, 134.

82. Corbin Scott Carnell, *Bright Shadow of Reality: Spiritual Longing in C.S. Lewis* (Grand Rapids: Eerdmans, 1974), 27, cited in Aalders, *To Express the Ineffable*, 156.

83. STE 3/13 (vii), letter from Steele to an anonymous woman, August 8, 1761, in Aalders, *To Express the Ineffable*, 35.

84. Aalders, *To Express the Ineffable*, 36.

5

Anne Steele's Hymns and Psalms in John Rippon's *Selection of Hymns*

Introduction

EVANGELICAL IN NATURE, THE revival that occurred in the English Particular Baptist community in the late eighteenth and early nineteenth centuries included a robust participation in hymn-singing.[1] This participation included both congregational singing in worship as well as the use of hymns and hymn-books as a part of private devotional practices. As the hymn-book, and most notably John Rippon's *Selection of Hymns*, functioned practically as a prayer book within the New Dissent,[2] it made a vital contribution to the evangelical Calvinistic piety of these reviving churches.[3] Anne Steele's fifty-two hymns and psalms that Rippon included in his hymnal reveal this fresh manifestation of evangelical Calvinism in both theology and piety, in both doctrinal basis and experiential character. Additionally, Steele's hymns display a theological cohesion with the *Second London Confession*,[4] the foundational document that systematically expounded the great truths of Scripture and that informed the preaching she heard from the pulpit of her uncle and father. They also exhibit the characteristics of the Evangelical Revival, such as a love and submission to the Holy Bible, a focus on the cross of Christ as the ground of the forgiveness of sinners, and an evangelistic thrust. In fact, each side of David Bebbington's well-known quadrilateral

1. Manley, '*Redeeming Love Proclaim*', 3–7.

2. The revived and Evangelically impacted Nonconformity, or Dissent, that emerged at the end of the eighteenth century.

3. See Manley, '*Redeeming Love Proclaim*', 84–85.

4. See Lumpkin, *Baptist Confessions of Faith*, 144–71 and 235–95.

of Evangelicalism is represented and illuminated through Steele's hymns in Rippon's *Selection of Hymns*.[5]

Steele's hymns are distributed quite evenly throughout the theologically and ecclesiastically organized hymnal for which Rippon is well-known. Not unlike a confession of faith or a volume of systematic theology, Rippon's hymnal is organized topically according to the loci of theology and church life.[6] In his dissertation concerning Baptist hymnody, Robert H. Young finds parallels between Rippon's hymnal and the *Second London Confession*.[7] Rippon's seventeen major headings are God, Creation and Providence, Fall of Man, Scripture, Christ, Spirit, Christian Life, Worship, World, Church, Baptism, Lord's Supper, Times and Seasons, Time and Eternity, Death and the Resurrection, Judgment, and Hell and Heaven. Steele is represented within thirteen of these sections.[8] Some of these sections contain subheadings, which will be indicated where appropriate below. Steele's proportionate placement throughout the hymnal illustrates the scope of her subject matter as well as that of this hymnal in promoting the theology and piety of the Particular Baptist community during their decades of revitalization and revival. These hymns demonstrate not only the orthodoxy of their evangelical and Calvinistic commitments, but also the resulting orthopraxy of such commitments.

God and Creation

John Rippon's *Selection of Hymns*[9] begins with twenty-eight hymns appearing under the major heading, God.[10] Two of Steele's hymns are included in Rippon's first section. Two more hymns by Steele are found in the second

5. See Bebbington, *Evangelicalism in Modern Britain*, 5–17, for his discussion of his quadrilateral of the four characteristics of Evangelicalism, namely, activism, biblicism, conversionism, and crucicentrism.

6. Upon examination, it also generally follows the flow of the Apostles' Creed, whether intentionally or unintentionally.

7. Young, "History of Baptist Hymnody in England from 1612–1800," 162.

8. The sections which do not include a hymn by Steele are Fall of Man, World, Baptism, and Judgment. Only Baptism contains more than ten hymns and that was not a subject about which Steele wrote.

9. Rippon's first edition included 588 hymns. He added sixty-two in the tenth edition and then 153 additional hymns in the twenty-seventh edition. An existing hymnal from its thirty-second edition is followed for this analysis. In counting the number of hymns in each section it should be noted that sometimes several hymns have the same hymn number in the book, but have been counted separately.

10. That is, according to the Analysis (found on a page numbered as 0). The top of each double page spread in this section reads, "The Being and Perfections of God."

section of this hymnal, Creation and Providence, out of a total of eleven. These two sections, which are made up of thirty-nine hymns, do not include subheadings. Steele is thus well represented in the first pages of the hymnal as Rippon begins, like the Bible, with God and his creative actions.

In Rippon's first section, each of the hymns generally considers an attribute of God.[11] The *Second London Confession* describes God as "infinite in being, and perfection, . . . immutable, immense, eternal, incomprehensible, Almighty, . . . having all life, glory, goodness, blessedness, in and of himself."[12] Steele's two hymns in this section consider God's eternity and goodness, respectively. In his theological analysis of the revival of the Particular Baptist community through a renewal of evangelical Calvinism, L. G. Champion notes four emphases he found in the teaching of the movement's leaders. Steele's first two hymns in Rippon's hymnbook illustrate the first line of emphasis revealed by Champion's analysis, "The absolute sovereignty of God over all His creation including mankind."[13]

Steele's first entry in the *Selection of Hymns*, the fourth hymn in the book, is her paraphrase of Psalm 90, which Rippon entitled "The Eternity of God, and Man's Mortality. Psalm xc."[14] Steele's original version of this hymn as found in her first published volume of hymns contains 17 stanzas, though Rippon only chose to include eight in his hymnal.[15] Due to the fact that this hymn is a paraphrase of a psalm, the theological content was already provided for Steele to take and craft into a paraphrased meter. In the case of this hymn, Rippon, for the most part, removed the verses that spoke of God's anger and judgment, subjects Steele was not afraid to tackle. As it stands, Rippon's shortened version offers a cohesive glimpse of God's eternity and humanity's mortality, but within petitions based on God's care for his finite children. Further, unlike Watts, who used Common Meter (86.86) double

---

11. In this case, Rippon follows the order of the *First London Confession*, which begins with the doctrine of God. The *Second London Confession*, more accessible in Rippon's day, follows the *Westminster Confession of Faith* by beginning with a chapter on Scripture followed by the doctrine of God and the typical loci of theology. See Lumpkin, *Baptist Confessions of Faith*, 144–71 and 235–95.

12. Lumpkin, *Baptist Confessions of Faith*, 252–53.

13. Champion, "Evangelical Calvinism," 199.

14. Rippon, *Selection of Hymns*, 4–5. Though she gave her own titles to most of her hymns, often including references to Scripture, Steele did not give titles to her paraphrases of Psalm texts.

15. For about one-fifth of the hymns of Steele published in Rippon's *Selection of Hymns*, he reduced the verses included by roughly one half of those originally written. When quoted in this book, the verse numbers are listed exactly as they were numbered in Rippon.

for his famous paraphrase of Psalm 90, Steele sticks with Long Meter for her stately treatment of such a majestic subject.[16]

A few characteristics of this hymn will be highlighted to show how Steele interacted with this most sobering of psalms. First, while paraphrasing a psalm concerning God's absolutely sovereignty, his eternity, and his power, Steele could not help but consider the intimate relationship between the Creator and his creatures. Even going beyond the strict words of the psalmist, Steele refers to human beings as God's children and to God as Father.[17] Second, she goes even beyond not only the passage, but also the *Second London Confession*, by describing God's creative acts as taking place through his word. The first two stanzas and two lines from verse 3 illustrate,

Lord, thou hast been thy children's God,
All-powerful, wise, and good, and just,
In every age their safe abode,
Their hope, their refuge, and their trust.

Before thy word gave nature birth,
Or spread the starry heavens abroad,
Or form'd the varied face of earth,
From everlasting thou art God.

Great Father of Eternity,
How short are ages in thy sight!

Notice in the first verse her descriptions of God as "All-powerful, wise, and good, and just" that echo the *Confession's* depiction of God, "Almighty, every way infinite, most holy, most wise, . . . abundant in goodness and truth, . . . most just."[18] Steele is conscientious in her word choice and demonstrates her reverent but also familial view of God the Father. Steele closes her paraphrase of the ninetieth Psalm with another interpretive set of lines, this time emphasizing the evangelical doctrine of living lives that adorn the gospel and faith in God's care. Steele writes, "Thy glorious image, fair imprest / Let all our hearts and lives declare; / Beneath thy kind protection blest, / May all our labours own thy care!" The *Confession* declares that any human works are good only through divine assistance, "because as they are good they proceed from his Spirit" and are acceptable in Christ, "he looking upon them in his Son

---

16. See Lovelace, *Anatomy of Hymnody*, 24–34, for a discussion of Long Meter.

17. Though Steele does not go so far as to make the psalm about Christ, yet she does show the characteristic of Isaac Watts, the one she chose to emulate, by taking the artist's prerogative to enhance the meaning according to theological conviction.

18. Lumpkin, *Baptist Confessions of Faith*, 252.

is pleased to accept and reward that which is sincere."[19] Steele's confessional paraphrase echoes the *Confession's* robust theology and so the Christian hope shines afresh in a sober hymnic paraphrase of Psalm 90.

The second selection by Steele found in Rippon is called "The Goodness of God. Nahum i. 7."[20] The biblical passage, placed in the title by Steele and retained by Rippon—which he often did—declares, "The Lord is good, a stronghold in the day of trouble; and he knoweth them that trust in him."[21] Like the prophets before her, including Nahum, Steele could offer words of praise and faith in God in the midst of messages of judgment. The verse is taken from Nahum's prophetic judgment by God against Nineveh, who had destroyed Israel's northern kingdom in 722 BC. Steele considers first and foremost God's goodness. Of this hymn's six verses, the first and last both declare that praise through song to God is most appropriate because of his goodness and his love. In between these verses of praise the second stanza considers God's "guardian care" over all of his creation while the third points out more specifically the wonder of love by which "He gave his Son, his only Son, / To ransom rebel worms." Such tender care gives way in verse 4 to her calling her Lord a "dear refuge" and "a safe defence, a peaceful home." The fifth stanza turns to God's perspective toward his people: "Thine eye beholds, with kind regard, / The souls who trust in thee." This hymn on the goodness of God immediately turns to the evangelical doctrine of the atoning work of Christ for "rebel worms," i.e., sinners needing salvation from their sins. Echoing Watts, Steele reveals her realistic view of humanity and exalted view of the one through whom mankind is redeemed. The singer/reader is left with little doubt that the hymn-writer truly believed "that Christ died as a substitute for sinful mankind."[22]

Steele's hymns illustrate both a theological breadth and depth along with their experiential elements. Her two hymns in this first section tackle first a more intangible or abstract attribute of God, his eternity, and second the more tangible attribute of goodness. Thus from the start, her wide range of theological concern is exemplified. Further, her assurance of God's care, a hallmark of the Evangelical Revival,[23] as well as her strenuous desire to offer praise to God as a caring Father are unmistakable. And Steele's lyrics betray a sense of the Particular Baptist doctrine of adoption. Steele would have been

---

19. Lumpkin, *Baptist Confessions of Faith*, 272.

20. Rippon, *Selection of Hymns*, 12–13. Rippon here includes all six of Steele's verses.

21. All biblical citations are from the Authorized Version.

22. Bebbington, *Evangelicalism in Modern Britain*, 15.

23. Bebbington, *Evangelicalism in Modern Britain*, 6.

happy to confess that the children of her Father in heaven "are pitied, protected, provided for, and chastened by him, as by a Father."[24]

Steele's two hymns in Rippon's second section, Creation and Providence, are "Creation and Providence" and "Praise for the Blessings of Providence and Grace. Psalm cxxxix."[25] These are two of the minority of hymns that Rippon effectively reduced by one half in order to include them in his hymnal. These each offer an illustration of Rippon's editorial wisdom. The reduction of "Creation and Providence" is clearly for purpose of eliminating redundancy. Five of the six verses Rippon cut are a cumulative reflection on various objects or phenomenon in the created order.[26] The theological and experiential point of the hymn is not at all lost, but is actually enhanced by the editor's decision to streamline the hymn and bring focus to its primary topic. In the second hymn under discussion here the omission of four verses is likewise for the sake of reducing redundancy, this time with regard to the theme of God's watch-care over one's growing life, the hymn's primary theme in Rippon's shorter version. The omission of the other three verses, however, appears to be for theological purposes. Three verses rehearsing Christ's atonement for sinners, which turn the theme somewhat away from that of Psalm 139, are removed since Rippon obviously addresses that theme in later sections of his hymnal.

Though Steele does not break much new ground in her third and fourth hymns in Rippon's *Selection of Hymns*, they do offer helpful insight into Steele's craft, theology, and faith. In "Creation and Providence"[27] Steele's gift for language is demonstrated as she meditates both on God's work in creation in general, but even more on his care of man, the crown of creation. Commenting on this hymn, J. R. Broome suggests that here Steele shows that "great love for nature" usually found in her more secular poetry.[28] First, she writes of creation's wonders,

> Lord, when our raptur'd thought surveys
> Creation's beauties o'er,
> All nature joins to teach thy praise,
> And bid our souls adore.

24. Lumpkin, *Baptist Confessions of Faith*, 267.

25. Rippon, *Selection of Hymns*, 34–35 and 39–40. In the first of these two hymns, Rippon retains eight of Steele's original fourteen stanzas and in the second he includes nine of sixteen. Further, Rippon added the reference to Ps 139 in the title to the second hymn.

26. See Steele, *Works*, 1:27–29.

27. Rippon, *Selection of Hymns*, 34–35.

28. Broome, *Bruised Reed*, 168.

Where'er we turn our gazing eyes,
　Thy radiant footsteps shine;
Ten thousand pleasing wonders rise
　And speak their source divine.

These first two stanzas highlight not only Steele's craft, but also her theology. First, note that this hymn is written in Common Meter (86.86) and with a cross-rhyming scheme. The well-crafted lyrics in the first two lines of each verse leave the reader or singer "with an expectancy, even a guessing, of the final two lines."[29] This scheme is in operation throughout the hymn. With such a subject, Common Meter offers Steele an opportunity to emulate Watts' work in "O God, Our Help in Ages Past." She does so admirably. Second, because Steele repeats the ABAB (cross rhyming) pattern from verse 1 to verse 2 both in rhyme, subject matter, and theology, there is a strong start to the hymn. This second point leads, finally, to the theological statement of these first two verses, that nature, or general revelation, reveals its Creator, which should result in praise. Like the *Second London Confession*, Steele bears witness to the fact that "the light of Nature, and the works of Creation and Providence do so far manifest the goodness, wisdom and power of God, as to leave men unexcusable."[30] Steele thus writes in verses 4 and 5,

Thy wisdom, power, and goodness, Lord,
　In all thy works appear:
And O! let man thy praise record,—
　Man, thy distinguish'd care!

From thee the breath of life he drew;
　That breath thy power maintains;
Thy tender mercy, ever new,
　His brittle frame sustains.

In these stanzas Steele continues to profess her theology through her poetic medium. She uses the same three words as the *Confession* to describe what the works of the Lord reveal. Second, she uses the simple poetic device of the dash to draw attention to the most important theme of creation, the creation of and then care of man by God. The dash in verse 4 is a visual device that highlights the duty of the reader of the hymn to praise God because of the distinguished care he receives. Steele expands this in verse 5 to include God's constant life-giving sustenance of his creatures which is a "tender mercy" needed to sustain such a "brittle frame." The verses reveal Steele's familiarity

29. Lovelace, *Anatomy of Hymnody*, 25. Lovelace is commenting on the value of the rhyme scheme itself in general, not on Steele's work.

30. Lumpkin, *Baptist Confessions of Faith*, 248.

with such passages as Genesis 2:7, Psalm 8:3–4 and 103:14, and Lamentations 3:22–23. But she also takes the theological teaching of this homiletical hymn even further by noting in the sixth verse that man is "By revelation's brightest rays / Still more divinely bless'd." So she again agrees with the *Confession*, that "yet are [the light of Nature, and the works of Creation and Providence] not sufficient to give that knowledge of God and His will, which is necessary unto Salvation."[31] The Bible, or "revelation's brightest rays," is needed for such knowledge. Thus Steele situates herself within the evangelical stream that includes a "devotion to the Bible" and the "belief that all spiritual truth is to be found in its pages."[32] Steele closes the hymn in the eighth stanza with a further evangelical thrust: "O may our lips and lives make known / Thy goodness and thy praise!" Steele's concern that the gospel be manifested in all of one's life is in line with the activism found in Bebbington's quadrilateral, the hope for the conversion of others to Christ.[33]

The first six stanzas of "Praise for the Blessings of Providence and Grace. Psalm cxxxix"[34] repeat and affirm the content of "Creation and Providence." Steele praises her "Almighty Father, gracious Lord!" for his "care," his being a "preserver," his "favours" and "the blessing of thy grace." But the last three verses advance Steele's contribution to Rippon's hymnal and Particular Baptist piety in at least two ways. Consider the final three stanzas that bring the hymn to a climactic close:

> Yes, I adore thee, gracious Lord!
>   For favours more divine;
> That I have known thy sacred word,
>   Where all thy glories shine.
>
> Lord! when this mortal frame decays,
>   And ev'ry weakness dies,
> Complete the wonders of thy grace,
>   And raise me to the skies.
>
> Then shall my joyful powers unite
>   In more exalted lays,
> And join the happy sons of light
>   In everlasting praise.

31. Lumpkin, *Baptist Confessions of Faith*, 248.
32. Bebbington, *Evangelicalism in Modern Britain*, 12.
33. See Bebbington, *Evangelicalism in Modern Britain*, 5–17.
34. Rippon, *Selection of Hymns*, 39–40.

These verses anticipate Steele's contribution to further sections of Rippon's hymnal: Scripture, Death and the Resurrection, and Hell and Heaven. Steele states her evangelical view of Scripture: it is God's "sacred word / Where all thy glories shine." This and the following two verses have a warmly evangelical and evangelically Calvinistic tone to them. She agrees with the *Confession's* "reverent esteem of the Holy Scriptures" and its teaching that the Scripture contains "all things necessary for [God's] Glory."[35] Further, the final two stanzas display Steele's hope in eternal life and include hints of resurrection faith. She poetically declares her belief that at the time of her death her soul "having an immortal subsistence [will] immediately return to God" and will be "received into paradise."[36] These two hymns further place Steele's literary achievements in the confessional stream of Particular Baptist theology with its exalted view of Scripture and of God's providential care over his creatures that will culminate in life everlasting. Their warm and intimate tone also reveals the evangelical nature of Steele's experience of her convictions.

In her first four hymns reproduced in Rippon's *Selection of Hymns* Anne Steele's literary ability and her vigorous theology both find their way into the sung piety of the Particular Baptist and broader Dissenting communities. These first few hymns also foreshadow evangelical themes Steele addresses more in depth in later sections of this hymn-book, such as Scripture and man's response to the divine initiatives of grace and mercy.

Revelation

Five of Steele's hymns appear in the section of his hymnal that Rippon simply entitled Scripture. This section of 105 hymns does include five sub-headings: Properties of [Scripture], Moral and Ceremonial Law, Gospel, Doctrines and Blessings, and Invitations and Promises. The large number of hymns is not surprising, as Scripture was at the very foundation of both Particular Baptist life and the Evangelical Revival. The first chapter of the *Second London Confession* is "Of the Holy Scriptures,"[37] and consists of ten sections that explain and apply the doctrine of Scripture to faith and practice. Further, as Bebbington explains, eighteenth-century Evangelicals were also driven by a high esteem of the Holy Bible: "Their devotion to the Bible has been the result of their belief that all spiritual truth is to be found

---

35. Lumpkin, *Baptist Confessions of Faith*, 250.

36. Lumpkin, *Baptist Confessions of Faith*, 293.

37. Lumpkin, *Baptist Confessions of Faith*, 248–52.

in its pages."[38] Steele's hymns in Rippon's hymnal demonstrate a similar reverent view of the Bible as inspired by God, a belief that true knowledge of Christ and salvation in him is found in its pages, and an illustration of the experience such views bring to the life of a believer. Some questions to consider while analyzing this section of hymns include: What is Steele's view of the Bible? What does she believe is its purpose for human beings, both before and after conversion? Does she believe it has authority? What does she believe about the glory and sufficiency of the sacred texts? Who or what, especially, do we find in the Bible?

Steele's most well-known hymn, "The Excellency and Sufficiency of the Holy Scriptures,"[39] or known today by its first line, "Father of Mercies, in Thy Word," is the fourth hymn of this section. It is in the subsection that considers the properties of Scripture. This hymn is a tremendous illustration of that characteristic of Particular Baptists (and their Puritan forbears) that may be called the "Spirituality of the Word,"[40] in which there is an ardent application of the Bible to a believer's faith and life. For the fourth time with the first five of Steele's compositions in the *Selection of Hymns*, Rippon edited out a sizeable number of the stanzas. He included only one-half of the hymn's twelve stanzas in his version.[41] And once again Rippon's editorial scissors result in a more tightly focused and doctrinally cohesive selection.[42] Written in Common Meter (86.86), the flow of the hymn helps accomplish its purpose.

"The Excellency and Sufficiency of the Holy Scriptures"[43] begins with a verse that states the thesis of the entire hymn, "Father of mercies! in thy word / What endless glory shines! / For ever be thy name ador'd / For these celestial lines." In these "excellent lines"[44] Steele walks verse-by-verse through her belief in the glory and sufficiency of the Holy Bible to the

38. Bebbington, *Evangelicalism in Modern Britain*, 12.

39. Rippon, *Selection of Hymns*, 48–49. Rippon added "and Sufficiency" to Steele's chosen title. See Steele, *Works*, 1:72. Though not found in recent editions of hymnals published by the Southern Baptist Convention, this hymn is still found, for example in *The Trinity Hymnal*, 144.

40. For a brief exposition of Baptist spirituality during the seventeenth and eighteenth centuries, see Haykin, "Draw Nigh unto My Soul," 54–73.

41. Of the next twenty-six hymns of Steele's, Rippon did not remove more than two stanzas in any given case and retained the full text of twenty-two hymns.

42. In this case the verses excluded by Rippon include an extended meditation on suffering and the Bible's answer to it. They are also a bit more earthy in tone and word choice. See Steele, *Works*, 1:72–74 for all twelve stanzas.

43. Rippon, *Selection of Hymns*, 48–49.

44. Manwaring, *Study of Hymn-Writing and Hymn-Singing in the Christian Church*, 115.

believer. In the first verse she addresses the Father and immediately speaks of the greatness of his written word. As J. R. Watson notes,

> The particular marks of her style are the use of nouns and adjectives to produce the expected—'endless glory,' 'celestial lines'—which, on second glance, prove to be slightly unusual: the endless glory is not heaven, but the word, the word on the page, and the celestial lines are not the lines of eternal life so much as the lines of Holy Scripture.[45]

In a word, Steele ascribes great honor to God's written word. Here again, she appears to be following the *Second London Confession*, which says that the "heavenliness," "efficacy," "Majesty," and unity of the Scripture all form part of its purpose to "give all glory to God."[46]

Steele continues,

> Here may the wretched sons of want
>   Exhaustless riches find;
> Riches above what earth can grant,
>   And lasting as the mind.
>
> Here the fair tree of knowledge grows,
>   And yields a free repast;
> Sublimer sweets than nature knows
>   Invite the longing taste.

Verse 2 uses the metaphor of riches to describe the value of the Bible. Watson believes that Steele's use of repetition here subtly conceals the art and the surprise of her statements. He sees this verse articulating "an expansion of the mind, from riches as an alternative to want, to 'Riches' that exceed all earthly possibilities."[47] Watson is pointing out the surprising view, on the surface, that for the Christian these *written words*, the special revelation of God, are words of life. The next verse, alluding to the Bible's wisdom literature, such as Psalm 1, teaches that in the Bible there is true knowledge that tastes good to the spiritual tongue. Christians, Steele implies, are not only physically, but also spiritually, dependent people. The Scriptures offer what believers need for "Faith and Life."[48] The *Second London Confession* says

---

45. Watson, *English Hymn*, 194.
46. Lumpkin, *Baptist Confessions of Faith*, 250.
47. Watson, *English Hymn*, 194.
48. Lumpkin, *Baptist Confessions of Faith*, 250.

that "the Holy Scripture is the only sufficient, certain, and infallible rule of all saving Knowledge, Faith, and Obedience."[49] Steele agrees.

This most well-known of Steele's hymns concludes,

> Here the Redeemer's welcome voice
>   Spreads heavenly peace around;
> And life, and everlasting joys,
>   Attend the blissful sound.
>
> O may these heavenly pages be
>   My ever dear delight;
> And still new beauties may I see,
>   And still increasing light!
>
> Divine Instructor, gracious Lord!
>   Be thou for ever near:
> Teach me to love thy sacred word,
>   And view my Saviour there!

There seems to be a skip in Steele's step as she concludes this poetic consideration of the Bible. To combat the conflicts in this life, the sixth verse claims that from the Redeemer's voice comes peace and life and joy—a blissful sound heard in the Bible. She concludes in the final two verses by offering the supplication that in the Bible she might ever find delight, light, beauty, and a Lord and Savior himself. So she asks for help in loving this word. The range of her theology of the Bible found in this hymn is wide.[50] The entire second half of the hymn, but especially the last two verses, is a reminder that the *Confession* finds in the Scripture all things necessary for "Man's Salvation, Faith and Life" as well as instruction for Christians within whom God's word dwells that "through patience and comfort of the Scriptures [they] may have hope."[51] Nancy Cho summarizes, "In this hymn, the Father's word, the Bible, is described as a luxuriant meeting place where the earth-bound Christian may encounter the abundant joys of heaven."[52] Thus Steele demonstrates from a variety of angles that all the spiritual truth and comfort needed for this life may be found in the pages of the Bible. Like her

---

49. Lumpkin, *Baptist Confessions of Faith*, 248.

50. It brings to mind such Scripture passages as Ps 119, John 1:1–18, 2 Tim 3:15–17, and Heb 1:1–4 and 4:12–13.

51. Lumpkin, *Baptist Confessions of Faith*, 250–51.

52. Cho, "Ministry of Song," 69.

fellow evangelicals, in this hymn Steele seeks to "bring home the message of the Bible and to encourage its devotional use."[53]

Two of Steele's hymns appear in the subsection of Scripture called Doctrines and Blessings: "Redemption by Christ alone. 1 Pet. i. 18, 19" and "Pardoning Love. Jer. iii. 22 and Hos. xiv. 1."[54] Two others appear in the subsection, Invitations and Promises: "Weary souls invited to rest. Matt. xi. 28" and "The Saviour's Invitation. John vii. 37."[55] Appearing in the larger section of Rippon's hymnal considering Scripture, these hymns further affirm Steele's relationship to the evangelical Calvinistic revival. They do this since they not only agree with the hymn just considered in its doctrine of Scripture, but they meditate on two specific teachings of both Scripture and the evangelical movement: the atonement of Christ through his cross and the invitation to confess Christ as he is offered in the gospel.

"Redemption by Christ alone. 1 Pet. i. 18, 19"[56] is written in Long Meter (88.88), the longer lines of which are suited for such heavy subject matter as sin and redemption. Redemption, in fact, is the heading listed at the top of the page upon which this hymn is printed in Rippon. The hymn begins, "Enslav'd by sin, and bound in chains, / Beneath its dreadful tyrant sway, / And doom'd to everlasting pains, / We wretched guilty captives lay." Displaying a Pauline understanding of sin and the sinful nature of the human condition as well as an understanding of Jesus's teaching on judgment and eternity, Steele places the sinner firmly in his "doom'd" predicament—unless faith in Christ intervenes. As the sixth chapter of the *Second London Confession* teaches, outside of Christ all are "by nature children of wrath, the servants of *Sin*, the subjects of *death* and all other miseries, spiritual, temporal, and eternal, unless the *Lord Jesus* set them free."[57] Commenting on this hymn, Watson helpfully observes that Steele's method of hymn-writing and the structure of many of her hymns, mentioned in the previous chapter, is relevant here. He says, "Whereas Doddridge [another follower of Watts] versifies a biblical text, like a preacher, she more frequently begins with experience."[58] She then follows by both

---

53. Bebbington, *Evangelicalism in Modern Britain*, 14.

54. Rippon, *Selection of Hymns*, 72–73 and 88, 90.

55. Rippon, *Selection of Hymns*, 134–35 and 137–38.

56. Rippon, *Selection of Hymns*, 72–73.

57. Lumpkin, *Baptist Confessions of Faith*, 259.

58. Watson, *English Hymn*, 195. At this point experience is not a negative aspect to the congregation's corporate worship, at least when it comes to hymns such as this one. These hymns under consideration are aiding the worshipers' experiential piety, and are not pushing them into subjectivity. Further, the question of what eventually leads from the more theologically grounded hymns of the eighteenth century to the more

interpreting the experience and pleading for further obedience, comfort, and praise to God in light of Scripture.

In the second, third, and fourth verses Steele offers a versified paraphrase of the passage noted from 1 Peter[59] as well as unpacking the teaching of the passage:

> Nor gold nor gems could buy our peace:
>   Nor the whole world's collected store
> Suffice to purchase our release;
>   A thousand worlds were all too poor.
>
> Jesus, the Lord, the mighty God
>   An all-sufficient ransom paid;
> Invalu'd price! his precious blood,
>   For vile rebellious traitors shed.
>
> Jesus the sacrifice became
>   To rescue guilty souls from hell:
> The spotless, bleeding, dying Lamb
>   Beneath avenging justice fell.

Steele shows a profound understanding of the penal substitutionary atonement made by Christ. None could possibly pay the price for redemption from their sins, but Jesus has fully paid the price of the transgressions of his sinful people.[60] It is helpful to note that an early Particular Baptist, Hanserd Knollys, who signed the *Second London Confession of Faith*, had written on the subject, "Christ as a Saviour [was] made sinne, made a Curse and crucified to redeem his Elect from the Curse due to sinne."[61] He later wrote "that Christ has made full satisfaction for the sins of all who the Father had given him to redeem."[62] Such teaching informs Steele's beliefs. Further, Steele makes allusions to the Levitical law of sacrifices and its interpretation in the book of

---

sentimentalized or subjective hymns of the next century is not the point of this study, but is a question worth asking.

59. "Forasmuch as ye know that ye were not redeemed with corruptible things, *as* silver and gold, from your vain conversation *received* by tradition from your fathers; But with the precious blood of Christ, as of a lamb without blemish and without spot" (1 Pet 1:18–19).

60. See Lumpkin, *Baptist Confessions of Faith*, 265–66 and 262.

61. Hanserd Knollys, *Christ Exalted: A Lost Sinner Sought; and Saved by Christ: Gods people are an Holy people* (London: 1646), 23, cited in Howson, "Hanserd Knollys," 53. Knollys's quote echoes 2 Cor 5:21 and Gal 3:13.

62. Hanserd Knollys, *The World that now is, and the world that is to come* (London: 1681), 6–7, cited in Howson, "Hanserd Knollys," 53. Knollys was a signer of the *Second London Confession*.

Hebrews. Jesus fulfilled the law—he was perfectly obedient—and as such is the unblemished sacrifice that can fully exhaust the wrath of God due to sinners.[63] In sum, Steele teaches the doctrine of the *Second London Confession,* "The *Lord Jesus* . . . hath fully satisfied the justice of *God,* procured reconciliation, and purchased an Everlasting inheritance in the Kingdom of Heaven, for all those whom the *Father* hath given unto him."[64]

In the fifth verse Steele reflects on the vast love of God for his people that should result in the grateful and obedient lives of those who have been ransomed and redeemed. She writes, "Amazing goodness! love divine! / O may our grateful hearts adore / The matchless grace; nor yield to sin, / Nor wear its cruel fetters more!" Here Steele is reminding those who read or sing this hymn that the evangelical commitment to faith must result in a changed and holy life.

Finally, in the last stanza she pleads with God on the basis of Philippians 1:6[65] to work in the believer's life, acknowledging the remaining sinful nature that must be constantly subdued in order that the believer may live as a devoted child of God: "Dear Saviour, let thy love pursue / The glorious work it has begun: / Each secret lurking foe subdue, / And let our hearts be thine alone." Echoes of the *Second London Confession's* chapters "Of Christ the Mediator" and "Of Good Works" are heard here for they teach that the Redeemer reveals his love for his own by "governing their hearts by his word and spirit, and overcoming all their enemies by his Almighty power, and wisdom; in such manner, and ways as are most consonant to his wonderful, and unsearchable dispensation."[66] And having been justified by faith and sanctified to good works, "These good works . . . stop the mouths of the adversaries, and glorify God, whose workmanship they are, created in Christ Jesus thereunto."[67] By rendering this teaching in hymnic form Steele dispels the claim that Particular Baptists are coldly dogmatic as she prays for a piety that accords with doctrine. And in the final line there is even a subtle offer of the gospel.

In "Pardoning Love. Jer. iii. 22 and Hos. xiv. 1"[68] Steele speaks as the backslider in need of a safe place of return. Having chosen a composition by Steele written in Long Meter (88.88) to rejoice in "Redemption," Rippon

---

63. See Lumpkin, *Baptist Confessions of Faith,* 260–63.

64. Lumpkin, *Baptist Confessions of Faith,* 262.

65. Paul writes, "Being confident of this very thing, that he which hath begun a good work in you will perform *it* until the day of Christ Jesus."

66. Lumpkin, *Baptist Confessions of Faith,* 263.

67. Lumpkin, *Baptist Confessions of Faith,* 271.

68. Rippon, *Selection of Hymns,* 88, 90.

next chose one, written in quicker moving Common Meter (86.86), to allow the reader now to feel the relief as a sinner receiving "Pardon" yet again.[69] This poem/hymn invites the reader or singer, feeling and knowing the fright and guilt of sin, to inhabit the world where forgiveness reigns. As is often her custom, Steele sets the stage early with a statement of a dire and personal situation followed by verses of prayer filled with emotion. The question marks and exclamation points reveal her Romantic impulse and her desire to express the inner reality of the theme of pardon from sin. This hymn follows in full:

> How oft, alas! this wretched heart
>   Has wander'd from the Lord;
> How oft my roving thoughts depart,
>   Forgetful of his word!
>
> Yet sovereign mercy calls, *Return:*
>   Dear Lord, and may I come?
> My vile ingratitude I mourn;
>   O take the wanderer home.
>
> And canst thou, wilt thou yet forgive,
>   And bid my crimes remove?
> And shall a pardon'd rebel live
>   To speak thy wondrous love?
>
> Almighty grace, thy healing power
>   How glorious, how divine!
> That can to life and bliss restore
>   So vile a heart as mine.
>
> Thy pardoning love, so free, so sweet,
>   Dear Saviour, I adore;
> O keep me at thy sacred feet,
>   And let me rove no more.

Steele is realistic about the sinner's predicament and yet bold to approach the One she has offended. Does she admit the hesitancy of a person who knows the distance between Creator and creature? Yes.[70] But she knows that "life"

69. "Pardon" is the sub-subheading in this case. Rippon also masterfully alternates between Long Meter and Short Meter hymns with his final two hymns by Steele in this section. Steele did not use many meters, but Rippon's alternating presentation allows for different aspects of her personality to be revealed.

70. In her research, Cynthia Aalders found "hesitancy" to be a significant characteristic of Steele's hymnody. Aalders writes, "[Steele] is hesitant yet determined; she

and "bliss" await at "thy sacred feet." She had strayed from the Lord's presence and word, but had now returned. For those needing personal revival, this hymn is written from the standpoint of one who has experienced it. For those in the midst of revival and renewal of faith and life, these prayerful lyrics serve to further encourage and affirm it.

Found in the sub-subsection, Scripture Promises, "Weary Souls Invited to Rest. Matt. xi. 28" and "The Saviour's Invitation. John vii. 37" are Rippon's final two choices of Steele's hymnic corpus as it relates Scripture.[71] Each of these hymns is a clear example of the characteristic of evangelicals and their Puritan forbears, "the call to conversion . . . to turn away from their sins in repentance and to Christ in faith."[72] The gospel is offered in each hymn and sinners are called, invited, and it could even be said, pled with, to come to Christ to find "promis'd rest," "To cleanse your guilt and heal your woes," and to find "life, and health, and bliss" and "heavenly joys" among other blessings. Each hymn dwells on the promised forgiveness from both sin's guilt and penalty, and also on the rest, both temporal and eternal, found in Christ alone. The opening stanza of each illustrates the thrust of these short five-verse hymns.

"Weary Souls Invited to Rest. Matt. xi. 28"[73] begins thus,

> Come, weary souls, with sin distrest,
> Come, and accept the promis'd rest;
> The Saviour's gracious call obey,
> And cast your gloomy fears away.
>
> Oppress'd with guilt, a painful load;
> O come and spread your woes abroad;
> Divine compassion, mighty love,
> Will all the painful load remove.

Cho's study of Steele's hymns leads her to say of these verses, "For Steele, languor and weariness induced a depressive heaviness of the spirit, and only Christ could lift the soul out of such states of despondency."[74] The singing of lyrics like these by local Particular Baptist congregations afforded Steele

---

does not doubt that her praise will fail to express properly what she wishes, but she has a strong sense of her vocation." Aalders, *To Express the Ineffable*, 94. See Aalders's full discussion in chap. 3, "'How Shall These Poor Languid Powers. . . Display the Grace My Soul Adores?': Anne Steele and the Problem of Language," 66–101.

71. Rippon, *Selection of Hymns*, 134–35, and 137–38.

72. Bebbington, *Evangelicalism in Modern Britain*, 5.

73. Rippon, *Selection of Hymns*, 134. "Come unto me, all that labour and are heavy laden, and I will give you rest" (Matt 11:28).

74. Cho, "Ministry of Song," 63.

an opportunity to contribute to her denomination's path out of stagnation and even despondent decline in the case of some churches.

"The Saviour's Invitation. John vii. 37" [75] begins in verse 1 and ends with verse 5 thus,

> The Saviour calls—let every ear
>   Attend the heavenly sound;
> Ye doubting souls, dismiss your fear,
>   Hope smiles reviving round.
>
> Dear Saviour! draw reluctant hearts!
>   To thee let sinners fly,
> And take the bliss thy love imparts;
>   And drink and never die.

Having noted the free offer of the gospel found in this hymn, which is one of the few Steele hymns still sung today, Sharon James observes, "The final verse expresses equally the firm belief in divine sovereignty, and that sinners would not actually respond to the free offer unless God enabled them." [76] Steele's words clearly exhibit one of the doctrinal emphases L. G. Champion identified as being present among Particular Baptist leaders during the Second Great Awakening, "The initiative of divine grace in man's salvation revealed and operative in Christ." [77] Steele is convinced that it is God's prerogative "effectually to call by his word, and Spirit, out of that state of sin, and death, in which they are by nature, [his own] to grace and salvation by Jesus Christ." [78] This robust theology effectively undergirded the offer of the gospel. Steele's hymns thus shared with the sermons that would have accompanied the singing of them an "emphasis on the initiative of God's grace in Christ [that] led to appeals for response" to "the gospel." [79]

Finally, three aspects of the structure and content of these two hymns are worth noting with regard to the way they would have contributed to the revival in Baptist life. First, each hymn begins with a call to those "with sin distrest," to "every thirsty longing heart," to come to Christ. Then each gives compelling reasons why "here" (i.e., to Christ) is the place to come, and each hymn closes with a heartfelt prayer for Christ to bring his people home. Steele effectively calls for personal and corporate revival, as it were.

75. Rippon, *Selection of Hymns*, 137–38.

76. James, *In Trouble and in Joy*, 154. She notes that this hymn is still sung as found in *Christian Hymns*, 476.

77. Champion, "Evangelical Calvinism," 199.

78. Lumpkin, *Baptist Confessions of Faith*, 264.

79. Champion, "Evangelical Calvinism," 199.

Second, each of these hymns makes a clear offer of the gospel. It was the High Calvinism of some Particular Baptists that had contributed to a declension in their spiritual vitality. But Steele had been influenced not only by her uncle and father, but also the stream of evangelical Calvinism that flowed from Bristol Baptist College and its alumni. She is not afraid to offer the gospel in her hymns and to call those who may read or sing them to faith in Christ. Finally, Bebbington suggests that the doctrine of assurance was a doctrine closely connected to conversion among evangelicals.[80] For all her eighteenth-century feminine sensibilities and whatever plaintive note her hymns may strike for some, Steele speaks very assuredly that in Christ not only is there the removal of the penalty and guilt of sin, but that "Here springs of sacred pleasure rise / To ease your ev'ry pain; / (Immortal fountain! full supplies! / Nor shall you thirst in vain."[81] For Steele, the promises of God declared in the Scriptures indeed find in Christ their yes and Amen.

Christ and His Work

A dozen hymns written by Steele are included in this lengthy section of Rippon's hymnal concerning Christ. Her hymns appear under four of the five subheadings. She has one in the subsection Incarnation and Ministry and another in the subsection Sufferings and Death. There are then two of her hymns in the subsection concerning Christ's Exaltation and Intercession plus another eight hymns in the final subsection that considers various aspects of Christ's character, names, and roles.

Incarnation and Atonement

Steele's "The Incarnation. John i.14"[82] comes fifth in this subsection, right after a Wesley hymn, known today as "Hark, the Herald Angels Sing." In total, there are thirteen hymns in this section considering Christ's incarnation and various significant points in his life. Steele begins, "Awake, awake the sacred song / To our incarnate Lord." The hymn goes on to proclaim three points of theology in particular: Christ's incarnation—the "awful Word" which was "once in flesh arrayed," Christ's humiliation—"to dwell with sinful worms" and "with misery," and the heavenly praise such an act

80. Bebbington, *Evangelicalism in Modern Britain*, 5.

81. Rippon, *Selection of Hymns*, 137.

82. Rippon, *Selection of Hymns*, 154. "And the Word was made flesh, and dwelt among us, (and we beheld his glory, the glory as of the only begotten of the Father,) full of grace and truth" (John 1:14).

elicits—"adoring angels tun'd their songs." Aalders notes the way Steele highlights how the incarnation of the Word prepares and anticipates the glorified worship of the saints in heaven: "In Christ, God brought near, the word breaks the silence, transfiguring human praise through the experience of divine love, and creating a way for the fulfillment of human longing—the promised presence of God and the eschatological perfection of praise."[83] Steele proclaims, "With rapture then let mortal tongues / Their grateful worship pay." Steele also longs to praise God in such a way.

Steele's thoughtful and poetic consideration of Christ's incarnation and humiliation shapes four of the six verses of this hymn of lively 86.86 meter, namely, verses 1 to 4:

> . . .Let ev'ry heart, and ev'ry tongue,
>   Adore th' eternal Word.
>
> That awful Word, that sovereign power
>   By whom the worlds were made,
> (O happy morn, illustrious hour!)
>   Was once in flesh array'd!
>
> Then shone almighty power and love
>   In all their glorious forms,
> When Jesus left his throne above
>   To dwell with sinful worms.
>
> To dwell with misery below,
>   The Saviour left the skies;
> And sunk to wretchedness and woe,
>   That worthless man might rise.

Two aspects of the hymn's theology deserve to be noted. First is Steele's affirmation of the *Second London Confession's* teaching about "the *Son of God,* the second Person in the *Holy Trinity,* . . . [who took] upon him mans nature, with all the . . . common infirmities thereof, . . . and underwent the punishment due to us, which we should have born and suffered, being made *Sin* and a *Curse* for us: enduring most grievous sorrows in his Soul; and most painful sufferings in his body."[84] This doctrine of the incarnation logically leads to an understanding of the great exchange Christ came into this world to accomplish—humanity's sins exchanged for the righteousness of Christ.

---

83. Aalders, *To Express the Ineffable,* 171.

84. Lumpkin, *Baptist Confessions of Faith,* 260–61.

Second, Steele uses no less than four poetic devices in these few verses to elucidate her theology.[85] Steele uses a type of repetition with stanzas 2 and 3.[86] The first half of each verse highlights the power of the Word. The second half of each verse declares the incarnation and then builds to relay the humiliation of it for Christ. Profoundly evangelical doctrines are thus poetically translated by Steele. "Poetic devices . . . [assist Steele in communicating] the spiritual intent of the hymn."[87] Steele then thoughtfully uses the third stanza, already in parallel with the second, to form a chiasmus with the fourth stanza.[88] In this she emphasizes Christ's incarnation and resulting humiliation within the declaration of the power and love toward man that such actions represented and communicated. A third device Steele effectively utilizes in these verses, is the "using words or ideas which end one stanza as the start of the next."[89] In this case Steele is masterful. She ends verse 1 and starts verse 2 with "eternal Word" and "awful Word," respectively. Word is a biblical and theological term pregnant with meaning. Then she closes verse 3 and opens verse 4 with "to dwell." Finally, the parentheses and exclamations in the second stanza emphasize the miraculous nature of the doctrine of the incarnation proclaimed in this homiletical hymn. With "The Incarnation. John i.14," Steele vividly illustrates what Manley suggests was Rippon's guiding maxim: "He wanted a selection of hymns that people would actually want to sing because the poetry captured their religious convictions and emotions and which they could together affirm in the unifying experience of worship."[90]

Found in the subsection, The Sufferings and Death [of Christ], "A dying Saviour"[91] illustrates how Steele processed and worked through her own physical and spiritual sufferings by considering those of Christ. The hymn's six stanzas dwell on the atonement, on how Jesus procured the salvation of his people. For example, Steele prays the question, "Can I survey this scene of woe

---

85. Lovelace lists and discusses twenty-eight such devices. Lovelace, *Anatomy of Hymnody*, 94–102.

86. This particular type of repetition is known as "Tautology—Repeating the same thing in other words." Lovelace, *Anatomy of Hymnody*, 102.

87. Lovelace, *Anatomy of Hymnody*, 93.

88. "Chiasmus—The crossing of lines or clauses, from the Greek 'Chi' or 'X.'" Lovelace, *Anatomy of Hymnody*, 96.

89. Lovelace, *Anatomy of Hymnody*, 94. This is known as anadiplosis.

90. Manley, "John Rippon and Baptist Hymnody," 103.

91. Rippon, *Selection of Hymns*, 163. Interestingly, Rippon includes a superscript after the title of this hymn, referring his readers to a footnote directing them to the pages where they could find hymns on Redemption and the Lord's Supper. These sections contain two and four hymns each from Steele, respectively.

/ Where mingling grief and wonder flow / And yet my heart unmov'd remain / Insensible to love or pain?" Looking upon the sufferings of Christ brings perspective to human sufferings. Further, beginning with the first verse, this hymn in its stately 88.88 meter is practically an exposition of section 4 of the *Second London Confession's* chapter, "Of Christ the Mediator." This section teaches that Christ "did perfectly fulfill [the Law], and underwent the punishment due to us, which we should have born and suffered, being made *Sin* and a *Curse* for us; enduring most grievous sorrows in his Soul; and most painful sufferings in his body; was crucified, and died."[92]

The hymn begins, "Stretch'd on the cross the Saviour dies; / Hark! his expiring groans arise! / See, from his hands, his feet, his side, / Runs down the sacred crimson tide!" In this first verse, Steele immediately focuses on Christ's cross, suffering, and blood, painting a lyrical picture of the drama. This death is different than any other and as described by Steele seeks to evoke the visual and auditory senses. She wants the reader to see, to hear, and to feel the moment. The next two verses quickly bring to remembrance that in Christ those who were once his enemies have now been given life and cleansed from their sins, for Jesus died in the place of "rebel foes" and "traitors":

> But life attends the deathful sound,
> And flows from ev'ry bleeding wound;
> The vital stream, how free it flows
> To save and cleanse his rebel foes!
>
> To suffer in the traitor's place,
> To die for man, surprising grace!
> Yet pass rebellious angels by—
> O why for man, dear Saviour, why?

Watson notes that the second verse moves "from dramatic presentation to theological reflection."[93] Like an evangelical "crucicentric" sermon, Steele illustrates theological truth with word pictures so that the theology may be understood. For all its poetic imagery, at its core this hymn, like many of those composed by Steele, is doctrinal. The death of Christ—his Crucifixion—brings life to those who receive it. These verses must be read with a full understanding of atonement theology.[94] In these stanzas Steele has echoes of Isaiah 53, which describes the work of the Suffering Servant by whose wounds sinners are healed. What we see here is a theological description of the atonement set

92. Lumpkin, *Baptist Confessions of Faith*, 261–62.

93. Watson, *English Hymn*, 192.

94. Watson, *English Hymn*, 192.

to verse, and having used a couplet describing the grace of substitution, she humbly asks, "Why?" echoing the psalmist in Psalm 8:4.[95]

The next two verses describe atonement by substitution and depict the creation's response to it:

> And didst thou bleed?—for sinners bleed?
> And could the sun behold the deed?
> No! he withdrew his sickening ray,
> And darkness veil'd the mourning day.

> Can I survey this scene of woe,
> Where mingling grief and wonder flow,
> And yet my heart unmov'd remain,
> Insensible to love or pain?

"Did you really do this for us?" Steele asks her Lord, reminiscent of her exemplar Watts and referring to the *Second London Confession's* teaching that Christ indeed did this "for us."[96] Next, she moves to creation as she mentions the historical occurrence of the darkness that came over the land as Christ hung upon the tree. She does this with a question followed by an exclamation. These lines build toward the description of supernatural darkness. In the fifth verse Steele's "sensibility" shows as she acknowledges the juxtaposition on Calvary of "grief" and "wonder" before quickly turning to apply this to the hearts of men and women with a probing question. Her question in this verse confirms Champion's observation that the revival in Particular Baptist life was "marked not only by clarity and coherence but also by its intimate association with living experience."[97] A spiritual view of Christ's passion cannot leave a "heart unmov'd."

The hymn closes in stanza 6 by calling upon the Lord not to leave the reader/singer unchanged by this reflection, but to change his or her heart and life by the power that flows from the cross: "Come, dearest Lord! thy grace impart, / To warm this cold—this stupid heart, / Till all its powers and passions move / In melting grief and ardent love."[98] As the *Second London Confession* teaches, "To all those for whom Christ hath obtained eternal redemption" he is found to be "persuading them to believe, and obey [and] governing their

---

95. "What is man, that thou art mindful of him? and the son of man, that thou visitest him?"

96. See Lumpkin, *Baptist Confessions of Faith*, 261–62.

97. Champion, "Evangelical Calvinism," 200.

98. Aalders notes that in this hymn Steele exhibits the "oxymoronic states of sentiment" of the Age of Sensibility as described by Davie, *Eighteenth-Century Hymn in England*, 126. See Aalders, *To Express the Ineffable*, 125–27.

hearts by his word and spirit."[99] Here then Steele contains more than a hint of the evangelical characteristics of conversionism and activism in a hymn that is thorough in its description of the atonement.

Exaltation and Intercession

Steele's next two hymns are found in Rippon's subsection concerning Christ's Exaltation and Intercession and each contains a fairly comprehensive focus on those topics, respectively. The first is called "The exalted Saviour,"[100] and covers six verses. The second, covering five verses, is "The Intercession of Christ. Heb. vii. 25."[101] Due to their theological weight and evangelical hope, each of these hymns will be considered in depth below.

With "The exalted Saviour,"[102] Steele considers in the first two stanzas the theme of Christ's reign as found in title she gave the hymn as she proclaims "our exalted Saviour reigns," and exhorts humans to join the angels in praising "the Saviour's glorious name." She begins,

> Now let us raise our cheerful strains,
> And join the blissful choir above;
> There our exalted Saviour reigns,
> And there they sing his wondrous love.
>
> While seraphs tune th' immortal song,
> O, may we feel the sacred flame;
> And ev'ry heart and ev'ry tongue,
> Adore the Saviour's glorious name!

As is often the case, the first verse here serves as a sort of thesis for the hymn and also takes the reader/singer to heaven, a place upon which Steele regularly reflected. The second stanza parallels the first thematically but also builds on and intensifies the theme both theologically and experientially. Believers ought to seek to spiritually—in this life—join the praise of Christ that is always existent in heaven. Steele then prays for an experience of the holiness of heaven that will result in internal and external praise.

---

99. See Lumpkin, *Baptist Confessions of Faith*, 262–63.

100. Rippon, *Selection of Hymns*, 174.

101. Rippon, *Selection of Hymns*, 179. "Wherefore he is also able to save them to the uttermost that come unto God by him, seeing he ever liveth to make intercession for them" (Heb 7:25).

102. Rippon, *Selection of Hymns*, 174.

Displaying Steele's ability as a poet and hymn-writer, the next two verses answer the question that the first two verses beg: Why should the Savior be exalted?

> Jesus, who once upon the tree,
> In agonizing pains expir'd;
> Who died for rebels—yes, 'tis he!
> How bright! how lovely! how admir'd!

> Jesus, who died that we might live,—
> Died in the wretched traitor's place,—
> O, what returns can mortals give
> For such immeasurable grace!

Structurally, Steele uses her poetry to focus the reader's eyes directly on Jesus and his cross. Both of these middle verses begins with "Jesus, who." The stanzas use thematic parallelism for an intense subject matter. Further, she continues with "Who died"—using this phrase at the beginning of a line in stanza 3 and then in the middle of a line in stanza 4 before dropping the "who" the third time as she begins a line with "Died." By the poetic strategy of repetition Steele emphasizes those for whom Christ died, "rebels." Steele's hymns thus betray her agreement with Bebbington's analysis: "The standard view of Evangelicals was that Christ died as a substitute for sinful mankind."[103]

Steele describes humankind as "rebels" and as "wretched traitor(s)." These word pictures reveal that Anne agreed with a younger contemporary like Andrew Fuller, who portrayed humans "as transgressors of the holy, just, and good law of God," and therefore "all, by nature, children of wrath. All the threatenings of God are in full force against us, and, were we to die in that condition, we must perish everlastingly."[104] That is the bad news the gospel of Jesus Christ addresses. So Steele paints a vivid picture of Christ's suffering in the place of men and women: "Upon the tree, / In agonizing pains [he] expir'd." "Jesus . . . died that we might live." Again Steele poetically captures a key aspect of Particular Baptist theology. Fuller also wrote of the good news though. He said, "All those threatenings which belonged to him heretofore no longer stand against him; but are reckoned, by the judge of all, as having been executed on Jesus his substitute, who was 'made a curse for us.'"[105] That

---

103. Bebbington, *Evangelicalism in Modern Britain*, 15.

104. Andrew Fuller, "Justification," in *The Complete Works of the Rev. Andrew Fuller*, ed. Joseph Belcher (1845 ed.; repr. Harrisonburg, VA: Sprinkle Publications, 1988), I:279–80, cited in Nettles, "Andrew Fuller," 110.

105. Fuller, "Justification," in *Works*, 1:279–80, cited in Nettles "Andrew Fuller," 110.

is why Jesus is exalted! And that is why Steele wrote her hymns. Through lines like these "Rippon's clear evangelical concern to encourage direct appeals to the conscience of sinners" is displayed while revealing "much of the piety and theology of Baptists at this time."[106] So Steele makes the appeal to "mortals" to cultivate a grateful spirit in response to "such immeasurable grace." These stanzas showcase Steele using the craft of poetry for the purpose of piety. In the second two stanzas she offers an explanation—both graphic and theological—as to why Jesus deserves such praise. Finally, she closes with the recognition that though unable to do so as well as one ought, each person's tongue should "proclaim thy praise!"

The hymn concludes with stanzas reminiscent of the work of Isaac Watts:

> Were universal nature ours,
> And art, with all her boasted store:
> Nature and art, with all their powers,
> Would still confess the off'rer poor!
>
> Yet, tho' for bounty so divine,
> We ne'er can equal honours raise;
> Jesus, may all our hearts be thine,
> And all our tongues proclaim thy praise!

While the following issues will be addressed in a bit more detail in the next chapter, it should be noted here that Aalders finds in the fifth stanza an example of what she terms Steele's self-conscious problem with "the ability of language to offer meaningful praise to God."[107] After commenting on the obvious influence of Watts on the language of the fifth stanza, Aalders says,

> But Steele adds her own self-conscious reflection on the art of hymn-writing. Not only is nature an inadequate gift to God, but the human act of creation and its outcome—art itself—are incapable of creating an offering worthy of God's acceptance. [Such] hymns demonstrate Steele's self-conscious feelings of hesitancy with regard to her own ability to use language to articulate praise to God.[108]

106. Manley, "John Rippon and Baptist Hymnody," 105, 104.

107. Aalders, *To Express the Ineffable*, 66. See Aalders's full discussion in chap. 3, "'How Shall These Poor Languid Powers . . . Display the Grace My Soul Adores?': Anne Steele and the Problem of Language," 66–101.

108. Aalders, *To Express the Ineffable*, 96. Aalders, however, after arguing her thesis throughout the third chapter, does say in her concluding comments of the chapter, "Impeded by the frailty of human language, recognizing the languidness of her praise, awed by inexpressible matters of divine mystery, Steele concludes, . . . she cannot remain

This book argues that Steele has a strong doctrine of human depravity and divine holiness, which does entail obvious limitations to man's ability to praise God. This hymn, written for the purpose of praising "the exalted Saviour," illustrates the problem. But three things must be noted regarding this human limitation. First, Steele still composed the hymn! The perceived hesitancy notwithstanding, Steele wrote such a hymn, which Rippon's hymnal disseminated. Second, the very next stanza offers the solution—in the face of such a problem, it is the help of "Jesus" that allows "all our tongues [to] proclaim thy praise." Finally, the next hymn in Rippon, aptly titled "The Intercession of Christ. Heb. vii. 25," reveals the lasting answer to the dilemma: "Our cause can never, never fail, / For Jesus pleads, and must prevail."[109]

"The Intercession of Christ. Heb. vii. 25"[110] is a sustained treatment of the *Second London Confession's* eighth chapter, "Of Christ the Mediator."[111] While more of this chapter's ten sections could be cited, its opening statement summarizes the doctrine: "It pleased God in his eternal purpose, to chuse and ordain the *Lord Jesus* his only begotten *Son,* according to the *Covenant* made between them both, to be the *Mediator* between *God* and *Man;* the Prophet, Priest and King . . . of his Church."[112] Three lines of analysis will shed light on this hymn's facility to shape piety: structure, poetic devices, and experiential theology. First, the hymn's content is built into a chiastic structure. The first and fifth verses address Christ with one of his biblical names and describe the subjective impact in believers of Christ's heavenly intercessions for them. The second and fourth verses juxtapose the experiential element of sin and guilt for the human being before God with the spiritual vision of Jesus the priest of his people. The third verse, the centerpiece of the chiasmus, situates the sinner in the depth of despair where only the power of the Intercessor brings relief. The hymn is listed below with analysis following:

> He lives; the great Redeemer!
> (What joy the blest assurance gives!)
> And now, before his Father God,
> Pleads the full merit of his blood.

---

silent. She must make her own 'raid on the inarticulate.' She is compelled to praise God."
Aalders, *To Express the Ineffable,* 101.

109. Rippon, *Selection of Hymns,* 179.

110. Rippon, *Selection of Hymns,* 179.

111. Lumpkin, *Baptist Confessions of Faith,* 260–63.

112. Lumpkin, *Baptist Confessions of Faith,* 260.

Repeated crimes awake our fears,
And justice arm'd with frowns appears;
But in the Saviour's lovely face
Sweet mercy smiles, and all is peace.

Hence, then, ye black despairing thoughts!
Above our fears, above our faults,
His powerful intercessions rise;
And guilt recedes, and terror dies.

In ev'ry dark distressful hour,
When sin and Satan join their power,
Let this dear hope repel the dart,
That Jesus bears us on his heart.

Great Advocate, almighty Friend—
On him our humble hopes depend:
Our cause can never, never fail,
For Jesus pleads, and must prevail.[113]

As was her custom, Steele uses a number of poetic devices to lay stress on the doctrine and spiritual experience she is attempting to convey. The chiastic structure of the hymn as a whole has already been noted. A part of that structure is the parallel of the message in the first and last stanzas of the Redeemer, Advocate, and Friend pleading the cause of the sinner successfully before the Father. The first verse also utilizes exclamations and a parenthetical remark to quietly remind the reader the point of all that follows: the evangelical doctrine and accompanying experience of assurance. Verses 1 and 5 together actually demonstrate faith of assurance as preached by Steele's father, William, who proclaimed it as "faith of relyance and dependence on Christ."[114] Further Steele makes artful use of personification: "Justice arm'd with frowns appears; / But . . . Sweet mercy smiles and all is peace." But how? By a look into the "Saviour's lovely face." Here, we see that Steele was among those whose subjectivity was described by Champion thus, "Their evangelical Calvinism derived from the realities and necessities of their personal experience."[115] Steele's hymns are often a dialogue between a sinner and the Word of God, especially the doctrines of grace emphasized

113. Rippon's hymnal contains a typographical error, listing this verse as the sixth verse.

114. William Steele, sermon on Ps 39:5, n.d., Angus Library, cited in Smith, "Covenant Life of Some Eighteenth-Century Baptists in Hampshire and Wiltshire," 174.

115. Champion, "Evangelical Calvinism," 200.

within her Particular Baptist context. With poetic emphasis Steele declares, "Our cause can never, never fail, / For Jesus pleads and must prevail."[116] Like the composer of the forty-second and forty-third psalms, Steele speaks to herself about God's truth. In a hymn like this one, Steele's poetic facility draws the reader in to do the same. Thus Steele invites those who sing her hymns to participate in the evangelical understanding that "the reality of faith – as opposed to belief about it – is the sole condition of acceptance by God."[117] Through lively faith the experience is genuine: "His powerful intercession rise; / And guilt recedes, and terror dies."

But this hymn also describes Steele's theological understanding of and spiritual experience resulting from the heavenly session of Christ. The *Second London Confession* states, "The *Lord Jesus* . . . sitteth at the right hand of *his Father*, making intercession; . . . making intercession for them.[118]" Seeing Jesus with the eyes faith, Steele indeed believed that "His powerful intercessions rise; . . . and must prevail." Steele practices her piety through verse. "Sin and Satan join their power" to inflict "guilt" and "terror" and "fears"[119] upon the redeemed. But through verse, Steele, like the *Confession*, owns that Christ, through his "Priestly office" serves "to reconcile us, and present us acceptable unto God and in his "Kingly office" to bring "security from our spiritual adversaries."[120]

Characters of Christ

Rippon included eight of Steele's hymns in the subsection called Characters and Representations of Christ Placed Alphabetically.[121] These hymns are alphabetized according to the name of the hymn, each of which describes a character or representation of Christ in Scripture. Steele has the first hymn in the subsection: "Advocate. 1 John ii. 1."[122] As its title and reference suggest, this hymn covers basically the same material as the last hymn

116. The repetition of never, never is an example of epizeuxis, or "immediate repetition of a word of phrase in the same line." Lovelace, *Anatomy of Hymnody*, 99.

117. Bebbington, *Evangelicalism in Modern Britain*, 22.

118. Lumpkin, *Baptist Confessions of Faith*, 262.

119. Rippon, *Selection of Hymns*, 179.

120. Lumpkin, *Baptist Confessions of Faith*, 263.

121. Rippon, *Selection of Hymns*, 183.

122. Rippon, *Selection of Hymns*, 183–84. Steele's title was "Breathing After God." She did not include a Scripture reference for this hymn. Rippon added 1 John 2:1: "My little children, these things I write unto you, that ye sin not. And if any man sin, we have an advocate with the Father, Jesus Christ the righteous."

assessed.[123] At the midpoint in the third stanza, it is again with the eye of faith that one looks to Jesus to receive the benefit of his heavenly session: "Look up, my soul, with cheerful eye, / See where the great Redeemer stands, / The glorious Advocate on high, / With precious incense in his hands." In the other hymn we considered Jesus was "Advocate" and "Friend"; here he is "Advocate" and "Redeemer." Addressing the persons of the Godhead by their biblical names was habitual in Steele's poetry.

There is a unique contribution, however, that this hymn makes to our consideration of Steele's piety. Steele asks in this hymn, "Are these weak breathings of desire / Too languid to ascend the skies?/ . . . / Teach my weak heart, O gracious Lord! / With stronger faith to call thee mine." She knows her own spiritual weaknesses. Steele's contemporary, the Welsh Baptist pastor, Benjamin Francis, similarly once wrote to a friend, "How languid my faith, my hope, my love! How cold and formal am I in secret Devotions!"[124] The corporate singing of hymns like this one offered an antidote to such admissions. It should also be noted that the context of Francis's words was prayer, a hallmark of Baptist spirituality.[125] In the hymn Steele sings of the hope of prayer through the mediation of Christ: "He sweetens every humble groan, / He recommends each broken prayer." This hymn also reveals that Steele shared with some of her Puritan forebears a proneness to doubt and introspection. Thus, she opens this hymn, "Where is my God? does he retire / Beyond the reach of humble sighs?" However, with fellow "Evangelicals [she] turned from . . . despondency to a calmer, sunnier devotional life"[126]— and so she finishes in joy: "Bid me pronounce the blissful word / *My Father, God*, with joy divine." Knowing the character of Christ made such assurance during a time of doubt possible.

Steele's second entry in the subsection Characters of Christ is "Our Example. John xiii. 15."[127] Rippon added the Scripture reference to the title, which reads, "For I have given you an example, that ye should do as I have done to you." Though the context of the verse is the service of foot-washing Jesus offered to his disciples on the night in which he was betrayed, Steele's hymn is an exhortation to others to be guided by the example of Jesus in all aspects of their human relationships. It is critical to note that Steele does not

123. The next chapter lists this hymn in full as published by Rippon.

124. "Queries and Solutions," vol. 1, Remarks on [Thomas'] answer to Query 48, cited in Haykin, "Draw Nigh unto My Soul," 68.

125. See Haykin, "Draw Nigh unto My Soul," 66–68 and the discussion below on "Watchfulness and Prayer. Matt. xxvi. 41."

126. Bebbington, *Evangelicalism in Modern Britain*, 47.

127. Rippon, *Selection of Hymns*, 193. Steele's title was "The example of Christ" and did not include a Scripture reference.

think such a life can be lived by human willpower alone, for in the last verse Steele offers a prayer to Jesus himself to make it so: "Make us, by thy transforming grace, / Dear Saviour, daily more like thee!"

The first three verses are a call for the believer to live by way of the example of the peace and self-control of Christ, particularly "Whene'er the angry passions rise, / And tempt our thoughts or tongues to strife, / To Jesus let us lift our eyes, / Bright pattern of the Christian life."[128] An evangelical Christian appropriately looks to Jesus to find out how to live, especially in life's difficulties. Steele also grounds her creative lyrics in the words of Scripture, suggesting that the content of the good news should guide Christian conduct in all circumstances: "And is the Gospel peace and love? / Such let our conversation be; / The serpent blended with the dove, / Wisdom and meek simplicity."[129] Steele's exhortation is derived from Matthew 10:16, where in sending out his disciples, Jesus said, "Behold, I send you forth as sheep in the midst of wolves: be ye therefore wise as serpents, and simple as doves."

The center of the seven-stanza hymn, verse 4, establishes the disciple's true hope in following the example of Christ, namely, his active righteousness: "To do his heavenly Father's will / Was his employment and delight; / Humility and holy zeal / Shone thro' his life divinely bright!" This hymn on sanctification is based first on Steele's understanding of the act of justification by faith. According to the *Confession*, faith receives and rests "on Christ, and his Righteousness" who by his "active obedience unto the whole Law, and passive obedience in his death" ". . . did fully discharge the debt of all those that are justified."[130] Of course justification logically leads to sanctification, which is a work of the Spirit in the redeemed, but still tempted, believer. Steele continues, "How frail! how apt to turn aside! / Lord, we depend upon thy care, / And ask thy Spirit for our guide." One is not alone in seeking to emulate Christ taught the *Confession*: "By his word and *Spirit* dwelling in them; . . . through the continual supply of the strength from the sanctifying *Spirit* of *Christ* . . . the Saints grow in Grace."[131] In this case Steele illuminates Champion's third emphasis found in evangelical Calvinism, "The responsibility of every believer to order his whole life according to the will of God made known by the Spirit through the Scripture."[132] And so following the example

128. Verse 2.

129. Verse 1.

130. Lumpkin, *Baptist Confessions of Faith*, 266.

131. Lumpkin, *Baptist Confessions of Faith*, 268.

132. Champion, "Evangelical Calvinism," 199.

of Christ means knowing him and his life and teaching through Scripture while pleading for the help of his Spirit and "transforming grace."

"King of Saints"[133] is one of Steele's many hymns that, in the words of James, expresses "devotion to Christ."[134] In this case, Steele takes the doctrine of the kingship of Christ as a vehicle for the rehearsal of the call of the Christian to worship and evangelism, which eventually leads to the eschatological "Glorious day! . . . When heaven and earth shall . . . celebrate thy praise." Hymns like this offer evidence for the evangelistic force that flows from the doctrines of grace properly expounded. The second and third stanzas suggest that certain connection between doxology and evangelistic outreach:

> Behold your King, your saviour, crown'd
>   With glories all divine;
> And tell the wond'ring nations round
>   How bright these glories shine.
>
> Infinite power, and boundless grace,
>   In him unite their rays:
> You, that have e'er beheld his face,
>   Can you forbear his praise?

Further, here Steele exemplifies in verse Champion's fourth emphasis upon which he found evangelical Calvinism in the eighteenth century to rest. Champion proposed that these Particular Baptists believed in "the obligation of all believers to bring the gospel to all men everywhere."[135] Steele fulfilled such obligation through song.

"Life of the Soul. John xiv. 19,"[136] is a hymn that declares that for the Christian, Jesus is himself the life of his or her soul.[137] This hymn reveals the theological cohesion shown between Steele's hymn and the *Second London Confession*. For example, the *Confession* describes Christ as Mediator:

> To all those for whom Christ hath obtained eternal redemption,
> he doth certainly, and effectually apply, and communicate the

---

133. Rippon, *Selection of Hymns*, 205, 207. Watson uses this hymn as an example of the influence of Watts upon Steele. He sees in this hymn an illustration of not only "her echoing of his phrases, but also her ability to accommodate the sense to the line." Watson, *English Hymn*, 197.

134. James, *In Trouble and in Joy*, 153.

135. Champion, "Evangelical Calvinism," 199.

136. Rippon, *Selection of Hymns*, 213. John 14:19 reads, "Yet a little while, and the world seeth me no more; but ye see me: because I live, ye shall live also."

137. Steele's title was "Christ the Life of the Soul. John xiv. 19."

same; making intercession for them, uniting them to himself by his spirit, revealing unto them, in and by the word, the mystery of salvation; perswading them to believe, and obey; governing their hearts by his word and spirit, and overcoming all their enemies by his Almighty power and wisdom.[138]

The quote is lengthy, but its doctrine is found poetically expressed throughout this hymn.

Commenting on this hymn, Aalders says, echoing Watson, that Steele "again relies on personal experience, beginning her hymn in that time 'When sins and fears prevailing rise, / And fainting hope almost expires.'"[139] Steele's experience, however, is informed by her theology, and so she continues by going to the only place one can in such a state: "Jesus, to thee I lift mine eyes— / To thee I breathe my soul's desires." Thus concludes the first verse. She goes to the one whom the *Confession* calls the "Mediator between God and man, . . . Christ, who is the Prophet, Priest, and King of the Church of God."[140] She knew upon whom to call in a state of spiritual distress, and in the hymn immediately does so.

And, like the quote above from the *Confession* teaches, Steele expresses the spiritual experience of various aspects of the work of Christ on her behalf, relying on both the knowledge that his word is true and sufficient for salvation and the faith that he is indeed the governor of her life:

> Art thou not mine, my living Lord?
> And can my hope—my comfort die,
> Fix'd on the everlasting word,
> That word which built the earth and sky?
>
> If my immortal Saviour lives,
> Then my immortal life is sure;
> His word a firm foundation gives;
> Here let me build, and rest secure.

But she also knows the certainty of what Christ has done for those for whom he died, the spiritual though very personal union she has with Jesus through

---

138. Lumpkin, *Baptist Confessions of Faith*, 262–63. Aalders, however, finds in this hymn an illustration of her thesis that Steele finds herself sometimes "incapable of addressing God using speech" and so "she continues to approach him in silence." Aalders, *To Express the Ineffable*, 99. In it Aalders also finds an example of Steele's "plaintive" tone and style reflected by "her experience of God's silence in the face of . . . suffering." Aalders, *To Express the Ineffable*, 128–29. Aalders's analysis of this hymn will be considered in the next chapter.

139. Aalders, *To Express the Ineffable*, 129. See also Watson, *English Hymn*, 195.

140. Lumpkin, *Baptist Confessions of Faith*, 263.

his Spirit, and the reality of his power and wisdom to overcome her enemies, even that last and most seemingly powerful enemy, death:

> Here let my faith unshaken dwell;
> Immoveable the promise stands;
> Not all the powers of earth or hell
> Can e'er dissolve the sacred bands.

> Here, O my soul, thy trust repose!
> If Jesus is for ever mine,
> Not death itself, that last of foes,
> Shall break a union so divine.

To lift the spirit of the struggling saint, Steele provides "the rich music of the gospel by which Christians of all ages have been inspired."[141]

A famous parable of Jesus related how a merchant, who, "when he had found one pearl of great price, went and sold all that he had, and bought it" (Matt 13:46). Steele, and likewise Rippon, declared Christ to be such. Steele's next hymn in the collection is called "Pearl of Great Price. Matt. xiii. 46."[142] The hymn contains six stanzas of sustained treatment of the contrast between "Ye glittering toys of earth . . . unworthy of my cares" and "A treasure all divine . . . Jesus, in thee . . . Wealth, honour, pleasure meet." Jesus, "The Pearl of Price immense!" is proclaimed against the backdrop "of earth's vain treasures [that] all depart." Expressing what John Julian calls her "intense personal devotion to the Lord Jesus,"[143] Steele concludes the hymn, "Dear Sovereign of my soul's desires, / Thy love is bliss divine; / Accept the wish *that* love inspires, / And bid me call thee mine."

The very next hymn in Rippon's hymnal proclaims both in content and title that Jesus is "Physician of Souls. Jeremiah viii. 22."[144] As with many of her hymns, Steele sticks closely to the imagery and teaching of the biblical passage accompanying her title. In Jeremiah 8:22, the prophet writes, "*Is there* no balm in Gilead; *is there* no physician there? why then is not the health of the daughter of my people recovered?" While Steele did write hymns that concerned physical health, though always with a view to its effect on spiritual health, this hymn is an exposition of sin's nature and effect: "Deep are the wounds which sin has made, / Where shall the sinner find a cure? / . . . Sin, like a raging fever, reigns / . . . The dire contagion fills the veins / And spreads its poison to the heart." Cho comments, "The

141. Champion, "Evangelical Calvinism," 207.

142. Rippon, *Selection of Hymns*, 219.

143. Julian, *Dictionary of Hymnology*, 2:1089.

144. Rippon, *Selection of Hymns*, 221. Steele's original title began with "Christ the."

conceit of sin as disease potently expresses the debilitating nature of sin on the health of the soul."[145] Steele, however, includes a clear view to the "sovereign cure": "The Saviour's dying blood . . . A cordial for the fainting heart, / A balm for ev'ry painful wound." "Where shall the sinner find a cure?" she asks. According to Steele, not in this world. She states emphatically and poetically, "In vain, alas! is Nature's aid; / The work exceeds all Nature's power."[146] And so Aalders argues that in this hymn "Steele uses the image of God as physician to convey an evangelical message of the need for salvation."[147] To the individual people of the world, each ruined by sin, Steele declares, "There is a great Physician near: look up, O fainting soul, and live." Like the Scripture which shapes Steele's verse, sin's "pointed dart" does not have the last word because "in the Saviour's dying blood, / Life, health, and bliss abundant flow."

Rippon gave the next hymn of Steele he included in his *Selection of Hymns* the title "Saviour—the only One. Acts iv. 12," adding the Scripture reference as well.[148] Echoing many of the themes of the other hymns of Steele in this subsection—the present joy that can be found in Christ ("joys divine . . . happiness"), the effects of the forgiveness of Christ ("Jesus . . . can save us from eternal woe"), and the eschatological victory and destination for those in Christ ("The blissful plains . . . where perfect joy for ever reigns")—this hymn also advances Steele's Christology as set forth in Rippon. In this hymn Steele highlights both the uniqueness of Christ and anticipates some of the hymns of the next section as she relates the work of the Holy Spirit to life in Christ. The second half of verse 1 and the first half of verse 3 are poetic statements of Steele's understanding of Jesus's teaching in John 14:6 and Acts 4:12. She writes, "Jesus, no other name but thine, / Can save us from eternal woe. / . . . No other name will heav'n approve: / Thou art the true, the living way." And so to follow "the living way" and "the heavenly path" Steele offers the petition, "O let thy Spirit, gracious Guide! / Direct our steps, and cheer our heart." Again, from John 14, this time verses 16 and 17, Steele presents her understanding of the work of the Spirit as Comforter and Spirit of Truth. Her Trinitarian theology ever shines as she acknowledges that through Jesus's name and the guiding of the Spirit is "the way to happiness and God."

145. Cho, "'Ministry of Song,'" 65.

146. Steele uses the poetic device here known as antanaclasis, "repetition with a slight difference in meaning, or a change in direction of thought." Lovelace, *Anatomy of Hymnody*, 95–96.

147. Aalders, *To Express the Ineffable*, 169n114.

148. Rippon, *Selection of Hymns*, 230. Steele's chosen title was "Christ the way to heaven." See Steele, *Works*, 1:68.

Appropriately enough Steele's eighth and final entry regarding the Characters of Christ is her paraphrase of the first three verses of Psalm 23. Rippon shortened Steele's original title of "The heavenly shepherd" to "Shepherd. Psalm xxiii. 1–3."[149] It is a fitting conclusion to the contributions of Steele to the hymns on Christ. There is an obvious interpretation being made by Rippon that this most famous of psalms is fulfilled by Christ. Steele, in fact, gives Rippon opportunity for his interpretation with her own Watts-like paraphrase. Foreshadowing where she is going, she begins in the first verse, "While my Redeemer's near, / My shepherd and my guide," before closing in the sixth and last, "Jesus, I plead thy gracious name, / For all my hopes are there." Steele's sense of the intimate care received from the Shepherd shows her embodiment of Karen Smith's description of Particular Baptist devotional life: "It involved *real sharing* in Christ."[150]

Written in Short Meter (66.86), Steele showcases her craft as she must briefly and crisply state her case in the first line and slowly build upon the theme in the second line before expanding in the third line of eight syllables before closing sharply with the fourth line. Steele begins, "While my Redeemer's near, / My shepherd and my guide, / I bid farewell to anxious fear, / My wants are all supplied." Having described "ever-fragrant meads" and "cool waters" in the second two verses, in the fourth she continues, "Here let my spirit rest; / How sweet a lot is mine! / With pleasure, food, and safety blest; / Beneficience divine!" Lovelace suggests that this meter allows for both an exhorting and an ecstatic nature to coexist, the "abrupt, direct opening line attracts attention," the author can "reinforce [his message] in the second, then develop it further in the last fourteen syllables."[151] In a paraphrase of such a familiar passage, Steele excels artistically as she brings out the delight the "unworthy" sheep takes in the Shepherd's "protecting care." This poetic paraphrase exudes with the rejuvenating life of the "Redeemer" and "Dear Shepherd" that "Jesus" brought to the Particular Baptists.

Summary

In a claim that Aalders finds remarkable, Hoxie Neale Fairchild said, "It would be difficult to find a writer of the period whose thought is more consistently Christ-centered than Theodosia's."[152] Well, these twelve hymns of Steele in this

---

149. Rippon, *Selection of Hymns*, 255–56.

150. Smith, "Covenant Life of Some Eighteenth-Century Baptists," 183.

151. Lovelace, *Anatomy of Hymnody*, 41–42.

152. Hoxie Neale Fairchild, *Religious Trends in English Poetry* (New York, 1942), 2:114, cited in Aalders, *To Express the Ineffable*, 168.

larger section on Christ collectively take the reader and singer chronologically through Christ's life as they reveal Steele's Christology, that is, both her doctrine of the person and work of Christ and her experience according to her belief in him. Further, they are clearly built upon the words of Scripture in the sense of their content, but also often in their very imagery. In these prayerful hymns based on the character and work of Christ for sinful people, Steele echoes the sentiments of her younger contemporary, pastor Benjamin Francis, as he also reflected on his relationship with Christ,

> In a nearness to God that is inexpressible, thro the Mediator, and in the enjoyment of God's favour and perfections, yielding nourishing satisfactions in God, as the souls full, everlasting portion and felicity. This enjoyment overwhelms the soul with wonder, glory, joy and triumph: it enflames it with vehement love to God and ardent wishes after his blissful [sic] presence in the heavenly world.[153]

Steele's "lived faith" was at the same time planted on this earth upon which the Word was made flesh and also uplifted to the heavenly places in Christ Jesus her Lord.

The Holy Spirit and His Work

Five hymns from the pen of Anne Steele are included in the section The Holy Spirit. The first, "The Influences of the Spirit experienced. John xiv. 16, 17,"[154] is in the subsection, his Influence. The other four hymns are found in the respective subsections concerning the graces of the Spirit: Hope, Humility, Repentance, and Resignation. Four more hymns by Steele are included in the next section concerning the Christian Life, which for the Christian is life under the influence of the Holy Spirit. Steele's hymns tend to support Particular Baptist pastor John Sutcliff's claim, "The outpouring of the divine Spirit . . . is the grand promise of the New Testament . . . His influences are the soul, the great animating soul of all religion."[155] A consideration of the hymns of Steele that Rippon chose to highlight the work of the Holy Spirit in the life of the Christian will illustrate this connection.

153. Benjamin Francis, "Queries and Solutions" (MS G.98.5; Bristol Baptist College Library, Bristol, England), vol. 1, Remarks on Query 55, cited in Haykin, "Draw Nigh unto My Soul," 68.

154. Rippon, *Selection of Hymns*, 255–56. Rippon slightly modified Steele's title, "The Influences of the Spirit of God in the Heart." See Steele, *Works*, 1:74.

155. John Sutcliff, *Jealousy for the Lord of Hosts illustrated* (London: W. Button, 1791), 12, cited in Haykin, "Habitation of God, Through the Spirit," 310.

The Influences and Graces of the Holy Spirit

"The Influences of the Spirit experienced. John xiv. 16, 17,"[156] one of the first hymns of the section, The Holy Spirit, is in the subsection, his Influence. This hymn is one that showcases how Steele's hymnody illustrates Champion's proposition, "Evangelical Calvinism provided a balanced and coherent theological system firmly rooted in Scripture."[157] There was a connection between the lived piety of the Particular Baptists and the Spirit's life-giving influence upon them. To illustrate, the hymn's first two stanzas display a humble approach to the Spirit, acknowledging his deity as the third person of the Trinity. They also deal with the tension of a Holy God dwelling spiritually within a sinful human being, who has both a sinful nature and who also experiences the internal consequences of individual sins:

> Dear Lord! and shall thy Spirit rest
> In such a wretched heart as mine?
> Unworthy dwelling! glorious guest!
> Favour astonishing, divine!

> When sin prevails, and gloomy fear,
> And hope almost expires in night,
> Lord, can thy Spirit then be here—
> Great spring of comfort, life, and light?

Having shown an understanding of her sinful nature and of the person and work of the Holy Spirit, Steele connects her experience to his work in the third stanza: "Sure the blest Comforter is nigh! / 'Tis he sustains my fainting heart; / Else would my hopes for ever die, / And ev'ry cheering ray depart." Particular Baptists were no strangers to spiritual struggles, and like John Bunyan in his *Grace Abounding to the Chief of Sinners* or John Wesley in his diary, they wrote of them in personal journals. Champion explains,

> It was this living, personal experience which required a theological explication different from that offered by the form of [High] Calvinism which [some] had known in their youth. So their evangelical Calvinism derived from the realities and necessities of their personal experience. This experience brought to life the word of Scripture, then the authority of Scripture confirmed

---

156. Rippon, *Selection of Hymns*, 255–56. Steele's title was slightly different: "The Influences of the Spirit of God in the Heart. John xiv. 16, 17." See Steele, *Works*, 1:74–75.

157. Champion, "Evangelical Calvinism," 201.

the authenticity of experience. On this foundation rose the new theological structure. From these roots grew a living tree.[158]

And so in the next three stanzas Steele relates her experience to the word ("promise") and authority ("Almighty") of Scripture (stanzas 4 and 6) while acknowledging the power of the Spirit of adoption to give her the assurance of her relationship to Christ (stanza 5):

> When some kind promise glads my soul,
> Do I not find his healing voice
> The tempest of my fears controul,
> And bid my drooping powers rejoice?
>
> Whene'er to call the Saviour mine,
> With ardent wish my heart aspires;
> Can it be less than power divine
> Which animates these strong desires?
>
> What less than thy Almighty word
> Can raise my heart from earth and dust,
> And bid me cleave to thee, my Lord,
> My life, my treasure, and my trust?

The sixth stanza's description uses similar imagery as Champion uses above, even if with a slightly different metaphor, to explain (by way of a prayer) the power of the Word of God ("What less than thy Almighty word") to pick up the despondent and sinful child of God ("Can raise my heart from earth and dust"), to place her upon the lap of her Heavenly Father ("And bid me cleave to thee, my Lord"), and to confirm in her heart the multifaceted role he assumes for her ("My life, my treasure, and my trust?").

Steele completes her prayer by confessing to God in the seventh stanza by way of a question that only God can confirm her sense of peace in him such that she can proclaim, "I love my God, and taste his grace." And the final stanza is an emphatic supplication based on her understanding of the Spirit's function within the Godhead: "Let thy kind Spirit in my heart / For ever dwell, O God of love! / And light and heav'nly peace impart,— / Sweet earnest of the joys above." Prayer was regarded by the Particular Baptists as a means of grace. The Spirit used it to draw God's people to himself. Singing such a prayer as this hymn sincerely to God and reading it meditatively contributed to the renewed life the congregations experienced who used Rippon's hymnal in worship and in family and personal devotions. Steele wrote and prayed of the personal experience of God's grace. As Champion

158. Champion, "Evangelical Calvinism," 200.

explains it, "The evangelical Calvinism [of which this hymn is an example] was marked not only by clarity and coherence but also by its intimate association with living experience."[159]

The first of Steele's four hymns concerning the graces of the Holy Spirit—in this case, hope—is a hymn called "Hope encouraged by a View of the Divine Perfections. 1 Sam. xxx.6."[160] The verse on which Steele based this hymn is instructive to have in mind as the hymn is examined. According to 1 Samuel 30, King David, having come upon a city burned to the ground and finding that all the women of the city had been carried away as prisoners, "was greatly distressed; for the people spake of stoning him, because the soul of all the people was grieved, every man for his sons and for his daughters: but David encouraged himself in the LORD his God." The biblical passage spoke of distress and despondency. Steele herself knew grief and doubt, facing such affliction not only by praying to God, but by speaking to her own soul based on the promises of God. Along with all the saints of all the ages before and after her who would suffer the trials of faith, Steele asks and hopes and prays. She begins this hymn of six stanzas with two pairs of related questions: "Why sinks my weak desponding mind? / Why heaves my heart the anxious sigh? / Can sovereign goodness be unkind? / Am I not safe if God is nigh?" Thus she emphatically admits the condition in which a believer may find himself or herself: dejected and disquieted. But she also more than hints at the answer to the "Why?" by asking the questions of faith. Yet, she does not immediately quit the "desponding mind" and "anxious sighs."

The next two and a half stanzas follow with poetic statements of theology—her doctrine of God—that alternate between the more abstract and the very personal:

> He holds all nature in his hand—
> That gracious hand on which I live,
> Doth life, and time, and death command,
> And has immortal joys to give.

> 'Tis he supports this fainting frame;
> On him alone my hopes recline;
> The wondrous glories of his name,
> How wide they spread, how bright they shine!

159. Champion, "Evangelical Calvinism," 198.

160. Rippon, *Selection of Hymns*, 286. Rippon slightly modified Steele's title: "Hope Encouraged in the Contemplation of the Divine Perfections." Steele chose the Scripture reference. Steele, *Works*, 1:93–94.

> Infinite wisdom! boundless power!
> Unchanging faithfulness and love! . . .

Steele recognizes both the transcendence and the immanence of God, and how these somewhat contrasting attributes operate in tandem to encourage the believer in the Lord. Steele was obviously in harmony with the *Confession* in these beliefs,[161] and also with other Particular Baptists. Pastor and historian Joseph Ivimey wrote in his diary in 1805, during the time of the regular use of Rippon's ministry and hymnal, "When I have been cast down, Thou hast lifted me up; when perplexed, Thou hast preserved me from despair. . . . O Lord, . . . Oh, forgive the want of zeal, of application, and spirituality of mind, which I have . . . felt."[162] Evangelical Calvinistic Baptist theology was grounded on the belief in and experience of grace, so that one of its poets could say and pray for all,

> . . . Here let me trust, while I adore,
> Nor from my refuge e'er remove.
>
> My God, if thou art mine indeed,
> Then have I all my heart can crave;
> A present help in time of need;
> Still kind to hear, and strong to save.
>
> Forgive my doubts, O gracious Lord!
> And ease the sorrows of my breast;
> Speak to my heart the healing word,
> That thou art mine—and I am blest.

The last part of the hymn is a sustained prayer to God based on his attributes earlier confessed. Steele dips here into a vast theological reservoir of belief and experience. She remembers her adoption, "My God, if thou art mine indeed, / . . . That thou art mine—and I am blest." Steele knows that she is a member of those who have "been taken into the number, and enjoy the Liberties, and privileges of Children of *God*; have his name put upon them, receive the *Spirit of Adoption*."[163] She clings to this in her time of need. Further, she reflects on and pleads based upon "the glory of God in his Attributes" that are "revealed in the *Word* . . . and the Power and fullness of the

---

161. See, for example, chap. 2, "Of God and the Holy Trinity," and chap. 8, "Of Christ the Mediator," in Lumpkin, *Baptist Confessions of Faith*, 252–53 and 260–63.

162. Joseph Ivimey, quoted in George Pritchard, *Memoir of the Life and Writings of the Rev. Joseph Ivimey, Late Pastor of the Church in Eagle Street, London* (London: G. Wightman, 1835), 61, cited in Doggett, "Joseph Ivimey," 120.

163. Lumpkin, *Baptist Confessions of Faith*, 267.

Holy Spirit in his Workings and Operations; and so [a Christian] is enabled to cast his Soul upon the truth thus believed."[164] For a covenant community with a theological tradition often thought arid, Steele makes a request to God for the Holy Spirit to "Speak to my heart the healing word." Now while she would have intended this "word" to be in line with the Scripture, it does not take away from the reality of the request. Such a petition is for Steele an illustration of the editor's concern for his hymnal, as Manley explains, "Rippon always emphasized, as did other evangelicals of this period, the work of the Holy Spirit."[165] The Holy Spirit is the divine Comforter for the Christian—and worthy of prayer of both petition and praise.

For the purpose of singing in order to cultivate the Christian grace of humility, Rippon included Steele's hymn, "Happy Poverty; or, the Poor in Spirit Blessed. Matt. v. 3" in his hymnal.[166] Rippon included all eight of Steele's verses in this hymn and kept her title fully intact.[167] The Sermon on the Mount, for which the Beatitudes are a preamble, is a sermon about the way of life in the Kingdom of God. Steele bases this hymn on the beatitude of the humble, or "poor in spirit." Steele uses a few poetic devices to drive home her own view of this kingdom in verses 4 and 5. She begins each verse with the same words—"A kingdom"—and thus defines in parallel two important aspects of the kingdom in each verse, respectively.[168] Having discussed the vanity of "the sons of wealth and pride" of the earth, she closes the third verse by saying of these "despisers" and "boasters," "Trifles are *theirs*, a kingdom *yours*:" and continues,

> A kingdom of immense delight,
> Where health and peace and joy unite,
> Where undeclining pleasures rise,
> And ev'ry wish hath full supplies:[169]
>
> A kingdom which can ne'er decay,
> While time sweeps earthly thrones away;

164. Lumpkin, *Baptist Confessions of Faith*, 269.

165. Manley, "John Rippon and Baptist Hymnody," 105.

166. Rippon, *Selection of Hymns*, 287. "Blessed *are* the poor in spirit: for they shall be comforted" (Matt 5:3).

167. He did, however, include brackets around verses 6 and 8, indicating that they might be left out in the singing of the hymn corporately without losing its basic sense.

168. "Repetition of a word at the start of successive lines" is anaphora. Further, Steele also ends verse 3 as she starts verse 4, thus also using the device known as anadiplosis. Lovelace, *Anatomy of Hymnody*, 94–95.

169. Broome notes that in verse 4 there is "another aspect of Watts' art" namely, "the accumulation of words." Broome, *Bruised Reed*, 168.

> The state, which power and truth sustain,
> Unmov'd for ever must remain.

For a Baptist, the earthly manifestation of this humble kingdom of shalom ("health and peace and joy") and of an abiding character ("which can ne'er decay") was in the covenant community of the local congregation or "gathered church." Steele's hymn offers a glimpse of the "now" of the kingdom as described by Smith in her discussion of the church covenant agreement: "As a 'gathered community' of saints, they joined together by mutual agreement, pledging their desire to live in the world and, yet, to be not of the world."[170] Only the Holy Spirit could bring forth a kingdom of such character.

With "Penitence and Hope"[171] the spiritual virtue of repentance is put to verse by Steele. Centering on the doctrine of repentance, its roots and fruits from first to last, this hymn demonstrates Broome's statement, "Besides a deep knowledge of Christ Anne had that deep knowledge of sin, which must precede it."[172] She also understood, as the *Confession* teaches, that "saving Repentance is an evangelical grace."[173] And so she prays thus in verses 1 and 4,

> Dear Saviour, when my thoughts recall
>   The wonders of thy grace,
> Low at thy feet asham'd I fall,
>   And hide this wretched face.
>
> But he, for his own mercy's sake,
>   My wand'ring soul restores:
> He bids the mourning heart partake
>   The pardon it implores.

Steele shows an intimate sense of the experience of the evangelical Calvinistic understanding that "the divine initiative in showing mercy to sinful man places upon all the obligation to receive the mercy."[174] She closes this hymn with the Calvinistic juxtaposition of the humility of the sinner and of the Saviour: "Then shall the mourner at thy feet / Rejoice to seek thy face: / And grateful own how kind, how sweet / Thy condescending grace."

170. Smith, "Covenant Life of Some Eighteenth-Century Baptists," 168.

171. Rippon, *Selection of Hymns*, 328, 330.

172. Broome, *Bruised Reed*, 170.

173. Lumpkin, *Baptist Confessions of Faith*, 270.

174. Champion, "Evangelical Calvinism," 199.

Finally, with his final selection by Steele regarding the graces of the Spirit, Rippon included her hymn, "Filial Submission. Heb. xii. 7."[175] The passage included in the title of this hymn reads, "If ye endure chastening, God dealeth with you as with sons; for what son is he whom the father chasteneth not?" Steele wrote often of her desire to receive the will of God through the work of his Spirit and to be content with his wise oversight of her life. "I would submit to all thy will," she writes. Ivimey also wrote on the theme of being submissive to God's will: "O Lord, grant me resignation to Thy heavenly will. Oh! how my heart has been lacerated with anguish . . . May this affliction work the peaceable fruits of righteousness; for at present 'tis very grievous. O Thou gracious God, assist me to devote myself anew to Thy service."[176] The four verses of "Filial Submission" read,

> And can my heart aspire so high,
>   To say, *My Father, God!*
> LORD! at thy feet I fain would lie,
>   And learn to kiss the rod.
>
> I would submit to all thy will,
>   For thou art good and wise;
> Let ev'ry anxious thought be still,
>   Nor one faint murmur rise.
>
> Thy love can cheer the darksome gloom,
>   And bid me wait serene
> Till hopes and joys immortal bloom,
>   And brighten all the scene.
>
> *My Father*—O permit my heart
>   To plead her humble claim,
> And ask the bliss those words impart,
>   In my Redeemer's name.

Steele loved her father William, who was also her pastor. She cared for him the nine years after the death of his wife, once writing to a relative that her work during that time was "to soothe a parent's care / In life's decline, his every grief to share, / By every act of cheerful duty prove / Sincerest gratitude and filial love. / . . . my ardent prayer, / . . . may heaven indulgent spare / His valued life!"[177] Noting that in the second verse of this hymn, "She promises

---

175. Rippon, *Selection of Hymns*, 335.

176. Ivimey, quoted in Pritchard, *Memoir of the Life and Writings of the Rev. Joseph Ivimey*, 63 cited in Doggett, "Joseph Ivimey," 120.

177. Steele, *Works*, 2:194.

filial duty to God," Cho suggests, "Steele's devotion for her earthly father may have informed her reverence of God as heavenly Father."[178] Steele acknowledges her need for fatherly discipline, expressing a desire—startlingly—to "learn to kiss the rod." Knowing God's fatherly love, care, and acceptance through Christ enables even "the darksome gloom" to give way to the experience of "the bliss" of being known by "my Redeemer's name."

The Holy Spirit and the Christian Life

Rippon chose to include four hymns by Steele, twelve percent of the unit, in the section of his hymnal known as The Christian.[179] Having been justified by grace through faith in Christ, the Christian seeks the power of the Holy Spirit for help in sanctification, for growth in holiness and faith in the Lord, especially in the face of life in a fallen world. Historically and in recent scholarship, it has been Steele's sufferings and reflections upon such sufferings in hymns, poems, prose, and letters that has dominated the discussion of the sanctifying influences in her life. The first two hymns in this section offer sustained examples of Steele's honest and probing lyrics regarding the difficult valleys of the Christian life. It has already been shown that many of Steele's hymns offer a diverse set of doctrinal and experiential material from which to draw out themes for analysis. These two hymns are no different. Yet two aspects of them stand out for reflection based upon their potential to influence the saints toward spiritual renewal. First, each of these hymns rehearses in detail the various spiritual afflictions through which God's people must pass. Simply acknowledging the reality of such circumstances shared by believers would bring relief to those experiencing just such situations. Second, the path through darkness is shone lit by the Word of God and is made passable by the hope and promise of the presence of God with his suffering children. A simple presentation of the verses of these hymns with brief comments interspersed will demonstrate these two points.

For the first of these two hymns, Rippon made a change to Steele's original title. Rippon lists it as "Walking in Darkness, and trusting in God. Isaiah i. 10"[180] though for the first part of the title, Steele called it, "Desiring the

178. Cho, "Ministry of Song," 67.

179. In his "Analysis of the Volume," Rippon calls this section Christian Life. See Rippon, *Selection of Hymns*, o.

180. Rippon, *Selection of Hymns*, 381–82. In this case, Rippon incorrectly has the Scripture reference as Isa i. 10 (or 1:10), when it was actually l. 10 (or 50:10), which reads, "Who *is* among you that feareth the Lord, that obeyeth the voice of his servant, that walketh *in* darkness, and hath no light? let him trust in the name of the Lord, and stay upon his God." The discerning reader of Rippon's day could have discovered and

Presence of God."[181] Steele presents an argument to God that the return of a sense of the Lord's presence to her would result in praise to him. She begins as one who knows that the Spirit intercedes on her behalf with groans too deep for words and that though the night is filed with sorrow yet there are mercies new in the morning: "Hear, gracious God! my humble moan, / To thee I breath my sighs; / When will the mournful night be gone, / And when my joys arise?" Having addressed God and asked a question based on Scripture,[182] Steele proceeds to both intimately and boldly address God again, this time alluding to his names, which, of course, express his attributes:

> My God—O could I make the claim—
> My father and my friend—
> And call thee mine by ev'ry name
> On which thy saints depend!—
>
> By ev'ry name of power and love,
> I would thy grace entreat:
> Nor should my humble hopes remove,
> Nor leave thy sacred seat.

The repetition having conveyed the person upon whom the hope of this prayer rests ("by ev'ry name . . . By ev'ry name"),[183] now she makes plain the source of the spiritual and emotional stability she seeks:

> Yet tho' my soul in darkness mourns,
> Thy word is all my stay;
> Here would I rest till light returns,
> Thy presence makes my day.
>
> Speak, Lord! and bid celestial peace
> Relieve my aching heart;
> O smile, and bid my sorrows cease,
> And all the gloom depart.

Only the words of Scripture could provide security in the darkness. The presence of God is that which makes a day worth living. The Word of God brings abiding peace and relief. A lifting of God's countenance toward her— there is found a new gladness. Evangelical and Calvinistic, experiential and

---

corrected the error. See Steele, *Works*, 1:136.

181. See Steele, *Works*, 1:136.

182. The second half of the verse is a paraphrase of Ps 30:5b. See also Rom 8:26–27 and Lam 3:22–23.

183. Note also its placement: at the end of a line and then the beginning of a line.

theological, this is Steele's approach to "darkness" and "sorrows." And so she closes with a final poetic argument, giving God a reason why he ought to answer her prayer! She pleads to her Advocate and Father, "Then shall my drooping spirit rise, / And bless thy healing rays, / And change these deep complaining sighs / For songs of sacred praise."

Like the psalmist Heman the Ezrahite, writer of the Psalm 88, who while praying through tears in the night and asking why God was hiding his face from him in the darkness, yet argued, "Lord if you let me die, will your lovingkindness and praise be declared in the grave?" Steele appeals to God.[184] "Lord," she seems to say, "your countenance upon me and presence with me will result in an uplifting of my spirit, my blessing you, my complainings coming to a cease, and your praise being raised." This hymn is a sincere prayer of faith.

With "Troubled, but making God a Refuge,"[185] Rippon again changed Steele's original title, but it seems in this case it was more for emphasis regarding the section within which he placed it. Steele's title was "God the Only Refuge of the Troubled Mind."[186] It seems that Rippon was including the hymn as a way for the believer to pray and cling to the Lord through difficult times, and thus changed the order in the title so that Trouble came first, both alphabetically and for emphasis.

Like the more than forty psalms that do the same, Steele begins by acknowledging God as "her refuge": "Dear refuge of my weary soul, / On thee when sorrows rise, / On thee, when waves of trouble roll, / My fainting hope relies." For a hymn that will deal with "fear," "gloomy doubts," "rising grief," and "sorrows," Steele begins with the answer, "On thee."[187] She continues, like the previous hymn considered, with the twofold sense of her intimate relationship with her Heavenly Father and her reliance upon his word: "To thee I tell each rising grief, / For thou alone canst heal; / Thy word can bring a sweet relief / For ev'ry pain I feel." But sometimes her own doubts push these two truths aside: "But, O! when gloomy doubts prevail, / I fear to call thee mine; / The springs of comfort seem to fail, / And all my hopes decline."

184. See Ps 88. Steele's hymns often have the ring of Psalms of lament (for example, 3, 5, 22, 42–43, 44, 58, 71, 74, 88, 137).

185. Rippon, *Selection of Hymns*, 391, 393.

186. See Steele, *Works*, 1:142.

187. Aalders, on the other hand, says, "As is typical in Steele's hymns, this hymn begins in a place of spiritual hesitancy, recognizing the reality of human sorrow." Aalders, *To Express the Ineffable*, 173. It does not, however, seem necessary to equate an acknowledgment of sorrow with spiritual hesitancy. Steele seems to have no hesitation with taking sorrow directly and boldly to the Lord in prayer.

Aalders rightly recognizes that here "[Steele] lingers over her grief."[188] But Steele's theology cannot help but spring up even if comfort has yet to do so: "Yet, gracious God! where shall I flee? / Thou art my only trust; / And still my soul would cleave to thee, / Tho' prostrate in the dust." She follows the lead of both her biblical and ecclesiastical fathers in the faith as she prays based on God's promises and her experience of them coming true for her. And so she continues with a renewed hope in the cherished relationship and in the basis of her salvation ("sov'reign grace"):

> Hast thou not bid me seek thy face?
>   And shall I seek in vain?
> And can the ear of sov'reign grace
>   Be deaf when I complain?
>
> No, still the ear of sov'reign grace
>   Attends the mourner's prayer;
> O my I ever find access
>   To breathe my sorrows there!

Steele knows that God hears her and will ultimately vindicate her and so she prays based on his own word to her and the foundation of her faith in him. Predicated on what she has professed in the previous two verses, she closes in a sort of summary, "Thy mercy-seat is open still, / Here let my soul retreat; / With humble hope attend thy will, / And wait beneath thy feet." There may not have been a specific answer to her troubles. Yet she seems to close with a sense that by settling in to an obedient and humble position before the Lord, at a place where she knows she can find grace and mercy to help in her time of need, waiting upon the Lord will be bearable. Aalders helpfully summarizes the scope and terrain covered by Steele here:

> Where this hymn began by engaging the full depth of human sorrow and then descended to a place of doubt, verging on despair, it makes a critical turn in order to focus again on God—a God who draws Steele forward in the spiritual life, a God of healing and grace, and a God full of mercy who consistently listens to her mourning prayer. And here is the source of Steele's "humble hope," which enables her to wait faithfully in the sorrow and silence.[189]

188. Aalders, *To Express the Ineffable*, 173.

189. Aalders, *To Express the Ineffable*, 176. Aalders actually concludes the quoted statement with a final phrase: ". . . in the sorrow and silence, and long for a presence that persistently alludes her." It does not seem necessary, either based on this hymn in particular nor on the other hymns of Steele in Rippon's *Selection of Hymns*, to detect in Steele a sense of a persistent experience of a lack of God's presence with her.

This hymn is a prayerful plea for personal revival and renewal, only possible through the "sov'reign grace" of a "gracious God."

For the third consecutive hymn in this section on The Christian, Rippon modifies the title somewhat significantly. In this case, however, he does more. "The Request"[190] is actually a cento taken from the last three verses out of ten from "Desiring Resignation and Thankfulness."[191] This short hymn is a personal prayer of supplication, briefly displaying how theology, experience, and relationship were three hallmarks of Steele's hymns as found in Rippon's hymnal. Further, it demonstrates what Broome calls "another aspect of her hymns, namely the desire for total submission to the Lord's will in her life"[192]:

> Father! what'er of earthly bliss
>   Thy sov'reign will denies,
> Accepted at thy throne of grace,
>   Let this petition rise:
>
> *Give me a calm, a thankful heart,*
>   *From ev'ry murmur free!*
> *The blessings of thy grace impart,*
>   *And make me live to thee.*
>
> *Let the sweet hope that thou art mine*
>   *My life and death attend,*
> *Thy presence thro' my journey shine,*
>   *And crown my journey's end.*

Aalders suggests that "the themes of resignation and longing can be traced throughout Steele's hymnody."[193] She finds in hymns such as this one "meaningful insight into Steele's spirituality, which is marked by both a humble acceptance of her limited capacity to know God while confined to earth, as well

---

Thus the quote is shortened above. The phrase "verging on despair" may also be an overstatement, but an analysis of hymns has an obvious subjective element as well as the presuppositions and temperament of the one making the analysis, the present author included.

190. Rippon, *Selection of Hymns*, 396, 398.

191. Steele, *Works*, 1:134–35. Aalders notes, "It has become part of the standard lore surrounding Steele's life that she composed this hymn in response to the drowning death of her fiancé." Aalders, *To Express the Ineffable*, 163n78. That "standard lore" was considered in chap. 3.

192. Broome, *Bruised Reed*, 167. Italics in original.

193. Aalders, *To Express the Ineffable*, 159. But, of course, other themes can be traced as well.

an unremitting desire to enjoy his presence in the future."[194] Three steps are made through these three short verses. First, Steele displays an evangelical Calvinistic understanding of sovereignty and prayer: though God may deny "earthly bliss" yet he receives her supplications. Next, she asks for divine grace in cultivating an attitude of thankfulness, a spirit devoid of complaining, and a determination toward obedience. Finally, she anchors these petitions to her experience of the doctrines of adoption and the Holy Spirit: the personal knowledge that she is a child of God inhabited by the divine Comforter is her hope in life and death. Aalders concludes, "She resigns herself to the will of God, but she maintains the "sweet hope" that she will recognize God's presence in her earthly life and be rewarded with a more complete knowledge of his presence at the end of her life."[195]

Anne Steele's hymns are often written directly as prayers or at least include stanzas that address God directly in prayer. J. R. Broome says of her, "Prayer was for [Steele] the breath of her life. To walk in the light of God's countenance was her one desire."[196] Haykin writes that among the means of grace, "Baptist piety and spirituality has also never doubted the centrality of prayer in the Christian life."[197] For example, he notes that in a sermon on 1 Cor 14:15, Benjamin Beddome declared,

> [Prayer] is . . . a constant duty; never out of season, never to be neglected, till faith is turned into vision, and prayer into praise. There is no duty we are more apt to omit, no duty which it is more our interest to perform, no duty which Satan more opposes, or with which God is better pleased. As a man cannot live without breathing, so it is certain that the Christian cannot thrive without praying."[198]

"Watchfulness and Prayer. Matt. xxvi. 41"[199] offers a glimpse into prayer as an expression of Steele's personal piety and an illustration of Beddome's words on prayer.

194. Aalders, *To Express the Ineffable*, 159. This book is making an argument for Steele's contribution to the revival in Particular Baptist life based specifically on Steele's hymns disseminated through Rippon's hymnal. Even for this hymn, only three of ten verses were retained. Aalders's argument is based on her assessment of the entire extant Steele corpus of writings.

195. Aalders, *To Express the Ineffable*, 161.

196. Broome, *Bruised Reed*, 166.

197. Haykin, "'Draw Nigh unto My Soul,'" 66.

198. Benjamin Beddome, "The Nature and Importance of Prayer," in *Sermons printed from the manuscripts of the late Rev. Benjamin Beddome, A.M.* (London: William Ball, 1835), 366, cited in Haykin, "'Draw Nigh unto My Soul,'" 66.

199. Rippon, *Selection of Hymns*, 398. "Watch and pray, that ye enter not into

Steele begins in the first verse with an acknowledgment that "hourly dangers" and "snares" deserve hourly watchfulness and prayer! Considering the first verses of this hymn, Watson suggests that Steele uses questions or exclamations for a specific purpose. They "probe further than [mere] statements themselves can do, because they gesture towards the unanswered, the mysterious, and the unknown."[200] Steele writes,

> Alas! what hourly dangers rise!
>   What snares beset my way!
> To heaven O let me lift my eyes,
>   And hourly watch and pray.
>
> How oft my mournful thoughts complain,
>   And melt in flowing tears!
> My weak resistance, ah! how vain;
>   How strong my foes and fears!

These verses find Steele "at her best," as through such verses, says Watson, "her hymnody celebrates not just the doctrine of grace, but the application of that grace to human experience."[201] Such application, and in a hymn on the grace of prayer, was part and parcel to a revival among Particular Baptists who sang such hymns.

Steele continues by first asking for divine help in the discipline of prayer. Then she follows by describing, within prayer to God, the fruits she desires from such watchful prayer:

> O gracious God! in whom I live,
>   My feeble efforts aid;
> Help me to watch, and pray, and strive,
>   Tho' trembling and afraid.
>
> Increase my faith, increase my hope,
>   When foes and fears prevail!
> And bear my fainting spirit up,
>   Or soon my strength will fail.
>
> Whene'er temptations fright my heart,
>   Or lure my feet aside,
> My God! thy powerful aid impart,
>   My guardian and my guide.

---

temptation: the spirit indeed *is* willing, but the flesh *is* weak" (Matt 26:41).

200. Watson, *English Hymn*, 198.

201. Watson, *English Hymn*, 198.

> O keep me in thy heavenly way,
>   And bid the tempter flee;
> And let me never, never stray,
>   From happiness and thee.[202]

In stanza 3, she acknowledges her shortcomings and pleads to the one with whom she is spiritually united, "Help me to watch, and pray, and strive." Having moved from the indirect seeking of divine assistance in her prayer life to more direct supplications, she confesses her lack of resistance to foes and fears from both within and without. Understanding the relationship of the creature to the Creator, she illustrates both the necessity of prayer for life and the complete dependence that the one praying has upon the one to whom the prayer is made. The second half of the hymn is a litany of supplications that illustrate her need for constant watchfulness and the one with power to help. Steele acknowledges those obstacles for which she needs help to face: foes, fears, weaknesses, temptations, and the tempter himself. She also appeals to God personally as having the power to remove these obstacles, as the one already watching and caring for her, and as the one in whom she has happiness. Finally, as an intense hymn has moved toward resolution, Watson finds the "never, never" to be "a most skilful way of introducing into the verse that kind of human sensibility which is the result of an interaction between doctrine and experience."[203]

Steele's hymns are often either prayerful poems or else hymns about prayer. And she writes both from the foundation of and toward an encouragement of dependence upon the Holy Spirit for all Christian piety. In Steele's prayerful hymns on the Christian life she illustrates where duty, need, benefit, and delight intersect in piety: in prayer.

The Church and Its Life

Steele is well represented among a number of sections of Rippon's hymnal that concern generally the church and its life: Worship, Church, Lord's Supper, and Times and Seasons. These hymns cover the gamut of the life of the Christian, from morning worship on the Lord's Day with God's people to both the ordinary and extraordinary events of daily life. Concerning the church, three of Steele's hymns are found under the heading, Worship, two under Church, and four under Lord's Supper.

202. Interestingly, in the case of this hymn's punctuation, Rippon inserted the exclamation points found in the final four stanzas. He thus possibly adds to the emotional elements of these heartfelt lyrics.

203. Watson, *English Hymn*, 198.

Worship

Steele's first hymn concerning the church and its life is found under the subheading Family Worship. This hymn, "The Christian's noblest Resolution. Joshua xxiv. 15,"[204] fits both its title and Scripture reference. Steele based these verses on a passage taken from Joshua's last sermon to the children of Israel as God's people prepared to receive their rest in the Land of Promise: "And if it seems evil unto you to serve the Lord, and, choose you this day whom ye will serve; whether the gods which your fathers served that *were* on the other side of the flood, or the gods of the Amorites, in whose land ye dwell: but as for me and my house, we will serve the Lord."

This hymn, as its title suggests, concerns the desire of the Christian for one's faith to result in good works. As the *Second London Confession* teaches in its chapter, "Of Good Works," and as Rippon even reveals in the very headings and subheadings he uses in his hymnal, for Christians,

> Their ability to do good works, is not at all of themselves; it is wholly from the *Spirit* of Christ; and that they may be enabled thereunto, besides the graces they have already received, there is necessary an actual influence of the same *Holy Spirit*, to work in them to will, and to do, of his good pleasure; yet they are not hereupon to grow negligent, as if they were not bound to perform any duty, unless upon a special motion of the Spirit; but they ought to be diligent in stirring up the Grace that is in them.[205]

The hymn, which includes a skillful and understated application of repetition throughout, begins with a statement of why those outside of Christ do not serve the Lord nor accomplish heavenly purposes: "Ah, wretched souls, who strive in vain, / Slaves to the world, and slaves to sin! / A nobler toil may I sustain, / A nobler satisfaction win." But it continues with the hope that the Spirit of Christ will instill a nobler purpose in the reader/singer's daily vocation. This hymn has a roughly chiastic structure with the second and fourth stanzas each stating and sometimes restating the resolution and grounding it in the power and precepts/commands of God. The third stanza, and center of the poem, is an exuberant versified restating of Jesus's exhortation, "Let your light so shine before men, that they may see your good works, and glorify your Father which is in heaven" (Matt 5:16). The middle three stanzas read,

> May I resolve with all my heart,
> With all my powers, to serve the Lord;

204. Rippon, *Selection of Hymns*, 416.
205. Lumpkin, *Baptist Confessions of Faith*, 271.

Nor from his precepts e're depart,
Whose service is a rich reward.

O be his service all my joy,
Around met my example shine,
Till others love the bless'd employ,
And join in labours so divine.

Be this the purpose of my soul,
My solemn, my determin'd choice,
To yield to his supreme controul,
And in his kind commands rejoice.

Here is the determination of the child of God to respond to the grace of God with a life lived for God under the authority of the Word of God and for the ultimate purpose of leading others to God.

Champion notes that the Particular Baptist and evangelical "emphasis on the divine activity of grace through Christ by the Spirit as the mean's of man's salvation . . . is capable of a wider interpretation."[206] Steele's third verse here with its joyful and personal tone but with a robust corporate vision poetically illustrates his claim. Champion elaborates, "The divine activity is discerned not simply in the restricted sphere of religious experience and activity but in all forms of human living, and salvation is understood not just in terms of the important relationship of the individual soul and God but in the larger terms of wholeness of life for both individual and society."[207] Steele expresses such sentiments through her hymns, especially those concerning worship, the Christian life, church life, and times and seasons.

Finally, this hymn is notable in that it includes a heavy dose of the sense of the believer's own striving in sanctification, an evangelistic theme at its center, the Scripture as the legs of the "nobler . . . serving," and a sense of movement rather than of hesitancy. The Christian life is lived by faith and in the strength of the Lord, but it is to be *lived*. Steele's hymns bear out such a belief, hope, and trajectory for the Christian.

In a short subsection with hymns specifically about Public Worship, Steele has two consecutive hymns featured in the *Selection of Hymns*: "The happiness of humble worship. Psalm lxxxiv"[208] and "Delight in God's House, and confidence in Him. Ps. xxvii."[209] Each of these hymns

---

206. Champion, "Evangelical Calvinism," 207.

207. Champion, "Evangelical Calvinism," 207.

208. Rippon, *Selection of Hymns*, 428–29.

209. Rippon, *Selection of Hymns*, 429, 431.

is actually a psalm paraphrase by Steele from which Rippon chose a few stanzas each to form hymns about the joy of the saints as they worship together on the Lord's Day.[210]

The first of these two hymns is an exuberant versification of the Psalm 84, containing the well-known cry, "My soul longeth, yea, even fainteth for the courts of the LORD: my heart and my flesh crieth out for the living God. . . . For a day in thy courts is better than a thousand" (Ps 84:2, 10a). Steele regularly has the same tone and mind as this psalmist, wholeheartedly desiring the presence of the Lord and a tongue with which to praise him. Considering the place of corporate worship, she writes, "Fain would my longing passions meet / The glories of thy presence there. / . . . To dwell in those abodes of joy, / And sing thy never-ceasing praise." This hymn is an example of Manley's claim about Particular Baptists, "Their convictions and aspirations were shaped and reinforced as they sang together."[211] Like other hymns in this section of the *Selection of Hymns*, this one "confirmed the value of their praising God together" in worship.[212]

Further, as elsewhere, Steele has a way of expanding on even the words of a psalm-writer as she reflects on the ways of the Lord. Here she adds the line about "revival" herself, "God is a sun: our brightest day / From his reviving presence flows; / God is a shield, thro' all the way, / To guard us from surrounding foes." And she translates the psalmist's short finish, "O LORD of hosts, blessed *is* the man that trusteth in thee" (84:12) into "O lord of hosts, thou God of grace / How blest, divinely blest, is he / Who trusts thy love, and seeks thy face, / And fixes all his hopes on thee!" Steele cannot help but draw attention to the intersection of faith and experience, of worship and a sense of God's presence. And so for Steele, like her Baptist forefather Keach, church was "a place where people give themselves to the Lord."[213]

The second of these psalm paraphrases puts to English the verses of David known as Psalm 27. David began this memorable psalm, "The LORD *is* my light and my salvation; whom shall I fear? the LORD *is* the strength of my life; of whom shall I be afraid?" (27:1). The fourth and fifth verses as found in Rippon offer a glimpse here of both Steele's earnest tone and her way of making the psalm her own:

> When thou, with condescending grace,

---

210. For the former, Rippon kept seven out of twelve verses and for the latter, six out of fifteen. Steele did not give titles to her psalm paraphrases. See Steele, *Works*, 2:57 and 2:26, respectively.

211. Manley, "John Rippon and Baptist Hymnody," 104.

212. Manley, "John Rippon and Baptist Hymnody," 104.

213. Smith, "Covenant Life of Some Eighteenth-Century Baptists," 170.

Hast bid me seek thy shining face,
My heart replied to thy kind word,
Thee will I seek, all-gracious Lord!

Should ev'ry earthly friend depart,
And nature leave a parent's heart,
My God, on whom my hopes depend,
Will be my father and my friend.[214]

The *Confession* says that through the *"Spirit of Adoption . . .* [believers] are enabled to cry *Abba Father,* are pitied, protected, provided for, . . . by him, as by a *Father."*[215] Steele's hymns consistently reveal that faith in such a reality was the very heartbeat of her spiritual life. And that reality was acknowledged in corporate worship.

Church

Steele has two hymns in Rippon's section, Church. They have similar themes. The first celebrates the coming of Christ and his spiritual presence even now with his own people while the second goes a step further by applying the power of that presence to the struggles of life. First, found in the subsection, Church: Described, Formed, etc., "The Presence of Christ the Joy of his People"[216] rehearses Christ's incarnation, the presence of his Spirit with his people during his current bodily absence, and the hope of his second coming. Steele puts her biblical theology to work in the first two verses by using her 88.88 meter to tell the story of Christ from the prediction of his coming to the incarnation and even to his ascension and heavenly reign:

The wond'ring nations have beheld
The sacred prophecy fulfill'd!
And angels hail the glorious morn
That shew'd the great Messiah born:

The Prince! The Saviour! long desir'd,
Whom men foretold, by heaven inspir'd,
And raptur'd saw the blissful day
Rise o'er the world with healing ray.

214. These are based on the verses: "*When thou saidst*, Seek ye my face; my heart said unto thee, Thy face, Lord, will I seek. . . . When my father and my mother forsake me, then the Lord will take me up" (Ps 27:8, 10).

215. Lumpkin, *Baptist Confessions of Faith*, 267.

216. Rippon, *Selection of Hymns*, 522.

Having set forth the global scope of Christ's person and the wonder of his coming, Steele makes her request of the Divine: please bring your "healing ray." Christ is needed. Steele then proclaims the meeting with Lord of corporate worship: "Oft, in the temples of his grace, / His saints behold his smiling face; / And oft have seen his glories shine / With power and majesty divine." Where is revival found? Within the church! Here in this hymn, located by Rippon within the context of the church described, Steele hints at one of the tenets of Baptist life Smith observed, "The idea that an individual's experience of faith is nurtured and shared within the context of the wider covenant community."[217] But living in the time between Christ's first and second advent is a reason that the covenant community is so necessary: "But soon, alas! his absence mourn, / And pray and wish his kind return; / Without his life-inspiring light, / 'Tis all a scene of gloomy night." Referring perhaps to both Christ's bodily absence between his advents and also the experience of God's seeming absence for the Christian, Steele mourns that absence. But she does not stay at the place of lamentation. Steele responds with two verses of prayer and presents her argument for an answer:

> Come, dearest LORD! thy children cry,
> Our graces droop, our comforts die;
> Return, and let thy glories rise
> Again to our admiring eyes:
>
> Till, fill'd with light, and joy, and love,
> Thy courts below, like those above,
> Triumphant hallelujahs raise,
> And heaven and earth resound thy praise.

Not afraid to admit both the "gloomy night" and that this side of heaven "graces droop" and comforts die," Steele yet knows the way to resolution: the "return" of her "dearest LORD." Steele expressed an experience of the need of renewal. She took her need to God in poetic prayer. She offers an opportunity for the reader or singer to go with her to the place of God's presence. And she even tells God why he ought to grant her request: that not only heaven, but also "earth resound thy praise."

Next, located in the subsection Church and Fellowship Meetings, "To whom shall we go but unto thee? Or, Life and Safety in CHRIST alone. John vi. 67–69"[218] is Steele's other hymn under Rippon's heading Church. He modified Steele's original title, which was the shorter "Life and Safety in Christ Alone. John vi. 68." John 6:68 reads, "Then Simon Peter answered

217. Smith, "Covenant Life of Some Eighteenth-Century Baptists," 166.

218. Rippon, *Selection of Hymns*, 580, 582.

him, Lord, to whom shall we go? thou hast the words of eternal life."[219] The title and Scripture reference anticipate that this hymn will traverse some difficult territory. And while it does do that, Steele yet begins with the answer to her quest—a person: "Thou only sov'reign of my heart, / My refuge, my almighty friend—." And so it is perhaps surprising that she spends the next several verses admitting herself: "A wretched wand'rer from my Lord," her habitation: "this dark world of sin and woe," and her temptation: "earth's alluring joys." But then she remembers Peter's confession and prays based on her foundation, "Eternal life thy words impart, / On these my fainting spirit lives" and the relationship upon which her hope lies, "One smile, one blissful smile of thine, / My dearest Lord, outweighs them all. / Thy name, my inmost powers adore, / Thou art my life, my joy, my care." For the tempted and tried Christian, Steele offers a prayer of hope both based upon Peter's confession, and also reminiscent of the Aaronic blessing: "The Lord make his face shine upon thee, and be gracious unto thee: the Lord lift up his countenance upon thee, and give thee peace" (Num 6:25–26). God's presence was the Old Testament hope fulfilled in Christ. And so Steele's reflections take her to a proper place of conclusion: "Low at thy feet my soul would lie, / Here safety dwells, and peace divine; / Still let me live beneath thine eye, / For life, eternal life is thine." The hope of eternal life is no pie in the sky, but assurance for the trials of the present. And eternal life is preached from the pulpit and sung from the pews at the Lord's Day gathering, because "believers are never believers alone, but [are] bound together in a covenant community."[220]

Lord's Supper

The *Second London Confession* lists baptism and the Lord's Supper as the two ordinances established and instituted by Christ.[221] Like her fellow Nonconformist hymn-writers, Steele did not tend to bring out denominational distinctions in her hymns, but subject matter about which most Protestant Christians agreed, thus the distinctive Particular Baptist emphasis on baptism is relatively absent from her hymns.[222] Steele's hymns do, however, offer

219. Rippon's addition of the other two verses of Scripture simply set the context of Steele's verse and complete Peter's statement. His addition to Steele's title again seems for the purpose of making sense of the hymn's placement in the section for the reader of the hymnal.

220. Smith, "Covenant Life of Some Eighteenth-Century Baptists," 166.

221. See chaps. 28–30 in Lumpkin, *Baptist Confessions of Faith*, 290–93.

222. Arnold, "Veil of Interposing Night," 383–84.

insight into the English Particular Baptist understanding of the Lord's Supper. In an essay concerning various aspects of Baptist spirituality, Haykin writes, "Another place that Baptists have historically regarded as being rich in spiritual nourishment is the ordinance of the Lord's Table."[223] Steele wrote several hymns especially for the Lord's Supper. Four of the nineteen hymns in Rippon's *Selection of Hymns* concerning the Lord's Supper were written by Steele. The content of the first, "An Invitation to the Gospel Feast. Luke xiv. 22,"[224] focuses on the call to come to the Table of the Lord. The second, "The Wonders of Redemption,"[225] concerns the work of Christ for sinners, illustrated by the Supper, as well as the proper response to Christ. "Communion with Christ at his Table"[226] offers further insight into Steele's confessional theology of the Lord's Supper. Steele's final contribution to this subject in Rippon, "Praise to the Redeemer,"[227] is a lively composition reminiscent of Charles Wesley rehearsing the glory of redemption through Christ. These four hymns collectively display Steele's multifaceted evangelical faith.

"Ye wretched, hungry, starving poor, / Behold a royal feast! / Where Mercy spreads her bounteous store / For every humble guest." Not one to mince words about sinners and their Savior, so Steele begins this Communion hymn.[228] Using a chiasmus,[229] thematically crossing the states of the guests with the splendor of the offer, Steele strikingly gains the readers attention. Then she paints a picture of the gospel, "See Jesus stands with open arms; / He calls, he bids you come: / Guilt holds you back, and fear alarms; / But see, there yet is room.—" In the gospel, sinners, estranged from their Creator, are reconciled to him through the work of another—their Redeemer. Salvation is received by grace. Bebbington identifies such a belief as foundational to the evangelical movement.[230] And an awakening of the conscience to one's sin

223. Haykin, "Draw Nigh unto My Soul," 63.

224. Rippon, *Selection of Hymns*, 619–20. Steele's title, modified by Rippon, was "Longing Souls Invited to the Gospel Feast. Luke xiv. 22." The Scripture reads, "And the servant said, Lord, it is done as thou hast commanded, and yet there is room." Interestingly, the passage is taken from a parable Jesus told comparing the kingdom of God to "a great supper."

225. Rippon, *Selection of Hymns*, 631–32. Steele's title includes a citation of 1 Pet 3:18.

226. Rippon, *Selection of Hymns*, 634.

227. Rippon, *Selection of Hymns*, 634–35.

228. "An Invitation to the Gospel Feast. Luke xiv. 22," in Rippon, *Selection of Hymns*, 619–20. This hymn's word choice and theological and experiential flow are reminiscent of John Newton's "Let Us Love and Sing and Wonder." *Trinity Hymnal*, 172. But with Newton's hymn written in 1774, Steele's would have come first.

229. See Lovelace, *Anatomy of Hymnody*, 96–97 for a discussion of this poetic device.

230. Bebbington, *Evangelicalism in Modern Britain*, 6.

could bring an overwhelming sense of guilt and fear[231]—perhaps even during a Communion service! So Steele continues,

> Room in the Saviour's bleeding heart,
> There love and pity meet;
> Nor will he bid the soul depart
> That trembles at his feet.

> In him the Father reconcil'd
> Invites your souls to come;
> The rebel shall be call'd a child,
> And kindly welcom'd home.

Steele offers the answer that brought relief to the agony and guilt through an offer of the gospel (to believers and unbelievers alike) and a reminder of the theologically and experientially rich doctrine of adoption. "All those that are justified, . . . receive the Spirit of Adoption, . . . [and are] never cast off,"[232] says the *Confession*. Steele naturally continues with "O come." The fifth stanza says, "O come, and with his children taste / The blessings of his love; / While hope attends the sweet repast / Of nobler joys above." Steele seems to acknowledge here the *Second London Confession's* teaching that "inwardly by faith" worthy receivers "spiritually receive, and feed upon Christ crucified and all the benefits of his death."[233] Fellow Baptist hymn-writers Joseph Stennett I and Samuel Stennett shared Steele's affection for the Lord's Supper. In the following two hymns in Rippon each Stennett describes the Table as a "rich banquet" and a "rich repast," respectively.[234] But her Particular Baptist confessionalism further interacts with her evangelical impulse for "experimental religion"[235] as she closes with an eschatological flurry,

> There, with united heart and voice,
> Before th' eternal throne,

> Ten thousand thousand souls rejoice,
> In ecstacies unknown.

---

231. Autobiographical conversion stories are a source for illustrations of this phenomenon. See Bebbington, *Evangelicalism in Modern Britain*, 5.

232. Lumpkin, *Baptist Confessions of Faith*, 267.

233. Lumpkin, *Baptist Confessions of Faith*, 293.

234. Joseph Stennett I, "Christ Dying, Rising, and Reigning," in Rippon, *Selection of Hymns*, 620–21; and Samuel Stennett, "My Flesh Is Meat Indeed. John vi. 53–55," in Rippon, *Selection of Hymns*, 629, 631.

235. See Bebbington, *Evangelicalism in Modern Britain*, 57–58.

> And yet ten thousand thousand more
>   Are welcome still to come:
> Ye longing souls, the grace adore!
>   Approach, there yet is room.

Steele displays here a catholic faith, an uncompromising offer for all who will to come, and a love for divine grace. For Steele, the Lord's Table shows forth for God and his people the temporal and eternal "pledge of their communion with him and with each other."[236]

"The Wonders of Redemption"[237] is Steele's second entry in this section. This hymn displays vintage Anne Steele when poetically, in a vibrant 86.86 meter, reflecting upon Christ's complete body of work accomplished for the sake of sinners as well their proper response to it. With the first half of this hymn of six verses she begins with questions and then moves to exclamations and parenthetical remarks. She uses a variety of names for God as well as graphic terms for sinful humans throughout the piece. The second half of the hymn is a prayer addressing the second person of the Trinity, acknowledging his sacrifice and its benefits for believers, and requesting his power to be at work in her life. Rippon published this as a Communion hymn. Smith comments, "Like the Puritans before them, Calvinistic Baptists related the Lord's Supper to redemption rather than to creation, and therefore, they emphasized God's gracious act of love and the forgiveness of sins rather than self-offering."[238] The hymn is listed in full below so that its impact may be felt and these poetic devices recognized as she expresses atonement theology:

> And did the holy and the just,
>   The Sovereign of the skies,
> Stoop down to wretchedness and dust,
>   That guilty worms might rise?
>
> Yes! the Redeemer left his throne,
>   His radiant throne on high,
>
> (Surprising mercy! love unknown)
>   To suffer, bleed, and die.

236. Lumpkin, *Baptist Confessions of Faith*, 291.

237. Rippon, *Selection of Hymns*, 631–32. Steele added a Scripture reference, 1 Pet 3:18, which reads, "For Christ also hath once suffered for sins, the just for the unjust, that he might bring us to God, being put to death in the flesh, but quickened by the Spirit." See Steele, *Works*, 1:168.

238. Smith, "Covenant Life of Some Eighteenth-Century Baptists," 179.

He took the dying traitor's place,
    And suffer'd in his stead;
For man, (O miracle of grace!)
    For man the Saviour bled!

Dear LORD! what heav'nly wonders dwell
    In thy atoning blood!
By this are sinners snatch'd from hell,
    And rebels brought to GOD.

JESUS! my soul adoring bends
    To love so full, so free;
And may I hope *that* love extends
    Its sacred powers to me!

What glad return can I impart
    For favours so divine?
O take my all—this worthless heart,
    And make it only thine.

The first two verses, one a question and the next an answer, work in parallel in proclaiming that it was indeed the "Sovereign" who was also the "Redeemer." The punctuation and grammar highlight the mystery and astonishment of such news. Taken together with the third and fourth verses, these lines of the hymn display when Steele is most bold in her lyrical development. Aalders explains, "These moments most often occur in the context of her devotion to Christ—that is, her joy as she hopes for redemption and her anticipation of spiritual fulfillment made possible by Christ's sacrifice."[239] The last two verses show that for Steele a consideration of the atonement contributed to her desire to commit her life in all its parts to Christ as "a living sacrifice"[240] in gratitude for his saving work. Further, she expresses an understanding of what the Apostle Paul desired: "That I may know him, . . . and the fellowship of his sufferings, being made conformable unto his death."[241] And so in a crucicentric hymn revealing Steele at her best she expresses both her evangelical emphasis on the cross of Christ and complements through poetry what Manley considers "the Christocentric emphasis of Baptist preaching."[242]

239. Aalders, *To Express the Ineffable*, 163.

240. From Rom 12:1.

241. Phil 3:10.

242. Manley, "John Rippon and Baptist Hymnody," 105.

"Communion with Christ at his Table"[243] offers further insight into Steele's confessional theology of the Lord's Supper. Because of its robust description of the experience of this ordinance in only five verses, it is listed below in full as found in Rippon's hymnal. Notice how each verse moves from adoration to confession to thanksgiving and finally to consecutive reverent notes of supplication:

> To Jesus, our exalted Lord,
> (Dear name, by heaven and earth ador'd!)
> Fain would our hearts and voices raise
> A cheerful song of sacred praise.
>
> But all the notes which mortals know,
> Are weak and languishing and low;
> Far, far above our humble songs,
> The theme demands immortal tongues.
>
> But while around his board we meet,
> And humbly worship at his feet,
> O let our warm affections move,
> In glad returns of grateful love!
>
> Let faith our feeble senses aid
> To see thy wondrous love display'd,
> Thy broken flesh, thy bleeding veins,
> Thy dreadful, agonizing pains.
>
> Let humble, penitential woe,
> With painful, pleasing anguish flow;
> And thy forgiving smiles impart
> Life, hope, and joy, to every heart.

Desiring to sing praise to Jesus, the one who instituted the Lord's Supper, takes up the theme of the first two stanzas. And in the second Steele confesses the failure of human tongues to praise such a worthy God properly. Next, note that Steele writes this from the vantage point of the communion of the saints as they are gathered both for worship and fellowship with Christ.[244] Further she prays for "warm affections" to be the human response to Christ's love illustrated at his table. She continues to pray, asking that God would enable "faith our feeble senses aid" to actually receive the spiritual nourishment offered in the spiritual feast. After all, Steele would have heard her own

243. Rippon, *Selection of Hymns*, 634.
244. See chaps. 22, 26–27 in Lumpkin, *Baptist Confessions of Faith*, 280–82, 285–90.

Particular Baptist pastor and father preach, "Christ . . . feeds his sheep with himself . . . the flesh and blood which he gives is food for our nourishment and life for our souls."[245] Thus she connects the physical sense of taste with the spirituality of feeding upon Christ by faith.[246] It is also clear that Steele sees the Lord's Supper as acknowledging Christ's death in history on the cross, the believers' union with Christ, and the believers' communion both with Christ and one another.[247] Her Romantic impulse even shows itself as she suggests the paradoxical description of "painful, pleasing anguish." Such a description calls to mind the Age of Sensibility[248] as Steele invites an experience: physical, emotional, and spiritual at the Lord's Table.

Steele's final contribution concerning the Lord's Supper in Rippon is "Praise to the Redeemer."[249] Like the second entry in this section, according to Rippon's alternating style, this hymn considers not the holy feast itself, but the center of the supper: the Redeemer and his person. This hymn does not break much new ground in the way of Communion theology, although the title is indeed a thesis for the hymn for it is a hymn of thanks and praise for the love of Christ composed in a lively 86.86 meter. It does, however, have an emphasis worth considering, stated boldly in the fourth of the five stanzas and applied globally in the fifth.

Steele first takes the first two stanzas to do what her hymns illustrate to be the passion of her spirituality: to seek to sing praise to God, even if one's tongue needs divine help in order to do so. She expresses this with her standard grammar of poetic device:

> To our Redeemer's glorious name
>   Awake the sacred song!
> O may his love (immortal flame!)
>   Tune ev'ry heart and tongue.
>
> His love, what mortal thought can reach!
>   What mortal tongue display!
> Imagination's utmost stretch
>   In wonder dies away.[250]

245. William Steele, sermon on John 10:11, n.d., Angus Library, cited in Smith, "Covenant Life of Some Eighteenth-Century Baptists," 179.

246. Rippon chose not to include Steele's fourth verse out of six original stanzas, which reads: "Yes, Lord, we love and we adore, / But long to know and love thee more; / And while we taste the bread and wine, / Desire to feed on joys divine." Steele, *Works*, 1:170.

247. See Lumpkin, *Baptist Confessions of Faith*, 291.

248. See Davie, *Eighteenth-Century Hymn in England*, 126 for an explanation of such a literary technique.

249. Rippon, *Selection of Hymns*, 634–35.

250. In the second stanza, Rippon replaced question marks with exclamation

Having stated the constant need of the hour, to offer praise, Steele then describes one of the key reasons why the "Redeemer's glorious name" deserves praise, his great exchange: "He left his radiant throne on high, / Left the bright realms of bliss, / And came to earth to bleed and die— / Was ever love like this." To the consternation of some hymn critics, Steele does not find it tedious—and apparently neither does Rippon—to use such "metaphors [that] require the singer constantly to prostrate himself before the divine majesty and give thanks for his deliverance by the blood of Christ from turmoil within and hell-fire hereafter."[251] Rather than avoiding such language, this language is one reason Rippon included this hymn as one for the service of the Lord's Supper. In the final two stanzas Steele gives another reason, which Rippon chose to italicize in his hymnal:

> Dear LORD! while we adoring pay
>   Our humble thanks to thee,
> May ev'ry heart with rapture say,
>   *The Saviour died for me.*

> O may the sweet, the blissful theme
>   Fill ev'ry heart and tongue:
> Till strangers love thy charming name,
>   And join the sacred song.

In his study of the revival in Particular Baptist life, Bebbington detects a more robust doctrine of assurance than he believes was present in their Puritan forebears. He cites particular Baptist pastor Abraham Booth as saying, "A Christian has as much warrant to believe as the hungry to feed."[252] Well, here, as the believers feed on Christ, the unbelievers present at the Communion service sing the prayer for their own conversion! Theology had a purpose for Steele. Here is the doctrine of Christ—atonement and adoption[253]—in the service of both praise and evangelism, and for Rippon, Communion.

Though Steele's Communion hymns do not mention the Holy Spirit by name, yet their tone and theological framework display a dependence upon him. They are really a poetic example of Medley's benedictory prayer to all present: "May the good Spirit of God quicken and renew your souls,

---

points. See Steele, *Works*, 1:164.

251. Adey, *Class Idol in the English Hymn*, 46. Adey seems impatient with the repetition of such metaphors in the English hymn. See also Manley, "John Rippon and Baptist Hymnody," 104.

252. Abraham Booth cited in Bebbington, *Evangelicalism in Modern Britain*, 46.

253. See chaps. 8 and 10–12 in Lumpkin, *Baptist Confessions of Faith*, 260–63 and 264–67.

and enable you to flee from the wrath to come to a dear and precious Jesus, while you are on mercy's ground, under mercy's sound, and within mercy's reach."[254] Steele also shows agreement with Sutcliff's observation that should the Holy Spirit withhold his influences, "divine ordinances are empty cisterns, and spiritual graces are withering flowers."[255] Taken cumulatively as a major portion of a relatively short section of the hymnal, these hymns demonstrate Steele's expression of Baptist eucharistic piety[256] while highlighting her contribution to the renewal of English Baptist piety.

Times and Seasons

The section Times and Seasons includes seven hymns composed by Steele. In the third chapter of Ecclesiastes, the Preacher says these immortal words, "To every thing there is a season, and a time to every purpose under the heaven: A time to be born, and a time to die; a time to plant, and a time to pluck up that which is planted; A time to kill, and a time to heal; a time to break down, and a time to build up; A time to weep, and a time to laugh; a time to mourn, and a time to dance . . . a time of war, and a time of peace." Steele's hymns tell this story dramatically and poetically. John Rippon sought to catch the sense of the Preacher's words in the structure of his hymnal. From the seasons of nature to the yearly national holidays and from seasons of youth to the challenges of adulthood—even the wars between the nations, Rippon has hymns through which one may sing and reflect upon God's work daily in the world he has made. Anne Steele's seven compositions are found throughout the more than fifty selections concerning Times and Seasons.

Steele's first composition in this section is called simply "An Evening Hymn."[257] Steele wrote it in L.M. (88.88), giving herself maximum room to rehearse the thoughts the end of a day brought to the thoughtful, if tried and tested, Christian poet. Step-by-step, through its five stanzas: It is an ode to the mercy and grace of God shown in the mere gift of life found each day in this world; a plea for forgiveness for thoughtlessly roaming and for failing to acknowledge it as such while the days pass; a Christ-centered atonement

254. Medley, cited in Sarah Medley, *Memoirs of the late Rev. Samuel Medley* (Liverpool: J. Jones, 1833), 259–60, cited in Ramsbottom, "Samuel Medley," 243.

255. Sutcliff, *Jealously for the Lord of Hosts Illustrated*, cited in Haykin, "Habitation of God, Through the Spirit," 310.

256. Haykin, "Draw Nigh unto My Soul," 65.

257. Rippon, *Selection of Hymns*, 642. Rippon includes five verses of Steele's original nine. The omissions allow for a more clear and crisp selection without changing its theme or tone. See Steele, *Works*, 1:42–43.

prayer; and, finally, a prayer for a safe night and a new prayerful spirit the next morning. This graceful hymn as found in Rippon reads,

> GREAT GOD! to thee my evening song
> With humble gratitude I raise:
> O let thy mercy tune my tongue,
> And fill my heart with lively praise.
>
> My days unclouded as they pass,
> And ev'ry gentle rolling hour,
> Are monuments of wondrous grace,
> And witness to thy love and power.
>
> And yet this thoughtless wretched heart,
> Too oft regardless of thy love,
> Ungrateful, can from thee depart,
> And fond of trifles, vainly rove.
>
> Seal my forgiveness in thy blood
> Of JESUS; his dear name alone
> I plead for pardon, gracious GOD!
> And kind acceptance at thy throne.
>
> Let this blest hope mine eyelids close,
> With sleep refresh my feeble frame;
> Safe in thy care may I repose,
> And wake with praises to thy name.

Much could be said about these deeply personal lyrics, but a few points must suffice. First, Steele asks her great God, "O let thy mercy tune my tongue." God's mercy in Christ was the lifeline of Steele's existence—and certainly of her craft. She wants her tongue to offer praise and she pleads for help in doing so. Further, she notes that even the days of life "Are monuments of wondrous grace." A sovereign God, as described by the *Confession*, "by the most wise and holy Counsel of his own will,"[258] providentially even orders the days as they pass. Steele relished such deep thoughts. Next, the only "blest hope," she prayed could "mine eyelids close" was none other than hope in the multifaceted work of her prophet, priest, and king, "Jesus." The cross cast its shadow across any manner of subject Steele chose to tackle. Finally, refreshed, safe, and awake in his care for another day, her desire was to live with "praises to thy name." Appropriate for corporate singing at an evening worship service, for family worship around an evening peat fire, or

---

258. Lumpkin, *Baptist Confessions of Faith*, 254.

for personal bedside devotion, a hymn with the mundane title "An Evening Hymn" surprisingly offers insight into the tone and texture of revival.

Steele wrote a number of hymns about the creation and nature. She enjoyed the simple pleasures of a pastoral life. Rippon included a number of hymns in the *Selection of Hymns* that were simply observations of the ordinary rhythms of life on the earth, such as Steele's "Winter."[259] Rather than receiving short shrift, this second consecutive hymn about the seemingly ordinary also merits closer attention than might be expected. Not unlike "An Evening Hymn," but perhaps with a bit more surprise, Steele relates the weather ultimately to the spiritual battle of the day. "Winter" begins with two stanzas that set the "icy" scene, though the last line of verse 2 begins the transition, "my heart." The middle two stanzas (and perhaps even the second) offer phrases that seem, characteristic of the Apostle John, for example, to be double entendres—the climate outside the house and the climate inside the heart set in parallel. The thoughtful reader may have seen it coming. Finally, the last two stanzas offer eschatological clarity: "Spring eternal reigns . . . where winter frowns no more." Steele reflected on a winter evening thus, with a shorter 86.86 meter,

> Stern Winter throws his icy chains,
> Encircling nature round;
> How bleak, how comfortless the plains,
> Late with gay verdure crown's!
>
> The sun withdraws his vital beams,
> And light and warmth depart;
> And drooping, lifeless nature seems
> An emblem of my heart—
>
> My heart, where mental winter reigns
> In night's dark mantle clad,
> Confin'd in cold inactive chains;
> How desolate and sad!
>
> Return, O blissful sun, and bring
> Thy soul-reviving ray;
> This mental winter shall be spring,
> This darkness cheerful day.

---

259. Rippon, *Selection of Hymns*, 655–56. Rippon retained six of the hymn's original eleven stanzas. He also changed the name. Steele called it "A Reflection on a Winter Evening." See Steele, *Works*, 1:322–24 where it is listed as an occasional poem of Steele's.

O happy state, divine abode!
  Where spring eternal reigns;
And perfect day, the smile of GOD,
  Fills all the heavenly plains.

Great source of light! thy beams display,
  My drooping joys restore,
And guide me to the seats of day,
  Where winter frowns no more.

"Winter" is warm with the hope of "Thy soul-reviving ray." It is really a parable of spiritual life. Particular Baptists could meditate unashamedly upon how the depressing effects of winter were a window into the depressing sinful nature's "chains; . . . desolate and sad." But they could do so with a spiritual glimpse of "spring eternal . . . the smile of God." What hope, what life, and what renewal such lyrics offered the congregation, the family, and the lonely individual with a copy of Rippon's hymnal in hand.

Following the lead of her hymn-writing model, Isaac Watts, Anne also penned hymns on issues of national importance.[260] Seven of these hymns were written during or just after the Seven Years' War (1756–1763) between England and France in response to special days of prayer and fasting as proclaimed by the king as he received news from the battlefront. This global conflict between the colonial empires of England and France included the battle for "supremacy of the seas" and also concerned "the jealousy between Prussia and Austria regarding the control of Germany."[261] Prussia eventually allied itself with England while Austria joined forces with France. Steele's stepmother's journals indicate a steady stream of news of the war making its way to Broughton through both newspapers and the business travels of the Steele men. Steele's war hymns offer a direct illustration of how a skilled and thoughtful Particular Baptist poet and hymn-writer reflected upon this war for the purpose of prayerful congregational singing. Among his "war hymns" Rippon included three of Steele's hymns concerning the Seven Years' War and a hymn concerning a time of national historical deliverance in this section of his hymnal.

Having heard on November 28, 1755, the "dreadful news" of a "major earthquake" in Portugal as well as news of impending war with France, on December 11 of that year the Broughton Baptists, as was their custom, set

260. Broome, *Bruised Reed*, 173. Steele in fact wrote nine hymns concerning national days of fasting and prayer as well as days of thanksgiving for national deliverance and the peace that followed war. She even wrote a hymn commemorating the coronation of George III in 1760.

261. Broome, *Bruised Reed*, 133.

apart a day for prayer for the nation.[262] The following year, prior to making the official declaration of war, which would come in May, King George II set apart February 6 "for a day of public fasting, humiliation and prayer to God on account of the dangers we are in from our encroaching enemies, the French, and the judgments that are abroad in the earth."[263] Though Steele's health did not allow her to attend the meeting, she composed a hymn to be sung at the service.[264] She called it "On the Publick Fast. February 6, 1756."[265] Rippon renamed it "For a Public Fast." Note both the rhetorical structure and the prayerful flow of the hymn's full text as found in Rippon's hymnal:

> See, gracious God! before thy throne
> Thy mourning people bend!
> 'Tis on thy sovereign grace alone,
> Our humble hopes depend.
>
> Tremendous judgments[266] from thy hand
> Thy dreadful power display,
> Yet mercy spares this guilty land,
> And still we live to pray.
>
> Great God! and why is Britain spar'd,
> Ungrateful as we are?
> O make thy awful warnings heard,
> While mercy cries, *Forbear!*
>
> What num'rous crimes increasing rise
> Thro' this apostate[267] isle!
> What land so favour'd of the skies,
> And yet what land so vile!
>
> How chang'd, alas! are truths divine
> For error, guilt, and shame!
> What impious numbers, bold in sin,
> Disgrace the Christian name!

262. Broome, *Bruised Reed*, 131–32.

263. Cited in Broome, *Bruised Reed*, 132.

264. Broome, *Bruised Reed*, 132.

265. "For a Public Fast," in Rippon, *Selection of Hymns*, 678–79.

266. Though not noted in the *Selection of Hymns*, Steele includes a footnote that these "judgments" are referring in particular to the earthquake at Lisbon, not to mention the battles at hand around the globe.

267. Steele used the word "wretched" here.

Regardless of thy smile or frown,
   Their pleasures they require;
And sink with gay indiff'rence down
   To everlasting fire.[268]

O turn us, turn us, mighty Lord!
   By thy resistless grace;
Then shall our hearts obey thy word,
   And humbly seek thy face.

Then should insulting foes invade,
   We shall not sink in fear;
Secure of never-failing aid,
   If God, our God, is near.

This hymn introduces all the major themes that will be revisited from different angles and with varying poetic devices in each of Steele's hymns composed in the context of wars between nations. The first stanza begins from a posture of humility. From the human perspective nations are dependent upon God. This first verse also acknowledges Steele's spiritual understanding of God's providence over nations and what the *Confession* says should be God's people's response to this: "We ought to make supplications and prayers for Kings, and all that are in Authority, that under them we may live a quiet and peaceable life, in all godliness and honesty."[269] The second verse turns to God's power, especially as displayed in his judgments, yet acknowledging his mercy. An evangelical trait was the belief that "judgment was expected on nations as well as individuals if they persisted in corporate sins."[270] The next three verses build the case for the sinfulness of the nation from the corporate aspect down to individual sinners committing individual sins. And she asks, "Why is Britain spared?" Admitting herself as among the citizens of a land in need of God's mercy displays in itself the evangelical Calvinistic impulse to break with an exclusive attitude for the sake of the gospel. This encouraged revival. In the seventh verse Steele's Calvinistic piety emerges as she calls on God's "resistless grace" to move their hearts to "obey thy word" and seek God's face. She closes with an expression of confidence in the face of invaders because of God being near to aid them in their desperate time of need.

268. This verse does not appear in Steele's published works. It appears to have been composed and added by Rippon.

269. Lumpkin, *Baptist Confessions of Faith*, 284. Each of Steele's "war hymns" affirms this.

270. Bebbington, *Evangelicalism in Modern Britain*, 61.

The hymn is characterized by an acknowledgment of the character of God as holy and gracious alongside an honest realism regarding the plight of sinful humanity, and indeed the nation of Britain, before him. Here is a land that has been blessed with the gospel now filled with "error, guilt, and shame." It appears that both Steele and King George II viewed the earthquake in Lisbon as a judgment from God. Is the war itself also a judgment against Britain or will the results of the war be that judgment or reprieve? The answer to this question remains to be seen. And so the hymn ends with a supplication made in faith. Steele expresses the optimism, even on the eve of war, of the evangelical doctrine of God's providence: "[God] is in active control of the world."[271]

"On a Day of Prayer for Success in War"[272] was written to commemorate the day appointed by King George II as "a day to be kept for thanksgiving for great mercies of our God."[273] These mercies included at least the British victories at Lagos and then at Quiberon Bay in 1759, following the loss of some battles to the French in previous months. Broome calls 1759 "a momentous year for Britain and her Allies in the Seven Years' War."[274] Having been just recently weak and ill during the midst of an outbreak of smallpox in Broughton and fearful of catching it, Steele penned another war hymn. This hymn follows the same general structure as the hymn considered above. The first two stanzas review earlier material as they reflect Steele's humble view of "wretched sinners" before the "bright terrors" and "dazzling glories" where there is yet "mercy" calling at the "throne of grace." The third verse brings out another aspect of her Particular Baptist spirituality: an understanding of the kingly, prophetic, and priestly roles of Christ on behalf of his people.[275] "O may our souls thy grace adore, / May Jesus plead our humble claim, / While thy protection we implore, / In his prevailing glorious name." With the fourth stanza, Steele calls upon "the Lord" as the one upon whose "arm" Britain depends. Steele's ability to apply her theology and piety to the craft of poetry in the midst of national need continues to mature and develop in this hymn. Having followed her basic outline through the first four stanzas, the final four break new ground:

> Let past experience of thy care
> Support our hope, our trust invite!

271. Bebbington, *Evangelicalism in Modern Britain*, 61.

272. Rippon, *Selection of Hymns*, 680–81.

273. Cited in Broome, *Bruised Reed*, 145.

274. Broome, *Bruised Reed*, 143.

275. See *Second London Confession*, chap. 8, "Of Christ the Mediator," in Lumpkin, *Baptist Confessions of Faith*, 263.

Again attend our humble prayer!
Again be mercy thy delight!

Our arms succeed, our councils guide,
Let thy right hand our cause maintain;
Till war's destructive rage subside,
And peace resume her gentle reign.

O when shall time the period bring
When raging war shall waste no more:
When peace shall stretch her balmy wing
From Europe's coast to India's shore?

When shall the Gospel's healing ray
(Kind source of amity divine)
Spread o're the world celestial day?
When shall the nations, Lord! be thine?

First, she implores God to remember his care of Britain in the past. Then she alludes to the everyday realities of war and says that its "destructive rage" can only be transformed into a reign of peace through the work of God's "right hand"—"from Europe's coast to India's shore." She finishes with an evangelistic flourish reminiscent of Psalms 67 and 117, asking when the gospel will transform the nations, taking revival even beyond Britain, so making them the Lord's.

Following the Seven Years' War, Steele wrote two further hymns of thanksgiving for peace. "Praise for National Peace, Psalm xlvi.9"[276] is included in Rippon's hymnal:

Great Ruler of the earth and skies,
A word of thy Almighty breath
Can sink the world, or bid it rise;
Thy smile is life, thy frown is death.

When angry nations rush to arms,
And rage, and noise, and tumult reigns,
And war resounds its dire alarms,
And slaughter spreads the hostile plains;

Thy sov'reign eye looks calmly down,
And marks their course, and bounds their pow'r;

276. Rippon, *Selection of Hymns*, 684, 686.

Thy words the angry nations own,
And noise and war are heard no more;

Then peace returns with balmy wing,
(Sweet peace, with her what blessings fled!)
Glad plenty laughs, the valleys sing,
Reviving commerce lifts her head.

Thou good, and wise, and righteous Lord!
All move subservient to thy will;
And peace and war await thy word,
And thy sublime decrees fulfill.

To thee we pay our grateful songs,
Thy kind protection still implore;
O may our hearts, and lives, and tongues,
Confess thy goodness and adore.

Of particular interest in this hymn are a sustained note of thanksgiving and joy and a lack of the petitions of the previous hymns. It simply consists of praise, adoration, and thanksgiving, using the prophetic images of nature singing and the Calvinistic emphasis of God fulfilling his "sublime decrees."[277] And as an evangelical believed in the divine judgment upon nations, "likewise mercies could be individual or national."[278]

"For the 5th of November"[279] was written by Steele to commemorate the foiling of the Roman Catholic Gunpowder Plot in 1605. Rippon included all eight of the stanzas Steele composed to celebrate God's saving power seen in the life of Britain—"While Britain (favour'd of the skies)"—through such providential occurrences. Cho suggests that this hymn "is a firmly Protestant work" which "reflected the 'generally-held position' of the majority of the Protestant British."[280] Verses 3 through 6 out of eight total stanzas offer the sense of such beliefs expressed in the hymn:

When Hell and Rome combin'd their pow'r,
And doom'd these isles their certain prey,
Thy hand forbade the fatal hour,
Their impious plots in ruin lay.

---

277. See *Second London Confession*, chap. 3, "Of God's Decree," in Lumpkin, *Baptist Confessions of Faith*, 254–55.

278. Bebbington, *Evangelicalism in Modern Britain*, 61.

279. Rippon, *Selection of Hymns*, 687–88.

280. Cho, "Ministry of Song," 81.

Again our restless cruel foes
Resum'd, avow'd their black design;
Again to save us GOD arose,
And Britain own'd the hand divine.

Why, gracious GOD! is Britain sav'd?
Why bless'd with liberty and light?
Nor by fell tyranny enslav'd,
Nor lost in superstition's night?

Not for our sake, we conscious own;
A wretched, vile, ungrateful race:
'Tis done to make thy glory known,
To show the wonders of thy grace.

The *Second London Confession* does directly and bluntly contradict Roman Catholic teaching concerning the pope and the Mass in its chapters "Of the Church" and "Of the Lord's Supper."[281] Cho concludes, "The interpretation reflects the contemporary view that God had graciously saved Britain from error and superstition."[282] Believing Britain as favored by God in this mercy and other deliverances, Steele displays that "evangelicals were sometimes more forward than their contemporaries in detecting the hand of God in particular events."[283]

Listed in the subsection Sickness and Recovery, "Desiring the Presence of God in Affliction"[284] is Steele's final hymn among those concerning Times and Seasons in Rippon. This is one of the hymns in Rippon that find's Steele in the time of doubt, discouragement, and maybe even despondence, for which she was characterized for centuries. This analysis of her hymns in Rippon has demonstrated that while this was an aspect of her personality and spirituality, it was certainly not the prevailing characteristic projected by her hymns in Rippon's *Selection of Hymns*. Listed in its entirety below for the purpose of

281. See Lumpkin, *Baptist Confessions of Faith*, 285–89 and 291–93.

282. Cho, "Ministry of Song," 81.

283. Bebbington, *Evangelicalism in Modern Britain*, 61.

284. Rippon, *Selection of Hymns*, 692–93. Rippon left out the first two of the original verses of this hymn that Steele named "The Presence of God, the Only Comfort in Affliction." They are "In vain, while dark affliction spreads / Her melancholy gloom, / Kind providence its blessings sheds, / And nature's beauties bloom. / For all that charms the taste or sight / My heart no wish respires; / O for a beam of heavenly light / When earthly hope expires." Steele, *Works*, 2:172–74. This composition is found in Steele's published writing among her "miscellaneous pieces" and it does not appear to have been meant for corporate singing.

getting its message in full, one should consider whether this hymn in Long
Meter (88.88) leaves the reader or singer in faith or doubt:

> Thou only centre of my rest!
> Look down with pitying eye,
> While with protracted pain opprest
> I breathe the plaintive sigh.
>
> Thy gracious presence, O my God!
> My ev'ry wish contains;
> With this, beneath affliction's load,
> My heart no more complains.
>
> This can my ev'ry care controul,
> Gild each dark scene with light;
> This is the sunshine of the soul,
> Without it all is night.
>
> My Lord, my life, O cheer my heart
> With thy reviving ray,
> And bid these mournful shades depart,
> And bring the dawn of day!
>
> O happy scenes of pure delight!
> Where thy full beams impart
> Unclouded beauty to the sight,
> And rapture to the heart.
>
> Her part in those fair realms of bliss,
> My spirit longs to know;
> My wishes terminate in this,
> Nor can they rest below.
>
> Lord! shall the breathings of my heart
> Aspire in vain to thee?
> Confirm my hope, that, where thou art,
> I shall for ever be.
>
> Then shall my cheerful spirit sing
> The darksome hours away,
> And rise on faith's expanded wing
> To everlasting day.

Steele named this hymn "The Presence of God, the only Comfort in Affliction."[285] As was her custom, Steele begins with a word of faith ("center of my rest"), but in this case she quickly relays her problem in prayer (she is "with protracted pain opprest"). But before closing the first verse, she remembers Romans 8:26, which says, "Likewise the Spirit also helpeth our infirmities: for we know not what we should pray for as we ought: but the Spirit itself maketh intercession for us with groanings which cannot be uttered."[286] So she acknowledges to God that though in pain she will still "breathe the plaintive sigh." She starts from a posture of pain? Yes. But also from the place of faith. She continues with a parallel verse that restates and advances her prayerful argument. She wishes for God's presence, for that is actually all she needs. But the way she concludes the second verse leaves the singer in suspense as to whether she is sensing that presence currently or still wishing for it. Still referring to God's presence as stated in the first line of the second verse, the third verse continues the theme. God's presence will take care of her needs. Contrasted with night and darkness, it is the "sunshine of the soul." So while in the darkness, yet she prays.

The fourth and fifth verses are clearly the apex of the hymn and its central prayer. The "reviving ray" of the Lord brings cheer, day, delight, beauty, and rapture, both to the sight and heart. Here is one of the reasons this hymn though dark is also light, it is a prayer with which the believer can pray with Steele, even from the depths. There is no shame in affliction and spiritual darkness if one takes it to the Lord by faith.

The sixth verse continues the theme, but steps aside to reiterate the writer's circumstance. She takes four lines to drive home—to the Lord, no less—that nothing less than the reviving presence of the Lord will do for her. Next she returns to the "breathings" of her heart and pleads for confirmation now that where he is she shall "forever" be. Still in the present, Steele now appeals based on eternity. It seems faith's dark path is giving way to spiritual sight. Referring to this verse of this hymn as an example of a certain type of hymn found within the Steele corpus, Aalders says, "Wondering where she can turn in her sorrow, she confronts God, trusting that her search for him cannot be futile since it is God himself who asks believers to seek him and, indeed, establishes that longing in their hearts."[287]

---

285. See Steele, *Works*, 2:172–74.

286. Perhaps Steele had that entire majestic chapter concerning life in the Spirit in mind as she composed this hymn.

287. Aalders, *To Express the Ineffable*, 176. Aalders finds Steele's sighs and breathings as ways by which she tries yet to pray even when language fails. See Aalders, *To Express the Ineffable*, 176. But based on biblical prayers and teaching on prayer it seems that "breathings" and "sighs" might simply be other words for explaining prayer, and

And so Steele acts, as it were, like the persistent widow of the parable from Luke 18, whose constant coming wearied the unjust judge into avenging her cause. Steele knew, it seems, "And shall not God avenge his own elect, which cry day and night unto him, though he bear long with them?"[288] The final verse begins thus, "Then shall my cheerful spirit sing / The darksome hours away." But perhaps Steele also knew Jesus's answer to his own question from the verse in Luke, for the passage continued, "I tell you that he will avenge them speedily. Nevertheless when the Son of man cometh, shall he find faith on earth?"[289] Steele has an answer. She finishes the eighth verse, "And rise on faith's expanded wing / To everlasting day."

The biblical ascription for Psalm 102 reads, "A Prayer for the afflicted, when he is overwhelmed, and poureth out his complaint before the Lord." Some of Steele's hymns, especially ones like "Desiring the Presence of God in Affliction,"[290] display her affinity with such psalmists. She put real life Particular Baptist piety to verse. And these verses offered an opportunity for spiritual benefit to those who read and sang them.

Final Events

Final events punctuates Rippon's *Selection of Hymns*. Steele is well-represented as Rippon closes his hymnal. She has two hymns each in three of the final four sections of hymns: Time and Eternity, Death and Resurrection, and Heaven and Hell. In these Steele emphasizes Christian perseverance and assurance of grace in the face of sin and suffering and death.

Time and Eternity

Steele paraphrased Psalm 39, which Rippon included in his hymnal and gave the title "The Shortness of Time and Frailty of Man. Ps. xxxix."[291] The hymn is a plea for human beings to spend the short time they have on earth to the glory of God. The first of Steele's four verses explains the theme of all four: "Almighty Maker of my frame! / Teach me the measure of my days; / Teach me to know how frail I am, / And spend the remnant to thy

---

not necessarily used by Steele due to a failure of language. Further, in "Happy Poverty; or the Poor in Spirit blessed. Matt. v. 3" Steele equates breathing to praying: "Jesus to thee I breathe my prayer!" Rippon, *Selection of Hymns*, 287.

288. Luke 18:7.

289. Luke 18:8.

290. Rippon, *Selection of Hymns*, 692–93.

291. Rippon, *Selection of Hymns*, 704.

praise."[292] She agrees with and pleads the spirit of her confession of faith: "God is to be worshipped every where in Spirit, and in truth."[293] She further writes that "vain" are both the "ambition" and "treasures" of this world and so she prays to God, "O, be a nobler portion mine!" Also included in this section and of the same theme is "Time and Eternity; or, longing after unseen Pleasures. 2 Cor. iv. 18."[294] Here Steele opines that in this world "These transient scenes will soon decay" but that hope remains as the believer looks to heaven where one finds "joys unseen to mortal eyes." The last two verses aptly summarize this poem of seven stanzas:

> LORD! send a beam of light divine
> To guide our upward aim!
> With one reviving touch of thine
> Our languid hearts inflame.

> Then shall, on Faith's sublimest wing,
> Our ardent wishes rise
> To those bright scenes where pleasures spring
> Immortal in the skies.

Here Steele, as is often the case, asks the Lord to revive the human heart. She wrote her hymns with a view to man's growth in the grace of God. She knew that those "united to Christ" would have "a new Spirit created in them."[295] And through God's Spirit renewal would come.

Death and Resurrection

Theology and spirituality, belief and piety, have been the hallmarks of the hymns of Steele included in Rippon's influential hymnal. Along with the Scripture, the ordinances, prayer, and suffering, Beddome also preached that God draws near to his children at death.[296] Fellow Baptist pastor Samuel Medley's final days illustrated Beddome's claim. Among his final

292. Steele's paraphrase includes thirteen total verses from which Rippon chose four. As a paraphrased psalm, Steele gave it no title of her own.

293. Lumpkin, *Baptist Confessions of Faith*, 281.

294. Rippon, *Selection of Hymns*, 706. Rippon composed the first part of the title, Steele, the latter, including the biblical passage. "And all things are of God, who hath reconciled us to himself by Jesus Christ, and hath given to us the ministry of reconciliation" (2 Cor 4:18).

295. Lumpkin, *Baptist Confessions of Faith*, 267.

296. Beddome, "Communion with God Our Security and Bliss," in *Sermons*, 399–401, cited in Haykin, "Draw Nigh unto My Soul," 55.

hours, Medley bore witness, "I never saw so much of my own unworthiness, or so much of the excellency, glory and the suitableness of Christ as an all-sufficient Saviour."[297] Steele's experience of this very near enemy translated into poignant verses on this most sober of subjects. As one, like her Particular Baptist forefathers and as those to follow her, acquainted with the reality and sorrows of death, she composed a number of hymns and poems discussing this theme, sometimes commemorating the death of a beloved family member or friend.[298]

"Victory over Death through Christ. 1 Cor xv. 27,"[299] focuses on Christ's victory over death and the glory of the believer's union with him. Steele starts with the confession that death is overwhelming to the human being in his or her own power: "When death appears before my sight, / In all his dire array, / Unequal to the dreadful fight / My courage dies away." But believing that Jesus her Mediator, as the *Confession* teaches, "sitteth at the right hand of his Father, making intercession,"[300] she can declare, "But see my glorious Leader nigh! / My LORD—my Saviour lives; / Before him death's pale terrors fly, / And my faint heart revives." The Spirit of Christ gives the believer a spiritual vision of Jesus and thus revival is possible. Steele lived and wrote her hymns in light of such a truth. Steele then commits her "soul to thee" until "that illustrious morning come" and "thy triumphant armies sing." And true to her custom, she closes with a flourish of praise, but this time from heaven itself: "O let me join the raptur'd lays! / And with the blissful throng / Resound salvation, power, and praise, / In everlasting song!" For in heaven, Arnold notes, the "traversable bridge to [the] articulation" of "inspired conceptions" will have been crossed.[301] Home at last, the worshiper's tongue is eternally loosened for glorified praise.

"At the Funeral of a Young Person,"[302] is a thorough meditation on death that offers an evangelically Calvinistic exhortation on how all those left behind at the death of a young one should respond. It is solemn and yet hopeful. Notice how Steele acknowledges the sad situation in the first stanza. The next three then build the case for living with eternity in view.

---

297. Samuel Medley, cited in Sarah Medley, *Memoirs of the late Rev. Samuel Medley*, cited in Ramsbottom, "Samuel Medley," 248.

298. See Broome, *Bruised Reed*, 151–75.

299. Rippon, *Selection of Hymns*, 717. "For he hath put all things under his feet. But when he saith, all things are put under him, it is manifest that he is excepted, which did put all things under him." 1 Cor 15:27. The hymn's third and fourth verses as they appear in Rippon were not a part of Steele's original hymn. See Steele, *Works*, 1:150–51.

300. Lumpkin, *Baptist Confessions of Faith*, 262.

301. Arnold, "Veil of Interposing Night," 377.

302. Rippon, *Selection of Hymns*, 722, 724.

Life on earth is short. This world will lead to a tomb—at any moment. Listen and pray. The final two stanzas are a clear offer of the gospel of Jesus and a reminder of God's providence in life:

> When blooming youth is snatch'd away
> By death's resistless hand,
> Our hearts the mournful tibute pay
> Which pity must demand.
>
> While pity prompts the rising sigh,
> O may this truth, imprest
> With awful power—*I too must die!*
> Sink deep in ev'ry breast.
>
> Let this vain world engage no more:
> Behold the gaping tomb!
> It bids us seize the present hour:
> To-morrow death may come.
>
> The voice of this alarming scene
> May every heart obey;
> Nor be the heavenly warning vain,
> Which calls to watch and pray,
>
> O! let us fly—to JESUS fly
> Whose pow'rful arm can save;
> Then shall our hopes ascend on high,
> And triumph o're the grave.
>
> Great GOD! thy sovereign grace impart
> With cleansing, healing power;
> This only can prepare the heart,
> For death's surprising hour.

These verses serve as a walk through Steele's piety, faith, and theology in the face of death. First she offers a mournful spirit at the inescapability of death for all. Second, she reinforces the sadness and personalizes the reality of death. So she offers a sober assessment of this sting of sin. But this is for a purpose, for in the third stanza she peers at this "gaping tomb" in order to flee the passing worldly pleasures of the present hour. Next she presses toward obedience, watchfulness, and prayer. It is noteworthy that her piety of prayer recurs again and again in this hymn about death. The fifth stanza takes the reader to Jesus in faith and hope, as in him is "triumph o're the grave." Notice again here the Christ-centered spirituality of Steele and the Particular Baptists. Finally, in the final stanza Steele directly addresses God, through whose "healing power" one can "prepare the heart For death's surprising hour." Steele's faith understands the frailty of the human condition, but with hope in a sovereign and gracious God.

Hell and Heaven

Steele wrote a number hymns about death, but also about the other side of death for the believer: heaven. "The Joys of Heaven"[303] and "The Worship of Heaven. John xvii. 24"[304] each describe all the ways life in heaven will be better than in this fallen world and how keeping an eye on heaven results in a well-lived life in the present for the glory of Christ.

In "The Joys of Heaven" Steele begins a poem in which she prays for present manifestation of the "joys of heaven" with a reminder that on this side of eternity even the hearts of believers need divine assistance in praise: "Come, Lord and warm each languid heart, / Inspire each lifeless tongue: / And let the joys of heaven impart / Their influence to our song." She also celebrates the wonder that the suffering of this life and the disunity, perhaps even thinking of denominational conflict, "shall cease" before heaven's throne. She says, "Sorrow and pain, and every care, / And discord there shall cease; / And perfect joy, and love sincere, / Adorn the realms of peace."[305] Just as the *Second London Confession's* hope for the church in this life, that "Saints . . . do willingly consent to walk together according to the appointment of Christ, giving up themselves, to the Lord & one another by the will of God,"[306] Steele knows, will be sure reality in her eternal home. The *Second London Confession*, the English Particular Baptist expression of confessional piety, concludes with two chapters covering the issues of death, heaven (paradise with Christ), resurrection, and judgment,[307] and this analysis of the hymns of Anne Steele in Rippon's hymnal does the same. Steele, in fact, catches the sense of the *Confession* regarding these themes: "The soul from sin for ever free, / Shall mourn its power no more; / But, cloth'd in spotless

---

303. Rippon, *Selection of Hymns*, 756, 758. Steele's original hymn had thirteen stanzas of which Rippon skillfully retains six for what appears to be the purpose of clarity and focus. See Steele, *Works*, 1:52–54 for the full hymn as originally written.

304. Rippon, *Selection of Hymns*, 762–63.

305. "The Joys of Heaven" in Rippon, *Selection of Hymns*, 756.

306. Lumpkin, *Baptist Confessions of Faith*, 286.

307. Chap. 31, "Of the State of Man after Death and of the Resurrection of the Dead," and chap. 32, "Of the Last Judgement," in Lumpkin, *Baptist Confessions of Faith*, 293–94.

purity, / Redeeming love adore."[308] As the *Confession* teaches, "Their souls
. . . return to God who gave them; the Souls of the Righteous being then
made perfect in holiness, are received into paradise where they are with
Christ."[309] In the next two stanzas Steele meditates on the joy of seeing
Christ in heaven where "The Exalted Saviour shines." Aalders comments on
such a vision for Steele, "Now glorified, the Lamb inspires eternal worship
in those whose powers of speech, and thus ability to praise were once com-
promised by a persisting sinfulness."[310] Next Steele closes by praying that
God himself would "tune our hearts to praise and love" until the believer
may "join the angelic choir." Like Medley, Steele believed of God, "He can
put heaven into the soul before he takes you there."[311] Finally, when thinking of heaven, the atoning work of Christ remains in Steele's mind, for there
believers will "Redeeming love adore."

Steele's final hymn in the *Selection of Hymns* is a meditation Rippon
called "The Worship of Heaven. John xvii. 24."[312] Steele begins, according to
her own spiritual character, with sanctified wishing: "O for a sweet inspiring
ray, / To animate our feeble strains, / From the bright realms of endless day,
/ The blissful realms where Jesus reigns!" True to form she prays for help
with holy worship, this time painting a picture of the place from which such
power comes—the eternal realm of Christ. Jesus is after all the "King of the
Church of God."[313] The second through the fourth stanzas consider the intimate relationship between the glorified creature and the Creator at heaven's
throne where angel and saint would "with delightful worship, own / His
smile their bliss, their heav'n, their all." She sought through her hymns to
have a taste of such worship on earth which would be made manifest fully in
heaven. The final two verses of this hymn's five highlight the Christ-centered
focus of Steele's literary efforts and her zeal for the praise of Christ and even
her dependence upon the Spirit of God for revival:

> There all the fav'rites of the Lamb
> Shall join at last the heav'nly choir:
> O may the joy-inspiring theme
> Awake our faith and warm desire!

---

308. "The Joys of Heaven" in Rippon, *Selection of Hymns*, 756.

309. Lumpkin, *Baptist Confessions of Faith*, 293.

310. Aalders, *To Express the Ineffable*, 171.

311. Samuel Medley, cited in Ramsbottom, "Samuel Medley," 241.

312. Rippon, *Selection of Hymns*, 762–63. Steele called it "The Glorious Presence of
Christ in Heaven." She did not include a biblical reference.

313. Lumpkin, *Baptist Confessions of Faith*, 263.

Dear Saviour! let thy Spirit seal
Our int'rest in that blissful place;
Till death remove this mortal veil,
And we behold thy lovely face.

Steele truly savored the beauties of creation, but even more she wanted to see her Savior face-to-face and praise him with a perfected tongue. At the end of life on this earth, the *Confession* teaches, "The Righteous go into everlasting Life, and receive fullness of Joy, and Glory, with everlasting reward, in the presence of the Lord."[314] Steele in fact called this hymn "The Glorious Presence of Christ in Heaven," for she cherished that hope of being with Christ in the paradise that awaits the believer.

This analysis of the hymns of Anne Steele published in Rippon's *Selection of Hymns* demonstrates the convergence of the beliefs and practices characteristic of the Evangelical Revival and those marks of Particular Baptist spirituality highlighted in the confessions, sermons, letters, and journals of the English Baptist community within the collection of hymns that formed the "sung piety" that nurtured the revival in Particular Baptist life between the 1780s and 1830s.

---

314. Lumpkin, *Baptist Confessions of Faith*, 294.

6

Conclusion

"O let thy mercy tune my tongue": Rippon's Steele

To ATTEMPT TO DESCRIBE what, or who, might be called "Rippon's Steele,"[1] is a task obviously fraught with danger. Every reader or singer of her hymns, as well any contemporary researcher or hymnologist, brought and brings a set of presuppositions regarding poetry and hymns, not to mention theology and Christian spirituality, to such an endeavor. Regardless of how much objective criteria may be utilized, there is always a large bias given the subjective nature of the task. Nevertheless, it is a useful exercise to try and paint the broad portrait of Anne Steele that may have been seen by that blessed company of individuals and congregations to whom a copy of Rippon's popular *Selection of Hymns* providentially made its way. Such a picture will offer a summary by which to bring the previous chapter's analysis into clearer focus.

This book argues for Anne Steele's contribution to the revival in English Particular Baptist life between the 1780s and 1830s. Steele's fifty-two hymns published in Rippon's popular hymnal are the basis for this research. These hymns would have made up the *textus receptus* of Steele for the popular and pious singing public. When recent research of the entire extant Steele corpus of hymns, poems, journals, and letters is considered and briefly compared, the question is raised: who is the Anne Steele to which the

---

1. The hymn lyric in the heading is from "An Evening Hymn," in Rippon, *Selection of Hymns*, 642.

evangelical worshipers, singers, and readers of Rippon's *Selection of Hymns* were introduced?[2]

A woman filled with awe at the wonders of God's creation and providence, confident in praise of such a benevolent Creator, and compelled to praise him emerges in Steele's hymns in Rippon's first two sections: God, and Creation and Providence. Further, in each of the first two hymns included Steele speaks of the "bliss" which is shared by God's servants and is divinely free, respectively. Having suffered physically, Steele yet saw the life of faith in Christ as one of glad joy. This is the first impression made as one works through Steele's hymns in Rippon.

Further, Steele's hymns tend to have a sort of thesis of praise, theology, or experience stated in the first stanza. There is often a closing note of praise, or a supplication for divine help in so doing, whatever one's circumstance, in the final stanza. A center, or theological or experiential peak, may often be detected somewhere in the middle of the hymn. In other words, singers of Rippon found coherent hymns based on a particular theme, and always from a posture of both submission to God and of praise.

The hymns by Steele in Rippon's *Selection of Hymns* often close with a verse that expresses that God is most worthy of the praise of human tongues, that these tongues should praise him eternally even if unable at the present to do so as well they ought, and that Steele, for one, finds such singing a delightful blessing: "On us that Providence has shone / With gentle smiling rays: / O may our lips and lives make known / Thy goodness and thy praise!"[3] With such words Steele concludes the third hymn found in Rippon's hymnal. Her next to last hymn closes, "LORD! tune our hearts to praise and love, / Our feeble notes inspire; / Till in thy blissful courts above, / We join the angelic choir."[4] Sinners may need God's help in praise, but it is such a duty and a privilege as to be worth the request. Steele's hymns consistently come to a close with such a note of praise and petition.

Steele's sense of her relationship to the Father through Christ by the ministry of the Holy Spirit regularly comes out throughout her hymns in Rippon. This occurs in a number of ways, namely, in addressing God by his various biblical names, the desire for his smile and presence, an acknowledgment that he is her life, and the request for God to tune her voice. Steele addresses God as God, Lord, Almighty Maker, Great God, Dear Saviour, Jesus, Lamb, Spirit, Great Father, Almighty Father, Redeemer, Word,

2. The following summary of the nature, form, and content of Steele's hymns is based strictly on the balanced selection of fifty-two hymns as they appear in Rippon's *Selection of Hymns*.

3. "Creation and Providence," in Rippon, *Selection of Hymns*, 35.

4. "The Joys of Heaven," in Rippon, *Selection of Hymns*, 756, 758.

Advocate, and Friend, among other names. And she often uses adjectives describing attributes and relationships along with these names. In "To whom shall we go but unto thee? Or, Life and Safety in CHRIST alone. John vi. 67–69,"[5] referring to the "vain" and "alluring joys of earth" Steele prays, "One smile, one blissful smile of thine, / My dearest LORD, outweighs them all. / Thy name, my inmost powers adore, / Thou art my life, my joy, my care."[6] In this one line the reader catches a glimpse of the comprehensive nature of Steele's approach to her God. Finally, in "An Evening Hymn"[7] she asks, "GREAT GOD! to thee my evening song / With humble gratitude I raise: / O let thy mercy tune my tongue, / And fill my heart with lively praise."[8] Such is Steele's way of moving toward God.

Concerning recent scholarship, the hymn "Praise for the Blessings of Providence and Grace. Psalm cxxxix" offers an illustration of areas of possible contrast between the Steele that was mediated through Rippon's hymnal and, for example, the picture of Steele found by Cynthia Y. Aalders's research of the entire Steele corpus.[9] As was mentioned in the previous chapter, Rippon included only half the verses of this hymn in his hymnal. Among the lines he omitted one finds "My highest praise, alas, how poor! / How cold my warmest love!" and "But frail mortality in vain / Attempts the blissful song."[10] Aalders uses these lines as an illustration of her thesis regarding Steele's sense that human language was incapable of offering adequate praise to God. She writes, "These hymns demonstrate Steele's self-conscious feelings of hesitancy with regard to her own ability to use language to articulate praise to God."[11] At least three things must be mentioned in response. First, while

5. Rippon, *Selection of Hymns*, 580, 582.

6. Rippon, *Selection of Hymns*, 582.

7. Rippon, *Selection of Hymns*, 642.

8. Rippon, *Selection of Hymns*, 642.

9. See Aalders, *To Express the Ineffable*. As was stated in the section of this book considering recent scholarship on Steele, Aalders immersed herself in the Steele Collection housed at the Angus Library, Regent's Park College, Oxford, and was given access to Karen Smith's unpublished DPhil thesis on the Calvinistic Baptists of Hampshire and Wiltshire. Examining all of Steele's extant hymns, poems, and works of prose, both published and unpublished, as well as journals and letters of both Steele and her stepmother, Aalders reached her conclusions. She outlines Steele's life, hymnody, and piety based on Steele's "Problem of Language," "Problem of Suffering," and "Faith in an Ineffable God." A brief word of discussion will follow concerning certain aspects Aalders's theses regarding Steele and how they may contrast with the view of Steele accrued by those who read and/or sang her hymns as found in Rippon's popular and accessible *Selection of Hymns*.

10. Steele, *Works*, 1:67.

11. Aalders, *To Express the Ineffable*, 95–96. Richard Arnold expresses similar sentiments in his innovative essay on Steele. See Arnold, "Veil of Interposing Night," 371–87.

Rippon's failure to use these words in his hymnal does not negate their value in revealing something of Steele's personality and view of writing, to call this a major emphasis in Steele's theology and writing philosophy would perhaps be to overstate the case. In any case, it is certainly not a prevailing characteristic of Steele's hymnody as it is found in Rippon. Second, one reviewer may offer a different, or at least modified, interpretation of Steele's use of words, questions, dramatic grammatical gestures, and prayers regarding the articulation of praise and God's presence. As a transitional figure in the literary world of her day, Steele demonstrated both the "sense" to have a sober and humble view of speaking words to or about God but also the "sensibility" of writing with a flair for drama and emotion. Third, this study argues that the "received texts" of Steele through Rippon to the person in the pew, the typical reader and/or singer of Steele's hymnody, reveal her to be within the stream of the evangelical Calvinism that contributed to the revival among Particular Baptist life between 1780 and 1830. Rippon's own selection of his material obviously contributed to this picture of Steele.

A hymn Steele called "Christ the Life of the Soul. John xiv. 19,"[12] appeared in Rippon unmodified except for his dropping of "Christ the" from the title.[13] It serves as an excellent example of how one hymn may be perceived differently by different people. And it may shed light on how Steele's hymns were perhaps received by Rippon's singing public. In Aalders's chapter, "Anne Steele and the Problem of Language," after discussing Steele's understanding of God's ineffability and how it affects her hymns, Aalders says,

> In her hymn, "Christ the Life of the Soul,"[14] . . . she again relies on personal experience, beginning her hymn in that time
>
> When sins and fears prevailing rise,
> And fainting hope almost expires
>
> The tone is thus set early on, as Steele creates a feeling of tenderness and vulnerability. As we saw in the previous chapter, in these times that verge on despair, Steele doubts her ability even to speak, instead opting to "breathe" her "souls desires."[15] By the second verse, Steele begins to pose her questions, which invoke the difficulties invoked by her "fainting hope" and her distant Saviour.[16]

12. Steele, *Works*, 1:137–38.
13. Rippon, *Selection of Hymns*, 213.
14. Steele, *Works*, 1:137–38.
15. Steele, *Works*, 1:138.
16. Aalders, *To Express the Ineffable*, 129.

The hymn continues to its conclusion,

> Art thou not mine, my living Lord?
> And can my hope—my comfort die,
> Fix'd on the everlasting word,
> That word which built the earth and sky?

> If my immortal Saviour lives,
> Then my immortal life is sure;
> His word a firm foundation gives;
> Here let me build, and rest secure.

> Here let my faith unshaken dwell;
> Immoveable the promise stands;
> Not all the powers of earth or hell
> Can e'er dissolve the sacred bands.

> Here, O my soul, thy trust repose!
> If Jesus is for ever mine,
> Not death itself, that last of foes,
> Shall break a union so divine.

Aalders finds each "if," the one in the third stanza and the one in the fifth stanza, as expressing Steele's "hesitant tendencies."[17] And so Aalders suggests that Steele concludes the hymn with a "sensitive and introspective" effect.[18] Aalders acknowledges that the "if" may mean "since" or may be more intentional, the former interpretation expressing certainty, and the latter hesitancy.[19] It must be admitted that this tends to be a matter of interpretation. This book, arguing a thesis based on the foundation of Steele's Calvinistic background as explicated in the *Second London Confession*, and the evangelical tendencies present in her hymns in Rippon's hymnal, has already examined this hymn, finding it to exude a convincing tone of certainty.[20] Steele's two hymns, "Hope encouraged by a View of the Divine Perfections. 1 Sam. xxx.6"[21] and "Happy Poverty; or, the Poor in

---

17. Aalders, *To Express the Ineffable*, 129.

18. Aalders, *To Express the Ineffable*, 130.

19. See Aalders, *To Express the Ineffable*, 129–30.

20. Aalders does affirm, however, based on her analysis, that "despite being troubled by an inability to understand God's nature and ways, Steele continued to attempt expression, to pursue meaning where it alluded her." Aalders, *To Express the Ineffable*, 134.

21. Rippon, *Selection of Hymns*, 286.

Spirit Blessed. Matt. v. 3" in his hymnal,[22] found consecutively in Rippon, corroborate such a conclusion.

In another chapter on Steele, Aalders considers from a number of directions Steele's "resignation" to the will of an "ineffable God."[23] Aalders writes, for example, "Even while she waited in silence, troubled by limitations and loss, she persistently longed for what eluded her: an understanding of the nature of God, the experience of his very near presence, and the ability to articulate meaningful praise."[24] Those who sang from Rippon's hymnal, however, found such hymns such as "Pardoning Love. Jer. iii. 22 and Hos. xiv. 1," "Weary Souls Invited to Rest. Matt. xi. 28," and "The Saviour's Invitation. John vii. 37"[25] by Steele, each of which has been considered in detail above. In these hymns, Steele boldly, though also humbly, approaches God in prayer, calling for others to do the same, based on an understanding of his character and a sense that his presence can indeed be experienced:

> Almighty grace, thy healing power
>   How glorious, how divine!
> That can to life and bliss restore
>   So vile a heart as mine.
>
> Thy pardoning love, so free, so sweet,
>   Dear Saviour, I adore;
> O keep me at thy sacred feet,
>   And let me rove no more.[26]

Further, Steele shows no hesitation to offer words of praise to God, even if she knows they are ultimately inadequate this side of glory: "Almighty Father, gracious Lord! / Kind guardian of my days, / Thy mercies let my heart record / In songs of grateful praise."[27] The Dissenting worshipers of the late eighteenth and nineteenth centuries sang such praises with Steele as a trusted guide. While Steele may have written in her journals and letters about a sense of inadequacy to the task of seeking to praise an infinite God within her context as an eighteenth-century English woman, she still did it—to the eternal benefit of those who sang her compositions. So even if a perceived

22. Rippon, *Selection of Hymns*, 287.

23. Chap. 5, "'Teach the Breathings of My Heart Dependence and Desire': Anne Steele's Faith in an Ineffable God," cited in Aalders, *To Express the Ineffable*, 136–71.

24. Aalders, *To Express the Ineffable*, 149.

25. Rippon, *Selection of Hymns*, 88, 90, 134–35, and 137–38.

26. "Pardoning Love. Jer. iii, 22 Hos. xiv. 1," in Rippon, *Selection of Hymns*, 88, 90.

27. Verse 1 of "Praise for the Blessings of Providence and Grace. Psalm cxxxix," in Rippon, *Selection of Hymns*, 88, 90.

hesitancy may be detected in a detailed study of the entirety of Steele's extant papers, an examination of her hymns as found in Rippon's *Selection of Hymns* reveals a woman who unhesitatingly praised God in poetic song. Perhaps Steele shares something of the spiritual DNA of Heman the Ezrahite, writer of Psalm 88, with which Steele would no doubt have been familiar. Though feeling the affliction, the wrath, as well as a perceived absence of God and his lovingkindness, yet Heman still prays. Day and night, even from such a position of affliction, Heman cannot help but cry out in prayer to the one whom he even says put "mine acquaintance into darkness" (Psalm 88:18). Steele did the same. She knew God in Christ through the Holy Spirit. Him she pursued—in life, in song, and in death.

One hymn listed in full[28] as found in Rippon illustrates each of these issues and offers an example of how Steele would instinctively answer the tough questions of faith and doubt within a single hymn.[29] "Advocate. 1 John ii. 1"[30] was the first of the hymns Rippon included concerning the Characters and Representations of Christ." The hymn begins with a sincere admission of Steele's questions for God. The second verse offers an emphatic answer. The third verse shows Steele talking to herself with the truth of God's promises rather than listening to herself in the times of doubt. The fourth verse reflects on the work of her Advocate and Redeemer. She concludes with a confessional prayer of supplication. Steele writes,

> Where is my God? does he retire
> Beyond the reach of humble sighs?
> Are these weak breathings of desire
> Too languid to ascend the skies?
>
> No, Lord! the breathings of desire,
> The weak petition, if sincere,
> Is not forbidden to aspire,
> But reaches thy all-gracious ear.

28. It was not listed in full in the last chapter.

29. Again, the illustration this hymn provides does not comprehensively answer the questions of Steele's overall view of human language and the praise of God or a hesitancy some may perceive in Steele to approach a holy and majestic God. It does, however, give an example of how the reading and singing public of Rippon's popular *Selection of Hymns* would have seen Steele wrestle with such dilemmas in a hymn.

30. Rippon, *Selection of Hymns*, 183–84. Rippon left out the second and third stanzas of Steele's original seven. In terms of content the second was basically parallel to the first as well as the fourth to the third. The hymn thus retains its intended meaning in Rippon's presentation.

Look up, my soul, with cheerful eye,
See where the great Redeemer stands,
The glorious Advocate on high,
With precious incense in his hands!
He sweetens every humble groan,
He recommends each broken prayer;
Recline thy hope on him alone,
Whose power and love forbid despair.

Teach my weak heart, O gracious Lord!
With stronger faith to call thee mine;
Bid me pronounce the blissful word,
My Father, God, with joy divine.

In a hymn called "Watchfulness and Prayer. Matt. xxvi. 41,"[31] which was considered in detail above, Steele writes and prays,

Alas! what hourly dangers rise!
    What snares beset my way!
To heaven O let me lift my eyes,
    And hourly watch and pray.

How oft my mournful thoughts complain,
    And melt in flowing tears!
My weak resistance, ah! how vain;
    How strong my foes and fears! . . .

O keep me in thy heavenly way,
    And bid the tempter flee;
And let me never, never stray,
    From happiness and thee.

Steele's hymns seek to apply the depth of Christian doctrine to the depth of Christian experience. She accomplishes this by skillfully building tension and then bringing it to resolution as the first and last verses of the above hymn above illustrate. J. R. Watson discusses at length the Steele he finds in such verses that encapsulates much of the current discussion:

Her poems and hymns indicate a distinct movement away from the generalized view of divine providence found in Addison, and from the Christian happiness found in Doddridge. She contemplates the world as a place where good and evil happen

31. Rippon, *Selection of Hymns*, 398. "Watch and pray, that ye enter not into temptation: the spirit indeed *is* willing, but the flesh *is* weak" (Matt 26:41).

(the deaths of children, [and others]), and recognizes its double nature feelingly: she is conscious of its beauty and fertility, but also of its unhappiness. Her solution is to enter into a personal relationship with the Saviour, in a way which parallels the writing of her contemporary Charles Wesley.[32]

While Puritanism and Evangelicalism actually share many common doctrines and characteristics, it is with the doctrine of assurance that they did tend to part ways. Bebbington posits, "Whereas the Puritans had held that assurance is rather rare, late and the fruit of struggle in the experience of believers, the Evangelicals believed it to be general, normally given at conversion and the result of simple acceptance of the gift of God."[33] Steele obviously had both Puritan and evangelical blood flowing in her spiritual veins. While Aalders does not suggest that Steele was unsure of her own salvation, she does find in Steele doubt and introspection and a desire to make sense of sufferings, though somewhat allayed by her Calvinistic theology. But even in discussing these things Aalders suggests a level of assurance in Steele. Aalders writes, "We see that despite her prolonged meditations on human suffering and human inarticulacy—despite her perception of God as ineffable—Steele's hymnody remains essentially hopeful, enabling her to make affirmations about God and the spiritual life."[34] Steele wrote, after all, "Dear Saviour! let thy powerful love / Confirm our faith, our fears remove; / And sweetly influence ev'ry breast, / And guide us to eternal rest."[35] Steele certainly found sanctification to be a difficult journey, but she could also see the finish line. And while it is beyond the scope of this study to examine and discuss every aspect of Steele as perceived by Aalders or Steele's other biographers, it is fair to say that according to the hymns included in his *Selection of Hymns*, "Rippon's Steele" was characterized more by an assurance in God than a focus on his ineffability.

Steele can also often pack a lot into a few short verses. In "Redemption by Christ alone. 1 Pet. i. 18, 19,"[36] for example, it has been demonstrated that Steele does several things at once. In this hymn's six verses, there are at least hints of each characteristic of evangelicalism as submitted by Bebbington. There is also a thoroughgoing Particular Baptist theology as found in the *Second London Confession* embedded within Steele's poetic

32. Watson, *English Hymn*, 198. Watson has just discussed Addison and Doddridge prior to his consideration of Steele.

33. Bebbington, *Evangelicalism in Modern Britain*, 43.

34. Aalders, *To Express the Ineffable*, 159.

35. "Weary Souls Invited to Rest. Matt. xi. 28," in Rippon, *Selection of Hymns*, 135.

36. Rippon, *Selection of Hymns*, 72–73.

lyrics. It displays the teaching of historic evangelical Calvinistic preaching, such as Keach's: "I mean to work Grace in them, and to change their Hearts, and vanquish the Power of Sin, and *Satan*, for this is and must be done by that Almighty Power which he exerts by his Spirit in their Souls, and so takes possession of them as King and Supream Ruler, whom as a Priest he purchased by his Blood."[37] Finally, there is the movement from human experience to a proclamation of the work of God in Christ to a proper response of faith, praise, and obedience.

For example, the first two stanzas depict humanity's devastating predicament due to the fall ("Enslav'd by sin, and bound in chains, / Beneath its dreadful tyrant sway"), the middle two Christ's overwhelming solution to the predicament through his active and passive obedience ("Jesus the sacrifice became / To rescue guilty souls from hell") and the final two verses a prayer/plea for a proper response from men and women ("Amazing goodness! love divine! / O may our grateful hearts adore"). The depth of both theology and experience as revealed within a pleasant poetic flow in such hymns by Steele is evident.

The depth of Steele's theological reflections and her sense of translating doctrine into experiential categories together shine in her hymns specifically focused on Christ. As the previous chapter showed, Rippon made liberal use of Christ-centered hymns from Steele's pen. Aalders explains, Steele's faith, and the expression of that faith in her hymnody, cannot be appreciated completely without some consideration given to her powerful devotion to the person of Christ."[38] Aalders notes further, "As with other eighteenth-century Calvinistic Baptists, Steele had a large view of her own sinfulness."[39] But she also knew where the only ultimate antidote for sin could be found: in the atonement of Christ for sinners. Steele believed her Christ "the Prophet, Priest, and King of the Church of God,"[40] as the *Confession* taught and her father preached.

As mentioned earlier, Steele often closes her hymns with an exhortation to all to lift their voices to the Lord in prayer. She believes that all people everywhere should offer praise to God with the very words of their mouths. She is not hesitant to pray in concluding a hymn exalting Christ, "Jesus, may all

---

37. Benjamin Keach, *The Display of Glorious Grace* (London: 1698), 70–71, cited in Nettles, "Benjamin Keach," 105.

38. Aalders, *To Express the Ineffable*, 168.

39. Aalders, *To Express the Ineffable*, 84.

40. Lumpkin, *Baptist Confessions of Faith*, 263.

our hearts be thine, / And all our tongues proclaim thy praise!"[41] The hymns of Rippon's Steele illustrate an evangelistic element to praise.

Rippon's Steele was marked by both realism and hope. While looking to a heavenly home she had her feet firmly planted upon the fruitful soil created by her God. Her hymns in Rippon's final sections concerning death and hell and heaven illustrate that it is Steele's theology that informs her understanding of human words and songs. It is her Calvinistic understanding that the doctrine of man relates to the doctrine of God that causes her to reflect as she does about language and praise. Rippon was willing to include such words from Steele: "Come, Lord and warm each languid heart, / Inspire each lifeless tongue: / And let the joys of heaven impart / Their influence to our song."[42] The *Second London Confession* teaches that because of the fall of man, all humans have a "*corrupted* nature" and are "by nature children of wrath, the servants of *Sin*, the subjects of *death*, and all other miseries, spiritual, temporal and eternal, unless the *Lord Jesus* sets them free."[43] Steele, likewise, believed in the depravity of man. But the *Confession* also teaches that those regenerated by the Spirit of Christ may do good works, but their ability to do so is "wholly from the *Spirit*."[44] Man will not sing words of praise to God in his own power. But Steele also believes in redemption through Christ: "Lord! send a beam of light divine / To guide our upward aim! / With one reviving touch of thine / Our languid hearts inflame."[45] To praise God aright humans need new hearts. And in saying so Steele even prays directly for revival!

Steele's understanding of the Creator/creature distinction even leads Steele to write, "What glory, Lord, to thee is due! / With wonder we adore; / But, could we sing as angels do, / Our highest praise were poor." [46] Yet in some sense, she also believes that in heaven itself, things will all ultimately be made right once and for all: "There shall the followers of the Lamb / Join in immortal songs; / And endless honours to sing his name / Employ their tuneful tongues."[47] As Aalders notes, "Even as Steele awaited the future healing of her various infirmities . . . she anticipated the eschatological

---

41. "The Exalted Saviour," in Rippon, *Selection of Hymns*, 174.

42. "The Joys of Heaven," in Rippon, *Selection of Hymns*, 756.

43. Lumpkin, *Baptist Confessions of Faith*, 259.

44. Lumpkin, *Baptist Confessions of Faith*, 271.

45. "Time and Eternity; or, longing after unseen Pleasures. 2 Cor. iv. 18," in Rippon, *Selection of Hymns*, 706.

46. "The Incarnation. John i. 14," in Rippon, *Selection of Hymns*, 154.

47. "The Joys of Heaven," in Rippon, *Selection of Hymns*, 756.

perfection of her praise."[48] And this inspires the praise of God's people even on this side of heaven: "There all the fav'rites of the Lamb / Shall join at last the heav'nly choir: / O may the joy-inspiring theme / Awake our faith and warm desire!"[49] The hymns of Anne Steele included in Rippon's *Selection of Hymns* offered Particular Baptist worshipers a vehicle through which to rehearse confessional theology, to renew acts of evangelical Calvinistic piety, and to respond to God's goodness and grace with tongues of praise.

"My Lord, my life, O cheer my heart / With thy reviving ray": Steele's Contribution to the Revival

Though largely forgotten by the end of the twentieth century, Anne Steele was once known as one of the best in her craft.[50] Steele was acknowledged as a giant not only among the highly talented group of Particular Baptist hymn-writer pastors of her generation, but was also mentioned alongside the pioneers of the English hymn such as Watts, Wesley, Newton, and Cowper. This book has argued for her contribution to the revival in English Particular Baptist life at the end of the eighteenth century that continued well into the nineteenth. More specifically it has demonstrated that Anne Steele's hymns illustrate and articulate eighteenth-century English Baptist piety in verse, particularly as expressed in the *Second London Confession*. The working definition of piety here is "devotion to religious practices and 'means of grace.'"[51] Piety may also be referred to as spirituality. Michael Haykin uses a host of Particular Baptist illustrations of piety, means of piety, or "means of grace" to zero in on three central expressions of this piety: the Scriptures (the Spirituality of the Word), the ordinances (baptism and the Lord's Supper), and prayer.[52] According to Karen Smith, Steele's father and pastor, William Steele, "described the Word and the ordinances as a 'means of grace when Christ is manifest and entertains the believer with Grace.'"[53] From

---

48. Aalders, *To Express the Ineffable*, 153.

49. "The Worship of Heaven. John xvii. 24," in Rippon, *Selection of Hymns*, 763.

50. The hymn lyric in the heading is from "Desiring the Presence of God in Affliction," in Rippon, *Selection of Hymns*, 692.

51. Means of grace are divinely ordained means by which God ministers to, communes with, spiritually nourishes, and/or grows the faith of his children through his Word and Spirit. See Haykin, "Draw Nigh unto My Soul," 54–73.

52. Haykin, "Draw Nigh unto My Soul," 54–73. As descendants of the Puritans, these three disciplines follow the Puritan "means of grace," namely, prayer, hearing the word, and the Sacraments. See Haykin, "Draw Nigh unto My Soul," 54.

53. Smith, "Covenant Life of Some Eighteenth-Century Baptists in Hampshire and Wiltshire," 179, quoting William Steele, Steele Collection, Angus Library.

Benjamin Beddome, Haykin lists two other ways in which "God draws near to his people," namely, in "'the time of affliction' and death."[54] Steele's hymns as published in Rippon's *Selection of Hymns* and thus received by the Baptist and the Evangelical public are a rich resource that illustrates these five aspects of English Baptist piety.

Anne Steele's hymns reveal convictions characterized by the Evangelical Revival, such as a focus on the Scripture, evangelism, the changed life, and the atoning work of Christ. They also reveal the Calvinistic doctrines taught in the *Second London Confession*. Her poetic expression of such beliefs helped fuel the revival of piety and a vibrant church life among Particular Baptists. Her understanding of the Scripture stands as a foundation of her influence. Using a term taken from Alister McGrath, Haykin describes the English Baptists as "Word-centered evangelicals."[55] He continues, "Given this prominence of the Scriptures in the life of Baptists, it is not surprising that hearing the Word preached was regarded by them as a vital spiritual discipline and *the* pre-eminent aspect of worship."[56] Steele's "homiletical" hymns as sung from Rippon's hymnal gave opportunity for this view of the Word of God and of worship to be both deepened intellectually and reinforced experientially. In "Life of the Soul. John xiv. 19,"[57] for example, Steele prays, "Art thou not mine, my living Lord? And can my hope, my comfort die, Fix'd on thy everlasting word, That word which built the earth and sky?" Here she displays the *Second London Confession's* declarations of the authority, power, and sufficiency of the Bible as well its instruction of the believer in the knowledge and foundation of Christian hope.[58] Steele's hymns formed a sort of singing companion to such other literary works as her contemporary Benjamin Beddome's exposition of Particular Baptist forefather and hero Benjamin Keach's catechism. Beddome asked of Scripture: "Is the Word of God a rule? Yes. It is *a light to our feet, and a lamp to our path*, Ps. cxix. 105. Do we need such a rule? Yes. For *we all like sheep have gone astray, Isa. liii. 6.* Is the word of *God* a sufficient rule? Yes. *The law of the Lord is perfect,* Ps. xix. 7."[59] Steele agreed, for her warm lyrics both taught and encouraged those who participated in worship through her hymns to view the Bible as

---

54. Haykin, "Draw Nigh unto My Soul," 55.

55. The term is taken from Alister McGrath, *Evangelicalism and the Future of Christianity* (London: Hodder & Stoughton, 1993), 66, and cited in Haykin, "Draw Nigh unto My Soul," 55.

56. Haykin, "Draw Nigh unto My Soul," 55.

57. Rippon, *Selection of Hymns*, 213.

58. See Lumpkin, *Baptist Confessions of Faith*, 248–52.

59. Benjamin Beddome, *A Scriptural Exposition of the Baptist Catechism* (Bristol: W. Pine, 1776), 11–12, cited in Haykin, "Benjamin Beddome," 177.

she did, "as a mine of wealth, a tree of knowledge, a wonderful feast, a spring of life-giving water."[60] Such is the very vocabulary of revival.

Rippon's four hymns by Steele that he included in his section on the Lord's Supper reveal a vigorous Communion theology. Two of them describe the partaking of the supper while describing what it represents and two of them focus on the one about whom the supper is a remembrance of and of whom one partakes in it. Smith records that Steele's father William wrote of the Lord's Supper, "Christ himself is the feast and persons by faith spiritually feed on him."[61] Manley notes that Rippon included nineteen Communion hymns, some of which he described as "Sacramental Hymns,"[62] but most of which were "appropriate meditations on the death of Christ."[63] Stanzas 3 and 4 from "The Wonders of Redemption"[64] illustrate,

> He took the dying traitor's place,
>   And suffer'd in his stead;
> For man, (O miracle of grace!)
>   For man the Saviour bled!

> Dear LORD! what heav'nly wonders dwell
>   In thy atoning blood!
> By this are sinners snatch'd from hell,
>   And rebels brought to GOD.

And for Steele, the assurance she found from the atonement, from her justification, regularly sprouted forth in evangelistic lyrics. Bruce Hindmarsh suggests, "A more robust assurance among evangelicals was the source of the tremendous energy they expended in mission."[65] Steele's fourth Communion hymn found in Rippon includes the prayer,

> Dear LORD! while we adoring pay
>   Our humble thanks to thee,
> May ev'ry heart with rapture say,
>   *The Saviour died for me.*

60. From Sharon James's analysis of Steele's hymn, "The Excellency and Sufficiency of the Holy Scriptures," in *In Trouble and in Joy*, 155.

61. Smith, "Covenant Life of Some Eighteenth-Century Baptists," 179, quoting William Steele, Steele Collection, Angus Library.

62. Rippon, *Selection of Hymns*, 619–37, in Manley, "John Rippon and Baptist Hymnody," 108.

63. Manley, "John Rippon and Baptist Hymnody," 108.

64. Rippon, *Selection of Hymns*, 631–32. Steele added a Scripture reference, 1 Pet 3:18, which reads, "For Christ also hath once suffered for sins, the just for the unjust, that he might bring us to God, being put to death in the flesh, but quickened by the Spirit." See *Works*, 1:168.

65. Hindmarsh, "Antecedents of Evangelical Conversion Narrative," 328.

> O may the sweet, the blissful theme
>> Fill ev'ry heart and tongue:
> Till strangers love thy charming name,
>> And join the sacred song.

And so there is a note of evangelism in an atonement hymn included for the service of the Lord's Supper. A monthly administration of the ordinance along with heartfelt singing of Christ, the Lamb slain for sinners, gave worshipers an opportunity for true spiritual renewal and even regeneration, should the Holy Spirit so move.[66]

Many, if not most, of Steele's hymns have a prayerful quality about them. But some stanzas and even some hymns in full are direct prayers to God covering the typical aspects of biblical prayer: adoration, confession, thanksgiving, and supplication. Like Particular Baptist pastors, John Ryland Jr. and John Sutcliff, Steele's prayerful hymns display that "the grand objective in prayer is to be that the Holy Spirit may be poured down on our ministers and churches, that sinners may be converted, the saints edified, the interest of religion revived, and the name of God glorified."[67]

Moreover, Steele's hymns that consider the atonement of Christ for sinners show that for Steele, "it would appear that in the sanctification of her life of suffering and weakness, she had often been led to meditate on the suffering sorrows of her Redeemer."[68] Steele's hymns display a Christ-centered and cross-centered view of suffering. Writing of the sufferings of her Redeemer and the redemption he provided through his blood, Steele found at the cross a place for suffering sinners. She approached suffering and death with her eyes fixed on Christ, and wrote hymns expressing faith in the face of the world, the flesh and the devil as well as the physical afflictions of her time. Steele showed no fear or discomfort at the prospect of singing about a Savior, Jesus Christ, who bore the wrath of God in the place of sinners that they might receive his perfect righteousness credited to them by faith. Further, as a member of a generation of Particular Baptists who believed in a "limited atonement" or a "particular redemption," Steele's hymns display no hesitation at freely offering the gospel of Jesus Christ by way of song.

Steele's hymns brimmed with both illustrations of and exhortations toward English Particular Baptist piety. For Steele, teaching and singing about the doctrines of the faith were meant to result in a life of gratitude and joyful obedience for the believer. One scholar notes that there was a "theological self-consciousness reflected in Baptist confessions" such as the *Second London*

---

66. See Smith, "Covenant Life of Some Eighteenth-Century Baptists," 179.

67. John Ryland Jr., *The Nature, Evidences and Advantages of Humility* (1784), 12, cited in Haykin, "Habitation of God, Through the Spirit," 310.

68. Broome, *Bruised Reed*, 169.

Confession.[69] Anne Steele illustrates this in her hymns. Steele's hymns demonstrate L. G. Champion's description of the evangelical Calvinism at the center of the revival in Particular Baptist life: It was "strongly grounded in a firm conviction about the nature of God, affirming the primacy of His grace in Christ and finding both strength and purpose through the personal responsibility brought by the obligation to respond in faith, to order life by a moral law and to bring the gospel to all mankind."[70] In summary, Richard Arnold says that eighteenth-century "hymns were expected to educate, arouse, or spiritually benefit or satisfy a congregation, to propagate and support certain religious and theological principles and specific orientations toward Christian experience, and to provide hope or assurance for one's beliefs and aspirations."[71] Anne Steele's confessional atonement hymns provide evidence for Arnold's claim, as she sang of the work of her Redeemer. J. R. Broome adds, "Simply to state doctrine in her hymns was a source of pleasure to Anne."[72] And in her approach to facing the sufferings of a fallen world with confidence, Anne Steele was firmly focused on the cross of Jesus Christ.

Steele's hymns, written by a committed Particular Baptist, often have an evangelistic thrust. Her pastor and father, William Steele "made a point of hearing and meeting George Whitefield."[73] And he preached thus of Christ's summons to sinners, "O how full is the invitation, how plain is the call to that soul to come unto the water."[74] Steele's hymns, like her father's sermons, confirm through sung piety Morgan Patterson's thesis: "The spirit of revival engendered by the Wesleys and Whitefield prompted a new evangelistic spirit among the Baptists."[75] In the early stages of the revival among the Particular Baptists, Robert Hall Sr. preached, "The way to Jesus is graciously laid open for every one who chooses to come to him."[76] Steele, likewise, pleads through her poetic verses with sinners to come to Christ. "Weary Souls Invited to Rest. Matt. xi. 28" and "The Saviour's Invitation. John vii. 37" are two examples of such hymns.[77] Comment-

69. Nettles, *Baptists*, 1:36.

70. Champion, "Evangelical Calvinism," 200.

71. Arnold, "Veil of Interposing Night," 374.

72. Broome, *Bruised Reed*, 175.

73. Broome, *Bruised Reed*, 194.

74. William Steele, sermon notes of a sermon on the text from Rev 22:17 housed in Angus Library, Oxford, in Broome, *Bruised Reed*, 195.

75. Patterson, "Evangelical Revival and the Baptists," 260.

76. Robert Hall Sr., *Help to Zion's Travellers*, in *The Baptist Library*, ed. Charles G. Sommers et al. (New York: Lewis Colby and Co., 1846), vol. III, 87, cited in Haykin, "Robert Hall, Sr," 207.

77. Rippon, *Selection of Hymns*, 134–35, and 137–38.

ing on the latter, Sharon James notes, "The Calvinism of the Particular Baptists did not preclude firm belief in the free offer of the gospel."[78] Steele wrote, for example, "Ye sinners, come; 'tis mercy's voice, / The gracious call obey: / Mercy invites to heavenly joys— / And can you yet delay?"[79] Such Calvinism not only did not hinder revival, it actually encouraged revival. As Bebbington submits, "The fulcrum of change was the doctrine of assurance. Those who knew their sins forgiven were freed from debilitating anxieties for Christian mission."[80] Steele's hymns in Rippon's hymnal are thus examples of such an offer and a biblical theology that contributed to a revived spiritual life among those who sang them.

Rippon's hymnal, organized according to theological and ecclesiastical concerns, showcases Steele's illustration of and contribution to the Particular Baptist piety and spiritual devotion of her generation and those that followed. Manley says, "All the evidence suggests that Rippon's book did meet the devotional and worshipping requirements of English Calvinist Baptists for more than one generation."[81] Hymn-writing was an expression of English particular Baptist piety undertaken especially by a number of pastors. Benjamin Beddome, for example, often composed "a hymn to be sung after his sermon on the Lord's Day morning."[82] Steele's hymns are an example of this piety as well. The *Second London Confession* has served as a theological control in this analysis of Steele's hymns. Teaching doctrine and instructing the religious affections, a purpose of the confession of faith, was also a purpose of the English hymn. Bebbington testifies both that "almost the whole Evangelical world read poetry" and that one aim of evangelical hymns was "to transmit doctrine to their singers."[83] It has been previously noted that Steele herself once commented on one of the purposes of her poetry, "'Sacred Poesy' is best employed 'in the service of Religion.'"[84] The poetry of Steele disseminated through Rippon's *Selection of Hymns* bears out her claim.

78. James, *In Trouble and in Joy*, 154.

79. Rippon, *Selection of Hymns*, 138.

80. Bebbington, *Evangelicalism in Modern Britain*, 74.

81. Manley, "John Rippon and Baptist Hymnody," 104.

82. Cramp, *Baptist History*, 519. Concerning Particular Baptist churches, Benson notes that "one effect of the use of [Isaac] Watts' hymns was to encourage the habit of employing the last hymn in the service as an application of the sermon." See Benson, *English Hymn*, 143.

83. Bebbington, *Evangelicalism in Modern Britain*, 67, 68.

84. Steele to anonymous woman, 8 August 1761, STE 3/13 (vii), in Aalders, *To Express the Ineffable*, 35.

It should also be briefly stated that poetry written skillfully for the purposes of praise and piety has the potential through its very form to bring fruit. Rhyming lyrics are memorable. Verses that draw the worshiper and the sinner, the disciple and the pilgrim, before the throne of God's grace are tools in the hands of the Spirit of Christ with which he does as he wishes to the glory of the Father and the good of his children. Poetic devices are more than mere aesthetic additions or dressings, but are powerful tools in the hands of a wordsmith. It is not an overstatement to suggest that Steele illustrates Austin Lovelace's claim, "There is more subtlety and craftsmanship in great hymns than meets the eye (or the ear)."[85]

Serving her Christ through songs proclaiming his great finished work and its ongoing benefits to believers and any who would simply come to him by faith, Steele made her contribution to the revival in Particular Baptist life in the decades immediately following her death in 1778. One writer said of Steele, No woman "has so largely contributed to the familiar hymnology of the church as the modest and retiring, but gifted and godly, Anne Steele."[86] Anne Steele, writing during the "golden age" of the English hymn and ushering in the golden age of Baptist hymnody, wrote evangelical hymns that directed the congregation to sing praises to God in worship, taught of the depth and richness of the theology of the Scriptures as taught in the *Second London Confession*, and gave believers a prayerful avenue through which to express their affections for God and the emotions that come from living in a sin-stained world. Through her hymns Steele meditated on the person and work of Jesus Christ for her and invited others to come to him alone for spiritual rest. Steele covered a wide breadth of doctrine and revealed a robust piety in her gospel-driven, biblically sound, articulately expressed, and emotionally compelling compositions showcased by Rippon in his popular hymnal.

85. Lovelace, *Anatomy of Hymnody*, 93.

86. Edwin F. Hatfield, *The Poets of the Church: A Series of Biographical Sketches of Hymn-writers with Notes on Their Hymns* (New York: Anson D. F. Randolph & Co., 1884), 570, cited in Burrage, *Baptist Hymn Writers and Their Hymns*, 46.

Bibliography

Aalders, Cynthia Y. "'In Melting Grief and Ardent Love': Anne Steele's Contribution to Eighteenth-Century Hymnody." *The Hymn* 60 (2009) 16–25.

———. *To Express the Ineffable: The Hymns and Spirituality of Anne Steele*. Studies in Baptist History and Thought 40. Milton Keynes, UK: Paternoster, 2008.

Adey, Lionel. *Class and Idol in the English Hymn*. Vancouver: University of British Columbia Press, 1988.

———. *Hymns and the Christian "Myth."* Vancouver: University of British Columbia Press, 1986.

Anderson, Jan. "Were Hymns Good Poetry?" *Christian History* 10 (1991) 29.

Arnold, Richard. *The English Hymn: Studies in a Genre*. New York: Peter Lang, 1995.

———, ed. *English Hymns of the Eighteenth Century: An Anthology*. American University Studies Series 4. English Language and Literature 137. New York: Peter Lang, 1991.

———. "A 'Veil of Interposing Night': The Hymns of Anne Steele (1717–1778)." *Christian Scholar's Review* 18 (1989) 371–87.

Ash, John, and Caleb Evans, eds. *A Collection of Hymns Adapted to Public Worship*. Bristol, England: W. Pine, 1769.

Bailey, Albert Edward. *The Gospel in Hymns: Backgrounds and Interpretations*. New York: Charles Scribner's Sons, 1950.

Baptist History Celebration Steering Committee. *Baptist History Celebration 2007: A Symposium on Our History, Theology, and Hymnody*. Springfield, MO: Particular Baptist, 2008.

Bebbington, D. W. *Evangelicalism in Modern Britain: A History from the 1730s to the 1980s*. London: Routledge, 1989.

Bell, Rob. *Love Wins: A Book about Heaven, Hell, and the Fate of Every Person Who Ever Lived*. New York: HarperOne, 2011.

Benson, Louis F. *The English Hymn: Its Development and Use in Worship*. Philadelphia: The Presbyterian Board of Publication, 1915.

———. *The Hymnody of the Christian Church*. The Lectures on "The L. P. Stone Foundation" Princeton Theological Seminary 1926. New York: George H. Doran Co., 1927.

Berkeley, George. "A Discourse Addressed to Magistrates and Men in Authority. Occasioned by the enormous License and Irreligion of the Times." In *The Works of George Berkeley*, 407–30. Oxford: Clarendon, 1901.

Bonner, Carey. "Some Baptist Hymnists: Part I." *Baptist Quarterly* 8 (1936–37) 256–62.

————. "Some Baptist Hymnists: Part II." *Baptist Quarterly* 8 (1936–37) 302–11.

Brackney, William H. "The Baptist Missionary Society in Proper Context: Some Reflections on the Larger Voluntary Religious Tradition." *Baptist Quarterly* 34 (1992) 364–77.

Brackney, William H., and Paul S. Fiddes with John H. Y. Briggs, eds. *Pilgrim Pathways: Essays in Baptist History in Honour of B. R. White*. Macon, GA: Mercer University Press, 1999.

Brawley, Benjamin. *History of the English Hymn*. New York: Abingdon, 1932.

Breed, David R. *The History and Use of Hymns and Hymn-Tunes*. Reprint, New York: AMS, 1975.

Briggs, John. "The Changing Pattern of Baptist Life in the Eighteenth Century." In *Pulpit and People: Studies in Eighteenth-Century Baptist Life and Thought*, edited by John H. Y. Briggs, 1–24. Studies in Baptist History and Thought 28. Milton Keynes, UK: Paternoster, 2009.

————, ed. *Pulpit and People: Studies in Eighteenth-Century Baptist Life and Thought*. Studies in Baptist History and Thought 28. Milton Keynes, UK: Paternoster, 2009.

Broome, J. R. *A Bruised Reed: The Life and Times of Anne Steele, Together with Anne Steele's Hymns, Psalms, and a Selection of Her Prose Works*. Harpenden, England: Gospel Standard Trust, 2007.

Burrage, Henry S. *Baptist Hymn Writers and Their Hymns*. Portland, ME: Brown Thurston, 1888.

Cecil, David, ed. *The Oxford Book of Christian Verse*. Oxford: Clarendon, 1940.

Champion, L. G. "Evangelical Calvinism and the Structures of Baptist Church Life." *Baptist Quarterly* 28 (1980) 196–208.

————. "The Letters of John Ryland to John Newton." *Baptist Quarterly* 27 (1977) 157–63.

————. "The Social Status of some Eighteenth Century Baptist Ministers." *Baptist Quarterly* 25 (1973) 10–14.

————. "The Theology of John Ryland: Its Sources and Influences." *Baptist Quarterly* 28 (1979) 17–29.

Cho, Nancy. "'The Ministry of Song': Unmarried British Women's Hymn Writing, 1760–1936." PhD dissertation, University of Durham, 2007.

Christian Hymns. Bridgend, Wales: Evangelical Movement of Wales, 1977.

Clark, Glenn. *Hymns and Hymn Writers of the Eighteenth Century*. Mayfield, KY: n.d., 1988.

Clements, K. W. "The Significance of 1679." *Baptist Quarterly* 28 (1979) 2–6.

Cramp, J. M. *Baptist History: From the Foundation of the Christian Church to the Close of the Eighteenth Century*. Philadelphia: American Baptist Publication Society, 1869.

Davie, Donald. *The Eighteenth-Century Hymn in England*. Cambridge Studies in Eighteenth Century English Literature and Thought 19. Cambridge: Cambridge University Press, 1993.

Davie, Donald, and Robert Stevenson. *English Hymnology in the Eighteenth Century*. Los Angeles: The William Andrews Clark Library, 1980.

Davies, Horton. *From Watts and Wesley to Maurice, 1690–1850*. Worship and Theology in England 3. Princeton: Princeton University Press, 1961.

————. *Worship and Theology in England.* 5 vols. Princeton: Princeton University Press, 1961–1975.

Dixon, Michael F., and Hugh F. Steele-Smith. "Anne Steele's Health: A Modern Diagnosis." *The Baptist Quarterly* 32 (1988) 351–56.

Doane, W. Howard, and E. H. Johnson, eds. *The Baptist Hymnal: For Use in the Church and Home.* 1883. Philadelphia: American Baptist Publication Society, 1902.

Doggett, J. C. "Joseph Ivimey (1773–1834)." In *The British Particular Baptists: 1638–1910,* edited by Michael A. G. Haykin, 3:113–31. Springfield, MO: Particular Baptist, 2003.

Dudley-Smith, Timothy. "Why Wesley Still Dominates Our Hymnbook." *Christian History* 10 (1991) 9–13.

Duffield, Samuel Willoughby. *English Hymns: Their Authors and History.* 3rd ed. New York: Funk and Wagnalls, 1888.

Duncan, Pope A. *Hanserd Knollys: Seventeenth-Century Baptist.* Nashville: Broadman, 1965.

Edwards, Jonathan. *The Works of Jonathan Edwards.* 2 vols. Peabody, MA: Hendrickson, 2003.

Eskew, Harry, and Hugh T. McElrath. *Sing with Understanding: An Introduction to Christian Hymnology.* Nashville: Church Street, 1995.

Ferguson, Sinclair B., et al., eds. *New Dictionary of Theology.* Downers Grove, IL: InterVarsity, 1988.

Fiddes, Paul S. "Daniel Turner and a Theology of the Church Universal." In *Pulpit and People: Studies in Eighteenth-Century Baptist Life and Thought,* edited by John H. Y. Briggs, 112–27. Studies in Baptist History and Thought 28. Milton Keynes, UK: Paternoster, 2009.

Forbis, Wesley L., ed. *The Baptist Hymnal.* Nashville: Convention Press, 1991.

George, Timothy. "William Carey (1761–1834)." In *The British Particular Baptists: 1638–1910,* edited by Michael A. G. Haykin, 2:143–60. Springfield, MO: Particular Baptist, 2000.

Gillman, Frederick John. *The Evolution of the English Hymn: An Historical Survey of the Origins and Development of the Hymns of the Christian Church.* London: George Allen and Unwin, 1927.

Green, Ian. "Anglicanism under Stuart and Hanoverian England." In *A History of Religion in Britain: Practice and Belief from Pre-Roman Times to the Present,* edited by Sheridan Gilley and W. J. Sheils, 168–87. Oxford: Blackwell, 1994.

Hall, Robert. *Help to Zion's Travellers: Being an Attempt to Remove Various Stumbling Blocks out of the Way, Relating to Doctrinal, Experimental and Practical Religion.* Edited by Nathan A. Finn. Dallas: BorderStone, 2011.

Hatfield, Edwin F. *The Poets of the Church: A Series of Biographical Sketches of Hymn-writers with Notes on Their Hymns.* New York: Anson D. F. Randolph & Co., 1884.

Hayden, Roger. *Continuity and Change: Evangelical Calvinism among eighteenth-century Baptist ministers trained at Bristol Academy, 1690–1791.* Chipping Norton, England: Nigel Lynn for Roger Hayden and the Baptist Historical Society, 2006.

————. *English Baptist History and Heritage.* Oxfordshire, England: Gem Publishing Company for The Baptist Union of Great Britain, 1990.

————. "Evangelical Calvinism among eighteenth-century British Baptists with particular reference to Bernard Foskett, Hugh and Caleb Evans and the Bristol Baptist Academy, 1690–1791." PhD dissertation, University of Keele, 1991.

Haykin, Michael A. G. "Benjamin Beddome (1717–1795): His Life and His Hymns." In *Pulpit and People: Studies in Eighteenth-Century Baptist Life and Thought*, edited by John H. Y. Briggs, 93–111. Studies in Baptist History and Thought 28. Milton Keynes, UK: Paternoster, 2009.

———. "Benjamin Francis (1734–1799)." In *The British Particular Baptists: 1638–1910*, edited by Michael A. G. Haykin, 2:17–29. Springfield, MO: Particular Baptist, 2000.

———. "British Particular Baptist Biography." In *The British Particular Baptists: 1638–1910*, edited by Michael A. G. Haykin, 1:15–19. Springfield, MO: Particular Baptist, 1998.

———, ed. *The British Particular Baptists 1638–1910*. 3 vols. Springfield, MO: Particular Baptist, 1998–2003.

———. "'Draw Nigh unto My Soul': English Baptist Piety and the Means of Grace in the Seventeenth and Eighteenth Centuries." *The Southern Baptist Journal of Theology* 10 (2006) 54–73.

———. "'A Habitation of God, Through the Spirit': John Sutcliff (1752–1814) and the revitalization of the Calvinistic Baptists in the late eighteenth century." *Baptist Quarterly* 34 (1992) 304–19.

———. "John Rippon (1751–1836) and the Calvinistic Baptists: A review article." *Eusebeia* 4 (Spring 2005) 105–10.

———. "John Sutcliff (1752–1814)." In *The British Particular Baptists: 1638–1910*, edited by Michael A. G. Haykin, 3:21–41. Springfield, MO: Particular Baptist, 2003.

———. *Kiffin, Knollys and Keach—Rediscovering Our English Baptist Heritage*. Leeds, England: Reformation Trust Today, 1996.

———. *One Heart and One Soul: John Sutcliff of Olney, His Friends and His Times*. Darlington, England: Evangelical, 1994.

———. "Robert Hall, Sr. (1728–1791)." In *The British Particular Baptists: 1638–1910*, edited by Michael A. G. Haykin, 1:203–10. Springfield, MO: Particular Baptist, 1998.

Haykin, Michael A. G., and C. Jeffrey Robinson. "Particular Baptist Debates about Communion and Hymn-Singing." In *Drawn into Controversie: Reformed Theological Diversity and Debates Within Seventeenth-Century British Puritanism*, edited by Michael A. G. Haykin and Mark Jones, 284–308. Göttingen: Vandenhoeck and Ruprecht, 2011.

Haykin, Michael A. G., and Kenneth J. Stewart. *The Advent of Evangelicalism: Exploring Historical Continuities*. Nashville: B & H Academic, 2008.

Hindmarsh, D. Bruce. "The Antecedents of Evangelical Conversion Narrative: Spiritual Autobiography and the Christian Tradition." In *The Advent of Evangelicalism: Exploring Historical Continuities*, edited by Michael A. G. Haykin and Kenneth J. Stewart, 327–44. Nashville: B & H Academic, 2008.

Holmes, Amanda. "Resurrecting the Anonymous: An Introduction to Mary Steele, the Author of Danebury and the Power of Friendship, A Tale with Two Odes by a Young Lady." MA thesis, Georgia Southern University, 2008.

Houghton, S. M. *Sketches from Church History*. Edinburgh: Banner of Truth Trust, 1980.

Howson, Barry H. "Hanserd Knollys (c. 1598–1691)." In *The British Particular Baptists: 1638–1910*, edited by Michael A. G. Haykin, 1:39–62. Springfield, MO: Particular Baptist, 1998.

Ivimey, Joseph. *A History of the English Baptists: Including an Investigation of the History of Baptism in England from the Earliest Period to Which It Can Be Traced to the Close of the Seventeenth Century. To Which Are Prefixed, Testimonies of Ancient Writers in favour of Adult Baptism: Extracted from Dr. Gill's Piece, Entitled, The Divine Right of Infant Baptism Examined and Disproved.* 4 vols. London, 1811–1830.

James, Sharon. "Anne Steele (1717–1778)." In *The British Particular Baptists:1638–1910*, edited by Michael A. G. Haykin, 3:1–19. Springfield, MO: Particular Baptist, 2003.

———. *In Trouble and in Joy: Four Women Who Lived for God.* Darlington, England: Evangelical, 2003.

Jeffrey, D. L. "John Bunyan (1628–1688)." In *Biographical Dictionary of Evangelicals*, edited by Timothy Larsen, 98–102. Leicester: InterVarsity, 2003.

Julian, John, ed. *A Dictionary of Hymnology.* 2 vols. Rev. ed. London: John Murray, 1907. Repr. New York: Dover, 1957.

Keeble, N. H. Review of *The English Hymn: A Critical and Historical Study*, by J. R. Watson. *The Modern Language Review* 94 (1999) 804–806.

Kurian, George Thomas, ed. *Nelson's Dictionary of Christianity.* Nashville: Thomas Nelson, 2005.

Larsen, Timothy. "The reception given *Evangelicalism in Modern Britain* since its publication in 1989." In *The Advent of Evangelicalism: Exploring Historical Continuities*, edited by Michael A. G. Haykin and Kenneth J. Stewart, 21–36. Nashville: B & H Academic, 2008.

Lawrence, D. H. "Hymns in a Man's Life." In *The Later D. H. Lawrence: The Best Novels, Stories, Essays, 1925–1930*, 380–85. New York: Knopf, 1952.

Leaver, Robin A. "The Hymn Explosion." *Christian History* 10 (1991) 14–17.

Lemon, Rebecca, et al., eds. *The Blackwell Companion to the Bible in English Literature.* Malden, MA: Wiley-Blackwell, 2009.

Lovegrove, Deryck W. *Established Church, Sectarian People: Itinerancy and the transformation of English Dissent, 1780–1830.* Cambridge: Cambridge University Press, 1988.

Lovelace, Austin C. *The Anatomy of Hymnody.* Chicago: GIA, 1965.

Lumpkin, William L. *Baptist Confessions of Faith.* Rev. ed. Valley Forge, PA: Judson, 1969.

Manley, Ken R. "John Rippon and Baptist Hymnody." In *Dissenting Praise: Religious Dissent and the Hymn in England and Wales*, edited by Isabel Rivers and David L. Wykes, 95–123. Oxford: Oxford University Press, 2011.

———. "The Making of an Evangelical Baptist Leader." *The Baptist Quarterly* 26 (1976) 254–74.

———. *'Redeeming Love Proclaim': John Rippon and the Baptists.* Studies in Baptist History and Thought 12. Carlisle, UK: Paternoster, 2004.

———. "'Sing Side by Side': John Rippon and Baptist Hymnody." In *Pilgrim Pathways: Essays in Baptist History in Honour of B. R. White*, edited by William H. Brackney and Paul S. Fiddes with John H. Y. Briggs, 127–63. Macon, GA: Mercer University Press, 1999.

Manning, Bernard Lord. "Congregationalism in the Eighteenth Century." In *Essays in Orthodox Dissent*, 171–95. London: Independent, 1939.

———. *The Hymns of Wesley and Watts: Five Informal Papers.* London: Epworth, 1942.

Manwaring, Randle. *A Study of Hymn-Writing and Hymn-Singing in the Christian Church.* Texts and Studies in Religion 50. New York: Edwin Mellen, 1990.

Marshall, Madeleine Forell, and Janet Todd. *English Congregational Hymns of the Eighteenth Century.* Lexington, KY: The University Press of Kentucky, 1982.

Martin, Hugh. "The Baptist Contribution to Early English Hymnody." *The Baptist Quarterly* 19 (1962) 195–208.

———. *Benjamin Keach (1640–1704): Pioneer of Congregational Hymn Singing.* London: Independent, 1961.

McBeth, Leon. *The Baptist Heritage.* Nashville: Broadman, 1987.

Miller, Kevin A. "Silent String." *Christian History* 10 (1991) 5.

Montgomery, James, ed. *The Christian Psalmist: or, Hymns, Selected and Original.* Glasgow: Chalmers and Collins, 1825.

———. "Introductory Essay." In *The Christian Psalmist: or, Hymns, Selected and Original*, edited by James Montgomery, v–xxxiv. Glasgow: Chalmers and Collins, 1825.

Moon, Norman S. "Caleb Evans, Founder of the Bristol Education Society." *Baptist Quarterly* 24 (1971) 175–90.

Morden, P. J. "Andrew Fuller and *The Gospel Worthy of All Acceptation.*" In *Pulpit and People: Studies in Eighteenth-Century Baptist Life and Thought*, edited by John H. Y. Briggs, 128–51. Studies in Baptist History and Thought 28. Milton Keynes, UK: Paternoster, 2009.

Mullet, Michael. "Radical Sects and Dissenting Churches, 1600–1750." In *A History of Religion in Britain: Practice and Belief from Pre-Roman Times to the Present*, edited by Sheridan Gilley and W. J. Sheils, 188–210. Oxford: Blackwell, 1994.

Music, David W. "America's Hesitation Over Hymns." *Christian History* 10 (1991) 26–29.

———. "Heroines of Baptist Hymnody." *Baptist History and Heritage* 29 (1994) 37–44.

Nance, Steven W. *Sing to the Lord: A Survey of Christian Hymnody.* Shippensburg, PA: This Ragged Edge, 1995.

Naylor, Peter. *Calvinism, Communion and the Baptists: A Study of English Calvinistic Baptists from the Late 1600s to the Early 1800s.* Studies in Baptist History and Thought 7. Milton Keynes, UK: Paternoster, 2003.

———. "John Collett Ryland (1723–1792)." In *The British Particular Baptists: 1638–1910*, edited by Michael A. G. Haykin, 1:185–201. Springfield, MO: Particular Baptist, 1998.

———. *Picking up a Pin for the Lord: English Particular Baptists from 1688 to the Early Nineteenth Century.* London: Grace, 1992.

Nettles, Tom J. "Andrew Fuller (1754–1815)." In *The British Particular Baptists: 1638–1910*, edited by Michael A. G. Haykin, 2:97–141. Springfield, MO: Particular Baptist, 2000.

———. *The Baptists: Key People Involved in Forming a Baptist Identity.* Vol. 1. Fearn, Scotland: Christian Focus, 2005.

———. "Benjamin Keach (1640–1704)." In *The British Particular Baptists: 1638–1910*, edited by Michael A. G. Haykin, 1:94–130. Springfield, MO: Particular Baptist, 1998.

Noll, Mark. *The Rise of Evangelicalism: The Age of Edwards, Whitefield and the Wesleys.* Downers Grove, IL: InterVarsity, 2003.

Nuttall, Geoffrey F. "Calvinism in Free Church History." *Baptist Quarterly* 22 (1968) 418–28.

Nutter, Charles S., and Wilbur F. Tillett. *The Hymns and Hymn Writers of the Church: An Annotated Edition of The Methodist Hymnal.* New York: The Methodist Book Concern, 1911.

Och, Carol. *Women and Spirituality.* Totowa: Rowman and Allanhead, 1983.

Oliver, Robert W. "Abraham Booth (1734–1806)." In *The British Particular Baptists: 1638–1910,* edited by Michael A. G. Haykin, 2:31–54. Springfield, MO: Particular Baptist, 2000.

———. *History of the English Calvinistic Baptists 1771–1892: From John Gill to C. H. Spurgeon.* Edinburgh: The Banner of Truth Trust, 2006.

———. "John Gill (1697–1771)." In *The British Particular Baptists: 1638–1910,* edited by Michael A. G. Haykin, 1:160–64. Springfield, MO: Particular Baptist, 2000.

Pailin, David A. "Rational Religion in England from Herbert of Cherbury to William Paley." In *A History of Religion in Britain: Practice and Belief from Pre-Roman Times to the Present,* edited by Sheridan Gilley and W. J. Sheils, 211–33. Oxford: Blackwell, 1994.

Patterson, W. Morgan. "The Evangelical Revival and the Baptists." In *Pilgrim Pathways: Essays in Baptist History in Honour of B. R. White,* edited by William H. Brackney and Paul S. Fiddes with John H. Y. Briggs. Macon, GA: Mercer University Press, 1999.

Pollard, Arthur. *English Hymns.* Writers and Their Work 123. London: Longmans, Green and Co., 1960.

Porter, Roy. *The Creation of the Modern World: The Untold Story of the British Enlightenment.* New York: Norton, 2000.

Porter, Roy, and Dorothy Porter. *In Sickness and in Health: The British Experience 1650–1850.* London: Fourth Estate, 1988.

Procter, W. C. *The Story of Sacred Song.* London: James Clarke, n.d.

Ramsbottom, B. A. "The Stennetts." In *The British Particular Baptists: 1638–1910,* edited by Michael A. G. Haykin, 1:133–43. Springfield, MO: Particular Baptist Press, 1998.

Reeves, Marjorie. *Pursuing the Muses: Female Education and Nonconformist Culture, 1700–1900.* London: Leicester University Press, 1997.

Reynolds, William J. "Three Hymnals That Shaped Today's Worship." *Christian History* 10 (1991) 36–37.

Richardson, Paul A. "Baptist Contributions to Hymnody and Hymnology." *Review and Expositor* 87 (1990) 59–74.

Rippon, John, ed. *A Selection of Hymns, from the Best Authors, including a Great Number of Originals; Intended to be an Appendix to Dr. Watts's Psalms and Hymns.* 32nd ed. London: self-published, 1830.

Rivers, Isabel. *Reason, Grace, and Sentiment: A Study of the Language of Religion and Ethics in England, 1660–1780.* 2 vols. Cambridge Studies in Eighteenth-Century English Literature and Thought 8. Cambridge: Cambridge University Press, 1991.

Rivers, Isabel, and David L. Wykes, eds. *Dissenting Praise: Religious Dissent and the Hymn in England and Wales.* Oxford: Oxford University Press, 2011.

Roberts, R. Philip. *Continuity and Change: London Calvinistic Baptists and the Evangelical Revival 1760–1820.* Wheaton, IL: Richard Owen Roberts, 1989.

Rogal, Samuel J. *A General Introduction to Hymnody and Congregational Song.* ATLA Monograph Series 26. Metuchen, NJ: The American Theological Library Association and Scarecrow, 1991.

Routley, Erik. *English Hymns and Their Tunes*. London: The Hymn Society of Great Britain and Ireland, 1981.

———. *Hymns and the Faith*. Grand Rapids: Eerdmans, 1968.

———. *Hymns and Human Life*. 2nd ed. Grand Rapids: Eerdmans, 1959.

———. *A Panorama of Christian Hymnody*. Chicago: GIA, 1979.

Ryden, E. E. *The Story of Christian Hymnody*. Rock Island, IL: Augustana, 1959.

Sharpe, Eric. "Bristol Baptist College and the Church's Hymnody." *Baptist Quarterly* 28 (1979) 7–16.

———. "The Language of Christian Worship." *Baptist Quarterly* 22 (1967) 143–56.

Smith, Allen E. "John Bunyan (1628–1688)." In *The British Particular Baptists: 1638–1910*, edited by Michael A. G. Haykin, 1:78–93. Springfield, MO: Particular Baptist, 1998.

Smith, Karen E. "Beyond Public and Private Spheres: Another Look at Women in Baptist History and Historiography." *The Baptist Quarterly* 34 (1991) 79–87.

———. "The Covenant Life of Some Eighteenth-Century Baptists in Hampshire and Wiltshire." In *Pilgrim Pathways: Essays in Baptist History in Honour of B. R. White*, edited by William H. Brackney and Paul S. Fiddes with John H. Y. Briggs, 165–83. Macon, GA: Mercer University Press, 1999.

———. "James Fanch (1704–1767): The Spiritual Counsel of an Eighteenth-Century Baptist Pastor." In *Pulpit and People: Studies in Eighteenth-Century Baptist Life and Thought*, edited by John H. Y. Briggs, 58–74. Studies in Baptist History and Thought 28. Milton Keynes, UK: Paternoster, 2009.

Steadman, Thomas. *Memoir of the Rev. William Steadman, D.D.* London: Thomas Ward, 1838.

Steele, Anne. *Poems on Subjects Chiefly Devotional by Theodosia*. Vol. 1. London: J. Buckland and J. Ward, 1760.

———. *Poems on Subjects Chiefly Devotional by Theodosia*. Vol. 2. Bristol: W. Pine, 1780.

———. *The Works of Mrs. Anne Steele, Complete in Two Volumes, Comprehending Poems on Subjects Chiefly Devotional and Miscellaneous Pieces in Prose and Verse: Heretofore Published under the Title of Theodosia*. 2 vols. Boston: Munroe, Francis and Parker, 1808.

Stevenson, W. R. "Baptist Hymnody, English." In *A Dictionary of Hymnology: Setting Forth the Origin and History of Christian Hymns of All Ages and Nations*, edited by John Julian, 110–13. Rev. ed. London: John Murray, 1907.

Temperley, Nicholas. *The Music of the English Parish Church*. 2 vols. Cambridge Studies in Music. Cambridge: Cambridge University Press, 1979.

Thomson, Ronald W. "Anne Steele, 1716–1778." *The Baptist Quarterly* 21 (1966) 368–71.

Tindall, William York. "Introduction." In *The Later D. H. Lawrence: The Best Novels, Stories, Essays, 1925–1930 by D. H. Lawrence*. New York: Knopf, 1952.

Torbet, Robert G. *A History of the Baptists*. Philadelphia: Judson, 1950.

Townsend, Jim. "The Forgotten Wesley." *Christian History* 10 (1991) 6–8.

The Trinity Hymnal. Suwanee, GA: Great Commission, 1990.

Walker, Austin. "Benjamin Keach (1640–1704): Tailor Turned Preacher." In *Pulpit and People: Studies in Eighteenth-Century Baptist Life and Thought*, edited by John H. Y. Briggs, 25–42. Studies in Baptist History and Thought 28. Milton Keynes, UK: Paternoster, 2009.

———. *The Excellent Benjamin Keach*. Dundas, ON: Joshua, 2004.

Ward, W. R. "The Baptists and the Transformation of the Church, 1780–1830." *Baptist Quarterly* 25 (1973) 167–84.

Watson, J. R., ed. *An Annotated Anthology of Hymns*. Oxford: Oxford University Press, 2007.

———. "Eighteenth-Century Hymn Writers." In *The Blackwell Companion to the Bible in English Literature*, edited by Rebecca Lemon et al., 329–44. Malden, MA: Wiley-Blackwell, 2009.

———. *The English Hymn: A Critical and Historical Study*. Oxford: Clarendon, 1997.

Watson, J. R., and Nancy Cho. "Anne Steele's Drowned Fiancé." *British Journal of Eighteenth Century Studies* 28 (2005) 117–21.

Watts, Isaac. *Hymns and Spiritual Songs*. London: J. Humphreys, 1707.

———. *The Psalms of David Imitated in the Language of the New Testament, and Apply'd to the Christian State and Worship*. London: J. Clark, 1719.

Watts, Michael. *The Dissenters: From the Reformation to the French Revolution*. Oxford: Clarendon, 1978.

Wellum, Kirk. "Caleb Evans (1737–1791)." In *The British Particular Baptists: 1638–1910*, edited by Michael A. G. Haykin, 1:213–33. Springfield, MO: Particular Baptist, 1998.

Whitley, W. T. "The Influence of Whitefield on Baptists." *Baptist Quarterly* 5 (1930–1931) 30–36.

Wilson, Paul R. "William Kiffin (1616–1701)." In *The British Particular Baptists: 1638–1910*, edited by Michael A. G. Haykin, 1:64–77. Springfield, MO: Particular Baptist, 1998.

Wright, Vinita Hampton. "Hymn Writers' Hall of Fame: The Poets Who Put Words in Our Mouths." *Christian History* 10 (1991) 20–23.

Young, Robert H. "The History of Baptist Hymnody in England from 1612–1800." PhD. dissertation, University of Southern California, 1959.

Index

Aalders, Cynthia Y.
  on effectiveness of a hymn, 17–18
  on examining hymns in cultural
    context, 101
  on the hymn as expression of
    both Christian doctrine and
    devotional experience, 24
  on a hymn-writer's approach to
    writing, 112–13
  on meaning of importance to the
    hymn-writer, 108
  researching the entire Steele corpus,
    203
  on scope and terrain covered by
    Steele, 164
  on Steele
    anticipating the eschatological
      perfection of her praise,
      211–12
    biblical approach of, 111
    comparing verses to Wesley and
      Watts, 38–39
    confronting God, 193
    continuing to attempt
      expression, 116
    doubt and introspection of, 209
    emotional expression of, 114
    encouragement to younger
      writers, 59

exhibiting the sentiment of the
  Age of Sensibility, 139n98
faith of Steele, 210
finding herself "incapable of
  addressing God using
  speech," 149n138
friendships nurturing her
  writing efforts, 58
"hesitancy" of, 132–33n70,
  163n187
highlighting the incarnation of
  the Word, 136
hymns of, 18, 113
joy and anticipation of spiritual
  fulfillment, 178
life and time of, 32
lingering over her grief, 164
problem of with "the ability of
  language to offer meaningful
  praise to God," 142, 203
relying on personal experience,
  149
"resignation" to the will of an
  "ineffable God," 206
sensitivity to God's response to
  suffering, 109–10
sighs and breathings of, 193n287
spirituality of, 33

Aalders, Cynthia Y., on Steele
(*continued*)
struggling with the "ability of
language to offer meaningful
praise to God," 115
tapping into "the developing
values of the evangelical
movement," 114
themes of resignation and
longing, 165
theses regarding, 203n9
understanding of God's
ineffability, 204
vision of the glorified Christ, 199
way of expressing sinfulness,
107–8
Aaronic blessing, in Numbers, 174
ABAB (cross rhyming) pattern, Steele
repeating, 123
*Abide with Me: The World of Victorian
Hymns* (Bradley), 30
Act of Toleration, 85
Act of Uniformity of 1662, 64n20, 65
activism, 3, 124
adoption
as doctrine of Christ, 181
Particular Baptist doctrine of,
121–22
Spirit of, 155, 172
Steele remembering her, 157
"Advocate. 1 John ii. 1" (Steele), 145–46,
207
affliction and spiritual darkness, taken
to the Lord by faith, 193
Age of Reason, 68n45
Age of Sensibility, 39, 180
American colonies, evangelical
Christianity in, 75n79
Anabaptists, 63n10
anadiplosis device, used by Steele,
158n168
anaphora device, used by Steele,
158n168
The Anatomy of Hymnody (Lovelace), 3
Anderson, Jan, 4
angelic choir, joining, 199
Anglican Church, response to
immorality, 70–71, 71n61

Anglicans, not extending civil equality
to Dissenters, 86
Annotated Anthology of Hymns
(Watson), 19n108
antanaclasis, poetic device used by
Steele, 151n146
Antinomianism, 73n65, 92
apocryphal story, of Steele's fiancé, 31,
54–55, 109n37
Apostle's Creed, 118n6
Arian views, 73
Arminianism, 73, 73n66, 75, 88
Arminius, Jacobus (1560–1609), 73n66
Arnold, Richard
essay on Steele, 203n11
on expectations for eighteenth-
century hymns, 4
on hymns as a verbal phenomenon,
11–12
on purposes of eighteenth-century
hymns, 216
on Steele's self-identification and
desire to find the right words, 41
on use the word "evangelical," 3
art, incapable of creating an offering
worthy of God's acceptance, 142
Ash, John (1724–1779), 5–6, 57, 60,
94, 95
associations of churches, 91, 95, 96, 99
assurance, doctrine of, 135, 144, 181,
209, 217
"At the Funeral of a Young Person"
(Steele), 196–98
Atkins, Abraham, 82n115
atonement by substitution, 130, 139
atonement of Christ
creation's response to, 139
as doctrine, 181
limited to the elect, 62n1
Steele's assurance from, 214
Steele's hymns considering for
sinners, 215
through his cross, 129
as the ultimate antidote for sin, 210
Augustan tradition, of Watts, 108

backslider, Steele speaking as, 131–32

baptism
 absent from Steele's hymns, 174
 by immersion, 81
 infant, 82
 of William and Anne, 48
Baptist Annual Register (1790–1802),
  100
Baptist chapel, at Broughton, 43
Baptist eucharistic piety, Steele's
  expression of, 182
Baptist hymn writers, number of hymns
  in Rippon's *Selection of Hymns*,
  1n4–2n4
The Baptist Hymnal of 1883, 2n4
Baptist Hymnal published in 1991, 2n4
Baptist Missionary Society, formation
  of, 99
Baptists
 divided into General and Particular
  Baptists, 44n6
 recognizing the need for the local
  church, 88
Baxter, Margaret (1639–1681), 28
beauty of creation, hymns of Steele
  reflecting, 111
Bebbington, David W.
 on characteristics of evangelicalism,
  3, 209
 on Christ dying for sinful mankind,
  141
 on the doctrine of assurance, 135,
  181, 209, 217
 on the emergence of Evangelicalism,
  75
 on esteem of the Holy Bible by
  Evangelicals, 125–26
 on Fuller's book, 98
 on Jonathan Edwards, 96, 97
 quadrilateral of, 3, 117–18, 118n5
 on salvation received by grace, 175
 on transmitting doctrine to singers,
  217
Beddome, Benjamin (1717–1795)
 boasting of church attendance,
  81n111
 as Bristol student, 95
 composing hymns to be sung after
  sermons, 4, 22–23, 23n129, 217

exposition of Benjamin Keach's
  catechism, 213
 familiar with Edwards's books, 97
 on God drawing near, 195–96, 213
 influenced by Watts, 22
 as a notable hymn-writer, 2
 on prayer, 166
 profiled by Watson, 39
 request of Steele's hand in marriage,
  57
"The Being and Perfections of God"
  section. *See* God section
belief, hymns speaking to, 15–16
Benson, Louis F.
 on Keach's hymns, 5
 on Rippon's *Selection of Hymns*,
  7n41
 on "the school of Watts," 3
 on Steele's feminine emotionalism,
  113
 on Steele's hymns, 2
 typology of the functions of hymns,
  3–4
Berkeley, George, 70
Bible
 Nancy Cho on, 128
 piety based on, 75n79
 reverent view of in Steele's hymn,
  126
 riches describing the value of, 127
 Second London Confession on, 213
 Steele situating herself with devotion
  to, 124
 Steele's view of, 213–14
biblical language, 21
biblicism, 3, 69
biography, of Anne Steele, 42–61
"bliss," shared by God's servants, 202
blood of Christ, as redemption, 130n59
Booth, Abraham (1734-1806), 84, 90,
  92, 181
Brackney, William H., 99n226
Bradley, Ian, 30
*The Breach repaired in God's Worship or
  Singing of Psalms, Hymns and
  Spiritual Songs* (Keach), 85
"Breathing After God" (Steele). *See*
  "Advocate. 1 John ii. 1" (Steele)

"breathings," explaining prayer, 193n287
Briggs, John, 84, 85, 89–90, 93, 95
Brine, John (1703–1765), 77–78, 79n99
Bristol Baptist Academy, 6, 43, 92, 93, 94
Bristol Baptist College, 91
Bristol Collection (Ash and Evans), 6,
    8n47, 60
Bristol Education Society, 94
Britain, 188, 191. *See also* England
Broome, J. R.
    on Baptist officers in the
        Parliamentary Army, 64
    biography of Steele's life, 24–28
    comparing Watts to Steele, 106
    on "Creation and Providence"
        (Steele), 122–23
    on doctrine in Steele's hymns, 216
    on the forebears of Anne Steele's
        church, 43
    on a generation of hymn-writing
        giants, 2
    on ill-health as sanctified to Steele,
        53
    on prayer for Steele as the breath of
        her life, 166
    on repentance, 159
    on the Seven Years' War, 188
    on the social caliber of Particular
        Baptist ministers, 45
    on Steele
        desire for total submission to the
            Lord's will, 165
        growing up singing out of Watts's
            hymn-book, 103
        handwriting of, 48
        ill-health over many years, 109
        as naturally depressive, 53
        relationship to Fanch, 60
    on Watts reaching great heights of
        grandeur, 105
    on William Steele, 44–45, 46, 112
"Broughton House," 61
Brown, John (d. 1800), 83, 84
Brown, Raymond, 94–95
*A Bruised Reed: The Life and Times of
    Anne Steele* (Broome), 24
Bunyan, John (1628-1688), 39, 66n37–
    67n37, 154

call to come to Christ, hymns beginning
    with, 134
call to prayer, genesis of Sutcliff's, 97
Calvinism, 67, 74, 75, 93, 217
Calvinistic
    emphases, of confessions of faith,
        44, 63
    preaching, teaching of, 210
    theology, combining with a passion
        for revival, 96
Carey, William, 98–99
catholic faith, of Steele, 177
Cator, Anne, love-letters from William
    Steele, 46
Cecil, David, on hymns, 10, 11
celestial lines, as the lines of Holy
    Scripture, 127
Champion, L. G.
    on divine activity of grace, 170
    on evangelical Calvinism, 154–55,
        156, 216
    on the initiative of divine grace, 134
    on "the obligation to bring the
        gospel to all men everywhere,"
        148
    on the subjectivity of Steele, 144
    on the teaching of Particular
        Baptists, 119
character study, of Steele by James,
    28–29
Characters and Representations of
    Christ Placed Alphabetically
    subsection, of Rippon's *Selection
    of Hymns*, 145–52
Charles II, restoration of, 64
chiasmus, 137, 137n88, 175
chiastic structure, 143, 144, 169
child of God, Steele's personal
    knowledge of, 166
Children of God, receiving the Spirit of
    Adoption, 157
Cho, Nancy
    chapter on Steele, 32
    on the conceit of sin as disease,
        150–51
    on the Father's word, the Bible, 128
    on God saving Britain from error,
        191
    insights on Steele, 31

on a "language of sensibility" in
Steele's lyrics, 115–16
on languor and weariness for Steele,
133
on the privileging of sympathy in
Steele's hymns, 114n69
on Steele
declaring that she is God's
instrument, 111
devotion for her earthly father,
161
encouragement to younger
writers, 59
following an established
devotional convention,
114–15
influencing later women writers,
114
reflecting the "generally-held
position" of the Protestant
British, 190
step-mother of, 110
unpublished PhD dissertation, 30
Christ. *See also* Jesus
died as substitute for sinful
mankind, 121
kingly, prophetic, and priestly roles
of, 188
real sharing in, 152
revealing his love for his own, 131
setting forth the global scope of, 173
Steele highlighting the uniqueness
of, 151
Steele on the suffering of, 141
theme of the reign of, 140
Christ and His Work section, of
Rippon's hymnal, 135–53
"Christ Dying, Rising, and Reigning"
(Stennett I), 176n234
"Christ the Christian's Life" poem, by
Anne Steele, 102–3
"Christ the Life of the Soul" (Steele),
204–5
Christ-centered focus, of Steele's literary
efforts, 199
Christian life, 161, 170
Christian Life section, of Rippon's
hymnal, 153

The Christian section, of Rippon's
hymnal, 161–68
"The Christian's noblest Resolution.
Joshua xxiv. 15" (Steele), 169–70
Christocentric emphasis of
Baptist preaching, Steele
complementing, 178
Christology, of Steele, 151, 153
Christ's cross, suffering, and blood,
Steele painting a lyrical picture
of, 138
church, 114, 171
Church and Fellowship Meetings
subsection, of Rippon's hymnal,
173
church and its life, sections of Rippon's
hymnal concerning, 168–94
church covenant agreement, as a
"gathered community" of saints,
159
Church of England, 43, 68
Church section, of Rippon's hymnal,
172–74
Clarendon Code, 64, 65, 72n62
closed communion, 63n12, 81–82, 83,
84
cloth trade, as the most important
industry in England, 48
*A Collection of Hymns Adapted to Public
Worship* (Ash and Evans), 5–6
Collins, Hercules, 100n231
Comforter, work of the Spirit as, 151
Common Meter (C.M.), or 86.86
"allowing a much more flexible and
expansive pattern," 104
allowing Steele to emulate Watts'
work in "O God, Our Help in
Ages Past," 123
"The Excellency and Sufficiency of
the Holy Scriptures" written in,
126
frequent in hymns, 15
hymns written in, 136, 177, 180
"Pardoning Love" written in, 132
used by Isaac Watts, 119–20
common nature, of hymns, 11–12
common worshippers, referred to as
"worms," 17

Communion theology, of Steele, 214
"Communion with Christ at his Table"
    (Steele), 175, 179–80
confession, that death is overwhelming,
    196
Confession. See also First London
    Confession of 1644; Second
    London Confession
    on the end of life on this earth, 200
    on making supplication and prayers
        for Kings, 187
    on repentance, 159
confessional atonement hymns, of Anne
    Steele, 216
confessional nature, to Steele's hymns,
    111–12
confessions of faith, 62, 215–16
confident assertions, lacking in Steele's
    hymns, 35, 37
confusion, over the nature of the
    authority, 69
congregational hymn-singing, 8, 11–12,
    27, 84–85, 108, 117
Congregationalists, accused
    Presbyterians of Arminianism,
    73
Conventicle Act of 1664, 65
conversion, 124, 133
conversionism, of early British
    evangelicals, 3
coronation of George III in 1760,
    Steele's hymn commemorating,
    185n260
corporate worship, Steele on the place
    of, 171
Corporation Act of 1661, 65
covenant community, 173, 174
Cowper, William (1731–1800), 2, 21, 22
Cramp, J. M., 44n12, 78, 78n97
created world, Steele wrote about the
    beauties of, 115
creation, 139, 200
creation and nature, Steele's hymns
    about, 184
Creation and Providence section, of
    Rippon's *Selection of Hymns*,
    118–19, 122–25, 202

"Creation and Providence" (Steele),
    122–24, 202n3
Creator God, relegated to being a
    remote caretaker, 68n45
Creator/creature distinction, Steele's
    understanding of, 211
Cromwellian government, Baptists
    supporting and benefiting from,
    64
cross of Christ, evangelical emphasis
    on, 178
crucicentrism, of early British
    evangelicals, 3
Crucifixion of Christ, 138

darkness, 139, 161
dash, used by Steele, 123
David, 156, 171
Davie, Donald, 7–8, 11, 22
Davies, Horton, 18, 21–24, 88
days of life, as monuments of wondrous
    grace, 183
"Dear Refuge of my Weary Soul,"
    Aalders's brief exposition of, 35
death
    of Christ bringing life, 138
    of family members and friends
        throughout Steele's life, 27, 42,
        56, 110
    overcoming, 150
    Steele approached with her eyes
        fixed on Christ, 215
    Steele's experience with translated
        into poignant verses on, 196
    Steele's piety, faith, and theology in
        the face of, 197
Death and Resurrection section, of
    Rippon's hymnbook, 195–98
"decay of religion," 76
deism, 71n57
"Delight in God's House, and confidence
    in Him. Ps. xxvii.," 170–72
dependence, of the one praying, 168
depravity of man, Steele believed in, 211
"Desiring Resignation and
    Thankfulness" (Steele), 165

"Desiring the Presence of God." *See*
　"Walking in Darkness, and
　trusting in God. Isaiah i. 10"
"Desiring the Presence of God in
　Affliction" (Steele), 191, 194,
　212n50
"destructive rage," of war, 189
"devotion to Christ," expressing, 148
dialogue, between a sinner and the
　Word of God in Steele's hymns,
　144–45
didactic function, of hymns, 4
Discourse on Method (Descartes), 68n45
Dissent, toleration of, 72–74
Dissenters
　community of, 43
　described as Puritan, Presbyterian,
　　or a non-Anglican Protestant,
　　64n20
　growing uneasiness of, 74
　highly disliked by most Churchmen,
　　86
　importance of the congregation
　　for, 18
　pastors interested in hymnody and
　　poetry, 57
　required to take the oath of
　　allegiance, 86
　restrictions on worship, 65, 85–86
dissenting baptisms, not recognized, 86
*The Distinguishing Marks of a Work of
　the Spirit of God* (Edwards), 97,
　97n214
disunity, of this life, 198
divine activity, in all forms of human
　living, 170
divine help, Steele asking for in the
　discipline of prayer, 167
divine love, eliciting joy, 108
Dixon, Michael F., 51, 52
doctrinal beliefs, revealed in the hymns
　of Steele, 112
doctrinal foundation, of the *Selection of
　Hymns*, 101
doctrinal nature, of Steele's hymns, 111
doctrine
　of assurance, 217
　of Christ bringing life, 181

of man, 211
　translating into experiential
　　categories, 210
Doctrines and Blessings subsection, of
　Scripture, 129
Doddridge, Philip
　awareness of the emotional power of
　　hymns, 23
　doubting traditional Trinitarian
　　formulas, 73–74
　influenced by Watts, 22
　subjective emphasis in, 18
　versifying a biblical text, 110, 129
"doom'd" predicament, of the sinner, 129
double entendres, of Steele, 184
doubt, 146, 163–64, 192
drowning incident, of Steele's fiancé, 31,
　54–55, 109n37
Duncan, Pope A., 63, 64, 65, 66
Dutton, Anne (1692-1765), 34
"A dying Saviour" (Steele), 137–40

earthquake, in Lisbon, Portugal,
　186n266, 188
Ecclesiastes, on times and seasons, 182
educated men, positively influenced
　Steele, 115
Edwards, Jonathan (1703–1758), 75n79,
　92, 94, 96, 97, 98
Edwards, Sarah (1710–1758), 28
effectiveness of a hymn, 18
"Eighteenth-Century Hymn Writers,"
　Watson's chapter on, 40–41
Eighteenth-Century Revival, in England
　and America, 75
Elcomb, James, as Anne's fiancée who
　drowned, 31, 54–55, 109n37
election, conditional on man's response,
　73n66
Eliot, T. S., 15
emotions, hymns allowed for Christians
　to express, 24
empathetic feeling, appealed to women,
　114n69
endless glory, as the word on the page,
　127
England, 68–71. *See also* Britain

English Baptist piety, aspects of, 213
English Baptists, hymn writers almost
    forgotten, 1–2
English Dissent, dispersion of the
    principles of, 99
English hymn
    as both literature and theology, 34
    congregational use and common
        nature of, 11–12
    literary value of, 14–18
    metrical form of, 10–11
    recent studies of eighteenth-century,
        10–24
    theological content and religious
        purpose of, 12–13
    value of eighteenth-century, 23–24
*The English Hymn: A Critical and
    Historical Study* (Watson), 14,
    30, 39–40
The English Hymn (Benson), 114
English Particular Baptists. *See*
    Particular Baptist(s)
English Presbyterians, Arian views
    among, 73
Enlightenment, 68, 68n45, 69
*An Enquiry into the Causes of the Decay
    of the Dissenting Interest*, 74
enthusiasm, 89
epizeuxis, example of, 145n116
Erlestoke congregation, in Wiltshire, 44
eschatological clarity, offered by Steele
    in "Winter," 184
eternal life, hope of, 125, 174
eternity attribute, of God, 121
"The Eternity of God, and Man's
    Mortality. Psalm xc.," 119–21
Evangelical Anglicans, as some of the
    best of the hymn-writers, 21
evangelical Calvinism
    breaking with an exclusive attitude,
        187
    Champion's third emphasis found
        in, 147
    derived from personal experience,
        144
    doctrinal basis and experiential
        character, 117
    legacy of the Bristol Academy, 95
    preachers, 75n79

revival, 129
    Steele influenced by, 135
    Steele within the stream of, 204
Evangelical Calvinistic Baptist theology,
    belief in and experience of grace,
    157
evangelical Christians, looking to Jesus
    to find out how to live, 147
evangelical commitment, to faith, 131
evangelical hymns, of Steele, 218
Evangelical Hymns and Songs (Wallin), 3
evangelical hymn-writing, 13, 34
evangelical nature, of Steele's experience,
    125
evangelical piety, endorsing, 6
Evangelical Revival, 74–89, 117
evangelical stream, Particular Baptists
    placed in, 3
evangelical vision, of sinners saved by
    grace, 107
Evangelicalism, characteristics of,
    118n5, 209
evangelicals, beliefs of, 191, 209
evangelism, in an atonement hymn by
    Steele, 215
evangelistic thrust, of Steele's hymns,
    216
Evans, Caleb (1737-1791), 5, 54, 57, 60,
    61, 96
Evans, Hugh (1713-1781), 93–94
Eve, John, 79
"An Evening Hymn" (Steele), 182–84,
    201n1, 203
Exaltation and Intercession subsection,
    of Rippon's *Selection of Hymns*,
    140–45
"The Exalted Saviour" (Steele), 140–43,
    211n41
"The Excellency and Sufficiency of the
    Holy Scriptures" (Steele), Steele's
    most well-known hymn, 126–29
exclamations
    emphasizing the miraculous
        nature of the doctrine of the
        incarnation, 137
    of Steele in "The Wonders of
        Redemption," 177
    Steele's use of, 108–9, 132, 144, 167
experience

of faith, 173
Rippon moving to the realm of
    Christian, 9
Steele frequently beginning with,
    110
Steele relating to the word and
    authority of Scripture, 155
of suffering, 110
experiential piety, hymns aiding the
    worshipers', 129n58
"experimental divinity," of the
    Evangelical Revival, 89
"experimental religion," evangelical
    impulse for, 176

"fainting hope," difficulties invoked by
    Steele's, 204
Fairchild, Hoxie Neale, 152
faith
    dark path giving way to spiritual
        sight, 193
    desiring to result in good works, 169
    evangelical commitment to, 131
    in God, 109
    receiving and resting on Christ, 147
    as the sole condition of acceptance
        by God, 145
    of Steele expressed more by
        questions, 37
    Steele starting from the place of, 193
    suffering the trials of, 156
"Faith and Life," Scriptures offering, 127
*A Faithful Narrative of the Surprising
    Work of God* (Edwards), 97
familial view, of God the Father, 120
family, of Steele, 45
family history, Steele's life and hymns
    reflecting her, 25, 25n140
family life, of Steele, 42, 46–50
Family Worship, subheading, 169
Fanch, James (1704–1767), 57, 60, 105
the Father, 120, 202
"Father of Mercies, in Thy Word." *See*
    "The Excellency and Sufficiency
    of the Holy Scriptures" (Steele)
"Father of the English Hymn," Isaac
    Watts as, 18–20
fatherly discipline, Steele's need for, 161
Fawcett, John (1739–1817), 2, 90

female hymn-writers, that followed
    Steele, 32
females, seeing life as more of a cyclical
    walk, 115n74
"feminine standpoint," introducing to
    hymns, 114
Fiddes, Paul S., 82
filial love, of Anne Steele, 160
"Filial Submission. Heb. xii. 7" (Steele),
    160–61
final events, Rippon's *Selection of
    Hymns*, 194–200
first Baptist hymnal, 6
First London Confession of 1644, 44n10,
    62, 63, 64, 119n11. *See also
    Second London Confession*
Five Mile Act of 1665, 65
foot-washing, service of, 146
"For a Public Fast" (Steele), 186–88
"For the 5th of November" (Steele),
    190–91
foreign missions, new vision of, 92
forgiveness, 133, 182
form, of the English hymn, 10–11
Foskett, Bernard (1685–1758),
    leadership of, 91, 93
Francis, Benjamin (1734–1799), 2,
    95–96, 146, 153
Francke, Hermann (1663–1727), 75n79
The Freedom of the Will (Edwards), 98
Frelinghuysen, Theodorus (1692–ca.
    1747), 75n79
friends and advisors, surrounding
    Steele, 56–57
Froude, Anne, 45
Froude, Edward (1645–1714), 44, 45
full life, lived by Anne Steele, 59
Fuller, Andrew (1754–1815)
    believer in closed communion, 84
    Booth's controversies with, 92
    conviction that all people should
        and could turn to God, 98
    on false Calvinism, 79–80
    on humans as transgressors of the
        holy, 141
Furneaux, Philip (1726–1783), 57, 58,
    60

"gathered community," of saints, 159

gender, addressed by studying Steele's work, 113

gender theory, 115n74

General Baptists, 62n1, 62n5, 63n10, 73, 100n231

General redemption, 44n6

George, Timothy, on Carey's tract, 99

Gill, John (1697–1771)
    High Calvinism of, 74n74, 77–79
    on lack of zeal and of an absence of able young leaders, 90
    on the Modern Question, 79n99
    relationship to High Calvinism, 79
    using imagery of "a garden enclosed," 87
    writings contributed to his denomination's decline, 80

"The Glorious Presence of Christ in Heaven" (Steele), 199n312, 200

Glorious Revolution of 1688, 43

God
    addressing by various biblical names, 202–3
    assurance of the care of, 121
    in Christ, 207
    confirming Steele's sense of peace in him, 155
    described, 119, 120
    as Father, 120
    gifts of, 31
    goodness of, 121
    grace of, 134
    human beings as children of, 120
    incomprehensibility and ineffability of, 115
    prerogative to effectually to grace and salvation, 134
    promises coming true for Steele, 164
    providence of, 187, 188
    Steele acknowledging as "her refuge," 163
    Steele intimately and boldly addressing, 162
    Steele longing to praise, 136
    Steele's way of moving toward, 203
    truth of, 145
    wishing for the presence of, 193

God section, of Rippon's *Selection of Hymns*, 118, 119–22, 202

"God the Only Refuge of the Troubled Mind" (Steele). *See* "Troubled, but making God a Refuge"

Godhead, addressing the persons of, 146

"Golden Age of Hymnody," 1, 1n3

goodness, of God, 121

"The Goodness of God. Nahum i. 7.," 121

gospel, hymns making a clear offer of, 135

The Gospel of Christ Worthy of All Acceptation (Fuller), 98

gospel of Jesus Christ, Steele's hymns freely offering, 215

gospel-focused sermons, preaching and publishing of, 92

grace
    application to human experience, 109, 167
    belief in and experience of, 157
    days of life as monuments of, 183
    evangelical vision of, 107
    evangelistic force flowing from, 148
    of God, 107, 170
    L. G. Champion on, 134, 170
    means of as divinely ordained, 212n51
    prayer as a means of, 155
    salvation received by, 175
    William Steele on, 212

Grace Abounding to the Chief of Sinners (Bunyan), 154

graces of the Spirit, subsections concerning, 153

"The Grandfathers" old family house, 46

gratitude for God's goodness, Steele's life characterized by, 29

Great Plague, in London of 1665, 65

Green, Ian, 70

"guardian care," of God over all of his creation, 121

guilt, Steele brought relief to the agony of, 176

gynocriticism, focusing on women as writers, 30n165

Hall, Robert, Jr. (1764–1831), 84

Hall, Robert, Sr., 93, 216

happiness, hymns of Steele expressing, 111

"The happiness of humble worship. Psalm lxxxiv," 170–71

"Happy Poverty; or, the Poor in Spirit Blessed. Matt. v. 3" (Steele), 158–59, 194n287, 205–6

"Hark, the Herald Angels Sing" (Wesley), 135

Harris, Howell (1714–1773), 75n79

Hastings, Selina, 1n3

Havergal, Frances Ridley (1836-1879), 28

Hayden, Roger, 63, 91, 98

Haykin, Michael A. G.
  on Baptists becoming a dynamic force, 99
  on Benjamin Beddome, 213
  on central expressions of piety, 212
  on the centrality of prayer in the Christian life, 166
  on the core problem with High Calvinism, 78
  on the decline of the Baptists and their reluctance to participate within the Evangelical Revival, 77–89
  on English Baptists as "Word-centered evangelicals," 213
  on expansion of the Calvinistic Baptist cause, 67
  on the *First London Confession*, 64
  on John Gill's thinking about faith and evangelism, 79
  on Jonathan Edwards, 96
  on the legal and social plight of the Particular Baptists, 86–87
  on the ordinance of the Lord's Table, 175
  on the *Second London Confession*, 101
  worship or evangelism outside of the Church of England, 65

headings, Rippon's hymnal, 118

health, of Steele, 27, 48, 48n26, 50, 52, 53, 109

hearing the Word preached, as the pre-eminent aspect of worship, 213

heart, finding within Steele's hymns, 113

heaven, 195, 198, 199, 211

"the heavenly path," following, 151

heavenly praise, of Christ, 135–36

heavenly session of Christ, 145, 146

"The heavenly shepherd" (Steele). *See* "Shepherd. Psalm xxiii. 1-3" (Steele)

hedonistic way of life, 70

Help to Zion's Travellers (Hall), 93

Heman the Ezrahite, 163, 207

Hervey, James (1714–1758), 84

hesitancy, of Steele, 115, 132–33n70, 142, 163n187, 205, 207

Hewling, Benjamin, sons executed, 65–66

High or Hyper-Calvinism, 74, 74n74, 77, 78, 78n95, 79, 135

Hindmarsh, D. Bruce, 214

his Influence subsection, of Rippon's *Selection of Hymns*, 153, 154

historical circumstances and familial structures, individuals as products of, 25

History of the English Baptists (Ivimey), 54

holiness of heaven, 140

Holy Scriptures. *See* Scripture

Holy Spirit
  deity as the third person of the Trinity, 154
  dependence upon, 181
  as the divine Comforter, 158
  as "felt" or "experienced," 89
  influences and graces of, 154–61
  relating the work of to life in Christ, 151
  seeking the power of, 161
  Steele's hymns concerning the graces of, 156

Holy Spirit section, of Rippon's hymnal, 153–68

holy worship, Steele praying for help with, 199

honesty, 29

hope, Steele offering a prayer of, 174

"Hope encouraged by a View of the Divine Perfections. 1 Sam. xxx.6" (Steele), 156–58, 205
"Hope Encouraged in the Contemplation of the Divine Perfections" (Steele), 156n160
hopefulness, Steele's hymnody remaining essential, 209
horse, Steele's fall from a, 55
Houghton, S. M., 70, 71
human beings, as God's children, 120
human depravity and divine holiness, Steele on, 143
human experience, application of grace to, 109
human heart, Steele asking the Lord to revive, 195
human loss and limitation, Steele acknowledging the existence of, 39
human needs, hymns satisfying deeply felt, 16
human reason, elevated to a place of supremacy, 68n45
human tongues, failure to praise God, 179
humanity
    predicament of due to the fall, 210
    sins exchanged for the righteousness of Christ, 136
An Humble Attempt (Edwards), 99
humiliation, of Christ, 135
humility, cultivating the Christian grace of, 158
"humors" or bodily fluids, sickness caused by an imbalance of, 51
Hussey, Joseph (1660–1726), 78–79
"hymn story" biographical sketches, 54
hymn-books, 92, 100
hymnody
    critic or student of needing a complex awareness, 17
    Dissenters pastors interested in, 57
    hymn-writing improving the quality of, 11
    "in-group" language of evangelical, 12–13
    ineffability of, 34

relationship with literature, 19
reviewers of Steele's, 204
Rippon's *Selection of Hymns* as a standard of Baptist, 7n41
of Steele, 7, 33
Victorian, 18n101
W. R. Stevenson on, 2
Watts's place in, 20
women hymn writers early in British, 30
hymns
    as both theology and literature, 24
    as both theology and poetry, 116
    characteristics of, 10
    close reading of individual by Cho, 30
    composed by Steele as a response to death, 110
    as a conduit for devotional experience, 113
    craftsmanship in great, 218
    encompassing all religious moods of the soul, 16
    expressing "the doctrines of faith and practice," 112
    functions in evangelical circles, 3
    on issues of national importance by Steele, 185
    making a deep and lasting impression, 23
    model of literary criticism directed at, 40
    modeled after Isaac Watts, 37
    needing to be commonplace, 11
    needing to use regular stresses, 10
    perceived differently by different people, 204
    of personal experience, 4
    purposes of, 216
    reasons for singing, 4–5
    simple form facilitating congregational singing, 11
    of Steele
        closing with an exhortation, 210
        distributed throughout Rippon's major sections, 9
        expressing that God is most worthy of praise, 202

as an expression of enduring
pain, suffering, and death, 27
found in Rippon's *Selection of
Hymns*, 7, 117, 207
introducing an expression of
faith, 36
offered to her father's Particular
Baptist congregation, 59
in response to the drowning of
Elcomb, 55
seeking to apply the depth of
Christian doctrine, 208
writing friends sought to have
them published, 59
theological and devotional nature
limiting their subject matter, 12
as "valuable pointers" to spirituality,
34
written by all kinds of persons,
except poets, 14n81–15n81
written by Particular Baptists, 62n4
Hymns and Spiritual Songs (Watts), 1n3,
5, 103
hymn-writers, 26, 34, 40, 102–16
hymn-writing, 11, 27, 29, 30
Hyper-Calvinism. *See* High or Hyper-
Calvinism

"I know that my Redeemer liveth," as
Steele's last words, 61
ideas, of an artist, 113
ill-health, common in eighteenth-
century England, 53
illnesses, of Steele, 52
immanence, of God recognized by
Steele, 157
immersion, as the proper mode of
Baptism, 63
"'In Melting Grief and Ardent Love':
Anne Steele's Contribution to
Eighteenth-Century Hymnody"
(Aalders), 36–39
*In Trouble and in Joy: Four Women Who
Lived for God* (James), 28–30
inadequacy, Steele's sense of, 206
incarnation, 135, 136

Incarnation and Atonement subsection,
of Rippon's *Selection of Hymns*,
135–40
"The Incarnation. John i.14" (Steele),
135–37, 211n46
incomprehensibility of God, Steele's
thoughts on, 35
Independent ministers, two prominent,
73
ineffability, of God, 33, 34, 115, 204, 206
infection, Steele's liability to, 51
"The Influences of the Spirit
experienced. John xiv. 16, 17"
(Steele), 153, 154–56
"The Influences of the Spirit of God
in the Heart. John xiv 16, 17"
(Steele), 153n154, 154n156
"The Intercession of Christ. Heb.
vii.25.," 140, 143–45
interplay, between observing Steele's life
and examining her hymns, 26
interpretation, of certainty or hesitancy,
205
intimate relationship, between the
Creator and his creatures, 120
invention, as the essence of poetry, 12
invitation, to confess Christ, 129
"An Invitation to the Gospel Feast. Luke
xiv. 22" (Steele), 175–77
Invitations and Promises subsection, of
Rippon's *Selection of Hymns*, 129
Isaiah 50:10, 161n180
"isolation and lack of communication,"
of Particular Baptists, 80
Ivimey, Joseph (1773–1830), 54, 93,
157, 160

James, Sharon
on Calvinism of Particular Baptists
not precluding free offer of the
gospel, 217
chronology of Steele's health for the
last part of her life, 52
on effects of Steele's experience of
suffering, 53
on firm belief in divine sovereignty,
134

James, Sharon *(continued)*
        on the impact of Anne Cator Steele
            on the lives of her children,
            50–51
        on medical remedies for Anne
            Steele, 51–52
        portrait of Steele based on the
            hymns, poems, and letters, 28
        on Steele and her friends advancing
            the rhetoric of the Romantic
            Movement, 115
        summary of her work on Steele,
            29–30
Jesus. *See also* Christ
        allowing "all our tongues [to]
            proclaim thy praise," 143
        died in the place of "rebel foes" and
            "traitors," 138
        fulfilled the law as the unblemished
            sacrifice, 131
        fully paid the price of the
            transgressions of his sinful
            people, 130
        guided by the example of, 146
        hope in the multifaceted work of,
            183
        on letting your light shine, 169
        as Mediator, 196
        as the pearl of great price, 150
        seen by Steele as behind Watts's
            successful hymnody, 103
        Steele's spiritual though very
            personal union with, 149–50
Joshua, 169
journals, of Anne Cator Steele, 47n21
journals and letters, offering a glimpse
        into life, 25–26
joy in the created world, of Watts, 105
joys of earth, referring to the "vain" and
        "alluring," 203
"The Joys of Heaven" (Steele), 198–99,
        202n4, 211n42, 211n47
judgment, on nations as well as
        individuals, 187
Julian, John, 150
justification, leading to sanctification,
        147

Keach, Benjamin (1640–1704), 2n11, 65
        catechism of, 213
        on church as a place, 171
        evangelical ways of, 90
        laying the foundation for hymn-
            singing, 5
        persecution of, 66
        profiled by Watson, 39
        promoter of hymn-singing, 85
        on the propriety of singing hymns, 2
        on singing as full of Instruction, 4
        on working Grace to change Hearts,
            210
Keeble, N. H., 10, 14
Kiffin, William (1616–1701), 44, 45, 63,
        65–66, 85
"King of Saints," 148
"King of the Church of God," Jesus as,
        199
Kinghorn, Joseph (1766–1832), 84
kingship of Christ, doctrine of, 145, 148
Kipling, Rudyard, 11n65
Knollys, Hanserd (ca. 1598–1691),
        3n11, 44, 65, 66, 130

language
        of love, 114
        problems pertaining to, 33
        understanding and, 34–35
Latitudinarian movement, 69, 69n49
Lavington, John (1690–1759), 57, 58
Lawrence, D. H., 23, 101, 113
leaders, of the Particular Baptists' first
        generation, 67
legal and social restrictions, placed
        upon Particular Baptists, 85, 87
"Let Us Love and Sing and Wonder"
        (Newton), 175n228
letters, of Steele, 36, 47
Levitical law of sacrifices, Steele's
        allusions to, 130–31
life, on earth as short, 56, 197
"Life and Safety in Christ Alone. John
        vi. 68." *See* "To whom shall we
        go but unto thee? Or, Life and
        Safety in CHRIST alone. John vi.
        67-69" (Steele)

life of faith in Christ, as one of glad joy
for Steele, 202
"Life of the Soul. John xiv.19" (Steele),
148–50, 213
literary analysis, of Steele's hymns, 40,
41
literary circle, of Steele with friends and
family, 102
literary criticism, in Watts book, 40
literary value, of English hymns, 14–18
literary women, with Steele as the
central figure, 57–58
"lived faith," of Steele, 153
living
with eternity in view, 196
for God, 28
"a living sacrifice," Steele committing
her life to, 178
living theology, Steele putting to verse,
27
"the living way," following, 151
local congregation, 159
Long Meter (L.M.), or 88.88, 15
hymns written in, 138, 172, 182, 192
with its longer lines, 104
"Redemption by Christ alone. 1 Pet.
i. 18, 19," 129
"Longing Souls Invited to the Gospel
Feast. Luke xiv. 22" (Steele),
175n224
Lord Hardwicke's Marriage Act of 1753,
86
Lord's Supper, 63n12, 83, 179, 180
Lord's Supper section, of Rippon's
hymnbook, 174–82, 214
love
of God, 131
of Steele
for her parents and siblings, 47
for nature, 122–23
Lovegrove, Deryck W., 81
Lovelace, Austin C.
defining a hymn, 3
on the hymn difficult to master, 17
on hymns as misunderstood and
unappreciated, 13
on making rhymes sound and feel
natural, 105

on the popularity of Watts and
Wesley, 4
on Short Meter, 152
on subtlety and craftsmanship in
great hymns, 218
on Watts's place in hymnody, 20
loving parents, raised Steele, 47
Ludwig, Nicholas (1700-1760), 75n79
lyrics of Steele's hymns, 26, 37

malaria, 29, 48n26, 51, 52, 109
males, seeing life as a linear journey,
115n74
Manfield, John James, 55
Manley, Ken R.
on affinity for Watts, 6
on corporate singing of Particular
Baptists, 171
on the emphasis of Baptist
preaching, 178
on Rippon, 39, 100
emphasizing the work of the
Holy Spirit, 158
guiding maxim of, 137
nineteen Communion hymns,
214
Selection of Hymns, 6, 7–8, 24,
217
Manning, Bernard Lord, 21, 99
Marshall, Madeleine Forell, 4, 19, 20, 22,
23, 101
masculine pattern, Steele's hymns
conforming to, 115
meaning, enhancing according to
theological conviction, 120n17
"means of grace," disciplines following
the Puritan, 212n52
Mediator, Christ as, 148–49
medicine, practice of in Britain during
Steele's life, 51
Medley, Samuel, 181–82, 195–96
membership practices, of Particular
Baptists, 81
men, among Steele's acquaintances, 57,
58
mercy, 159, 183
metaphors, 104, 181

Methodist movement, within the
    Anglican church, 21n115
metrical form, 10–11, 15
mind, affected by physical pain, 52
ministers. *See also* pastors; preachers
    in Salters' Hall in London in 1719,
        73
"'The Ministry of Song': Unmarried
    British Women's Hymn Writing,
    1760-1936" (Cho), 30–32
Modern Question, first asked by Hussey,
    79n99
monotony, avoiding, 15
Montgomery, James, 14, 21n115,
    23n129
"moral ability," of humankind, 98
moralism, 71n61
morality of everyday life, 69–70
Morden, P. J., 78, 80
More, Hannah (1745–1833), 58
"mother" of English women hymn
    writers, Steele as, 31
Mrs. Steele. *See* Steele, Anne Cator
    (Steele's stepmother)
Mullett, Michael, 74
The Music of the English Parish Church
    (Temperley), 21
"My Flesh Is Meat Indeed. John vi. 53-
    55" (Samuel Stennett), 176n234
"mysterious meeting," of God and the
    human person, 113

Nahum, 121
Nanny, Anne Steele known as in the
    family, 46
Napoleonic Wars (1804–1815), 68n45
national days of fasting and prayer,
    Steele wrote nine hymns
    concerning, 185n260
nations, as dependent of God, 187
"natural ability," of humankind, 98
naturalism, 69
nature, revealing its Creator, 123
Naylor, Peter
    on congregational singing as a point
        of contention, 84–85
    on Fuller leading the reaction
        against High Calvinism, 98
    on Kiffin's fear of singing, 85

on nonconformist suffering after
    1660, 64
on Particular Baptists's attitude
    towards the Evangelical
    Awakening, 90
on twilight years for the Baptists, 68
nervous disorder, in Steele's fortieth
    year, 52–53
Nettles, Tom J., 2n11, 44, 66, 78n95, 98
network of friends and advisors, of
    Steele, 42
Newton, Isaac, 68n45
Newton, John (1725–1807), 2, 21, 22,
    95n201, 175n228
Noll, Mark, 68, 71, 72, 78, 98
Nonconformist tradition, English
    eighteenth-century hymns in,
    21n115
Nonconformists, 22, 43, 64n21, 72
nonresidence, linked to pluralism,
    71n60
Northampton Association, missionary
    spirit of, 96
Northamptonshire Baptist Association,
    missionary endeavor in, 99

"O God, Our Help in Ages Past," 123
obstacles, Steele needed help to face, 168
"On a Day of Prayer for Success in War"
    (Steele), 188–89
"On a Stormy Night" (Steele), 104
"On the Publick Fast. February 6, 1756"
    (Steele). *See* "For a Public Fast"
    (Steele)
open communion, 83
open membership, 82n115
ordinances, as a central expression of
    piety, 212
Orthodox Confession of 1678, 62n5
"Our Example. John xiii. 15." (Steele),
    146–48

paedobaptists, Turner on, 82–83
Pailin, David A., 69
parables, 150, 194
"Pardoning Love. Jer. iii. 22 and Hos.
    xiv. 1." (Steele), 129, 131–33

"Pardoning Love. Jer. iii.22 and Hos. xiv. 1" (Steele), 206, 206n26
parenthetical remarks, Steele's use of, 108, 109, 137, 144, 177
Particular Baptist(s)
  believed the atonement is limited to the elect, 62n1
  cause advanced after the Glorious Revolution, 77
  Christ-centered spirituality of, 198
  congregational hymn-singing in worship service, 112
  in declension at the time of the Evangelical Revival, 77
  denomination growth of from 1790 to 1838, 100
  as early pioneers of the English hymn, 100
  emerged from English Puritanism, 44, 62
  evidenced little spiritual vigour in London, 91
  fell into a hardened hyper-Calvinism, 78
  hymnody carried forward to our own time, 7n41
  influence of Edwards, 96
  maintained an evangelical Calvinistic theology, 90
  ministers refused to baptize Taylor as he was an Arminian, 88
  as a minority denomination within a minority dissenting movement, 81
  negative attitude towards the Evangelical Awakening, 90
  not appreciating emotional aspects of crying and weeping, 89
  not yet in line with Evangelicalism, 87
  notable hymn-writers, 2
  pastors, 25, 45, 76, 95n201
  piety of, 215
  putting piety to verse, 194
  renewal and revival of, 89–99
  responding to the evangelical appeal, 92
  reverted gradually to original Calvinism, 99
  serious about theology and ecclesiology, 82
  spiritual state of at the time of the Evangelical Revival, 76
  Steeles as a family of, 43
  Steele's contribution to the revival, 201
  understanding of the theological emphases of, 9
  wedded themselves to the word "evangelical," 3
Particular Baptist ancestors, of Steele, 72n62
Particular Baptist churches, many founded by Baptist officers, 43–44
Particular Baptist community
  affinity for Watts, 6
  Anne Steele as a beloved daughter of, 61
  background of, 62–68
  congregational system of government, 111–12
  High Calvinism spreading through, 78–79
  placed beyond the religious life of fellow Dissenters, 82
  revival included hymn-singing, 117
  Rippon's hymnal as the introduction to the hymns of Anne Steele, 8
  teaching of, 119
  theology of, 81
Particular Baptist Missionary society, 92
Particular redemption, 44n6
pastors. *See* ministers; Particular Baptist(s), pastors; preachers
Patterson, W. Morgan, 216
Paul, on the fellowship of his sufferings, 178
peace and life and joy, coming from the Redeemer's voice, 128
peace and self-control, of Christ, 147
"Pearl of Great Price. Matt. xiii. 46" (Steele), 150
pedagogical device, viewing the hymn as, 18–19

penal substitutionary atonement made
  by Christ, Steele's profound
  understanding of, 130
"Penitence and Hope" (Steele), 159
perceived silence of God, in the midst of
  suffering, 35
persistent widow, wearied the unjust
  judge, 194
personal experience, hymns of Steele
  expressing, 4, 109
personal hymns, of Steele "expressing
  her emotion, 39
personal revival and renewal, prayerful
  plea for, 165
personification, Steele making artful use
  of, 144
perspective, of God toward his people,
  121
Peter, Steele remembering the
  confession of, 174
physical and emotional trials, viewing
  Steele's response to, 53
physical and spiritual experience,
  Steele's ability to communicate,
  26–27
physical pain, Steele dealing with her
  own constant, 27
physician, image of God as, 151
"Physician of Souls. Jeremiah viii. 22"
  (Steele), 150–51
Pietists, in Germany, 75n79
piety
  based on the Bible, 75n79
  definition of, 212
  evangelical Calvinism, 6
  experiential, 129n58
  prayer as an expression of Steele's
    personal, 166
  of prayer recurring in a hymn about
    death, 197
  Scriptures as central expression of,
    212
  of Steele in the face of death, 197
  Steele practicing through verse, 142,
    145
  Steele's hymns brimmed with, 215
The Pilgrim's Progress (Bunyan), 72

pioneers of the English hymn, Steele
  mentioned alongside, 212
"plaintive" tone and style, of Steele,
  149n138
pleasures of the rural life, hymns of
  Steele reflecting, 111
*Poems on Subjects Chiefly Devotional,
  by Theodosia* (Steele), 8, 31, 33,
  36, 60
poetic argument, of Steele giving God a
  reason to answer her prayer, 163
poetic devices, 137, 144, 158, 187, 218
poetic form, of the hymn, 13
poetic medium, Steele professing
  theology through, 123
poetic meters. *See also* Common Meter
  (C.M.), or 86.86; Long Meter
  (L.M.), or 88.88; Short Meter
  (S.M.), or 66.86
  of Steele's day, 103–4
poetic quality, Keach's hymns lacked, 5
poetic virtue, of honest lyrics of
  Newton, 22
poetry
  as best employed "in the service of
    Religion," 217
  of certain hymns as bad, 17
  composed by Steele as a response to
    death, 110
  hymns deserving to be considered
    as, 14
  reading hymns as, 10–11
  Steele both inherited and cultivated,
    102
  Steele using to focus the reader's
    eyes, 141
  written skillfully having potential to
    bring fruit, 218
Pollard, Arthur, 20
poor health, of Steele throughout her
  life, 27
"poor in spirit," beatitude of, 158
Porter, Roy, 69, 70, 71
Portugal, "major earthquake" in, 185
praise
  of Christ, 140
  to God, 34, 206

praise and faith in God, in the midst of messages of judgment, 121

"Praise for National Peace, Psalm xlvi.9" (Steele), 189–90

"Praise for the Blessings of Providence and Grace. Psalm cxxxix" (Steele), 122, 124–25, 203, 206n27

"Praise to the Redeemer" (Steele), 175, 180–81

prayer
    as a central expression of piety, 212
    Edwards's call for fervent, 96–97
    as an expression of Steele's personal piety, 166
    fruits desired by Steele from, 167–68
    as a hallmark of Baptist spirituality, 146
    illustrating the necessity of for life, 168
    as a means of grace, 155
    Steele approaching God in, 206
    Steele's evangelical Calvinistic understanding of, 166

prayer book, Rippon's *Selection of Hymns* functioned as, 8, 117

Prayer Call, of 1784, 97

prayer of hope, Steele offering, 174

prayerful hymns, of Steele, 215

preachers. *See also* ministers; pastors
    biblical warrant to freely offer salvation, 90

Presbyterians, 44n10, 73

presence
    of God, 162
    of the Lord, 171

"The Presence of Christ the Joy of his People" (Steele), 172–73

"The Presence of God, the Only Comfort in Affliction," 191n284

"The Presence of God, the only Comfort in Affliction" (Steele), 191–94

presuppositions, 25, 33, 201

"priestly office," of Christ, 145

Principia (Newton), 68n45

private devotional practices, hymn-books as a part of, 117

professions of faith, of William and Anne, 48

Protestant scripturalism, refined into a new rational faith, 69

Prussia, allied itself with England, 185

Psalm 23, paraphrase of the first three verses of, 152

Psalm 27, putting to English the verses of, 171

Psalm 39, paraphrased by Steele, 194

Psalm 84, versification of, 171

Psalms, Steele's paraphrases of, 7, 117, 119, 152, 171, 171n210, 194

Psalms and Hymns (Watts), 103

Psalms of David (Watts), 5, 103

pseudonym, publishing under a, 60

Public Worship subsection, of Rippon's *Selection of Hymns*, 170

quadrilateral, of Bebbington, 3

Quakers, 67n38

question marks, of Steele revealing her Romantic impulse, 132

questions, Steele's use of, 108, 109, 167, 177

"raid on the inarticulate," Steele making, 143n108

Ramsbottom, B. A., 5

"reason," 69

"rebel worms," as sinners needing salvation, 121

"rebels," Steele describing humankind as, 141

"received texts," of Steele through Rippon, 204

Rede, John, 43, 45

'Redeeming Love Proclaim': John Rippon and the Baptists (Manley), 39

"Redeeming Love" (Steele), 116n80

"Redemption by Christ alone. 1 Pet. i. 18, 19" (Steele), 129–31, 209–10

redemption through Christ, Steele believing in, 211

redundancy, Rippon reducing by the omission of verses in Steele's hymns, 122

"A Reflection on a Winter Evening"
(Steele), 184n259
Reign of Grace (Booth), 92
religious leaders, positively influenced
Steele, 115
religious purpose, of the English hymn,
12–13
renewal, Steele expressed an experience
of the need of, 173
repentance, spiritual virtue of put to
verse by Steele, 159
repetition
emphasizing those for whom Christ
died, 141
examples of the use of by Watts and
Steele, 104
known as Tautology, 137n86
skillful and understated application
of, 169
Steele's use of, 104, 137, 162
Watts's use of, 104
"The Request" (Steele), 165–66
resolution, Steele bringing, 208
rest, found in Christ alone, 133
restricted communion, 84
revelation, from hymns, 125–35
reviewers, of Steele's hymnody, 204
revival
coming to the Particular Baptist
movement, 92
eighteenth-century, 75
evangelical, 74–89, 117, 129
ministers in the Church of England
as early key leaders of, 88
in Particular Baptist life, 139, 218
personal, 165
preachers, 87–88
Steele calling for personal and
corporate, 134
Steele's contribution to, 212–18
taking beyond Britain, 189
within the church, 173
"reviving ray," of the Lord, 193
rhyme, Steele consistently used in her
hymns, 104–5
rhyming lyrics, as memorable, 218
riches, describing the value of the Bible,
127

Rippon, John (1751–1836)
alternating between Long Meter and
Short Meter hymns of Steele,
132n69
at Carter Lane in 1772, 94
chose to supplement Watts, 6
contributed to the Baptist cause, 100
editing by, 126
emphasizing the work of the Holy
Spirit, 158
guiding maxim of, 137
included forty-five of Steele's
hymns in the first edition of his
Selection of Hymns, 60
included Steele's hymns about daily
life and life in England at the
time, 111
innovative in his careful
arrangement, marking, and
indexing of hymns, 9n49
inserted exclamation points adding
to the emotional elements
heartfelt lyrics, 168n202
knew the power of hymns to
inculcate the faith through
poetry, 101
liberal use of Christ-centered hymns
from Steele, 210
removed Steele's verses that spoke of
God's anger and judgment, 119
Rippon's *Selection of Hymns*
first edition contained 588 hymns
including 45 by Anne Steele, 6
first published in 1787, 100
illustrative of the devotional content
of Baptist worship for the
period, 7
included six of Steele's hymns
concerning death, resurrection,
and heaven, 110
interpreted the Christian faith for its
generation, 9
as the key introduction of Anne
Steele's hymns to Particular
Baptists, 8
made its way across denominational
lines, 9
Manley's analysis of, 39

meeting and worshipping
    requirements for more than one
    generation, 217
number of hymns in editions of,
    118n9
organized into seventeen
    distinct subjects with various
    subheadings, 9, 112, 118
sections not including a hymn by
    Steele, 118n8
showcasing Steele, 217
as a standard of Baptist hymnody,
    7n41
Steele's hymns and psalms in,
    117–200
success of, 6
widespread use of, 8
"Rippon's Steele," 201, 209, 211
Rivers, Isabel, 66n37–67n37
Roberts, R. Philip, 94
Robinson, Robert (1735–1790), 83
"Rock of Ages, cleft for me" (1776), with
    explicitly Calvinist theology, 13
Rogal, Samuel J., 5, 19, 20
Roman Catholic Gunpowder Plot in
    1605, 190
Romantic literature's sense of aspiration
    and longing, Steele expressed,
    116
Romantic Movement, rhetoric of, 115
Routley, Erik, 10, 12–13
Rowe, Elizabeth Singer (1674–1737), 34
Rowland, Daniel (1713–1790), 75n79
Ryland, John Collett, 84
Ryland, John Collett, Sr. (1723–1792),
    83
Ryland, John, Jr. (1753–1825), 2, 78,
    95n201

salvation, 90, 121, 170, 175
sanctification, 147, 170, 209
"The Saviour's Invitation. John vii. 37."
    (Steele), 129, 133, 134–36, 206,
    216
"Saviour-the only One. Acts iv.12"
    (Steele), 151
Savoy Declaration in 1658, 44n10, 67

scholarship, on Anne Steele, 24–41
"school of Watts," members of, 103
Scot, Mary, known as "Myra," 58
Scripture, 73, 111, 125, 162, 212
Scripture Promises sub-subsection,
    Steele's hymns found in, 133
Scripture references, included with
    Steele's hymns, 111
Scripture section, of Rippon's hymnal,
    125–35
*Second London Confession. See also
    Confession; First London
    Confession* of 1644
on the authority, power, and
    sufficiency of the Bible, 213
Calvinistic emphases, 62–63
change to the *Westminster
    Confession of Faith*, 112
chapters
    "Of Christ the Mediator," 138,
        143
    "Of Good Works," 169
    "Of the Holy Scriptures," 125
on Christ as Mediator, 148–49
on Christ persuading to believe and
    obey, 139–40
concluding chapters, 198
contradicting Roman Catholic
    teaching, 191
crystallized theological convictions
    of the Particular Baptists, 44
describing God, 119
following the *Westminster
    Confession of Faith*, 119n11
on Holy Scripture, 127–28
on humans having a "corrupted
    nature," 211
introductory words to, 76
on "inwardly by faith," 176
Knollys a signer of, 130, 130n62
listing baptism and the Lord's
    Supper as ordinances, 174
on the Lord Jesus making
    intercession, 145
placing Baptists in the stream of
    evangelical theology, 67
on the religious worship of God, 112

Second London Confession (continued)
  as a response to the trials of
    persecution, 67
  Steele
    following on Scripture, 127
    hymns displaying a theological
      cohesion with, 117
    hymns preserved the orthodoxy
      of, 101
    teaching the doctrine of, 131
    well acquainted with the
      theology of, 45
  teaching
    about the Son of God, 136
    that Christ indeed did this "for
      us," 139
    that outside of Christ all are by
      nature the servants of Sin,
      129
  as a theological control in analysis of
    Steele's hymns, 217
  theology of as part and parcel of
    Steele's poetic output, 112
*A Selection of Hymns, from the Best
  Authors* (Rippon). *See* Rippon's
  Selection of Hymns
self-fulfillment, as more beneficial than
  self-denial, 70
sense of humor, of Steele, 29
"sensibility," of writing with a flair for
  drama and emotion, 204
sermon, as crucial for Particular
  Baptists, 62n4
Sermon on the Mount, 158
sermonic hymn, J. R. Watson on, 4
Seven Years' War (1756–1763), hymns
  written during or just after, 185
sewing, Steele learning to do elegant,
  48n23
"Shepherd. Psalm xxiii. 1-3" (Steele),
  152
Shepherd's "protecting care," of the
  "unworthy" sheep, 152
Sheppard, John, 26, 61
Short Meter (S.M.), or 66.86, 15, 104,
  152
shortness of breath, Steele suffering
  from, 53

"The Shortness of Time and Frailty of
  Man. Ps. xxxix" (Steele), 194–95
Sickness and Recovery subsection, of
  Rippon's hymnal, 191
"sighs," as a word explaining prayer,
  193n287
"Silvania," pseudonym of Steele, 58
simplicity and clarity, as marks of both
  Watts and Steele, 108
sin
  guilt and, 143
  human, 35
  nature and effect of, 150–51
  Pauline understanding of, 129
  ultimate antidote for, 210
sinful nature, 129, 131
sinfulness, 108, 187, 210
singers, of Rippon's hymnal, 202
singing, 18, 202
singleness, of Steele, 29, 57
sinners
  finding a cure, 151
  Holy God dwelling spiritually
    within, 154
  needing God's help in praise, 202
  plight of, 188
  reconciled through the work of their
    Redeemer, 175
  situating in the depth of despair, 143
  Steele pleading for, 216
  Steele realistic about the
    predicament of, 132
Skepp, John (1675–1721), 78n93, 79
slave trade, sermons preached against,
  92
Smith, Karen E., 24, 105, 152, 177,
  203n9
Society of Friends, 67n38
Socinianism, 92
"souls desires," Steele on, 204
Souls of the Righteous, made perfect in
  holiness, 199
sound doctrine, as the heart of Wesley's
  religion, 21
"Sovereign," as also the "Redeemer," 178
"sovereign cure," for sin, 151
sovereign God, orders the days as they
  pass, 183

sovereignty, 119, 166
Spirit
    of Adoption, 155, 172
    of Christ, 196
    maketh intercession for us with
        groanings, 193
    of Truth, 151
spiritual afflictions, rehearsing in detail,
    161
spiritual decay, 69
spiritual emotion, Steele giving voice
    to, 114
spiritual experience of Steele, in her
    hymns, 26
spiritual hesitancy, of Steele, 163n187
spiritual life, "Winter" as a parable of,
    185
spiritual nourishment, receiving,
    179–80
spiritual renewal, need for, 76
spiritual struggles, of Particular Baptists,
    154
spiritual vitality, fostered by the
    associations, 95
spiritual weaknesses, Steele knowing her
    own, 146
spirituality
    gender theory of, 115
    hymns as pointers to, 34
    piety referred to as, 212
    prayer as a hallmark of, 146
    of Steele, 33, 165–66, 198
"Spirituality of the Word," 126
stability, of hymns, 16
Standard Confession of 1660, 62n5
state churches, as institutions ordained
    by God, 68
Steadman, William, 81n112
Steele, Anne (1717-1778)
    as the "all-time champion Baptist
        hymn-writer of either sex," 2
    bearing the will of God, 54
    bedridden for the final years of her
        life, 61
    biography of, 42–61
    birth of, 43
    cared for her father at the end of his
        life, 56

celebrated as "the female 'Poet of the
    Sanctuary,'" 1
constantly explored Christ's works,
    106
constructing hymns of praise to
    God, 35
current scholarship on, 24–41
death of, 61
enjoyed visiting and receiving visits,
    57
equaled Watts in matters of the soul,
    28, 106
followed Watts in using a few
    standard meters, 103
gave titles to her poems and hymns,
    110–11
hymns
    evaluating as printed in Rippon,
        Selection of Hymns, 7n41
    first stanza having a sort of
        thesis of praise, theology, or
        experience, 202
    not published in the *Baptist
        Hymnal* published in 1991,
        2n4
    one of the few still sung today,
        134
    related to both "the head and the
        heart" of Christianity, 101
    as resolutely Evangelical
        encouraging a personal
        relationship with Christ, 111
    testifying her love for Christ, 106
as a hymn-writer, 102–16
knowing that God hears her, 164
letters
    to her brother William, 49
    to her suffering sister-in-law,
        Mary Bullock Steele, 53
life of sorrows beginning at the age
    of three, 46
literary corpus, entire, 8
loved her family, 48
mother-figure to her niece Polly,
    54, 56
not composing hymns in a solitary
    vacuum, 57

Steele, Anne (1717-1778) *(continued)*
  not giving titles to paraphrases of
    Psalm texts, 119n14
  only recently receiving the study she
    is due, 23
  pleading with the Lord to give her
    the same inspiration as Watts,
    103
  poem about friendship's influence
    on writing and publishing
    efforts, 58–59
  as a poet from a family of poets, 59
  remained single, 29, 57
  represented within thirteen of the
    seventeen sections of Rippon's
    hymnal, 118
  seeking to reach great heights in
    "Praise for National Peace,
    Psalm xlvi:9," 105–6
  as seen by users of Rippon's popular
    Selection of Hymns, 201
  spent time writing drafts and
    improving her verse, 105
  suffered from shortness of breath
    and severe headaches, 52
  theological and spiritual role in
    Baptist faith and life, 7
  as a transitional figure between an
    Augustan era of literature and
    the Romantic period, 115
  used Long Meter for her treatment
    of Psalm 90, 120
  writing
    of heaven, 106
    hymns to supplement those sung
      in her father's congregation,
      2
    hymns while suffering from
      illnesses, 52
    of mourning and reflecting upon
      the lives and deaths of those
      she loved, 56
    as a natural outlet to
      communicate about
      common experiences, 53
    verse for practical spiritual
      concerns, 103
Steele, Anne Cator (Steele's stepmother)
  on Anne's spiritual sensitivities and
    her regular struggle with ill
    health, 48
  caring for the two children as her
    own, 46
  constant care of as crucial in the
    lives of Steele and her siblings,
    50
  died in 1760, 56
  journal entries of, 25, 47, 47n21
  mentioning Anne having trouble
    with Molly, 49
  recording falls from a horse for
    Steele, 55
  on Steele's patient endurance of
    suffering, 110
  surviving journals of, 46n20
Steele, Anne Froude (1684–1720)
  died apparently while giving birth to
    Thomas, 46
  Steele's mother, 43
Steele, Henry (1655-1739), Steele's great
    uncle, 43
Steele, Little Mary or Molly (1724–
    1772), 46, 49–50, 57, 58
Steele, Mary Bullock (1713-1762),
    sister-in-law of Anne Steele, 52
Steele, Polly (Steele's niece), 54, 56, 61
Steele, Thomas, Anne Steele's younger
    brother, 46
Steele, Uncle Henry, 50
Steele, William (1689–1769)
  Anne Steele's father, 43, 144
  hearing and meeting George
    Whitefield, 216
  on the Lord's Supper, 214
  love-letter to Anne Froude, 46
  on means of grace, 212
  Steele cared for after the death of his
    wife, 160
  in the throes of sorrow, 46
Steele, William (1715–1785), 46, 49, 58
Steele, William, Sr., died in 1769, 56
Steele Collection, housed at the Angus
    Library Regent's Park College,
    Oxford, 24

Steele's family, financed the publishing
    of Anne's poems and hymns,
    59–60
Stennett, Joseph, I (1663–1713), 2, 5, 39,
    85, 176
Stennett, Samuel (1725–1795), 2, 39,
    61, 176
Stevenson, W. R., 2, 100n231
stomach problems, endured by Steele,
    109
"The Strange Case of James Elcomb of
    Ringwood," 54
"strict Baptist," referring to closed, or
    restricted, communion, 84n125
subject matter, vastness of for hymn-
    writing, 17
"sublime decrees," Calvinistic emphasis
    of God fulfilling, 190
suffering
    of Christ, 138
    of hymn-writers as over emphasized,
        31
    as a means for God to bring Steele
        closer, 29
    problems pertaining to, 33
    sanctified to Steele, 27
    "shall cease" before heaven's throne,
        198
    of Steele, 42, 51, 109, 161
    Steele's hymns displaying a Christ-
        centered view of, 215
Suffering Servant, of Isaiah 53, 138
The Sufferings and Death [of Christ]
    subsection, 137
Sutcliff, John, 96, 97, 153, 182

Tate, Nahum, 5
Taylor, Dan, 88
Temperley, Nicholas, 13, 18, 21
tenderness and vulnerability, feeling
    of, 204
Tennent, Gilbert (1703-1764), 75n79
tension, Steele building, 208
Terrill, Edward, 93
Test and Corporation Acts, repealed in
    1828, 86

thanksgiving and joy, sustained note
    of, 190
thanksgiving for peace, hymns of,
    189–90
thematic parallelism, 141
themes, of Steele's life, 27, 42
Theodosia, Steele's pseudonym meaning
    "gift from God," 2, 31, 54, 111
theological
    beliefs, 27, 112
    content, 12–13
    controversy, 82
    convictions, 111
    reflections, 210
    truth, 109, 138
theology, 81, 149, 156–57, 211
thesis, for Broome's work on Steele, 26
thesis and methodology, of this book,
    7–9
"Thoughts in Sickness, and on
    Recovery" (Steele), 52
"Time and Eternity; or, longing after
    unseen Pleasures. 2 Cor. iv. 18"
    (Steele), 195, 211n45
Time and Eternity section, of Rippon's
    hymnbook, 194–95
Times and Seasons section, of Rippon's
    hymnbook, 182–94
Tindall, William York, 101, 113
titles, of Steele's poems and hymns,
    110–11
*To Express the Ineffable: The Hymn
    and Spirituality of Anne Steele*
    (Aalders), 32–39
"To whom shall we go but unto thee?
    Or, Life and Safety in CHRIST
    alone. John vi. 67-69" (Steele),
    173–74, 203
Todd, Janet
    on accomplishments of the English
        eighteenth-century hymn, 22
    on hymns
        as artful expressions of religious
            truth, 4
        incorporating the common
            poetic values of its day, 23
        revealing the religious climate of
            their time, 101

Todd, Janet *(continued)*
  on Watts, 19, 20
Toleration Act of 1689, 44
toothaches, endured by Steele, 109
topical index, of Rippon, 9
Toplady, Augustus, 21
tradition, within which Steele was born
    and raised, 42
"traitor(s)," Steele describing
    humankind as, 141
transcendence, of God recognized by
    Steele, 157
transitional figure in the literary world,
    Steele as, 204
*A Treatise Concerning Religious
  Affections* (Edwards), 97
Trinitarian faith, of "classical Christian
    theology," 68
Trinitarian theology, of Steele, 151
Trinity, hymns on, 16
Trinity Church, Steele's hymns in the
    hymnal of, 61
The Trinity Hymnal, 126n39
"Troubled, but making God a Refuge,"
    163–65
Turner, Daniel (1710-1798), 57, 60, 82,
    83–84, 88
Turner, James, 82n113

uncertainty and hesitancy, in Steele's
    writing style, 115
unhappiness of the world, Steele
    conscious of, 209
Unitarianism, 73, 73n71
universality, of hymns, 16
unregenerate, having no duty to believe
    in Christ, 78
usefulness, of Steele far distanced her
    fame, 26

Vanity Fair, 72
"A 'Veil of Interposing Night': The
    Hymns of Anne Steele (1717-
    1778)" (Arnold), 41
Venner, Thomas, 64n21
verses, 39, 158
versifiers, as hymn-writers, 17

Victorian hymnody, 18n101
"Victory over Death through Christ. 1
    Cor xv. 27" (Steele), 196
virtue, 70

Wakeford, Joseph (1719-1785), 58, 60
Walker, Austin, 65
"Walking in Darkness, and trusting in
    God. Isaiah i. 10," 161–63
Wallin, Benjamin (1711-1782), 2, 3,
    88, 90
war hymns, of Steele, 185
Ward, W. R., 84n129
"warm affections," 179
warships, Steele's family sold timber to
    the Navy for, 110
"Watchfulness and Prayer. Matt. xxvi.
    41" (Steele), 166–68, 208
Watson, J. R.
  answering criticisms of hymns, 14
  citing Steele's hymn "On a Stormy
      Night," 104
  describing poetic meters, 104
  on Doddridge, 23
  examining the English hymn, 14
  hymn study of, 30
  on hymns
    dismissed by literary critics as
        "restricted and churchy," 10
    given to the Church by those
        who wrote them, 12
    as the only poetry that some
        have ever known, 23
    as a part of popular culture and
        also a religious and literary
        culture, 101
    speaking to those are united in a
        common belief, 15
  on Isaac Watts, 19, 108
    careful observation of the ways
        in which words behave, 104
    influence upon Steele as
        "considerable," 103
    joy in the created world, 105
  on lack of organization of other
      hymn books, 9n49
  listing hymn topics, 16

on meters in the eighteenth-century
    English hymn, 15
on "never, never" introducing
    human sensibility, 168
on Steele, 39
    beginning with experience, 129
    celebrating the application of
        grace to human experience,
        167
    poems and hymns moving
        away from Addison and
        Doddridge, 208
    using questions or exclamations
        for a specific purpose, 167
on Steele asking questions and
    making exclamations, 108
on Steele's
    use of nouns and adjectives, 127
    use of repetition, 127
Watts, Isaac (1674-1748)
    on the Clarendon Code, 65
    departed from all precedent, 19n108
    "doctrinally acceptable" hymns of, 4
    doubting the adequacy of the
        traditional Trinitarian formulas,
        73–74
    on Edwards, 96, 99
    English Hymn after, 21–23
    evangelical hymns of, 75
    on the evangelical revival, 75, 99
    as the "Father of the English Hymn,"
        18–20
    on God as Redeemer, 106
    on High Calvinism, 78–79
    hymnal of, 1n3
    hymnodists influenced by, 20–23
    hymns of as dignified and didactic,
        37
    influence upon Steele, 27, 102,
        148n133
    inspiration behind his Christ-
        focused hymns, 106
    inspired those who came after, 19
    on Joseph Stennett I, 5
    large view of his sinfulness, 108
    leading hymn writer, 1
    moving the English hymn from
        literature to poetry, 113

    paraphrased psalms from the
        vantage point of their fulfillment
        in Christ, 106
    poetic talents of, 19, 20
    publication of his *Hymns and
        Spiritual Songs*, 5
    realization of the majesty and glory
        of God, 27–28
    roused his singers from indifference,
        22
    sought clarity, order, and simplicity
        in his use of language, 104
    on the source of the evangelical
        revival, 74–75
    stanzas of Steele reminiscent of, 142
    Steele
        following the lead of, 185
        longing to write like him, 109
        poem of about, 102–3
    subjective emphasis in, 18
    transformed the hymn form, 19
    used Common Meter (86.86) double
        for his paraphrase of Psalm 90,
        119–20
    wrote as a well-studied theologian,
        20
Watts, Michael, 64, 72
"Weary Souls Invited to Rest. Matt.
    xi. 28" (Steele), 129, 133–34,
    135–36, 206, 209n35, 216
weather, Steele relating to spiritual
    battles, 184
Wesley, Charles (1707–1788)
    Aalders comparing to Watts, 38
    call to conversion and spiritual
        fervor, 22
    characteristics of, 21
    evangelical hymns of, 75
    on the glory of redemption through
        Christ, 175
    hymn themes of, 21n115
    hymns of, 18, 37
    leading hymn-writer of
        evangelicalism, 1
    regarded as an Evangelical
        [Anglican] quite as much as a
        Methodist, 21
    Steele paralleling the writing of, 209

Wesley, Charles *(continued)*
  writer of thousands of hymns, 1n3
Wesley, John (1703–1791), 75, 82, 154
Wesley, Watts, 2
West Country Baptist ministers, as
    representative of Particular
    Baptists, 91
Western Association, training
    institution of Bristol Baptist
    College, 91
Westminster Confession of Faith, 44n10,
    63, 67
"When I Survey the Wondrous Cross"
    (Watts), 37–38
Whitefield, George (1714–1770), 75,
    216
will of God, Steele's desire to receive,
    160
William III, 67–68
"Winter" (Steele), 184–85
woman of faith and good humor, Steele
    as, 28
women, studied by James, 28
women hymn writers, early in the
    history of British hymnody, 30

"The Wonders of Redemption" (Steele),
    106–9, 106n28, 175, 177–78,
    214
Word, 137
Word of God, 155, 162
word of ideas, ending one stanza and
    starting the next, 137
"Word-centered evangelicals," English
    Baptists as, 213
words, used by Steele, following Watts,
    107
words of life, written words as, 127
works, 120, 131, 169
The Works of Mrs. Anne Steele, published
    in 1808, 61
worldliness, of Church of England
    bishops and parish clergy, 71
"The Worship of Heaven. John xvii. 24"
    (Steele), 106n27, 198, 199–200,
    212n49
Worship section, of Rippon's hymnal,
    169–72
"wretched sinners," plight of, 188
writing, self-conscious process of
    Steele's, 41

Young, Robert H., 118

Printed in Great Britain
by Amazon